PARKS, RECREATION AND LEISURE SERVICE MANAGEMENT

Hilmi M. Ibrahim
Whittier College

Kathleen A. Cordes
Executive Director
American Association for Leisure and Recreation

D1396732

eddie bowers publishing co., inc.

Exclusive marketing and distributor rights for U.K., Eire,
and Continental Europe held by:

Gazelle Book Services Limited
Falcon House
Queen Square
Lancaster
LA1 1RN
U.K.

eddie bowers publishing co., inc.
P.O. Box 130
Peosta, Iowa 52068-0130 USA

ISBN 1-57879-016-6

Printed in the United States of America.

9 8 7 6 5 4 3 2 1

PREFACE

During the past few decades, administration courses dealing with parks, recreation, and leisure services focused on the public sector. With the 21st century upon us, the student who is majoring in these fields will be dealing with new arrangements whether in structure or offerings. The shrinking role of the public sector on all levels--federal, state and local--is accompanied by a rise in new structural arrangements in the fields of parks, recreation and leisure services. This new era requires that the focus in administration courses extend beyond the public sector to include new possibilities. This book is written with this approach in mind.

THE APPROACH

This textbook begins with introducing the student, the future manager and leader in the fields of parks, recreation and leisure services, to the concept of a profession and its role in the human society. As a professional, the future manager/ leader is reminded that he or she will abide by a code of ethics through which the professional becomes responsible to society as well as to his or her place of employment.

The approach of this book emphasizes that the future leader/ manager in parks, recreation and leisure services should be able to understand the dynamics of good leadership and to master the elements of strategic management. This will be done by emphasizing interaction between leader and employee and through the fundamentals of strategic management.

In his or her capacity as a leader in the fields of parks, recreation and leisure services, the future professional will understand the intricacies of these delivery systems. He or she will grasp the significant contribution and the rich heritage of these fields. The future professional will be able to develop an awareness of the cultures of different agencies in the leisure delivery system.

Through our approach, the future manager will be able to manage personnel, facilities, equipment, and natural resources as well as develop programs for a variety of people of different ages and backgrounds.

Due to the importance of fiscal and legal aspects in parks, recreation and leisure services, a special place is afforded them in our approach. For instance, creative marketing and fund raising are emphasized because a large number of the future professionals will be employed in the private and semi-public sectors, which depend on these two techniques. Accordingly, entrepreneurial and recreation businesses are discussed in detail in this volume because it is felt that the future leader/manger should be equipped with the techniques utilized in business, in general, and in entrepreneurial activities, in particular.

An important aspect of management and leadership depends on up-to-date tools and information that can be used in providing quality programs. Our approach includes the utilization of technology, the use of public relations, and methods of evaluation as means of achieving quality programs.

Awareness of present day issues and comprehension of future trends in parks, recreation and leisure services are essential components of a dynamic leadership and effective management. Our approach underscores the importance of these areas in the professional life of the future leader/manager.

THE FEATURES

- An important feature in this book is the comparison between leadership and management.

- A novel feature on the culture of human organizations with an emphasis of leisure services organizations is included.

- An emphasis on creative marketing is provided in light of the need to market leisure services, whether they are public, semi-public, or private

- The management of the technological environment is an added feature in this volume.

- The importance of office management and its impact on public relation is provided in this work.

- The important feature of entrepreneurial and recreation business speaks to the future trends in leisure services.

THE PEDAGOGY

- **Learning Objectives:** Each chapter is provided with a number of objectives that the instructor could use as means of enhancing the quality of his or her teaching.

- **Summary:** Each chapter is provided with a summary in which its salient points are given in short sentences.

- **Learning Activities:** At the end of each chapter, a list of activities are provided in the form of assignment that can be distributed to the class members individually or in groups.

- **References:** Comprehensive references are provided at the end of each chapter which can be utilized in both learning activities and other assignments as deemed necessary.

We dedicate this work to:

Bianca and other future professionals and to the Fellows of the American Leisure Academy.

Acknowledgment

Communications today are swift and often brief. In fact, in a survey of some 1,200 workers from receptionists to top executives, Pitney Bowes found that employees handle an average 204 messages a day, counting e-mail, voice mail, snail mail, and memos. It is a wonder, then, that any of us can find the blocks of time needed to accomplish that which we intend to do. It is in the midst of these hundreds of communications, that whenever a substantial task is completed, many people deserve a big round of applause. It is befitting that the last words we write for this book are words of gratitude extended to those who have contributed their talents to the project and supported us along the way.

We want first to thank Bianca Urquidi for her dedication to this project. Since we both use different computer formats, we really needed someone like Bianca who could streamline our manuscript into one integrated presentation. We will always be grateful to her. We would like also to thank Jane Lammers, Shelly Urbizagastegui, Dave Sanderlin, and Bob Bacon for their valuable input and insightful reviews. Our heartfelt thank you go to Cynthia Ibrahim for her support and encouragement. We extend our gratitude to Eddie Bowers for his patience and faith in our project. Thank you, Eddie.

We acknowledge, too, the recreation and leisure managers of today and those of the future who contribute to a healthy employee/employer relationships by providing an atmosphere of trust where talent, creativity, and innovation can flourish in a healthy environment. And we extend our professional admiration and gratitude to the fellows of the American Leisure Academy for their enduring professional contributions and inspiration for which we are all indebted.

CONTENTS

Chapter 3
DYNAMICS OF LEADERSHIP   47

Chapter 4
MANAGEMENT   73

Chapter 5
PERSONNEL MANAGEMENT   109

Chapter 6
FACILITIES AND EQUIPMENT 151

Chapter 7
MANAGEMENT AND NATURAL RESOURCES 185

Chapter 8
MANAGEMENT IN THE TECHNOLOGICAL ENVIRONMENT 215

Chapter 9
FISCAL MANAGEMENT 233

Chapter 10
MARKETING 267

Chapter 11
PROMOTING PARKS, RECREATION, AND LEISURE SERVICES 291

Chapter 12
THE LEGAL ASPECTS OF MANAGEMENT 325

Chapter 13
ENTREPRENEURIAL AND
RECREATION BUSINESS   363

Chapter 14
EVALUATION, RESEARCH,
AND LEISURE SERVICES   391

Chapter 15
CURRENT ISSUES AND FUTURE TRENDS 417

CHAPTER 1
INTRODUCTION

Learning Objectives

After studying this chapter, you should be able to do the following:

1. Understand the difference between a profession and an occupation.
2. Develop an understanding that the leisure profession needs a code of ethics.
3. Appreciate the need for a leader/manager in the agencies dealing with parks, recreation, or leisure services.
4. Appreciate the responsibilities of a leader/manager in the agencies dealing with parks, recreation, or leisure.

This book is concerned with management in parks, recreation, and leisure services. Management differs from leadership in that a manager is a person who directs others to achieve agreed-upon objectives. On the other hand, leader has the ability to motivate and direct the efforts of others toward new alternatives and unchartered paths. Can a person heading a parks, recreation, or leisure agency be a leader and a manager at the same time? It may seem that these two roles are incompatible and in direct conflict with one another. There is a dire need for a manager who directs others toward achieving the goals of the agency, but in the ever-changing parks, recreation, and leisure services, there is as much a need for a leader who motivates and directs his or her staff toward new alternatives and unchartered paths. Can one person fulfill these two roles?

At this point in the evolution of parks, recreation and leisure services such a person is sorely needed. These services are going through fundamental changes, that are significant to the professional as well as and the consumer of these services. Responses to these changes critical for the administration of an agency dealing with parks, recreation, or leisure services.

For this volume the review of the literature reveals that of the many changes taking place in this field, five seem to have a greater impact on discipline. In this chapter, these five changes, listed below, are supplemented with some possible responses as follows:

1. The internal social milieu of an agency providing parks, recreation, and leisure services has gone and is still going through changes. The scope of the changes in the structure and functions of human organizations is presented in Chapter Two. With the arrival of the new century, understanding the culture of the agencies in parks, recreation, and leisure services is a must for an effective leadership and for an efficient management.

2. The recent advances in technology have impacted organizations such as parks, recreation and leisure agencies. While technology facilitates many a process in the management of an agency, it can also create a life of its own. The leader/manager of such an agency should be cognizant of this reality as shown in Chapter Eight.

3. Fundamental changes are taking place in both the source and the method of ending public parks, recreation, and leisure services. Chapter Nine is devoted to presenting the fiscal aspect of an agency dealing with these services. In addition, Chapter Ten discusses creative marketing techniques. Although creative marketing techniques have been used by professionals in semi-public and private agencies, these elements are somewhat new to the recreation professionals.

4. Changes have taken place not only in the profile of the typical consumer of parks, recreation, and leisure services but also in his or her expectations which, must be addressed. The leader/manager and the staff must deal with these important changes. Other chapters discuss some of the ramifications of these changes on the services of an agency offering parks, recreation and leisure programs.

5. One of the most dramatic changes found in the parks, recreation, and leisure services is the growth of entrepreneurial and commercial recreation. Today enterprises using these approaches to serve consumers are becoming fixed scenes in the United States and in many other countries. Although small, these two approaches have helped in part to serve consumers in the evolution of parks, recreation, and leisure system. Their recent unprecedented growth, the impact of which is already being felt, requires the attention of the leader/manager in this field. Chapter Thirteen deals with entrepreneurial and commercial recreation.

KEY CONCEPTS

The staff in most agencies dealing with parks, recreation, and leisure services, including the administrators, are called professionals. What does this mean? Understanding the nature of professionalism, in general, and the parks, recreation, and leisure profession, in particular, is important at this point. Also since this book is written for the future professional who may become a leader/manager in parks, recreation, and leisure services; professionalism, leadership, and management will be considered key concepts in this work. These concepts will be explored inthis first chapter.

Though aprofession often indicates acertain status in social life, but it also requires one to take on certain responsibilities. In order to explore what status means, a brief historical background on the professionalization of occupations will be given to help shed some light on the subject.

One of he earliest attempts at professionalizing an occupation took place in ancient Greece when Hippocrates, the father of medicine, was successful in creating a profession for the c'medicine men" of this time. These men adhered to a code of ethics. It is still used today in the medical profession and is named after its founder, the Hippocratic Oath. What was the purpose behind Hippocrates' attempts?

The idea was and still is that members of a profession would first be well prepared for the tasks ahead ofthem; and secondly, they would do their best in the service of their clients. While these two principles still hold true for today's professions, an additional principle has evolved over the years, and it has added another form of responsibility, directed this time towards our entire society i.e. a shift from occupations to professions. While crucial to status hierarchy and often used as a status symbol, this shift carries with it a very important social responsibility. And a code of ethics for the profession becomes necessary.

In 1957, the seminal article by Ernest Greenwood laid the foundation in the determination of what constitutes a profession. The distinguishing factors of a profession includes a body of knowledge; practitioners who have a monopoly of judgement based on that knowledge; institutions of learning; an ethical code; and a professional culture and association.

In the case of the leisure profession, its members are trained and prepared to perform their duties with competence audio serve their clientele to the best of their abilities. These commitments lie at the core of mission of the profession. There are, of course, other important aspects of the mission of the leisure profession to which the professional is committed, e.g., safety, personal integrity and honesty.

When a professional is granted status, whether implicit or explicit, a social contract between the professional and the society he or she serves is formed, and "That contract, written on the soul of the professional, contains the moral imperatives that promise to benefit the citizens of the society" (Fein 1991:320). Inscribed to the leisure professional is the commitment that leisure is a right for each citizen.

Leisure as A Human Right

Almost half a century ago, the General Assembly of the United Nations adopted the Universal Declaration of Human Rights including the following important principle which goes to the heart of the mission of the leisure professional:

> Every citizen has the right to rest and leisure ...including reasonable limitation
> of working hours and periodic holiday with pay ...and the right to freely par-
> ticipate in the cultural life of the community... to enjoy the arts(UN 1978)

If the mission of the education profession is to have everyone in school and if the mission of the health profession is to make every one healthy, what then is the mission of the leisure profession? In a matter patterned after goals of the education and health, the mission in the leisure profession is to see that recreational opportunities are available for everyone. This is, of course, a very tall order.

In today's climate of shrinking public funds, it is difficult if not impossible to meet this social responsibility. In the case of education, not every child is in a public school. While laws of the land determine that every child should be in school be it pubic or private, at a particular time in his or her life, no such law exists for leisure and recreation. Here lies the dilemma of the leisure professional.

How could his or her mission, that envisions ample recreational opportunities for everyone, be fulfilled with the ever shrinking public and even private funds. The need for the professional to provide effective leadership in securing funding is very clear. This leadership goes beyond a single agency or single service. The leadership goes into the heart of the mission and its social responsibility. The playground movement that began over a century still goes on today.

Another dilemma for the leisure professional and his or her mission is the fact that not all the participants in park settings, recreational activities, or leisure pursuits are served under the watchful eyes of a professional. For example, many communities organize after-school sports programs, which are sponsored by local businesses and are manned by staff who have no professional training in the fields. How can a case be made that all these activities could come under the watchful eyes of a well-prepared and well-trained professional staff?

A Decline in Leisure Opportunities?

In the meantime, recent statistics are not very encouraging for the profession and its mission. It is rather disheartening that the United States, which led the world in human rights within and outside the United Nations, has the lowest rate on leisure rights among the industrial nations of the world. A recent study shows that American industrial workers put in 1,994 hours a year; followed by the Japanese,1,964,theCanadian,1,898;theDanish, 1,581; and finally the German, 1,527. This translates into a 38.3 hours per week for the American worker and 29.3 hours for the German worker (L.A. Times, 1995).

Yet statistics also show that Americans are spending more on leisure as shown in the following Table 1-1.

TABLE 1-1

Personal Consumption Expenditures for Recreation: 1990 to 1998

[In billions of dollars (284.9 presents $284,900,000,000), except percent. Represents market value of purchase of goods and services by individuals and nonprofit institutions]

[In billions of dollars (284.9 represents $284,900,000,000), except percent. Represents market value of purchases of goods and services by individuals and nonprofit institutions]

Type of product or service	1990	1993	1994	1995	1996	1997	1998
Total recreation expenditures	**284.9**	**340.1**	**368.7**	**401.6**	**429.6**	**457.8**	**494.7**
Percent of total personal consumption [1]	7.4	7.6	7.8	8.1	8.2	8.3	8.5
Books and maps	16.2	18.8	20.8	23.1	24.9	26.6	27.8
Magazines, newspapers, and sheet music	21.6	23.1	24.9	26.2	27.6	29.5	31.9
Nondurable toys and sport supplies . . . . [2]	32.8	39.5	43.4	47.2	50.6	53.7	57.7
Wheel goods, sports and photographic equipment [2]	29.7	32.5	35.2	38.5	40.5	43.2	47.1
Video and audio products, computer equipment,							
and musical instruments	52.9	62.6	71.0	77.0	80.0	84.0	92.6
Video and audio goods, including							
and musical instruments	43.9	48.1	53.0	55.9	56.4	57.8	62.2
Computers, peripherals, and software	8.9	14.5	18.0	21.0	23.6	26.2	30.4
Radio and television repair.	3.7	3.3	3.3	3.6	3.7	3.9	3.9
Flowers, seeds, and potted plants	10.9	12.5	13.2	13.8	14.9	15.6	16.5
Admissions to specified spectator amusements	14.8	17.5	18.2	19.2	20.7	22.2	23.8
Motion picture theaters . . . . [3]	5.1	5.0	5.2	5.5	5.8	6.4	6.8
Legitimate theaters and opera, and entertainments							
of nonprofit institutions [3]	5.2	6.8	7.2	7.6	8.0	8.7	9.4
Spectator sports [4]	4.5	5.7	5.8	6.1	6.9	7.1	7.6
Clubs and fraternal organizations except insurance [5]	8.7	11.1	11.8	12.7	14.0	14.4	14.9
Commercial participant amusements [6]	24.6	34.0	38.6	43.9	48.3	52.3	56.2
Pari-mutuel net receipts.	3.5	3.3	3.4	3.5	3.5	3.6	3.7
Other [7]	65.4	81.9	84.7	93.1	100.8	109.0	118.6

[1] See Table 723.   [2] Includes boats and pleasure aircraft.   [3] Except athletic.   [4] Consists of admissions to professional and amateur athletic events and to racetracks, including horse, dog, and auto.   [5] Consists of dues and fees excluding insurance premiums.   [6] Consists of billiard parlors; bowling alleys; dancing, riding, shooting, skating, and swimming places; amusement devices and parks; golf courses; sightseeing buses and guides; private flying operations; casino gambling; and other commercial participant amusements.   [7] Consists of net receipts of lotteries and expenditures for purchases of pets and pet care services, cable TV, film processing, photographic studios, sporting and recreation camps, video cassette rentals, and recreational services, not elsewhere classified.

Source: U.S. Bureau of Economic Analysis, *The National Income and Product Accounts of the United States, 1929-94*, Vol.1, and *Survey of Current Business*, June 2000.

With shrinking funds perhaps one explanation for the rise in leisure spending might be that the semi-public and the private sectors are picking up the slack. If this is true, the inclusion of a section in this book on nonpublic agencies is justified. As shown in the above table the increase in leisure spending is taking place not only in dollars and cents (From 284.9 billion dollars in 1990 to 494.7 billion dollars in 1996), but also in the percent of total personal consumption (from 7.4% to 8.5% respectively.) Most of the increase is found in commercial participant amusement.

LEADERSHIP

Keeping the aforementioned five changes in mind, the social milieu of the agency, the advent of advanced technology, the changes in sources and methods of funding public service, the changing profiles of the consumers of these services, and the increased interest in entrepreneurial and commercial recreation, how should the manager/leader of today's and tomorrow's parks, recreation, and leisure agency be prepared? From the literature used in the course of writing this book, five answers have been derived. These answers come from the experience of practitioners and researchers in parks, recreation, and leisure services. The detail of these findings can be found in the following sixteen chapters.

1. Let us first discuss the social milieu in the parks, recreation, and leisure agency. The new work force of any agency will help achieve the objectives of the agency, but only if it can achieve its own personal goals as part of the bargain. This means that the manager as an order-giver is passe. The new manager/leader is a consensus-maker and not merely a decision-maker. He or she is a facilitator, one who knows how to draw the best out of co-workers.

2. Where technology is concerned, the manager/leader must serve as a role model in utilizing advanced technology in the work of the agency. The she or he must also keep current with the state of the art in this area.

3. With the decline of public funds, attempts should be made by public agencies dealing with parks, recreation, and leisure service to acquire funds from sources that have in the past been utilized solely by non-public agencies. The competition over the non-public funds is going to be fierce. In the continual search for funding, other unchartered paths need to be explored. This can be done through the initiative and the creativity of a well-prepared manager/leader.

4. The demographic shape of America is changing. The changes are not only limited to age groups but also in the ethnic composition of the country. In the past managers/leaders knew the important of the characteristics of age groups in constructing a program. Today more

than ever, understanding of the values, customs, and traditions of an increasing number of ethnic groups is a must for the effective leadership and the efficient management of an agency dealing with parks, recreation, and leisure services.

5. At one point in the history of the recreation movement, people who were working in public agencies were not concerned about others who are engaged in similar services, either through semi-public agency such as the YMCA or through the private sector such as a health spa. As the increasing competition over funds between public and semi-public agencies and as the number of entrepreneurial and commercial recreation enterprises increases, more attention is now being given to these two sectors of leisure services: the semi-public and the private.

In addition, the limited number of vacancies in the shrinking public recreation sector has compelled many of the graduates of departments of parks, recreation, and leisure studies, who were once being prepared for the public recreation market, to join semi-public and private agencies. It seems that an interaction is taking place among these three sectors, and each of the three will benefit from the experience of the others. Together these factors make it necessary to think in terms of combining leadership skills that seek alternatives and are willing to try unchartered paths with the traditional management skills as presented in the next section. More on leadership in this chapter as well as chapter three.

MANAGEMENT

There is a tendency to play down management and to elevate leadership as the best model in heading an agency, nonetheless, skillful management is still needed. The day by day operation of an agency is not going to stop while the search is going on for alternatives or looking for the unchartered paths. At this point per- haps an understanding of what managers do is in order.

Long ago, one of the pioneers in parks, recreation, and leisure service, Luther Gulick, suggested "POSDCORB" as a memory device to list the functions of a manager of an agency in these services. These letters stand for planning, orga- nizing, staffing, directing, coordinating and budgeting (1937). Other acronyms have been used over the years to point out the tasks required in management. For example, MBO stood for Management by objectives; PPBS stood for Planning-Program-Budgeting-System; and PERT stood for Program Evaluation Review Techniques.

BBM, or Benefit-based Management in Park, Recreation and Leisure Services is the recognition that they are integral part of community life (Alien et al, 1997).

Some people advocate that management is ascience, while others see it as an art." In either case, management in parks, recreation, and leisure agencies should follow four basic principles as suggested Kraus and Curtis (1986:25):

1. Division of labor and task specialization: Here operational functions are separated and placed in different departments, which in turn could be divided in turn its based on the tasks they perform.

2. Assignments of authority and accountability: If the authority is legitimate, i.e., the boss has the right to command and the subordinate to obey, then, accountability is possible.

3. Scalar principle and unity of command: This means that the authority on top is supported by unity of command and therefore every subordinate directly responsible to only one superior.

4. Span of Control: This principle refers to the number of immediate subordinates with whom the supervisor is charged. The numbers suggested range from six to ten.

It is also important to know that the interactive process in management is both vertical as well as horizontal. On the vertical plane, the hierarchy is delineated as discussed above. On the horizontal plane, the departments and or units are placed next to each other. This means that not only should the line of authority be known, but also the tasks of each department or unit and its relationship to other departments or units should be clearly spelled out.

Responsibilities of the Leader

As is shown in Chapter Three, " Dynamics of Leadership," it is difficult to develop a list of tangibles for the effective leadership in parks, recreation, and leisure services. When compared to the responsibilities of the manager, the responsibilities of the leader are very hard to list and quantify. This difficulty is due in part to the role of the leader being more or less "spiritual". No one can see the "spirit" of an agency, but one can feel it. Nonetheless, there are important elements to the leadership of an agency dealing with parks, recreation, and leisure services. For instance the leadership should concern itself with the vision of the agency, the standards of operation, and the integrity and ethical behavior of the staff.

The Leadership and the Vision: As will be discussed more in details in Chapter Three, the vision of an agency goes beyond everyday reality. This is one of the tasks of the leadership. While management takes care of the reality of everyday operations, leadership requires the setting aside of some time in which things "beyond" the everyday tasks are contemplated. Where the agency is going. Why?,..and how?... would be examples of the contemplative queries to be pondered by the leadership.

Since the mission and objectives of the agency are usually in place, the next task of the leadership is to relate the vision to the mission of the agency.

The Leader and the Led: Successful leadership relates the vision of the agency to its mission. The leadership also tries to motivate those who engage in the operation of the agency to become an integral part of both the mission and the vision. Energizing the staff into action is not an easy task. Perhaps crucial to the leadership's success in this endeavor is the understanding of human nature in general and the integral culture of the agency.

In the meantime, leadership serves as the guardian of integrity and ethical behavior. With the growth of entrepreneurial and commercial recreation; concerns have been voiced that parks, recreation, and leisure services, in their current market-oriented mode, are drifting toward a "merchant mentality." Are the ethical guidelines different for the public and private sectors in parks, recreation, and leisure services? In the business world, many corporations realize that it is not in their long-term interest to behave in a "merchant mentality." Some believe that their primary interest is to protect the consumers, above the interests of stockholders, employees, and others (Wolff, 1991:289).

Entrepreneurial and commercial recreation providers must be aware of this aspect of business. If not maybe they should be reminded of it and be urged to join public recreation providers in their endeavors to follow a code of ethics.

The Leader and Ethics: According to Bedini and Henderson (1991:291),

> Professional ethics' relates' to what one ought to do, one's duty as a member of a socially responsible profession, which includes one's responsibility to consumers, to the profession, and to society.

A code of ethics was suggested for leisure professionals and approved by NRPA Board of Directors in 1994 (See p. 69).

Another code of ethics could be adopted by the agency itself. But the mere adoption of a code of ethics, be it the national one or the local one, is not in itself sufficient. Larry Williams writes:

> "Exemplary action is required, as -well as an understanding of the conflicts and royalties and the gray areas of ethical decisions "which individual managers face. " (1991:244-5).

It is incumbent upon the leadership of an agency in parks, recreation, and leisure services to see that not only a code of ethics is adopted, but also that it is alive and it is being followed in letter and in spirit.

Responsibility of the Manager

Detailed through the chapters of this book are the duties and responsibilities pertaining to the administration of an agency in parks, recreation, and leisure services. While Chapter Four gives an overview of the duties of a manager, the day by day operations that are necessary for the efficient functioning of an agency are covered in most of the remaining chapters. An overview of these duties is provided below.

Personnel Management: Staffing the agency with the needed personnel is a task that falls on the shoulder of the management. The manager should familiarize himself or herself with the important elements of hiring, retaining, and promoting processes. Perhaps an important question that has nothing to do with job analysis and qualifications for the job is whether the person, being considered for the job, can fit within the internal culture of the agency and how amenable he or she is to the mission and the vision of the agency (see Chapter Five).

Facilities and Equipment: Although the manager of an agency, particularly a large one, dealing with parks, recreation, and leisure services, will not be the immediate custodian of facilities or equipment, he or she are ultimately responsible for the planning, execution, and maintenance of the facilities. Attention should be given to two aspects of planning facilities. The first is consideration of the needs of special populations, above and beyond what the law required. The second is the possibility of a joint power agreement, which reduces the cost for both agencies. Where equipment are concerned, the manager is ultimately responsible for his or her agency's purchases and maintenance(See Chapter Six).

Fiscal Management: This may be the most difficult task for an administrator of an agency in parks, recreation, and leisure services. Granted, there may be specialists in accounting, auditing, and other fiscal matters working in the agency, but sometimes decisions have to be made which fall on the shoulder of the person in charge of the agency. Keeping expenditure under control requires continual vigilance. Mechanisms used in such control are given in Chapter Nine. As important is the recent trend of enhancing revenues through means other than the main source of financing. In the case of a private, profit-oriented agency, the concept of creative marketing has gained ground due to competition (see Chapters Ten and Eleven).

Promotion of the Agency: The notion of public relations has given way to the idea of promoting the agency. Promotion is thought of as an attempt to overcome inertia, and to add a perceived value to its offerings. Public relations is one aspect of promoting the agency. Promotion should be a continuous effort by the whole staff and not merely through publications such as news releases, fact sheets, or news conferences. It is advocated that special events are a good method of promoting the agency. All these activities may be the responsibility of a staff member or two; nonetheless, the final responsibility falls on the manager of the agency (see Chapter Eleven and Twelve).

The management of natural resources is given special attention in Chapter Seven. Chapter Eight provides information on technology as applied to recreation, and leisure services. Evaluation, an important function for both the leader and the manager in parks, recreation, and leisure services is discussed in Chapter Fourteen. The final chapter, Chapter Fifteen, discusses present issues and future trends. A glossary of terms is provided at the end of the book along with the needed appendices.

SUMMARY

- There is a need in parks, recreation, and leisure services to have a unique combination of a manager/leader to be in charge of the individual agencies. The need for leadership has been expedited by the changes that have taken place and have affected both the structure and functions of these agencies.

- The newly approved leisure profession must follow a code of ethics, which is expected by most of society. The National Recreation and Park Association has adopted a code which could be used by the individual agencies, and they can develop codes of their own.

- The professional has a commitment to society which is reflected in " the leisure right," which underscores the right of each citizen to a reasonable time off from work and opportunities for recreational participation.

- While the leader of a parks, recreation, or leisure agency is responsible for the energy, morals, and standards of conduct of the staff, he or she is also responsible for the every day operations as its manager.

LEARNING ACTIVITIES

1. Read the code of ethics that the National Recreation and Park Association has adopted. React to it in writing,

2. Invite the administrator of a nearby public agency in parks, recreation, or leisure services to attend your class. Have him or her talk about his or her responsibilities. See if there is a difference between leadership and management in the performance of these duties.

3. Invite the administrator of a semi-private agency dealing with parks, recreation, or leisure service. Have him or her react to the code of ethics adopted by the National Recreation and Park Association.

4. Invite a professor of philosophy to present his or her views on ethics in services and business.

REFERENCES

Alien, L. et al.(1997) **Benefit-Based Programming**. Salt Lake City, Utah: NPRA Congress.

Bedini, L.A. and K.A. Henderson (1991) "Methods of Teaching Ethics in Leisure Studies Curricula", in G. Fain (Editor) **Leisure and Ethics**. Reston, VA: American Association for Leisure and Recreation.

Fein, G. (1991) "Moral Leisure: the Promise and Wonder" in G. Fain (Editor) **Leisure and Ethics**. Reston, VA: American Association for Leisure and Recreation.

Gulick, L. and L. Urwick (Editors) (1937) **Papers in the Science of Administration**. New York: Institute of Public Administration.

Ibrahim, H, and K. Cordes (1993) **Outdoor Recreation**. Dubuque, IA: Brown and Benchmark.

Kraus, R. and J. Curtis (1986) **Creative Management in Recreation, Parks, and Leisure Services**. St. Louis: Mosby Year Book, inc. **Los Angeles Times**(1995)"U.S. Worker's Hours Longest, Study Shows' September 27.

United Nations (1978) **Human Rights: Acompilation of International Instruments**. New York: United Nations

Williams, Larry (1991) "Ethics in Management" in G. Fain (Editor) **Leisure and Ethics**. Reston, VA: American Association for Leisure and Recreation.

Wolff, R.M. (1991) "Private vs. Public Recreation Ethics: Is the Vision

Different" G. Fain (Editor) **Leisure and Ethics**. Reston VA: American Association for Leisure and Recreation.

CHAPTER 2

HUMAN ORGANIZATIONS AND THEIR CULTURE

Learning Objectives

After studying this chapter, you should be able to do the following:

1. Understand the intricacies of the leisure delivery system.

2. Differentiate between the types and levels of leisure delivery agencies.

3. Understand the underpinning of different types of agencies in the leisure delivery system.

4. Describe the cultural factors that affect the functions and effectiveness of agencies dealing with parks, recreation, and leisure.

5. Explain how groups are formed in human organizations and in particular the ones dealing with parks, recreation, and leisure services.

6. Appreciate how decisions are made in human organizations and particularly the ones dealing with the areas covered in this volume.

What is a human organization? What does organizational culture mean? And what do these two terms mean to the recreation profession? The term human organization refers to the formal association of a group of persons for the purpose of performing specific tasks as they relate to specific objectives. There are many kinds of these organizations: economic, political and social. In this work, the main interest is in service-oriented organizations, particularly those providing leisure services.

These organizations develop their own cultures since they are made of people who interact and try to deal with everyday tasks. It is, therefore, inevitable that each organization will develop a culture which may not seem to outsiders as being different from the cultures of the agencies that deal with the same type of service. Granted these organizations may share similar values since they offer the same service; yet each will develop a culture uniquely its own. When a recreation professional joins an agency dealing with leisure service, he or she must acquaint himself or herself with the dominant culture of the agencies providing leisure services as well as with the culture of the particular one he or she is joining.

The organizational culture of a leisure delivery agency and its sub- units depends to a great extent on the kind and level of service. It is therefore necessary to review the kinds and levels of the agencies that are providing leisure services before delving into their cultures.

THE LEISURE DELIVERY SYSTEM

What is meant by the leisure delivery system? This is a system that provides leisure services in a given society. Typically, this system is composed of three types of services that are provided at three levels as shown in the following chart:

LEVELS:

TYPES:	LOCAL	STATE/REGIONAL	NATIONAL
Public:	Community centers	Beaches/Lakes	Parks/Forests
Semi-public:	Day Camps	Tournaments	YMCA/YWCA
Commercial:	Miniature Golf	Resorts/Hotels	Amusement Parks

The following describes these agencies and their affiliates.

Local Leisure Services

On the local level, there are three kinds of agencies that provide leisure services to the members of the community: public, semi-public/ nonprofit, and commercial.

Public Agencies: Numerically, these agencies dominate leisure services and receive the most attention from scholars of leisure. Corresponding with the growth of suburban America and Canada, local public agencies providing leisure services witnessed phenomenal growth after World War II. Established through what is commonly known as enabling legislation, the state enables local government, whether it is city or county, to provide a leisure delivery unit as part of the local services. The law enacted in this case is permissive, not mandatory, since it does not force the local government to offer the service but allows it to do so if a need exists. This is not the case with other services, which are mandatory such as education, police and fire.

The legal basis for a local leisure delivery unit goes back to the Tenth Amendment of the Constitution of the United States which stipulates that the powers not delegated to the Federal Government are reserved for the states. The states, in turn, create counties to administer the policy of the state, and towns and cities are then empowered to deliver services. Accordingly, several public entities provide a public leisure delivery unit where there is a real need to improve local conditions one of the following administrative arrangements may be followed.

County Agencies: There are over 3,000 counties in the U.S., and since their populations are growing at a faster rate than in metropolitan areas, the counties role in providing services has increased dramatically in the last few decades. Under a county structure, leisure service could be offered in many different ways. Possibilities include combining parks and recreation into one department or providing parks and recreation services as separate functions within the county structure. Also municipalities within the county provide local recreation and park services.

Special Districts: Enabling legislation allows counties to offer services through special districts. School districts are a good example of a service provided for the residents of a county. Another example is the transportation district which provides a service to a number of cities and towns. Recreational services can be provided in the same way. A number of cities could join together to provide these services. Illinois has legislation that enables local governments to establish two types of agencies that have a direct impact on the leisure delivery units. These agencies include the forest preserve districts such as the Cook County Forest Preserve district and the park districts such as the Chicago Park District. There are also districts which combine parks and recreation.

Municipal Leisure Delivery Units: Similarly, there are a number of ways through which leisure delivery can be established in a city or town. The dominant method is to combine park and recreation authority under one unit in the local municipal government as is the case in county and special district delivery units.

Semi-Public/Nonprofit Agencies: Some of these organizations predate the public agencies in providing leisure services to the young and old of both genders. In 1851 the Young Men's Christian Association was introduced to Boston from England; the first Boys' Club was established in Hartford in 1860; and the first Young Women's Christian Association was established in Boston in 1866. Today there are a number of these agencies including the following that are providing recreational activities in local communities.

The Local YMCA & YWCA: Despite the growth of the public delivery system of leisure services that has taken place since the inception of the first Y, this voluntary agency has gained solid ground in America and Canada. The local Y is often housed in specified buildings or through a school, a house or even a storefront. According to Kraus and Curtis there were 964 YMCAs operating 1,233 units with a combined budget of 2.3 billion dollars.(2000:6)

The Local Boy and Girl Scouts: In the United States there are close to four million members in the Boy Scouts and close to three million members in the Girl Scouts. While the boys' ages range from 8 to 20 in the 130,000 units, the girls ages range between 6 and 17 in the 104,000 units. These units are sponsored by religious groups, civic clubs, and public and private schools.

The Local Boys and Girls Club: Established on the East Coast of the United States by volunteers to serve underprivileged boys in urban centers during the second half of the 19th century, today these clubs welcome both boys and girls to their 700 local units.

Other Local Agencies: There are a number of other local private nonprofit units that provide leisure services to young and old. The Young Men's Hebrew Association and local 4H Clubs are examples of leisure providers. The 4H Clubs were organized according to the Smith Lever Act of 1914, which provided for cooperative extension work in agriculture and home economics.

Another example of a youth agency serving local needs is the Campfire Organization, which was established in 1910 with a strong American motif revolving around Indian lore. The local church, synagogue, temple, or mosque could also become involved in providing activities for its young members. Although the emphasis is on the religious aspects, a number of recreational activities are planned for the youth of the congregation, and are frequently open to others in the community.

Commercial Enterprises: There are many local small businesses that cater to the leisure pursuits of local residents. Since the tendency is toward a free market economy, there is a growth in entrepreneurial approaches to leisure services. Therefore, understanding the organizational culture of these enterprises is important. On the local level, the following commercial enterprises are engaged in providing local leisure services:

Nightclubs and Cafes: It is only recently that leisure scholars discovered the importance of the nightclub and the cafe in the leisure lifestyle of the community. While the number of nightclubs may not be dramatically increasing in the United States, cafes are gaining grounds. Both these enterprises are places for socialization, entertainment, and recreation. These places allow for active participation in dominoes, billiards, darts, and similar activities.

Health Spas: In the last few decades, local health spas have witnessed a phenomenal growth in North America. The spa, previously limited to the wealthy, is now available to members of all classes in society. The concentration is on health and fitness through the use of equipment that is developed with state-of-the-art technology. Serving as a meeting place for individuals, the social element of health spas has become increasingly important in the lives of many people.

Private Clubs: There are hundreds of clubs in North America catering to a number of leisure pursuits from traveling and hiking, to sports and hobbies. Among these clubs are the country clubs serving the well to do. Recently, some of these clubs has been criticized for discriminatory practices, and so most have changed their policies according to the prescriptions of the law.

Movies and Theatres: There are about 10,000 walk-in and drive-in movie theatres in the United States. However with the introduction of television, the number of movie theatres has declined. The same decline was seen in legitimate theatres due to the same reason. But by 1970, the number of these theatres began to increase again, as is the case for movie theatres, with the exception of drive-ins, which continue to become increasingly scarce. This may be due in part to the advent of home movie rentals and satellite and cable television which allows people to watch recent movies in the comfort of their own homes.

Regional and State Leisure Services

Other leisure services are provided regionally and statewide through agencies that may have affiliation with local or national agencies. They are the following.

Public Agencies: The number of public agencies that provide leisure services on a regional or statewide basis is not as high as those providing services locally. Nonetheless, their services are as important and as effective as the services of the local units.

Parks: The acreage of state parks does not exceed one-fifth of the national parks acreage in the United States, yet because of their accessibility, they are used three times as much. Compared to its American counterpart, the Canadian provincial park is more autonomous because public domain land, known as Crown's land, is available to the provinces under Canadian laws while the public domain land in the United States is controlled totally by the Federal Government.

Forests: State and provincial forests serve as intermediary resources between the limited local and the distant federal resources. There are a number of state forests that are easily accessible to the residents of the Northwest, New England, and South Atlantic regions of the United States. In Canada, provincial forests are close to urban centers, thus allowing more choices in leisure.

College and University Campuses: The need for recreational outlets among college students helped in the formation and expansion of the student union.

While there are ample opportunities for leisure pursuit in activities sponsored by other entities on campus, such as the departments of music, drama, physical education, and literature; the student union concentrates on providing participatory activities to the students. The student union may have a building of its own or share a building with another division of the college. Colleges and universities organize intramural and sports clubs.

Semi-Public/Nonprofit Agencies: Although the number of these agencies is smaller on this level than the number of its local units that provide direct services to the members of the community, these agencies are worth discussing.

Residential Camps: A number of private nonprofit organizations provide camps that are used by its local units as well as other groups. There are at least 6,000 resident camps in the Unites States, most of which are run by nonprofit organizations such as the Young Men's Christian Association and the Boy Scouts. Some northern and/or mountain residential camps are winterized to receive campers in the winter, but most of them are summer camps in which the season is divided up into one to two week sessions. The camps have permanent features such as cabins, dining facility, pool, and meeting rooms.

Resorts: These are self-contained facilities, which provide more than room and board. Although most of resorts are commercial enterprises, some are run by private nonprofit organizations. This includes health and beauty resorts as well as ski resorts. Some resorts provide specific activities such as the Pinehurst Resort in North Carolina, which has a 200-mile trail for horseback riding.

Commercial Enterprises: There are a number of commercial enterprises that cater to the leisure needs of the citizens. Though some of them may have national and sometimes international orientation, many of these enterprises only serve regional and state groups.

Amusement Parks: From modest beginnings two centuries ago, the amusement park has become an important feature in the leisure delivery scene of the 20th century. The original amusement parks were simple moveable rides. Even now these can be seen in many of the Third World countries. Today, modern technology has allowed rides and other features to consist of elaborate nonmovable mechanisms. There are over 300 amusement parks in the United States with an annual revenue of close to four billion dollars.

Campgrounds: While many of the campgrounds may fall the under public and the private/nonprofit domain, almost two thirds of the campgrounds in the United States are commercial enterprises. There are a number of ways in which the commercial campgrounds are administered. Many are units of a large business entity; others are small businesses.

National Leisure Agencies

On the national level, there are a number of agencies that provide leisure services: public, semi-public/nonprofit, and commercial agencies.

Public Agencies: The public agencies that provide recreational activities for the citizens include parks, forests, and wilderness areas.

National Parks: The concept of national parks, a place distinguished for its natural uniqueness, is a recent idea, which is gaining ground worldwide. The idea behind a national park is preservation. Today there are 79 million acres and 32 million acres of national parks in the United States and Canada, respectively.

National Forests: The United States has an extensive national forest system totaling over 186 million acres. Contrary to the idea of preservation which is behind the establishment of national parks, national forests are administered with the idea of multiple use that includes recreational activities such as camping, winter sport, fishing, and hunting. There are close to 5,000 campgrounds in the national forests with the capability of catering to about half a million people at the same time.

Wilderness Areas: These are "primitive" areas within the national forests of the United States, and are now designated to stay this way. Wilderness areas are used by die-hard hikers and campers who are willing to stay overnight or for a few days without modern conveniences.

Semi-Public/Nonprofit Agencies: Most of the volunteer and youth organizations have national offices that provide services to their regional and local organizations and chapters. For instance, the YMCA national office develops standards to be followed by the different Ys. These offices do not provide direct services.

Commercial Enterprises: There are a number of enterprises that offer leisure services such as tourism or what is also called pleasure travel. Tourism and pleasure travel have increased dramatically in the last two decades. There are more American tourists traveling abroad than there are tourists coming to the United States. The ratio of 1:0.6 U.S. tourist to other tourists may be due to the fact that the United States does not have a tourism office in other countries while many countries have such an office in the United States. However, there are state tourist offices to promote tourism from other states, making domestic tourism a thriving business.

The Gaming Industry: Gambling has become legal in many states. It is done on riverboats, on native American Land, and in many other local and regional areas across the United States. This despite the fact that gambling on-line is gaining popularity as a form of leisure pursuits.

Whether a recreational professional is hired in local, regional, state; or national agency, be it public, semi-public or private, understanding the culture of the leisure delivery system in general, and the culture of the specific agency in which he or she is working is important.

THE CULTURE OF THE LEISURE DELIVERY SYSTEM

By understanding the components of the leisure service agency's culture the recreation professional can better adjust to the agency. These agencies are human organizations, which according to Trice and Beyer (1993), develop cultures that have two main components. The first component includes the shared values, norms, myths, symbols and taboos of the agency. The second component refers to observable ways through which the members of the agency express themselves either formally or informally, depending on the type of agency. Since many of the shared values, norms, myths, symbols, and taboos of the agency are derived from the society in which it functions, an understanding of the relationship between leisure and the dominant societal values and ideology is important.

Values, Ideology, And Leisure

Organizations are governed by ideologies that stem from a belief system usually derived from adopted values. Values are at the core of belief systems of individuals, groups, and societies, since they determine goals and the means to achieve these goals. Values are usually held in high esteem, and are protected because they serve as the general guidelines for behavior. Although values are not in themselves tangible, they can be observed through a second layer of cultural traits known as cultural norms. Cultural norms are specific guides for behavior which are usually observable. For instance, motherhood, culturally valued in American society, is played out by specific behavioral guidelines. Calling one's mother on Mother's Day and buying her flowers are expected norms. This can be validated by witnessing the amount of flowers purchased on that day and how it has become the busiest day of the year for telephone companies.

Although slow in changing, values and norms are not static. Within two hundred years, the values of play, recreation, and leisure have changed drastically in both America and Canada--changes that have left an impact on the development and function of the leisure delivery systems in North America. Three levels of values affect the leisure delivery system. The first level is the dominant societal values--the ones affecting society in general. The second level includes the shared values of the leisure delivery system, and the third level is related to the internal organizational values of a particular agency.

Societal Values and Leisure

In the early 1800's, the dominant values in the United States and Canada were not amenable to leisure pursuits. Accordingly, public systems for the delivery of such pursuits did not materialize for almost a century after the establishment of these two nations. Even then, with the establishment of the first public systems of urban parks, it was clear that they were intended to provide natural vistas in the growing urban centers of North America and not necessarily be used as playgrounds. Although maintained by human beings, the urban parks of New York, Philadelphia, Boston, Ottawa, and Toronto were meant to be extensions of nature.

In these early years play was frowned upon originally, but it was gradually accepted as an important aspect of human life. It was through the efforts of a few individuals toward the end of the 19th century when awareness of the role of play in human life took hold. Play had been observed among the young and also the old; yet publicly and privately, organized playforms took some time to develop in North America. Efforts of volunteers, who saw the Industrial Revolution creating urban slums, introduced the need for supervised playgrounds. The value behind such provision was service.

In the meantime, two factors played important roles in raising some focus on the importance of play. The first factor was increased free time of the new white middle class that resulted from the Industrial Revolution paving the way for the "willingness to accept participation in a wide variety of sporting activities as a legitimate way to spending it " (Levine 1989:18). The second factor was growing interest in health, particularly among women. "Health was important for everyone, but it was particularly important for women in their role as progenitors and nurturers of new life" (Mechikoff and Estes, 1993:212). Organized play, which became known as recreation, was becoming valued by individuals for its impact on hygiene and personal improvement.

The change in attitude toward play in some segments of American society resulted in the growth of voluntary associations that dealt with organized play. The leading thrust came from the formation of the Boston Sand Garden in 1885 (Butler, 1940:61). The idea of providing organized play was extended to adults as well. Despite the efforts of the dedicated individuals who volunteered to provide recreational outlets for young and old, these volunteer efforts did not fill the demand for supervised recreational programs. The gap was filled in the second half of the 19th century with what Mclean et al. call unsavory commercial recreation such as pool halls, nickelodeons, shooting galleries, vaudeville attractions, horse racing, professional baseball, and prize fighting (1985: 45). The reaction to this tendency was swift in that "the worthy use of leisure" became an important objective of education. Leisure was the term used for the free time created by the change in the lifestyle of the growing urbanized population of North America. The worthy use of leisure was advocated by the National Education Association as one of the Seven Cardinal Principles of Education in 1918. Thus schools became involved in providing leisure education.

Although local sponsorship of recreational programs and leisure activities increased in the first two decades of the 20th century through both public and private organizations, the role played by state and federal government was limited to providing outdoor recreational resources. A few years later, during the Depression years, the role of the federal government in providing recreational outlets increased dramatically using "recreation as a means of maintaining public morale, particularly of the unemployed and also is a means of actually providing employment" (Kraus, 1984:66). Leisure and recreation were not valued for whatever they could do for the individual but rather for stimulating a staggering economy.

Expansion in recreational services took place after World War II with the rapid mobility of the populace, which was coupled with an increase in the population. The number of municipal agencies providing recreational services in the newly expanding communities increased drastically. On the other hand, local school programs, which provided extensive recreational programs as mandated by the Seven Cardinal Principles of 1918, were dropped. Municipal public recreation became part of the lexicon of local governments. The feeling, then, was that leisure and recreation were valued for themselves, a step in the right direction, but this was a short-lived euphoria.

The euphoric feeling that recreation was an individual right and not a privilege continued into the 1960s when the Federal Government expanded its role by establishing the Bureau of Outdoor Recreation. Additionally, the passage of the Land and Water Conservation Fund allowed for federal assistance to local and state recreation programs. More assistance to the local and state offerings came about with the creation of the National Endowment for the Arts. It was during this time that recreation for special populations was gaining ground. But progress was stalled in the recession of the 1970s. A decade later, the assumption that leisure services were valued enough to deserve public financial support was overthrown. Unlike education, the public leisure delivery units on the local level found it necessary to raise funds through aggressive marketing efforts. This drastic shift in orientation left its impact on the value orientation of the ideology of the total leisure delivery system.

Values Of the Leisure Delivery System

Granted, the roots of the leisure delivery system started at a time when such pursuits were not supported by the Puritanical orientation of American society. Nonetheless, the system grew over the years to provide activities that became an important part of the lifestyle of almost all citizens of this country. The same thing occurred in many other countries. In this pursuit, the leisure delivery system is composed of three subsystems: the public, the semi-public/nonprofit, and the commercial subsystems. Today, each one of these subsystems is dominated by certain values. It is safe to state that although the core value of the public and the semi-public/nonprofit subsystems is service, the core value of the commercial subsystem is profit. At the same time, the core value of the public subsystem is in a state of flux. This subsystem started at a time when the concept of play was not *de rigueur* and playforms evolved around some convoluted notion that play was rehabilitative for the unfortunate and was therapeutic for the unhealthy. Other values were added over the years, such as the value of the "perfect" community and the economic value of recreational offerings to the community. Both the profession and professional training were swayed accordingly. Leisure, valued for itself and by itself, was not adopted except briefly and haphazardly.

Today, it is hard to determine if there is indeed a core value for the leisure delivery system, and in particular where the leisure pursuits offered by the public sector on the local, regional, state and national levels are concerned.

Values and the Leisure Delivery Units

The leisure delivery units are local ones that provide service to the members of the local community. These are local public units, provided by counties and municipalities, youth service organizations, and commercial enterprises such as health spas and private clubs. It is clear that the value orientation of these units vary according to affiliation. The following section discusses the value orientation of these units.

The Culture of Small Governmental Units: As was previously stated, the public leisure delivery subsystem is in a state of flux because of the continual change in orientation. For instance, social work values played an important role in launching the projects which were the forerunners of what is the recreation movement (Butler, 1940:60). The movement, started in 1885, was in response to the deteriorating conditions resulting from the industrialization of the country. Recreation was valued as a means of solving social problems.

Initially, philanthropy was one of the dominant values in the public sector. Even the establishment of Central Park was seen in this light. Frederick Law Olmsted stated that the park was designed to "supply those who have no opportunity to spend their summers in the country, a specimen of God's handiwork that shall be to them, inexpensively, what a month is.., at a great cost, to those of easier circumstance" (Udall, 1963;139).

Granted there was an aesthetic value sought in attempting to preserve America's great natural heritage; but on the local level, once the playgrounds were handed to the local authorities, a change in the view of recreation was formalized. Within the first two decades of the 20th century, the need for professionals to handle the growing municipal departments resulted in the hiring of personnel from the service sector who were still dedicated to the service-oriented value of recreation programs and resources.

Particularly after World War II, communities gradually began to include recreational offerings and build parks and community centers. These facilities were seen as amenities that no community could be without. Authors felt that the recreation staff seemed to have been charged not with service to the community but instead with the supervision of the grounds (Gray and Pelegrino, 1973:288).

During the 1960s, the spirit that began the recreation movement resurfaced (Benest et al., 1983:20). However, this time, the value was not that of service to the needy but rather service to the needs of the individual. The term leisure had just come into use, and the concept focused exclusively on the individual and his or her right of self actualization. Benest et al. suggest that municipal recreation departments in this country continued to program traditional recreation activities in order to serve the needs of the 1920s industrial society (1983:10). Although a change was taking place in the attitude and orientation of local leisure delivery units, these changes were short lived.

In the late 1970s, tax cutting initiatives resulted in reduced recreational offerings. During this period self-help replaced institutional help (Naisbitt, 1982). Murphy and Howard state that the leisure delivery system expanded to "incorporate an enabling approach which transfer the responsibility for leisure choices, decisions and behavior to the individual" (1977:208).

Values and the semi-public/nonprofit agency: The nonprofit agencies that provide recreational activities to their members did not start with leisure pursuits in mind. Originally, the idea of many of these nonprofit agencies was to help the individual who needed to cope with the demands of modern living resulting from the Industrial Revolution, in particular the urban decay in the inner cities. There, rapid changes took place that led to many social problems. The motivational factor behind the establishment of a nonprofit service agency was to provide a place set up to deal not with social problems at large but with people who were experiencing problems in the management of their own personal lives. The provision of recreational activities, offered by some of these agencies, is to reach individuals with problems. Many of the original philosophies of the nonprofit agencies changed over the years to include specific services such as recreational activities and not necessarily as a means of reaching the individual.

Values and the commercial enterprise: A commercial enterprise dealing with leisure service is managed with a different set of values. Its aim is to provide the service through the market sector of the economy. The service is organized as a business so that the enterprise strives to obtain a price for the goods it sells and/ or the service it provides. The price should be adequate enough to pay the costs of materials, labor, and capital plus an incentive to continue providing the service, i.e., a profit. In the meantime, if the enterprise is faced with competition, it would have to organize itself in such a way that it would still make at least a 10 percent profit.

The value or values adopted by a parks, recreation, or leisure agency serve as a general guide. It is crucial that all the persons involved in providing the service or goods in such an agency are cognizant of its guiding principles. The vision and mission of the agency are derived from these values. It is therefore imperative that the leadership of the agency make a concerted effort to see that the values, mission, and vision of the agency are clear to everyone.   The values adopted by the agency are not the only cultural elements of an agency. Other elements that have important bearing on its tradition should be explored. Following are some of these elements.

RITES, CEREMONIALS, AND THE LEISURE PROFESSION

To further understand the culture of the leisure delivery system, specific acts and interactions of the persons involved need to be examined. Since all human groups develop rites which stem from the daily life of their members, so will the group dealing with leisure services.

Rites of Individual Focus

The three rites in organizations that focus on the individual include the rite of passage from a previous role or social position to another, the rite of degradation or reduction in social position and power, and the rite of enhancement of one's position or increase in status. All three are witnessed in almost all human societies.

One of the most important acts in the life of the individual member of an organization as well as in the daily routine of the organization is his or her passage through a number of significant events such as joining the group, promotion, or retirement.

According to Van Gennep (1960), in the rite of passage, the individual goes through three phases. First is the separation from the old role and position; this phase is followed by a transitional phase; and finally, an incorporation into the new position or role takes place.

In applying these principles to the recreation profession, once a young professional joins an agency dealing with leisure services, he or she will go through a separation phase from his or her previous role of a student, and acquires the new role of a novice professional. A veteran recreation professional changing jobs will also go through a separation phase from the old job, followed by a transitional phase between the two jobs. This phase is followed by the incorporation phase that takes place in the new agency. This period should be used to facilitate the process of incorporation and to help the new colleague overcome the difficulties encountered during the separation and transition phases. The current agency should make it possible for the newcomer to understand his or her role during the incorporation phase and that he or she is being accepted in the new work environment. In-service training is a very appropriate tool in the incorporation phase of the rite of passage.

At the other end of the scale is the rite of degradation which according to Trice and Beyer (1993:113) is used by organizations to demote an individual from a certain professional status to a less important one. They suggest that this rite also has three phases: separation, discrediting, and removal. The first phase publicly associates the person with the agency's problems and failures. This is followed by substantial decrements in the person's power and end in his or her removal from the position. The rite of degradation should be handled with utmost care. Perhaps a news conference, an open meeting, or a simple announcement can be used in an attempt to reduce embarrassment.

Contrary to the rites of degradation, the rite of enhancement represents a joyous occasion in which the enhanced person receives a concrete symbol of his or her enhanced status. Prizes, awards, and certificates are the usual symbols used in American organizations. Needless to say that a ceremony is appropriate at this point.

Rites of Group Focus

As was previously stated, rites of group focus include rites of renewal, conflict reduction, and integration. Rites of renewal could be organized around periodic and annual meetings. Although the manifest purpose of this rite may be to refurbish the organizational structure and improve the functions of its units, it could be used to reassure the staff that something is being done about the problems facing the agency. On the other hand, Trice and Beyer suggest that a number of latent purposes could be at work. For instance, the rites of renewal could be used to disguise the nature of the problems or to focus attention towards some problems away from others. Also, these rites are sometimes used to legitimatize and reinforce existing centers of power and authority (1993:114).

Annual meetings of professional associations represent good opportunities for a rite of renewal that would help members of the agency to function as professionals. In these annual meetings, new information may be acquired that would be helpful in solving persistent problems. Leisure services delivery agencies should endeavor to send their members to the national and regional professional meetings since they represent an important aspect of the rites of renewal in the life of the recreation professional.

Rites of conflict reduction can be used to reestablish equilibrium in disturbed social relations. The most used means in this case is the committee. The committee agenda should provide opportunities for airing tension. On the other hand, the rites of integration are used to allow for group cohesiveness and to bind the members to the culture of the agency. Although Christmas parties may be the most used means to achieve the goals of integration, other means such as retreats, picnics, and sporting activities are utilized.

The Importance of Rites

The rites listed above are important tools in facilitating the smooth functioning of the social interactions at work. The absence of rites in the life of any organization makes the socialization and enculturation processes rather difficult. Trice and Beyer believe that the rites of passage are perhaps the most important cultural form used in organizational socialization (1993:366). While the rites of enhancement tell the members which behavior is valued, the rites of degradation signal the opposite. These three rites focus on the individual. The other three rites--the rites of renewal, conflict reduction, and integration--should become part of the professional lives of the recreation professionals. The leisure delivery system, its agencies and local units, are well advised to practice what they preach: these are activities that are very useful in enhancing cohesiveness. Recreation professionals serving a local unit, whether it is public; semipublic/ nonprofit; or commercial, will be able to work more harmoniously if rites of renewal, conflict reduction and integration are utilized.

Ceremonials and the Leisure Delivery System

Rites describe activities that are limited to the staff and special guests. Ceremonials, on the other hand, are activities to which the public is either invited or is welcome to attend. Ceremonials are part of public relations (see Chapter Eleven).

LEISURE, SYMBOLS, MYTHS AND TABOOS

Among the many things shared in local, regional, or national agencies dealing with parks, recreation, or leisure services are the symbols, myths, and taboos observed in the agency or by its members.

Symbols in the Recreation Place: A symbol is something that stands for something else. A gold medal stands for some athletic achievement, the significance of which is in the eyes of the beholder and in the eyes of a specific circle of people who are familiar with the importance of such achievement. In an organizational culture, there are a number of symbols that need to be understood.

Organizational symbols are seen in a number of objects such as the manner of dress. For instance, a male recreation professional who comes to work dressed in a suit and tie symbolizes a particular level of professional status, management. Women also at the same level of professional status dress in a particular fashion. Uniforms are symbols of what the person is doing. Custodial staff usually wear particular uniforms that distinguish them from other employees as do referees of sport events whose uniforms distinguish them from the athletes. Should the local, regional, or national agency dealing with leisure services look into a dress code?

Should uniforms and other attires be required? Do they symbolize certain activities in the workplace? Will certain values be given to certain dress code or codes? Does a receptionist dressed informally project a warmer feeling to the visitors of a recreation center?

Other than the manner of dress, the settings in the workplace are also symbolic. It seems that the presence of reading material, potted plants, decorative pictures, and soft couches are symbols of warmth in the reception area. Among the staff, the office arrangement can have an impact on morale. For instance, an open office that has no interior walls is a symbol of egalitarianism which appeals to the lower level employees; yet it is not often favored by high status managers (Trice and Beyer, 1993:89).

The office furnishings of the top level executives have been a bone of contention in organizations for years. However, what is important is the culture of the organization that can be detected from the settings in the workplace. For example, an agency that follows status distinction in its settings tends to be hierarchical. On the other hand, an agency that eschews status symbols tends to be more democratic.

The use of logos is important in that they provide continuity. Mull suggests that the logo symbol should be used to identify the agency in every possible way such as, in promotional activities, programs, publications, as well as avenues such as T-shirts, entrances, and bookmarks (1997: 306).

Myths in Leisure and Recreation: Myths are also important in the life of an agency. A myth occurs when a story is placed beyond doubt and is freed from argument (Trice and Beyer, 1993: 105). Are there myths in the leisure delivery system, its subsystems, and the local units providing services? At one point one of the leisure delivery system myths was that the activities it provided were a panacea for social ills. This myth started at the beginning of the recreation movement in the final years of the 19th century. Recreation was looked upon as the answer to the many ills created by the Industrial Revolution. The idea was to provide the young and old with "constructive activities" and all would be well. This, of course, was found not to be true. Recreational activities are but one variable, among many, in the life of a human being.

Another myth encountered by the public and private sector was the preservation policy--a principle adopted for national parks and other natural resources that they be maintained for future generations--which was considered as the best means of their protection. Experience leads us to conclude otherwise. Other measures, such as carrying capacity, had to be adopted to protect recreational natural resources. Recently, one of the authors took a trip to Mt. Whitney in California, and found himself to be among 265 others also hiking its well-trodden trail that day!

Myths about leisure service at the local levels may have been perpetuated also, and continuous evaluation of the service's progress is necessary to avoid the traps of these myths. Yet on the local, regional, and national levels certain topics may become taboo.

Taboos in the Workplace: Taboos are unspoken and unwritten prohibitions. Yet they specify in a very unique way those things which should be avoided, such as a certain topic or behavior. For instance, some managers instill in his or her employees the taboo of discussing salaries. In many organizations salaries are not topics for discussion at office hours, coffee breaks, or during other social activities. Another common taboo is the expression of one's feelings and emotions. They are considered private matters that should not be discussed in the workplace. Dating a person from the same organization is often considered a taboo. These may be localized taboos, and the newcomer is well advised to discover for himself or herself, which topics, subjects, and behaviors are prohibited and which are not.

THE HUMAN SIDE OF THE LEISURE DELIVERY SYSTEM

In this section the discussion will center on the human side in parks, recreation, and leisure services. The human side in any organization includes topics such as group dynamics, power and ethics, and decision making mechanisms.

Group Dynamics

A professional in parks, recreation, and leisure services performs his or her duties not in a vacuum but as a member of many groups. Understanding group dynamics is important in one's professional growth and development. Also, the manager of such service should be aware of the impact of group dynamics on the performance of his or her staff and in achieving the desired goals.

A group is a unique social unit that exists in all human societies. But the mere meeting of three or more persons does not constitute a group in the sociological sense. For these people to be called a group, they must establish a stable pattern of relationships and share some common goals. A group requires three or more persons, since an interactive twosome is called a dyad in sociology.

Types Of Groups

There are many types of groups that take shape in an agency dealing with parks, recreation, and leisure services. The distinction among these groups arises from their origin. Formal groups are organized by the management for a particular purpose and are controlled to a great extent by it. On the other hand, informal groups maybe formed in the workplace, and their impact on the smooth functioning of the agency should be taken into consideration by the management. There are other groups that may be formed in the workplace which will be discussed later in this section.

Informal Groups: Informal groups vary in size and purpose. For instance, friendships may emerge in the workplace which are usually based on positions and status. A friendship group may be formed among high status employees of the agency on the bases of certain characteristics and symbols. On the other hand, other employees initially base their friendship grouping not on status but proximity. These groups are harmless and should be differentiated from cliques in that the latter uses collective resources to achieve certain aims. Sometimes these aims may not be compatible with the smooth functioning of the agency. While friendship groups are directed towards camaraderie and cabals, on the other hand, there are groups that attempt to realize some temporary gains. In the meantime coalitions may be formed to pool a number of groups into a well-defined interest group who is committed to achieving a common goal. The management of an agency in parks, recreation, and leisure services is well advised to understand the differences among these groups.

Formal Groups: A formal group, also known as a work team, may be formed by the management for a particular purpose such as planning a tennis tournament, developing the next schedule, or organizing a special event. Tuckmann and

Jensen (1977: 419-427) suggest that a formal group may go through five stages of development:

1. Forming: Members get to know each other and seek to establish ground rules.

2. Storming: Members come to resist control by leaders and show hostility.

3. Norming: Members work together developing close relationships and feelings of camaraderie.

4. Performing: Group members work toward getting their job done.

5. Adjourning: The group may disband after either meeting their goals or after member start to leave.

To be effective, the management of an agency dealing with parks, recreation, and leisure services should see that its formal groups, or work teams, are given the following opportunities (Baron and Greenberg (1990:266):

1. Prework: What work needs to be done?

   Is a group necessary?

   What authority should the group have?

   What are group goals?

2. Create performance conditions:

   Provide all needed material and equipment.

   Provide all needed personnel.

3. Form and build teams:

   Establish boundaries-who and who is not in the group.

   Arrive at an agreement regarding tasks to be performed.

   Clarify expected behaviors.

4. Provide ongoing assistance:

   Intervene to eliminate group problems (certain members?)

   Replenish or upgrade material resources.

   Replace members who leave the group.

Other Forms of Groupings: Management should also be aware of the other types of groupings that occur as a result of line and staff distinction. In the case of an agency which deals with both parks and recreation, two distinct groups may occur, one dealing with parks and the other with recreation. Hopefully, distinction among groups will not stand in the way of cooperation. Though it may seem that staff distinction is acceptable and is amenable to the smooth functioning of the agency, research has shown that staff and line distinction tends to undermine cooperation and coordination as each group develops its own set of values and norms (Trice and Beyer, 1993: 234). It is important that the management emphasizes, now and then, that the ultimate goal of the agency includes the particular goals of its two distinct units.

As a result of hierarchical difference, another form of grouping may occur in the agency. Such a grouping may seem to be healthy for the agency because the formal authority given to the supervisor may create a form of desirable social distance between him and his subordinates. On the other hand, total absence of authority may also be harmful. It seems that a position between these two extremes of social distance and absence of authority should be practiced. For example, although planned social functions may reduce extreme social distance, periodical announcements praising and emphasizing the role played by the leaders may reduce impressions of absence of authority.

Structure Of Work Teams

How a work team is structured is very important in achieving the objectives of the team. The following four aspects of this structure are crucial to the desired success (Baron and Greenberg, 1990:267-278).

Role of the Recreation Professional: The term "role" describes the typical behavior that characterizes a person in a particular social or work position. In the parks, recreation, or leisure agency, the role played by each professional and staff members is assigned by virtue of one's position in the agency. A member of the agency is supposed to play a particular role that is differentiated from other roles. Sometimes it seems that two roles played by two different members are identical, as in the case of two recreation leaders who are hired under the same job description.

In reality, because of the different work and social settings of each of these two professionals, their roles are to some extent differentiated. Novice and veteran professionals should realize that roles are not cast in stone and that they will vary slightly. These two roles will vary due to the special work setting of each individual, the social atmosphere in their work place, and individual differences of the employees.

Despite these differentiations and even with the best attempts to avoid them, role conflict results when competing demands are made on the roles a person plays. Baron and Greenberg suggest that employees may experience *intrarole* conflict when contradictory demands occur within a single role (1990). Ambiguity in defining the role leads to this kind of conflict. Management in a parks, recreation, or leisure service agency must carefully review the assignments given to its individual professionals and staff members.

Another type of conflict is called *interrole*, which occurs when there are incompatible demands made on someone playing two roles. A good example in the fields of parks, recreation,, and leisure services occurs when a friendship develops between a supervisor and a subordinate. In this situation, the relationship could result in a role conflict with negative results. A firm discussion by the manager over this issue may help defuse it.

Norms and The Agency: As stated earlier in this chapter, norms are the specific behavioral guides that are derived from values, the general guides for behavior. Norms of many professions differ from the rules of the agency in that they are not necessarily formal. While many professions have developed a code of ethics to which the professional is sworn, others do not have such a formal, written code. Since the behavior of the professional often has an important impact on how the profession is judged by others, certain expectations from the person who joins it are required. A code of ethics has been adopted by the National Recreation and Park Association (See p.11). The agency dealing with parks, recreation, and leisure services, be it public, semi-public/nonprofit or even commercial, may use this code as its modus operandi. Of course, the agency is free to develop its own code of ethics.

Other than a code of ethics that should be observed by all who serve in any capacity in an agency dealing with parks, recreation, or leisure services, individual agencies usually develop their own norms which should be taken into consideration by the novice. According to Feldman (1985), other than the carryover from the professional standards of the profession, there are three ways in which group norms can develop:

1. Precedent set over time: For example, the seating location of the members around a meeting table.

2. Explicit statements from others: A novice may be told that this is how the task is done.

3. Critical event in the group's history: A norm may develop concerning control over interviews with the media especially after one which was considered negative.

Status Ladder in the Agency: How does the rank and/or social positions of each member of the agency affect work relationships and productivity? The rank or social position given or acquired by a person determines his or her status in the agency. There are two ways of looking at status. First is the formal status, the one that gives a person a degree of formal authority. Status symbols in this case include title, work conditions, and type and number of assistants given. Another type is the informal status, the one acquired because of certain characteristics such as age, skill, gender, or ethnicity. For instance, older workers are considered more experienced, and may be afforded some informal status within the agency. Persons with certain skills, as is the case with gifted athletes, may gain a higher status among the workers.

A recreation professional joining an agency must be aware of its status ladder. How to communicate with the persons occupying the two ends of the ladder is important. Some persons in high status positions like to be treated a certain way such as using their title, or being addressed as sir or madam. Lower "rung" employees deserve appropriate if not equal respect from higher management. With the advent of the Civil Rights movement in the 1960's, the low status, from which certain minorities and women frequently suffer, has been ameliorated.

Also, a person with high status, be it formal or informal, has greater influence in the decision making process. What is important is that the agency or the service unit must develop an *"esprit de corps"* as shown in the next section.

Cohesion in Work Teams: Cohesion, the ability of staff to work cooperatively to achieve agreed upon outcomes, tends to be greater among smaller groups. In smaller units or agencies dealing with parks, recreation, and leisure services cohesion can be accomplished easier than in the larger ones. Other factors can also lead to group cohesion. In a larger unit or agency, the amount of time that the members spend together should be emphasized. If work conditions do not allow for greater interaction among members, management should endeavor to bring the employees together on as many occasions as possible. For instance, a bowling league will help in this direction as will occasional lunches, and the ubiquitous "company" picnic can prove beneficial for employees.

Although group cohesion is thought of in a positive way, Baron and Greenberg (1990:277) warn that a phenomenon known as group thinking may occur. Here the group becomes so cohesive that the members lose sight of the ultimate goal of the agency. However, studies cited by them show high productivity in highly cohesive groups under a supportive managerial style.

Decision Making

Decision-making is very important in the management of parks, recreation, and leisure services. Wedley and Field (1984) suggest that a number of steps could be used by management.

1. Identify the problem: Low enrollment in skiing course

2. Define objectives: Increase enrollment

3. Make a pre-decision: Decide to look at total enrollment

4. Generate alternatives: Reduce fees/Change time/Replace instructor

5. Evaluate alternatives: Difficult to replace instructor/reduce fees

6. Make a choice: Reduce fees anyway

7. Implement choice: Reduce fees slightly

8. Follow up: Talk to future participants.

An important question that faces the management in parks, recreation, and leisure services is whether the decision making procedure should be made by an individual or a group.

Group Decision-Making: Decision making by groups has become an established fact in the life of most organizations, whether they are public, semipublic, or commercial. According to Delbeq et al. (1975:497), 80 percent of a manager's time is spent in committee meetings. Baron and Greenberg suggest that despite the advantages of group decision making, which includes pooling of resources and acceptance of the decision, there are a number of disadvantages. These include possible group conflict and intimidation by leaders. Moreover, a great amount of time is spent by the group on a decision which may have been utilized more effectively (1990: 498).

If the management of an agency dealing with parks, recreation, or leisure services sees that the advantages of group decision making outweighs the disadvantages, a number of variables should be considered, which according to research helps in the success of the group. The group must be heterogeneous, and members of the group should have complementary skills.

Individual Decision-Making: In the case of individual decision making, there are a number of factors that should be taken into consideration. For example, there may be a cognitive bias on the part of the decision-maker. According to Baron and Greenberg, human beings tend to frame the problem, as in the case of emphasizing the positive gains over the negative ones apriori (1990:499). Another problem is that human beings tend to base their judgment on available information, although it may be incomplete or inaccurate. Time constraint may be a factor in both individual and group decision making. Baron and Greenberg (1990) suggest that decision-makers should assess their decision style by answering the following questions:

1. When performing my job, I usually look for

   a) practical results.   b) the best solutions to problems.

   c) new ideas or approaches.   d) pleasant working conditions.

2. When faced with a problem, I usually

   a) use approaches that have worked.   b) analyze it carefully.

   c) try to find a creative approach.   d) rely on my feelings.

3. When making plans, I usually emphasize

   a) the problems currently faced.   b) attaining the objective.

   c) future goals.   d) developing my career.

4. The kind of information I usually prefer to use is

   a) specific facts.   b) complete and accurate data.

   c) broad information.   d) data that are limited and simple.

5. Whenever I am uncertain about what to do, I

   a) rely on my intuition.   b) look for facts.

   c) try to find a compromise.   d) wait and decide later.

6. The people with whom I work best are usually

   a) ambitions and full of energy.   b) self-confident.

   c) open-minded.   d) trusting and polite.

7. The decisions I make are usually

   a) direct and realistic.   b) abstract or systematic.

   c) broad and flexible.   d) sensitive to other's needs .

This test will shed light on one's decision style and is scored as follows: 1 point for each a, 2 points for each b, 3 points for each c, and 4 points for each d. The added points will reveal the following about the decision style:

The Directive Style (7-10 points): This style characterizes people who prefer simple solutions and avoid ambiguity. They tend to make decisions rapidly because they use little information and do not consider many alternatives. They tend to rely on existing rules to make their decisions and aggressively use their status to achieve results.

The Analytical Style (11-17 points): Persons of this style are more willing to consider complex solutions based on ambitious information. They tend to carefully analyze their decisions using as much data as possible. Such individuals enjoy solving problems, finding the best possible answers and willing to use innovative methods to achieve them.

The Conceptual Style (18-24 points): Persons of this style are more socially oriented in their approach to problems. Their approach is humanistic and artistic. They tend to consider many broad alternatives when approaching problems and value commitments, and they use their creativity to find solutions. They have a strong future orientation and like initiating new ideas.

The Behavioral Style (25-28 points): The individuals in this group have deep concern for the organization in which they work and for the personal development of their co-workers. They are highly supportive of others and are very concerned about others' achievement; frequently helping them meet their goals. They tend to be open to suggestions from others, and therefore tend to rely on meetings for making decisions.

Regardless of the form through which decision-making is followed; Janus and Mann (1977) suggest a preferable way of predicting whether a given decision is likely to lead to satisfaction or regret. Although their work was published sometime ago, their seven criteria have been quoted in recent publications. Koteen (1997:89) states that the decision-maker or makers should:

1. thoroughly canvass a wide range of alternative courses of action,

2. survey the full range of objectives to be fulfilled and the values implied by the choice,

3. carefully weigh whatever the costs, risks and negative consequences of each alternative,

4. intensively searches for new information relevant to further evaluation of the alternatives,

5. correctly assimilate and takes into account any new information or expert judgment to which the agency is exposed, even when the information or judgment does not support the course of action initially preferred,

6. re-examines the positive and negative consequences of all known alternatives including those originally regarded as unacceptable, before making a final decision, and

7. make detailed provisions for implementing or executing the chosen course of action, with special attention to contingency plans that might be acquired if various known risks were to materialize. More on decision making in Chapter Four.

SUMMARY

- This chapter points out the existence of a leisure delivery system in this and other societies. This system is seen to exist on three levels-- national, state, and local--as well of three kinds--public, semi-public/ nonprofit and commercial.

- All agencies dealing with parks, recreation, and leisure services are organized along the same lines as other human organizations. This means that each agency will develop its own unique cultural elements.

- Values are the basic guidelines for both society and its subsystems including human organizations. Values from the main culture will affect the work within an organization, and the values adopted by the organization are important to its smooth functioning.

- Rites, ceremonies, myth, and taboos are important ingredients of the culture of any organization. Parks, recreation, and leisure agencies are well advised to utilize these cultural tools in facilitating the fulfillment of their missions and visions.

- The human side of the leisure delivery system examines the roles that groups and work teams play in the life of an organization. Special attention is given to the process of decision making and its impact on morale.

LEARNING ACTIVITIES

1. Make a quick survey of your community. Find out how many agencies dealing with parks, recreation, or leisure services exist. Keep in mind the three kinds of services: public, semi-public/ nonprofit, and the commercial.

2. From the list above, find the closest agency to your home with some national affiliation. Find the charter of the mother organization and discuss with the class the type of affiliation it has with the national office.

3. Interview a professional, whether he or she is in parks, recreation, or leisure services or any other service. Find out the most dominant value in the service for which he or she is engaged.

4. Find out from the professional interviewed about the types of symbols, myths, and taboos observed in his or her agency.

5. Enumerate the rites and ceremonies that you have personally gone through. Reflect on how they have impacted your life.

6. Invite a group of friends to your residence and then suggest that you go out. Take notes on how a decision was reached on where to go.

REFERENCES

Baron, Robert A. and Jerald Greenberg (1990). **Behavior in Organizations: Understanding and Managing the Human Side of Work**. Boston,MA: Allyn and Bacon.

Benset, Frank, Jack Foley and George Welton (1983). **Organizing Leisure and Human Services.** Dubuque, IA: Kendall/Hunt.

Butler, George D. (1940). **Introduction to Community Recreation.** New York, NY : McGraw-Hill.

Delbeq, A.L., Van de Ven and D.H. Gustafson (1975). **Group Techniques for Group Planning.** Glenview, IL: Scott, Foresman.

Feldman, D.C.(1985). "The Development and Enforcement of Group Norms," **Academy of Management Review**, 9, 47-53.

Gray, David and Donald Peligrino (1973). **Reflections on the Recreation and Park Movement.** Dubuque, IA: Wm. C. Brown Company, Publishers.

Janus, Irving and Leo Mann (1977) **Decision-Making.** New York, NY: Free Press.

Koteen, Jack (1997) **Strategic Management in Public and Nonprofit Organizations.** London: Praeger.

Kraus, Richard (1984). **Recreation and Leisure in Modern Society.** Glenview, IL: Scott, Foresman.

Kraus, Richard and Joseph Curtis (2000) **Creative Management in Recreation, Parks, and Leisure Services.** St Louis: McGraw-Hill

Levine, Peter (1989) **American Sport: A Documentary History.** Englewood Cliffs, NJ: Prentice Hall.

Mechikoff, Robert and Steven Estes (1993). **A History and Philosophy of Sport and Physical Education.** Madison, WI: Brown and Benchmark.

McLean, J., J. Peterson and D. Martin (1985). **Recreation and Leisure: A Changing Scene.** New York, NY: MacMillan.

Mull, Richard et al (1997) **Recreational Sport Management.** Champaign, IL: Human Kinetics.

Murphy, James and Dennis Howard (1977**). Delivery of Community Leisure Service: A Holistic Approach.** Philadelphia, PA: Lea and Febiger.

Naisbitt, John (1982). **Megatrends.** New York, NY: Warner Books.

Trice, H. M. and J. M. Beyer (1993) **The Cultures of Work Organizations.** Englewood Cliffs, NJ: Prentice Hall.

Tuckman, B.W. and M.A. Jensen (1977). "Stages of Small Group Development Revisited," **Group and Organization Studies**, 2:419-427.

Turner, Victor (1969). **The Ritual Process: Structure and Antistructure.** Chicago, IL: Adeline.

Udall, Stuart (1963) **The Quiet Crisis.** New York, NY: Avon Books.

Van Gennep, A. (1960). **The Rites of Passage.** London, England: Routldge & Kegan

Wedley, W.C. and R.H. Field (1984) "A Predecision Support System,"**Academy of Management Review**, 9, 696-703.

CHAPTER 3
DYNAMICS OF LEADERSHIP

Learning Objectives

After studying this chapter, you should be able to do the following:

1. Understand the importance of leadership.

2. Define the role of the leader.

3. Use a process to develop a vision for an organization.

4. Describe the skills and characteristics of leaders.

5. Describe several leadership styles.

6. Recognize the dynamics of teamwork.

7. Understand the importance of balance between leadership and management within an organization.

Parks, recreation, and leisure service professionals today are faced with the challenge of being effective as both leaders and managers. A leader-manager strives to motivate and direct the efforts of others toward new alternatives and uncharted paths. With this in mind, it is not surprising that whenever change is imminent, publications about the positive aspects of leadership begin to appear. This was seen in the United States during such times as the Great Depression and World War II. The term leadership is again at the forefront as explosive new technology creates a need for leaders to chart new paths, spark innovative ideas, and sculpt new relationships and interactions (Hargrove 2001:6-9).

During times of change, there is often a tendency to react with reservation or even fear and resentment. Nonetheless, change is a constant that forces new reactions, responses, and ideas. Once change is viewed as a necessary part of life, energy can better be directed toward positive options and outcomes. These options can be exciting, rewarding, and inspirational especially in democracies where people are given choices. In these instances, leaders emerge who convince and persuade others to tackle new pathways and to work together toward a mission that the group supports and finds worthy of their energy. This strong leadership is needed in leisure service organizations where changes may be necessitated by increased visitor use, demands for higher quality and more diverse programs, stagnant budgets, and environmental protection.

TABLE 3-1
_____
A Historical Look at Leadership
_____

1. *Age of Conquest Leadership.* People looked to their leader for safety, and in return offered their loyalty and taxes.

2. *Age of Commerce Leadership.* By the Industrial Age, people began looking for leaders who could show them how to raise their standard of living. These leaders, though skilled at bargaining, eventually lost their followers because they exploited them by giving them less and less for their performance.

3. *Age of Organization Leadership.* As standards of living rose, people looked for leaders who could organize and give them a place to belong.

4. *Age of Innovation Leadership.* Creative employees, needed to help organizations push ahead, were attracted to innovative leaders. These leaders needed to handle the speed at which methods and products became obsolete.

5. *Age of Information Leadership.* People needed leaders who could make the most intelligent sense of information, using it in the newest and most creative way.

6. *New Leadership.* People look to leaders who will lead them, not projects. While they still must know how to use new technologies and be effective in analyzing and synthesizing information, their commitment is focused on the individual. To keep ahead of competition, short-term and long-term planning is essential.

Source: Culligan, M., Deakins, C., and Young, A. *Back to Basics Management* (New York: Facts On File, Inc., 1983).
_____

The direction of leadership has evolved over the years. In the 1950s, leaders were autocratic, and few individuals were given leadership opportunities. Most of their decisions were impacted by the immediate, and the results tended to be short-term without much heed given to the future. In time, as more and more individuals became better educated and aware of their human, civil, and economic rights, leadership styles evolved and became responsive to the independent thinker. People, less motivated by control, were now more receptive to the democratic process. Their needs had shifted causing them to desire and to require shared decision-making and more leadership responsibilities. The necessity of long-term planning, innovation, and foresight became more apparent (Hamel 2000:20-23). Leadership continues to evolve in today's knowledge-based organizations where employees must decipher and use the large amount of information generated by modern technology in their decision-making (Tecker, et. al. 1997:1). In fact, today's leaders are more like entrepreneurs than stewards who coach, mentor, or guide others toward achieving a dream of what is possible (Jacobson 2000:22,27).Six ages of leadership are identified on the previous page.

THE ROLE OF THE LEADER

Leaders take charge, make things happen, dream dreams and then translate them into reality. Leaders attract the voluntary commitment of followers, energize them, and transform organizations into new entities with greater potential for survival, growth and excellence. Effective leadership empowers an organization to maximize its contribution to the well-being of its members and the larger society of which it is a part. If managers are known for their skills in solving problems, leaders are known for being masters in designing and building institutions: they are the architects of the organization's future. (Nanus, 1989: 7)

In this description the role of the leader is differentiated from that of the manager. Leaders innovate, bring about major changes, and inspire followers to pursue goals with extraordinary effort. They are concerned with making sure that the organization is doing the right thing. Ultimately, the effective leader's task is to create human vision and human energies. Managers are skilled at doing the same thing over and over, implementing the tasks that are assigned, and making sure that the work is done efficiently. They are concerned with doing things right and achieving goals and objectives. The challenge today is for the leisure service professional to be a good leader and a good manager.

THE LEADER-MANAGER

In some organizations, the Chief Executive Officer (CEO) or President is the designated leader and the Vice-President is the designated manager.   More commonly, one individual must take on both roles, combining the characteristics and skills of each.   Although the role of the manager is discussed in the next chapter, it should be noted that to be an effective one, the manager must be a leader (Ibrahim and Cordes 1996:41).   The functions of each are noted above, but the major difference between a leader and a manager is that the leadership title must be earned.   This is only accomplished by building successful relationships with those being led.   According to Cox (1992:12), a true leader, even with the commitment of only a few individuals, can ultimately become more effective than the manager who lacks these skills.

TABLE 3-2

Characteristics of Leaders and Managers

LEADERS:	**MANAGERS:**
Innovate	Administer
Are original	Copy
Inspire trust	Rely on control
Have a long-range perspective	Have a short-range view
Ask what and why	Ask how and when
Have an eye on the horizon	Have an eye on the bottom line
Originate	Imitate
Challenge the status quo	Accept the status quo
Is his/her own person	Are good soldiers
Do the right thing	Do things right

Source: Bennis, W. *On Becoming a Leader* (Reading, MA: Addison-Wesley, 1989), p. 45.

The Positive Leader

A leader is someone who impacts others. A leader has insight, takes initiative, is in control, is charismatic, gives direction, offers help, creates hope, takes on responsibility, sacrifices, transforms, and contributes. A leader takes others on a journey by establishing a vision or direction for the future, a vision that incorporates the opinions and needs of others (Ibrahim and Cordes 1996:42). A leader challenges others to work toward that vision and brings out their best qualities and dreams. When the leader orients around challenge, potential, and the betterment of humankind, the leader is referred to as a positive leader (Reynolds 1994:24). Positive visionary leaders are needed in public service agencies, nonprofit organizations, commercial recreation enterprises, and throughout organizations at all levels. One does not need to wait to be assigned a management position in order to be a leader, but once this challenge is accepted, the novice must work to acquire and develop the skills of a leader (Korfhage 2001: 40-43).

The Vision

Leaders strive to stay a step ahead of the current reality, dreaming about what the future holds and what role their organization should play in it. To be inspiring in this capacity, the visionary leader needs an agenda or a vision which encompasses organizational values. The vision becomes a guiding light or direction, pointing out possibility and potential. Much more than a revelation, it is a rational, objective, and intuitive understanding of current reality as it relates to the future direction. This does not mean that it is factual. A vision may, in fact, never be realized as originally imagined. Because a vision is neither true nor false, it can only be evaluated in terms of whether it is still suitable, too risky, or not good enough. A vision, then, changes and evolves.

Powerful and transforming visions tend to have special properties such as faith and possibility (Cox 1992:25-27). They are idealistic and have the power to inspire and energize others. Most importantly, a vision must be acted upon or it is simply a leader's dream. To be acted upon, the vision must be desirable, strategically developed, communicated, and published.

Commitment to the Vision: Without a vision, leadership and the organization loses its thrust. A vision alone, however, is not enough. A leader must recognize the importance of working with others to realize the vision. First, it becomes the duty of a leader to persuade others to accept the vision, and then to help them commit, perform, and contribute to it. In order for this to happen, employees will need to understand the benefits of the dream. The leader-manager will communicate, seeking the employee's advice, input, and support, even at the developmental stage. Furthermore, it is the leader's duty to coach employees to work together and to encourage them to take on visionary leadership roles throughout the organization (Jacobson 2000:22) . When employees become empowered to make decisions to get things done, they are more involved in the process. And the more involved they are in the process, the more likely it is that the dream will become a reality. The more highly skilled and educated the employee the more potent this tactic is.

Relating the Vision to the Mission and Goals: A successful vision must be compatible with the purpose or mission of the park, recreation, and leisure delivery service system. The mission defines what the organization has been established to accomplish. Every mission statement should reflect opportunity, competence, and commitment. The mission is the purpose, not the direction or vision, of the organization. Normally, the mission and principles of an organization do not change, and the implications of the mission are clear-cut and easy to understand. For example, the mission of the Nature Conservancy is narrowly defined: to buy and protect lands with rare and endangered species. The Conservancy believes that their membership increased in the 1990s at a time when many other environmental organizations lost support because they stayed focused on their mission which is easily definable.

The goals or strategies that are needed to accomplish the mission and the vision are flexible. In this way the organization can respond to change or take advantage of new or existing opportunities. Therefore, goals and strategies are temporary, while the mission is stable. For example, after the Girl Scout Council surveyed the nation's population, they found a need to provide a program for girls as young as age five. Their former goal, to serve girls age seven to seventeen, changed. The Brownie age was lowered to six and a successful new program, Daisy Girl Scouts, was formed for five year olds.

According to management leader Peter Drucker (1992:121), a key element of effective leadership is to clearly and visibly define the organization's mission and goals. Leaders see goals as progressions rather than obstacles. Managers develop the necessary strategies needed to make the dream come true. Leader-managers do both. They are more concerned with achieving results and with the managerial mechanics needed to get the results.

Creating Human Energies

Many persons have the potential to be or may have been leaders. To the surprise of many, however, no one is a naturally-born leader. Leaders learn their craft through experience, continuous study, and never-ending observation. When attempting to understand the qualities of leadership, a number of skills and attributes displayed among leaders should be reviewed.

Leaders tend to focus on the future and on achieving results. They have a basic understanding of the nature of humankind, and learn to work skillfully with those inside and outside of their organization. They help others to achieve their goals and the goals of their organization. They encourage innovation and strive to nurture excellence in others without demanding unreasonable perfection. Leaders learn when and how to take calculated risks that involve strategic decision making based on fact, intuition, and faith. Their decisions are not based on chance or whim. They learn to rise above criticism and self-doubt. Leaders have courage and a knack for bringing order to chaos. They are sensitive to diverse and special populations, encourage inclusiveness and collaboration, and promote joy in the workplace. Leaders have integrity and hold ethical standards as a fundamental priority (Cordes and Ibrahim 1999:245-46).

In the Field...

Walt Disney's Vision As He Described It

The Disney Company, a leading organization from which others might learn, had no difficulty taking action to make dreams a reality (Capodagli and Jackson 1999:9). *Dreamovations*, a visionary, holistic, management approach, is based on Walt Disney's credo: *Dream, Believe, Dare, Do* (Capodagli and Jackson 2000:396). Consider the vision of Walt Disney as he described it.

> *The idea of Disneyland is a simple one. It will be a place for people to find happiness and knowledge. It will be a place for parents and children to spend pleasant times in one another's company: a place for teachers and pupils to discover greater ways of understanding and education. Here the older generation can recapture the nostalgia of days gone by, and the younger generation can savor the challenge of the future. Here will be the wonders of Nature and Man for all to see and understand. Disneyland will*

be based upon and dedicated to the ideals, the dreams and hard facts that have created America. And it will be uniquely equipped to dramatize these dreams and facts and send them forth as a source of courage and inspiration to all the world. Disneyland will be something of a fair, an exhibition, a playground, a community center, a museum of living facts, and a showplace of beauty and magic. It will be filled with the accomplishments, the joys and hopes of the world we live in. And it will remind us and show us how to make those wonders part of our own lives (Thomas 1976:246-247).

When Disneyland opened in Anaheim, California on July 17, 1955, it was a 20-year-dream come true for its creator. It was a triumph for a man who reached boldly beyond his contemporaries. After its debut the *Minneapolis Tribune* wrote: "If it's an amusement park it's the gosh-darndest, most happily inspired, most carefully-planned, most adventure-filled park ever conceived. No ride or concession in it is like anything in any other amusement park anywhere" (Walt Disney Productions 1979:11). Today, approximately 2,000 Imagineers are the inspiration for Disney Company *Dream Retreats* based on the *if you can dream it, you can do it* concept. Dream Retreats help employees understand their company's vision, but they also spark innovation and new ideas (Capodagli and Jackson 1999:17,21).

In The Field...

CREATING A VISION

Sometimes a vision seems obvious, and at other times, it seems to be an endless kaleidoscope of variations. The challenge is to select the right vision for the organization. The organization's mission must, therefore, be fully understood. In the following situation, a new director seeks to energize a Department of Parks and Recreation in a medium sized state with a challenging new vision that will guide its activities over the next five years. The following questions help her frame her vision. Sample answers for each question are provided in an abbreviated form.

The Vision Audit*:*

1. *What is the current stated mission or purpose of your organization?* The essence of the mission is to work with other public and private agencies, to provide recreational opportunities and programs for all citizens and visitors to

the state, to operate and maintain the state park system, and to administer state and federal funds allocated for these purposes.

2. *What values does the organization provide to society?* The department provides access to a broad range of recreational opportunities. Recreation is recognized as a basic societal need, enriching lives, developing skills, and so on.

3. *What is the character or institutional framework within which your organization operates?* The department's mandate is broad because it is responsible to all citizens, and it must coordinate its activities with other federal, state, and local agencies.

4. *What is your organization's unique position in that institutional structure?* It is a cabinet-level department reporting to the governor of the state, and it is charged with providing leadership to other agencies in managing lands, facilities, and services which help to meet the recreational needs of the state population.

5. *What does it take for your organization to succeed?* The department must be fair to all and use its resources efficiently and wisely.

6. *What are the values and the organizational culture that govern behavior and decision making?* The values include a strong dedication to public service, ethical management of state resources, and careful adherence to legal and legislative guidelines.

7. *What are the operating strengths and weaknesses of the organization?* The strengths include excellent facilities and an increasing demand for services. Weaknesses include poor maintenance of park roads and insufficient staff.

8. *What is the current strategy, and can it be defended?* The department tries to comply with all of its legislative mandates as best it can with limited staff and a declining budget. Emphasis is on efficiency and cost reduction.

9. *Does the organization have a clearly stated vision? If so, what is it?* No. Its legislative mandates tend to be broad and somewhat unrealistic. "Providing a full range of high-quality recreation to all residents, while ensuring protection of all species and the environment."

10. *If the organization continues on its current path, where will it be heading over the next decade?* Its staff will be cut by at least 50 percent and most of the parks will have to close for most of the year. Tourism in the state will be adversely affected. Another vision is needed.

11. *Do the key people in the organization know where the organization is headed and agree on the direction?* In the absence of a more encouraging vision, morale is low. They recognize that the ability to serve is declining rapidly with increased budget cuts.

12. *Do the structures, processes, personnel, incentives, and information systems support the current direction of the organization?* No. The department remains organized and staffed as it was in an earlier time of more ample budgets.

The Vision Scope

1. *Who are the most critical stakeholders—both inside and outside your organization—and of these, which are the most important?* A diverse population of users; governmental and nongovernmental providers of recreation services such as federal agencies, the tourist industry, and taxpayers etc. (A list of critical stake holders would be listed according to their importance.)

2. *What are the major interests and expectations of the five or six most important stakeholders regarding the future of your organization?* User expect a wide diversity of recreational opportunities, easy access, economical activities, etc.

3. *What threats or opportunities emanate from these critical stakeholders?* Users may be willing to pay more, but if any interests are neglected they may lobby for their special needs and seek media coverage of their grievances.

4. *Considering yourself a stakeholder, what do you personally and passionately want to make happen in your organization?* I would like to cut costs and leave the job with a reputation for responsible stewardship of natural resources.

5. *What are the boundaries to your new vision? For example, are there time, geographical, or social constraints?* There are state requirements to provide facilities and services for *all potential users.*

6. *What must the vision accomplish? How will you know when it is successful?* The success of the new vision can be measured by the extent to which it promotes public satisfaction, public good, accessibility of services and facilities, efficiency of service delivery, service quality, and collaboration.

7. *What critical issues must be addressed in the vision?*   How will the activities be funded? How can the increasing demand for recreational services be reconciled with the need to protect the public lands from crowding and environmental damage? Etc.

The Vision Context

1. *What major changes can be expected in the needs and wants served by your organization in the future?* More concern should be given for the health and wellness aspects of recreation, as opposed to diversion or amusement. The organization will see increased participation in riskier recreation activities such as rock climbing, more...

2. *What changes can be expected in the major stakeholders of your organization in the future?*   Users will demand more family recreation; expansion of group tours; etc.

3. *What major changes can be expected in the relevant economic environments in the future?*   There will be a major recession in the state as companies downsize, etc.

4. *What major changes can be expected in the relevant social environments in the future?*   One can expect a continued growth in environmentalism, an increase in volunteerism, more...

5. *What major changes can be expected in the relevant political environments in the future?* There will be more cooperation between public agencies; increased federal standards for safety and environmental protection in parklands; more...

6. *What major changes can be expected in the relevant technological environments in the future?* A growth will occur in the computerization of park reservation and services, more...

7. *What major changes can be expected in other external environments that could affect your organization in the future?* There will be increased contracting for services and facilities, more....

8. *Which future developments would have the most impact on your choice of vision, and what are the probabilities of these high-priority developments actually occurring?* There will be a shift in values in favor of a higher quality of life; pollution; more...

Vision Choice

Analysis: The State Department of Parks and Recreation intends to make enormous progress over the next decade by...

A. Becoming the most efficient agency of its kind, offering the greatest amount of public recreation services per budgeted dollar.

B. Being a "Wellness Agency" dedicated to healing the ills of an urban society by contributing to physical, mental, and spiritual wellness, etc.

C. Emphasizing the preservation and enhancement of public lands, etc.

D. Becoming family centered.

E. Stressing access and diversity of users, activities etc.

F. Stimulating the development of private and nonprofit sector recreation programs through a variety of joint arrangements, including leasing of public lands, etc.

G. Reducing the public cost of recreational services by developing innovative means to develop financial support for recreation.

H. Stressing local empowerment and an urban focus by developing state management authority for recreational services to regional and local authorities and acting mainly as the standard setter, facilitator, etc.

Adapted from Nanus, B. *Visionary Leadership* (San Francisco: Jossey-Bass Inc., Pub., 1992), pp.189-217.

Integrity and Ethical Standards: Every organization should attempt to be recognized as an asset to the community. It is up to the leader to represent the organization's values, as they relate to ethical and legal codes of conduct, and to clearly communicate them to others within the organization. When a leader possesses a personal ethical standard which appropriately represents the values of the organization, the leader earns the trust of his or her associates, and the parks, recreation, and leisure delivery system earns the respect of its customers or guests. Even its products and services are branded in this favorable light (Nilson 1999:9,50,226).

Leadership does not confer privileges, it entails responsibilities and the need for personal integrity. Ethical standards should be developed early in the career, because it is difficult, if not impossible, to establish an ethical foundation once a significant position of leadership is attained. Drucker (1992:116) makes this point by referring to the following English jingle, "The higher up the monkey goes, the more of his behind he shows." Certainly, the lack of a strong ethical framework is difficult to mask, and various studies have shown that the leader with a reputation for integrity is better received and less likely to be misinterpreted than the leader with excellent skills who has not established this aspect of their character. If sound character and integrity are lacking, the unity and respect of followers are apt to be sacrificed. If this is lost, there is no leadership.

Defining Terms: To fully understand principled leadership, a basic understanding of some important terms is necessary. Ethics, simply put, is a commitment or duty to do right things. Values are the standards that help people decide what is worthwhile or desirable. Within an organization, values represent abstract ideas that personify images of what matters or should matter in terms of performance and in the ways that an organization satisfies its responsibilities to its constituencies - workers, customers, taxpayers, investors, and the rest of society (Nanus 1989:34). The values of a leader influence the leader's decisions, direction, and guidance. Character reflects one's thoughts, values, and attitudes. Sound character is developed through thought, choice, courage, and determination. Working with *integrity* means working with conscience and conviction (See values and the leisure delivery system p.31).

A Framework of Principle: According to Stephen Covey, author of Principle-Centered Leadership and other best selling books on leadership, leaders obtain power by demonstrating an honorable character,(1991). He believes that through the use of certain principles, leaders will attract loyal followers because they are trusted, and will not need to coerce their employees or provide them with lavish benefits. He defines these principles as proven enduring guidelines or ideals for human conduct which govern human effectiveness. Examples of these principles include fairness, kindness, dignity, charity, integrity, honesty, quality service, and patience. Principles, he finds, can be distinguished from values which are more subjective and internal. Therefore, Covey advocates that when employees are trained through principles, they can make their own decisions because the decisions are based on principle. In this manner, employees assume a greater opportunity to expand their expertise, creativity, and shared responsibility at all levels of an organization because they are empowered to act without constant monitoring, evaluating, correcting, or controlling. When they are trained through practices or specific actions, they are limited because rules and regulations cannot possibly cover all situations. By training through principle, Covey finds that it is easier to set a moral and ethical framework throughout the organization.

Leadership Skills

The following skills are attributed to leaders. Though often recognized as traits or qualities, they are also considered skills because they can be learned or developed. To acquire them, they must be practiced on a daily basis. If they are not accepted as important, they generally cannot be developed.

Commitment: A leader is service-oriented and dedicated to the vision and mission of the organization. He is loyal and work with others, striving to develop commitment in them as well. Leaders can be counted on to follow-through on their projects and not to fold under negative or external pressures.

Openness: Leaders constantly grow, learn, and expand their abilities. They show interest in making new discoveries about life and others. Recognizing that life and events are ever changing, they are adaptable and flexible. Every situation is turned into a learning experience. Their base is increased through observation and by listening, questioning, and trying. Leaders explore and seek out better and simpler ways to reach a higher order. They separate the unimportant from the important, then integrate and apply new-found knowledge to the future by looking at the past and the present.

Empathy: Leaders see potential in others. They want them to succeed and develop. Another's strength is not seen as threatening. Rather, they capitalize on these strengths by offering support or even sacrificing time and energy to help them grow and cultivate. Positive leaders do not carry grudges or stereotype others. They strive to achieve unity. They are humble and give credit where credit is due. Leaders acknowledge their mistakes, without placing blame. They aid others in becoming more insightful. As competence grows, they help others gain experience by giving them more power and authority. In turn, they are held responsible and accountable for their duties and performances.

Courage: Leaders have the courage to be creative, to try new ideas, to take calculated risks, and to hold to their convictions. They sacrifice, take abuse, and make corrections when needed. Leaders make efforts to develop courage in their followers, encouraging them to try new directions and to face change when necessary.

Confidence: Leaders have confidence in themselves, and they know that others are confident in them. Their loyalty, calmness, and ability to anticipate help them to inspire confidence when needed. In addition, leaders help others build confidence in themselves by sharing information and offering alternative plans and options. They encourage and help others to overcome failure with sound advice.

Enthusiasm: Leaders have a strong desire or urgent interest that compels them and others into action. When enthusiasm is genuine, it is contagious. Leaders are sensitive to what inspires others thus encouraging the spread of enthusiasm.

Communication: Leaders communicate clearly and succinctly. Their communications are supported with appropriate visual material. As excellent communicators they are persuasive motivators and networkers who are completely present when dealing with others. Their directions are clear and beneficial; questions are welcomed and answered precisely. They admit mistakes, negotiate fairly, and try to reach synergistic solutions, rather than relying on give and take.

Peacemakers: As peacemakers leaders realize that conflict is inevitable. They work to resolve incidents of conflict with minimum hostility, and work toward favorable outcomes by listening, remaining calm, and by proposing reasonable and brief solutions. Leaders do not complain about others or attack their intelligence, character, or motives. As optimists they radiate positive energy and hope.

Harmony: Leaders strive to achieve harmony and balance in their lives by creating symmetry between the mental, physical, spiritual, and emotional dimensions. Externally, they balance proportionate energies into career, family, community, and self which helps them create a healthier broader outlook. Centered leaders react less to negative conditions and radiate a sense of security and poise. They are not extreme. Their actions and attitudes are balanced. They consider the inter-working of the entire being and life process when making leadership decisions. Leaders look for the good and place their energies accordingly.

In the Field...

NRPA Code of Ethics

The National Recreation and Park Association (NRPA) members carry special responsibilities to the public at large, and to the specific communities and agencies in which
recreation and park services are offered. These obligations are set forth in the following NRPA Code of Ethics:

- As a member of the National Recreation and Park Association, I accept and
  agree to abide by this Code and pledge myself to:

- Adhere to the highest standards of integrity, truthfulness and honesty in all
  public personal activities to inspire public confidence and trust.

- Strive for personal and professional excellence and encourage the
  professional development of associates and students.

- Support the efforts of the Association and profession by participating in and
  supporting continuing education opportunities, publications, certification, and
  accreditation.

- Support the efforts of the Association and profession by participating in and
  supporting continuing education opportunities, publications, certification, and
  accreditation.

- Strive for the highest standards of professional competence, fairness,
  impartiality, efficiency, effectiveness, and fiscal responsibility.

- Avoid any interest or activity which is in conflict with the performance of
  responsibilities.

- Promote the public interest and avoid undue personal gain or profit from the
  performance of duties and responsibilities.

- Support equal employment opportunities for all elements of society.

- Support and participate in state affiliate and national/branch/section functions.

THE LEADER AND THE EMPLOYEE

Some organizations have difficulty relating to change, especially when employees feel powerless and vulnerable. Yet, it is the employees who are the organization's most important asset because they are the programmers and producers who achieve the organization's goals. As a natural resource, they cannot be wasted and should be included by the leader in the decision-making process. Their motivation levels and levels of inspiration are better met when their basic human needs for achievement, a sense of belonging, recognition, self-esteem, a sense of control over their lives, and the ability to live up to their ideals are satisfied (Kotter 1990:107). These feelings touch deeply and elicit powerful responses.

The successful leader prioritizes the needs of the employees along with the needs of the organization. Many times there is overlap. When the needs of the employees are satisfied, then the needs of the organization are met as well through increased productivity or efficiency. For example, a problem that has proved difficult for National Park Service employees has been the lack of adequate shelter. In some instances old trailers and tent-cabins in national parks have inadequate insulation which makes the basic heating needs of park employees difficult to satisfy. The Department of the Interior is rectifying this situation and other morale roadblocks to performance with the hope that ultimately the parks will be better serviced by more satisfied employees.

A study by the University of Maryland found that employees ranked the following needs in order of importance: being appreciated, being considered an insider, personal sympathy, job security, wages, interesting work, promotions, loyalty, work conditions, and tactful discipline (Reynolds:1994:109). While each person has his or her own unique needs and desires, it falls on the leader to shepherd individuals toward harmonious relationships. They must then be united to many variables including environment, systems, time, change, roles, and education so that the vision, mission, and goals of the organization can be successfully executed.

Leadership Styles

Because leaders work with people, leadership studies lean more toward the humanistic and philosophic. Leadership is, in fact, often compared to an art form rather than a science because no one answer can serve all people at all times. And since each individual is different, unpredictable, and inconsistent, there can be no direct leadership style that is recommended for every occasion. There is, however, one key ingredient used in working with others that does remain constant. This important element is respect for others. Respect is paramount to all leadership styles. Three broad styles have been identified.

Autocratic: The first, autocratic, was once in greater vogue. In this style the leader issues orders in a straightforward manner and makes decisions without consulting others. It is highly effective when quick decisions are needed, if employees need direction, and if the leader can enforce the decisions. The downside is that employees tend to lose their motivation.

Democratic: More popular today are the democratic and laissez-faire styles. The democratic leader allows a free flow of communication and encourages employee participation. So, the leader has less control over workers, but maintains the final decision- making authority.

Laissez-Faire: The laissez-faire style comes from a French term which means "hands off." In this style, the leader becomes a consultant who provides encouragement, insight, opinion when asked, and allows each employee to express himself or herself freely and creatively. However, every employee must clearly understand the mission and goals of the organization.

The use of one of these three style or any combination herof depends on the follower readiness as shown in the following section.

Follower Readiness: The Center for Leadership Studies recommends the use of four leadership styles as seen in Figure 3-1. These are utilized by leaders according to employee performance readiness. In general, the more participatory the style used, the more developed is the employee's innovation, initiative, and commitment but also the more unpredictable the employee's behavior. Leaders must weigh the benefits of participatory styles against those establishing more control (Covey 1991:184). At each level the employee is coaxed into greater performance and development. As the performance at each level changes, so does the style of leadership. Eventually, when the leadership style matures, the individual's self-leadership potential also matures. As this maturity develops, employees become more empowered by leaders to work in a freer environment and to use their own judgment to a greater extent.

FIGURE 3-1

Four Recommended Leadership Styles Based on Follower Readiness

Level I — Democratic Employee is able, willing, confident	**Level IV — Autocratic** Employee is unable, unwilling or insecure
Level II — Democratic/Autocracy Employee is able, but unwilling, or insecure	**Level III — Autocratic/Democracy** Employee is unable, but willing or confident

Source: Reynolds, J. *Out Front Leadership* (Austin: A Bard Productions Book, 1994), p. 105.

The Structure

The structure is the framework of the organization. It is designed to effectively, efficiently, and cooperatively meet the organization's mission. Leaders select the structure which best suits their environment. For example, leaders in new or smaller organizations may be driven by tasks. This gives them less room for flexibility even if desired. Since decisions must be made quickly, the structure itself is less hospitable to democratic decision-making. As an organization grows, time-frames allow employees to participate in the decision making process, thereby, creating a more adaptable, democratic structure.

Leaders respond to change and new environments by periodically reevaluating organizational structures. If an evaluation is delayed too long, total restructuring may be required in order to prevent or to respond to a crisis situation. The proper structure also considers employee needs.

Service Sector Structures: In the service sector, success is rated on customer satisfaction. If tension or low levels of trust exist among employees or volunteers, obstacles tend to form in the path of quality service for the customer. To combat this negative environment and to respond to the needs of employees, the organizational structures of park, recreation, and leisure service delivery systems have become less centralized. This means that they have taken on more of a horizontal rather than a vertical appearance (see Figure 3-2). In these flatter structures, individuals are more involved in the creative process and are granted more respect.

When employees are treated with respect they are likely to treat customers or guests with greater respect. According to Loden and Rosener (1991:8-9) there is an interdependence on the value of the customer and the value of the employee.

Making changes to meet the needs of employees, then, can enhance customer satisfaction indirectly. Consider that in one survey (McClenahen 1991:28) nearly 63 percent of the employee respondents did not enjoy their working conditions. The reason most frequently cited was the absence of teamwork. Others charged that their was a lack of leadership and care (see Table 3.3). Another study found that job setting is a key factor in the satisfaction of volunteers (Silverberg, Marshall, and Ellis 2001:79-92). Leaders respond by incorporating more team work to enhance the job setting and overall satisfaction.

Teams: When the team or collaborative approach is interspersed with a nonteam or a hierarchical approach, a more flexible, balanced leadership effort can be established (Katzenbach 1998:5). Teams are very different than groups. A *team* is a small number of people with complementary skills who are committed to a common purpose, performance goals, and approach for which they hold themselves mutually accountable (Katzenbach 1998:4). In order for people to move in the same direction, they need to be aligned but not necessarily organized. This becomes the challenge of the team leader who must be a communicator rather than a manager (Kotter 1990:107). In fact, cooperative, efficient, smooth-functioning work teams can maintain consistent, high-quality service over a prolonged period of time (Loden and Rosener 1991:8-9). Collaborating together, teams have the capacity to outperform a group of individuals (Stasca 1994:20), and diverse employees learn to work together. Teams also provide opportunities for leaders to emerge from within the ranks. The stronger leadership is at lower levels, the more effective leadership can be at higher levels.

TABLE 3-3

Work Could Be Enjoyable Again If....	
24%	we abolished titles and worked as a team.
22%	My work was recognized.
17%	I had a boss who cared.
13%	I were given more direction.
8%	I were paid more.
7%	I were left alone to do the job.

Source: McClenahen, J. *It's No Fun Working Here Anymore* Industry Management. Vol 240, No 5. March 4, 1991(Cleveland: Penton Publishing).

The Team Leader's Role: Team leaders keep meetings productive by advising members of the purpose and agenda. They allow each member time to prepare for the meeting by encouraging them to submit additional agenda items as needed. This promotes the free expression of ideas and individual communication and leadership throughout the team. Team leaders keep the meetings moving at an appropriate pace, and they communicate the team's progress and future agenda items to members and upper management. Their job is to work with, but not to dominate, the team who elected them leaders. Team leaders create unity.

The Organizational Leader's Role: The organizational leader-manager is also involved in the team process. He acts as coach or facilitator, striving to create synergy among the team. Synergy is the ability to produce and achieve results beyond the normal capacity of each individual. Coaches as facilitators enhance the team's endeavors by building on the strengths of the individual members and by attempting to complement any of their weaknesses. They openly give the team necessary information needed to complete its assignment. They are also willing to hear what the team has to communicate and to grant the necessary power to implement the change. This process, known as empowerment, encourages the team to unite toward its purpose and the organization's mission. See Table 3-4 for ways that leader-managers empower teams.

Four Stages of Team Work: Reynolds (1994:135) finds that teams work in four stages. During the first, or start-up stage, teams need the organizational leader's direction. At this stage a more autocratic form of leadership is required. The second stage, which often involves *conflict* and *frustration* among team members, requires the leader-manager to be a team builder who can help define the goals and help to smooth out conflict. The third stage or *nonproductive* stage, requires a motivator who can create harmony. At this stage, the leader-manager supports each individual and leads the team into an exploratory mode. In the final or fourth stage, the leader-manager *empowers* team members and encourages innovation as the team is now a cohesive and productive unit.

TABLE 3-4

TEN LEADERSHIP ACTIONS FOR EMPOWERING TEAMS

1. Communicate Honestly
2. Follow through on Commitments
3. Hold Employees Accountable
4. Remove Barriers
5. Recognize and Reward Desired Behaviors
6. Create a Supportive Environment
7. Coach Your Employees
8. Identify and Schedule Required Training
9. Determine the Scope of Empowerment
10. Examine Your Own Attitude

Source: "Ten Actions for Empowering Teams," Leaders Digest Vol. VIII, No. 1, (Washington DC: Department of the Treasury, Summer 1994).

The Leadership-Management Equilibrium

Leadership skills tend to be more important than management skills during the early stages of an organization's development. The role of management increases with the growth of the parks, recreation, and leisure service delivery system until it reaches equilibrium with leadership. Despite the rise in importance of management, leadership is always needed to maintain the vision and to devise new and innovative strategies. Too often, there is a tendency for most organizations to be over-managed and under-led (Kotter 1990:103). When leadership falters, management dominates and the rules and regulations of management begin to stifle communications and creativity. This atmosphere allows for fewer calculated risks and less innovation. Morale is soon lowered, and the competitive capacity of the organization depreciates (Reynolds 1994:121-122). Strong leadership with weak management, on the other hand, is no better. Just as the inevitable barriers to change demand leadership skills, complex situations demand managerial skills. The skills of each must be combined to create balance.

In The Field...

Creating Teams to Implement the Vision

The new director of the Department of Parks and Recreation wants his staff to take on leadership roles and to be empowered to implement the agency's vision. Department managers are organizing employees into teams so that they can help with the decision making process and propose new ideas and formulas to help the department modernize and energize. To do so:

1. Teams of five to ten insiders (employees representing varying departmental functions) and outsiders (individuals selected from outside sources with a vested interest) were composed. The team to help the department become more family oriented had one member from Social Services and another from the State Board of Education. Insiders understood the present process and its strengths and weakness while outsiders provided a creative link to different procedures and new ideas.

2. Each team selected a captain or facilitator who enabled the others to communicate, problem-solve, create, synthesize ideas, and make plans.

3. The outer core was composed of one supervisor, one customer, and a representative from marketing, information services, or public relations to provide input and information when needed. The Family Team's outer core included culturally diverse customers representing various family structures, children, adolescents, young adults, adults, and seniors.

4. Teams reported their progress to the outer core supervisor.

5. Supervisors met with the Director at regular department meetings. Team progress was reported which enabled the director to help coordinate team efforts into a workable whole.

Source: Hammer, M. and Champy, J. *Reengineering the Corporation* (New York: Harper Collins Publishers, Inc. 1993), pp. 110-111.

SUMMARY

- The leader is responsible for creating and communicating the vision of the recreation agency or organization. Through the vision, the leader conceptualizes the future role and operations of the entity and incorporates its mission and goals.

- Integrity and ethical standards are foundations of leadership that need to be developed throughout the leader's career. Other leadership skills, often considered attributes, can be developed through daily experiences.

- Leadership styles from autocratic to laissez-faire can be effective depending on the orientation and qualifications of the employees and the complexity and immediacy of the task.

- Building unity and empowering others has occurred through flatter organizational structures. These structures tend to eliminate layers of reporting, are oriented around collaboration, and encourage the development of natural leaders.

- Demonstrating respect and care for employees earns profound loyalty.

- Teams are committed to a common purpose, performance goals, and approach. Through the team effort, diverse employees learn to work together with the capacity to outperform individuals.

- There is a tendency for organizations to be overmanaged and underled. This causes rules to stifle communications and innovations. A balance between leadership and management is required.

LEARNING ACTIVITIES

1. Locate and read the mission statement of an organization in the recreation field. Then imagine that you are the leader of this organization and create a vision for it. Please write an overview of the key parts of your vision. Does it relate to the mission?

2. Identify a leader in the history of the recreation field. Describe the skills this person used to lead others. Would these same leadership skills be effective for a leader in any field? Describe why or why not.

3. Identify a famous leader throughout all of history. Describe the skills this person used to lead others. Would these same leadership skills be effective for a leader in the recreation field? Describe why or why not.

4. Review the list of leadership skills and characteristics in this chapter and identify five that you would like to develop in yourself. How will you do this?

5. As a future leader in recreation, would you empower teams of employees to accomplish a task? If you were an employee would you want the leader to assign you to a team? Why or why not?

REFERENCES

Bartol, K. and Martin, D. (1994) **Management.** New York: McGraw-Hill, Inc.

Cordes, K. and Ibrahim, H (1999) **Applications in Recreation and Leisure.** New York: WCB McGraw-Hill, Inc.

Capodagli, B. and Jackson, L. (1999) **The Disney Way** New York: McGraw-Hill, Inc.

Capodagli, B. and Jackson, L. (2000) **The Disney Way Fieldbook.** New York: McGraw-Hill, Inc.

Cox, D. (1992) **Leadership When the Heat's On.** New York: McGraw-Hill, Inc.

Covey, S. (1991) **Principle-Centered Leadership.** New York: Simon and Schuster, Inc.

Drucker, P. (1992) **Managing for the Future.** New York: Penguin Books USA, Inc.

Hamel, G. (2000) **Leading the Revolution.** Boston: Harvard Business School Press.

Hargrove, R. (2001) **E-Leader.** Cambridge, MA: Perseus Publishing.

Heller, B. (2000) " Don't Vegetate Innovate." **Parks and Recreation** Vol. 35 No. 1 January p. 77.

Ibrahim, H. and Cordes, K. (1996)" Leader or Manager?," **JOPERD** Vol.67/ No.1. January 1996.

Jacobson, R. (2000) **Leading for Change.** Boston: Butterworth Heinemann.

Katzenbach, J. (1998) **Teams at the Top.** Boston: Harvard Business School   Press.

Korfhage, J. (2001) "Leadership Dynamics in Parks & Recreation in the 21st Century, Lessons We Have Learned from Great Leaders, Writers, and History." **Parks and Recreation** Vol. 36 No. 6 June p. 40-43.

Kotter, J.P. (1990) **What Leaders Really Do.** Harvard Business Review. May-June 1990.

Loden, M., Rosener, J. (1991) **Workforce America! Managing Employee Diversity as a Vital Resource.** Homewood, IL: Business One Irwin.

McClenahen, J. (1991) "Its No Fun Working Here Anymore," **Industry Management** Vol. 240, No. 5. Cleveland: Penton Publishing Company.

Nanus, B. (1989) **The Leader's Edge: The Seven Keys to Leadership in a Turbulent World.** Chicago: Contemporary Books.

Nilson, J. (1999) **Competitive Branding** New York: John Wiley and Sons.

Reynolds, J. (1994) **Out Front Leadership.** Austin, TX: A Bard Productions Book.

Silverberg, K.E., Marshall, E.K. and Ellis, G.D. (2001) "Measuring Job Satisfaction of Volunteers in Public Parks and Recreation." **Journal of Park and Recreation Administration** Vol. 19.(1): 79-92.

Stasca, A. (1994) **Is a Team Ready for Team Building.** Leaders Digest Vol VIII No 1, Washington D.C.: Department of the Treasury.

Tecker, G., Eide, K., and Frankel, J. (1997) **Building a Knowledge-Based Culture.** Washington, D.C.: American Society of Association Executives.

Thomas, B. (1976) **Walt Disney, An American Tradition.** New York: Simon and Schuster.

Walt Disney Productions (1979) **Disneyland the First Quarter Century.** Anaheim, CA: Walt Disney Productions.

CHAPTER 4
MANAGEMENT

Learning Objectives

After studying this chapter, you should be able to do the following:

1. Understand the importance of management.
2. Define the role of the manager.
3. Describe the four key management activities.
4. Understand the concept of organizational development.
5. Describe motivational theories and current motivational tools.
6. Understand the unique aspects of managing a nonprofit entity.

Inevitably the ultimate success of any organization is dependent upon the development and unity of leadership and management. As seen in the last chapter, the leader dreams and guides the organization into the future. It is the manager, though, who keeps the operation running in the present and gets the job done on a daily basis. The skills of both the leader and manager can and should be developed by an individual manager although management hierarchies encourage this in varying degrees. Eliciting results, managers in parks, recreation and leisure service delivery systems focus on efficiency, logistics, methods, policies, procedures, and the bottom-line, whether it is on customer service or the financial status of an agency. Once the mission, vision, and goals are in place, management techniques are used to implement the strategies. To build their agencies and organizations into more efficient, productive, and results oriented institutions, managers make decisions and plan, organize, direct, and control. Management as defined by Thomas Bateman and Scott Snell (1999:6) is the process of working with people and resources to accomplish organizational goals. Good managers do those things both effectively and efficiently. Effective managers achieve organizational goals in an efficient manner. Efficient managers achieve goals using a minimum amount of resources or by making the best use of time, money, materials, and people.

THE FUNDAMENTALS OF MANAGEMENT

Management has been studied for centuries, and general principles and concepts have been drawn from the effort. Management, for some, is considered a developing science, while others refer to it as a practice comparable to medicine or law. Interestingly enough, because managers must also be leaders, management will never cease to remain an art or craft. This unlikely combination makes management one of the most interesting disciplines today.

Though management undoubtedly impacted great undertakings of society such as the building of the pyramids in Egypt and Central and North America as well as the construction of the Great Wall of China, the roots of the modern discipline go back a mere 200 years. Even then it was not until after World War I that the first real management boom took place. But because this period between the two World Wars was replete with political, social, and economic tensions, this new management vision was not compatible with the times (Drucker 1992:21,24). Nonetheless, foundations for the sweeping management boom of the post-World War II period were set in place with the establishment of management as a discipline at Harvard and the Massachusetts Institute of Technology. Soon new approaches to business included strategic planning, working through objectives, personnel management, organizational structures, accounting, marketing, decision making, psychology, and human relations. Recognized as a boom in business management, it ultimately became clear that all institutions needed to be managed for performance. This included public service institutions where it was discovered that the manager faced the same tasks as the manager in business. With today's service sector facing increased expectations from constituents, taxpayers, and customers, it is more imperative than ever that these agencies be properly managed for service and results. This often means removing bureaucratic steps known to interfere with effectiveness, and the reevaluation of programs in terms of the needs of present society. In this section, we will concentrate on the fundamentals of the management process while approaching some new innovations in management.

Management Levels

Except in the smallest organizations, there is generally more than one manager charged with overseeing the activities of employees. In general, there are three levels of management with each level relying on three basic types of managerial skills: conceptual, human relations, and technical. The first refers to the ability of the manager to analyze and coordinate organizational objectives and activities throughout the agency. Decision making is one example of a managerial activity that takes conceptual skills. The second involves the ability of the manager to want to lead and motivate people in order to accomplish the organization's goals. Human relations skills are needed in countless situations including work with supervisors, customers, the public, and other work related contacts. One of the major human skills needed by all managers is the ability to communicate or transfer necessary information. The third skill involves the manager's ability to use certain methods and tools to accomplish specific tasks. A manager of Therapeutic Recreation Specialists must understand the task in order to correct problems that may arise. Each level of management uses these skills but to a different extent.

Top Level Management: Top level managers in parks, recreation, and leisure service delivery systems are typically appointed, elected, or designated by the agency's board or commission. Managers at this level are generally referred to as the Executive Director, Director, Chief Executive Officer (CEO), or Chairman. Two individuals sharing this position at the top may serve as a President and Vice President. At this level, managers are expected to be more conceptual, analyzing information, studying trends, and considering economic factors in order to make decisions. Because they are in the most powerful level, they are the individuals held responsible for all decisions made.

Middle Management: Middle management includes managers of specific divisions such as the Director of Recreation, the Director of Parks, or the Director of Marketing. They analyze information received from top management and supervisory managers. Because they have the responsibility to implement organizational plans, human relations skills are particularly important at this level.

Frontline Management: Frontline managers coordinate the work of all who are not managers. They lead and direct the organization's employees by encouraging, motivating, teaching, and communicating. These managers tend to be more technical. They may charged with the direction of community centers, the youth division, or special activities. They are often called upon to show how it must be done or to participate in the actual task to be carried out by their section or unit.

In the Field...

Management in Action

The Executive Director of the YMCA has studied the clientele of the district and believes that the Y is not attracting a culturally diverse audience, and everyone agrees. This observation became a stated goal, and it was agreed that the Director of Recreation would take on the responsibility to increase diversity through appropriate program planning. She believes that the frontline manager in charge of Special Events can help. Both managers select a team of employees and individuals from the community to consider various possibilities. They decide to begin their efforts with a Festival of the Arts. Middle management consults with the top management. Together they decide on an appropriate date and budget. The Executive Director receives approval from the city. With the help of the Special Events manager, the team decides how to hold try-outs, who will need to be hired, and the specifics of production. They keep to the specific budget and make arrangements for volunteers, parking attendants, concessions, and tickets sales. They will arrange for evaluations and statistics which will be forwarded to the Executive Director for review.

The Manager's Role

Managers at each level continuously set goals and objectives, but in order to accomplish them they have to coordinate the objectives with sufficient resources in order to produce the desired results. They consider materials that are needed and how they might be integrated with the human efforts that are necessary to accomplish the task. If that is not enough, managers must also make decisions about the objectives within the context of a larger environment. For example, they consider public demand, city ordinances, and so on. When considering all of these duties, it becomes clear that management is the process of setting and accomplishing goals through the coordination of people and use of other resources within the context of the environment.

In the Field...

The Managerial Process in Action

Executive Director of the San Diego Zoo and Wild Animal Park Douglas Myers claims that he was influenced by a colleague who was determined not to listen to killer phrases such as "that's the way we've always done it," or "we tried it before, and it doesn't work." Taking a positive approach, he rejuvenated ideas that had been discarded and three successful programs emerged: the Butterfly Encounter, the Nighttime Zoo, and Roar & Snore.

The Butterfly Encounter was the result of a 1960's donation given to the zoological society with the assurance that there would one day be an insect exhibit. Held for 25 years, the gift was activated by Myers to fund a new exhibit which opened at the Wild Animal Park in 1992. The success of the Butterfly Encounter soon led to the expansion of an enlarged display of insects and to a proposal for a permanent insectarium. The promise made in the 1960s was fulfilled and an extremely popular program was founded.

The second idea, the Night Time Zoo, was not ever previously developed because it was believed that slumbering animals might be disturbed and that the lighting and security needed would be too expensive. Myers believed in the possibility and tested the idea. The popularity of the event soon led the way to plans for a seasonal Nighttime Zoo.

The third idea came to fruition from a brainstorming session which paved the way for camping opportunities at the Wild Animal Park. The program, called Roar & Snore, ranges from simple hookups for recreational vehicles to an elaborate safari-style encampment. Its successful pilot program was an immediate sellout. Due to popular demand a special camp manager was assigned to work with the reservation list already in line for the following year.

Myers was a leader, but he also had to be a manager who had to plan, organize, direct, and control. To make these programs happen, there were many preparations that were needed including experiments with animal bedtimes, new shows and menus, additional hiring and training, installation of special lighting, and other amenities. As Executive Director, Myers had to be sure that his innovative ideas coordinated with the entire operation. The zoological business had to integrate smoothly with the restaurant business, the entertainment, displays, and even with other zoos around the world. There were environmental responsibilities, marketing and public relations considerations, unexpected events, and a diverse staff to train and direct including the skilled entertainers, veterinarians, vendors, trainers, office workers, and many newly hired individuals. Finally, the new programs had to be analyzed and measured.

THE MANAGEMENT PROCESS

The environment which concerns leisure service managers generally includes customer demands, any imposed government restrictions, competition, the state of the economy, and other overall conditions. Each environmental factor tends to help, hinder, or influence the parks, recreation, and leisure service delivery system in some manner. If it were not for the changes, threats, and opportunities that the environment imposes, management would be far less demanding and much more stable. Because management requires a variety of applications and interpretations in order to accomplish its objectives, managers in small, large, for profit, and nonprofit organizations go through the same steps in order to start or maintain their operations. They plan, organize, direct, and control. This is known as the managerial process.

To fully understand the management process, it is important to look at each of the four basic functions individually.

Planning

Planning is the first management function and the one in which all others depend. It is the process by which leader-managers envision the future, develop goals, and set a course of action. Although focus on achieving goals and objectives, they can only be made after managers consider budgets, schedules, data, existing resources, and the general economy. This function is particularly important to parks, recreation, and leisure service delivery systems in the government sector and nonprofit arena because they often lack the clear financial bottom-line that businesses tend to translate into goals.

In the Field...

Is it a Symptom or the Problem

Birds were attracted to a monument in the city park. As a result, a portion of the budget was being spent to keep it clean. Cleaning the monument, however, only addressed the symptom and not the problem. The first step in the problem-solving effort was to find out why the birds were so attracted to the monument in the first place. The Fiscal Improvement Team studied the situation and found that the lights on the monument were going on an hour earlier than other lights in the area. The lights attracted insects which attracted the birds to the monument. By simply turning on the lights an hour later, the source of the problem was addressed and safety was not compromised. By responding to the problem, rather than the symptom, the monument no longer needed excessive cleaning. The money saved each month was now available for community events.

Short-Range Plans: In order to achieve long-range plans, many short-range plans or tactics are necessary. These plans are generally devised by middle and frontline managers to span a day, a week, a month, or less than one year. Besides taking less time to implement than a long-range plan, short-range plans affect fewer people, are less complex, and involve smaller budgets. Employees may be given specifics about what needs to be done and in what order, or they might be involved in the formulation of these decisions. Procedures may be accompanied by certain principles, practices or methods, and an array of rules or ethical standards that employees are expected to follow. These relate to the organization's values.

Addressing Problems: Appropriate planning keeps the organization competitive if accompanied by sound problem-solving. Traditionally problems have been viewed as barriers to the achievement of organizational goals. In actuality, problems or complaints may highlight underlying areas that need managerial solutions in order to improve service to the customer. To determine a solution, managers must first understand the problem. This means distinguishing it from mere symptoms. Symptoms are only indicators that a problem exists. Stated another way, problems give rise to symptoms. The difference between the two can be illusive. If the two are confused, inadequate solutions may result. Only after the total problem is defined and understood can a manager formulate a solution based on a sound decision making process (See box on previous page).

Making Decisions: As previously stated managers are continually engaged in decision making activity. A decision is a judgment or choice between two or more alternatives (Heller 1998:6). After identifying the problem, managers generate alternative solutions and analyze their options. If enough information is available to predict the outcome, some decisions are relatively easy to make. Many decisions tend to be challenging, however, because they involve risk, uncertainty, lack of structure, or conflict (Bateman and Snell 1999:80). Whenever there is insufficient information, a decision becomes risky. In response, the manager will draw upon knowledge, skills, experience, and intuition to reach conclusions. Intuitive thinking - a hunch led by emotion and sensitivity - is always balanced with sound logical analysis (Heller 1998:10). The manager also considers whether a decision is even necessary. If low impact aerobic dance classes are popular at 6:30 A.M. and 12:00 P.M., then there is probably no reason to change the schedule. When uncertain decisions must be made, managers may seek the advice of others. Groups may be able to bring in more information for brainstorming purposes, and the organization as a whole is more likely to accept the uncertain outcome. After the decision is made, the manager is committed to its successful implementation and evaluates the outcome (Refer to Chapter Two for details).

Managing Priorities: Although planning is key to an organization's success, it is not unusual for managers to find that they have too little time to devote to the planning process. This phenomena has evoked the outpouring of numerous articles and publications offering managers suggestions about how to manage their time more efficiently. In fact, Americans are getting 60 to 90 minutes less sleep each night than they did 10 to 15 years ago (Cook 1999:6). Based on the belief that efficiency improves effectiveness, manager's are encouraged to establish priorities. These priorities aid managers in guiding their time more efficiently. By sorting essential tasks from nonessential ones, for example, managers find that they can devote larger portions of time to their priority items. It may also be necessary to decide what priority takes precedence over another. To do this effectively, managers are encouraged to set goals and prioritize activities that will help them meet their goals. Deadlines are then scheduled and adhered to. They filter themselves from unnecessary distractions. When time is well managed, the management process can begin with a stronger foundation through appropriate planning. When time is not well managed, stress often leads to procrastination and indecision, two chief robbers of time.

Organizing

Once the plans are made, managers are challenged to accomplish goals by using the resources that are available to them in the most efficient way possible. To do this, they consider the entire organization and the individual employees including their activities, potential, and needs. A need might include the equipment that is necessary to carry out the organization's plan. Through the process of organizing, managers determine the tasks that their employees are to do.

In the Field...

Engaging in Renewal

The National Park Service (NPS) is looked upon globally as a model of conservation and preservation management. Yet, an ever-growing population continues to impact its park units, often bringing traces of economic and social activities that are inimical to the purpose of the parks. Visitor levels and demographic mixes are growing and changing as are the number of sites that the NPS manages. To perform capably under these kinds of pressures, the NPS must be innovative and well-managed. To address these issues and others, the NPS initiated an intense review of its responsibilities and prospects in cooperation with other leading institutions concerned with management of the NPS.

At the Symposium called *Our Parks: Challenges and Strategies for the 21st Century* issues included increased bureaucratization, eroding independence, autonomy, the sense of efficacy of many employees, and the desire for organizational renewal. The Working Group on Organizational Renewal formed to focus attention on the question of how the administrative capacities of the NPS might be adapted to enhance the organization's resilience and ability to meet the challenges ahead. Healthy organizations continually engage in renewal.

Generally, the top management establishes the organizational structure, middle management organize the structure needed for their area, and frontline management organizes the training necessary to suit the structure. This requires a division of labor that best suits organizational goals and objectives, including staffing positions, selecting well-suited people for various tasks, training them so they know what to do, and helping them to do it. Organizing these functions becomes particularly difficult when organizations face rapid change. In these instances, staff and equipment may need to be updated, customers may no longer be satisfied with the same programs or products, and new economic trends may call for new actions. In a fast-paced society changing circumstances challenge leader-managers.

Organizational Change: To remain viable, all agencies go through organizational change or some amount of restructuring. Change is precipitated by environmental factors and internal events, such as a decreasing number of customers or failure to meet organizational goals. In this challenging but crucial process, the leader-manager serves as the change agent. They determine what ingredients will make the change a successful one and investigate where resistance is likely to occur. They consult with employees throughout this process to help move them toward change and new goals.

Reengineering: Reengineering is a fundamental rethinking that results in a total redesign of the inner working processes of an organization. The purpose is to achieve dramatic improvements in critical measures of performance such as quality, service, cost, and speed (Hammer and Champy 1993:33). Many public parks and recreation agencies at the federal, state, and local levels have undergone reengineering efforts to become more efficient and productive. Like many government agencies, park, recreation, and leisure service delivery systems have been accused of being run for the convenience of the employee rather than for the convenience of the customer. If this is the case, appropriate reorganization may lead to increased productivity at lower costs. If it is not the case, reorganization can lead to failure. Reengineering failed when some of the nation's corporations used it as a means of cost reduction and downsizing. Leading to a loss in morale, it also lead to a loss of trust, loyalty, and productivity. Reengineering should be customer driven or used as a means to change goals to meet changing needs. When total restructuring is necessary, management executes the plan with speed and precision throughout the organization. Doing so in increments may lead to confusion and agitation (Knight 1995:24).

Organizational Development: Organizational development, referred to as OD, is a planned approach for organizational change. This includes the movement toward a more productive system in which all of the parts of the organization are integrated into a more effectively functioning whole. The goal of the OD process is to achieve a self-renewing, learning organization, where managers and teams utilize leadership skills (See box on previous page).

Ultimately, the successful OD process will lead to a healthier leisure service organization that is better able to meet its goals, serve its customers, and motivate its employees in a cost effective manner. Newer trends focus on achieving the best from the individual for the benefit of the agency or organization, and achieving the best agency for the benefit of the people. Because team building incorporates the team in the decision making process and improves human relations, morale, effectiveness, and group performance, it is one of the most popular organizational development approaches used today.

To become a healthy, whole, and complete agency is not necessarily done without pain, and because change takes time to implement, its success cannot be measured quickly. Avoidance, on the other hand, can lead to denial and organizational dysfunction and paralysis. Thriving agencies and organizations are realizing that human potential and systems thinking are fundamental to the modern organizational development process and to its success.

Systems: Organizations used to be viewed as closed systems that operated without any exchange with the environment. This meant that managers needed to create highly specialized and departmentalized structures to carry out the work of the organization. Today's open systems stress the need for organizations to remain flexible so that they can respond quickly to changes within the environment. Managers in open systems organize their employees according to their specializations, and various employees are integrated in ways that their efforts will be coordinated rather than segregated.

Within both systems managers are given a certain amount of authority or power to act; they influence, make decisions, carry out responsibilities, and make subordinates accountable. In a vertical hierarchy, typical of the closed system, managers coordinate and communicate effectively with superiors above them and subordinates below in order to keep the line of flow unbroken. In horizontal or flat structures, typical of open systems, managers serve as liaisons and leaders, linking the groups together and helping them integrate their efforts more effectively. In either case, leader-managers are often called upon to settle conflicts.

Conflict: Managers realize that it is inevitable that the wishes, preferences, or rights of individuals will from time to time be compromised by the actions of others. This is not always bad, however. Conflict may serve as a motivator for necessary change. With more human interaction and change occurring in organizations, managers are called upon to settle personal and organizational conflicts more often than in the past. Though conflict may simply come with the territory of daily life, if left unattended, it can escalate. The manager attempts to channel the energy into positive outcomes with minimal hostility. To do so, factors such as personality and level of conflict are considered before a course of action is taken. Whether dealing in interpersonal conflict, person-group conflict, or intergroup conflict, there are four basic methods of response: avoidance, accommodation, competition, and collaboration (Wisinski 1993:18-20). Though the first choice may suppress the symptoms, it will not resolve the issues and may lead to a lose/lose situation. The next two options are also usually ineffective because they cause delays and indecisiveness and create a winner and a loser. The fourth, collaboration, is the preferred method because both parties strive to understand the other's point of view while seeking to reach an acceptable solution. Leader-managers encourage collaboration by helping those in conflict define and analyze the situation, select and agree on alternatives, and implement a system of evaluation.

> " The ultimate measure of a man is not where he stands in moments of comfort and convenience, but where he stands at times of challenge and controversy"
>
> > Martin Luther King, Jr.
> > Minister, Civil Rights Activist

In the Field...

Conflict Management: Tips for People in Charge

Conflict is a by-product of change. Knowing how to effectively manage conflict is crucial to a successful organization. When managing conflict, consider these three major areas: yourself, others, and the process for reaching agreement.

MANAGING OTHERS	MANAGING YOURSELF
Acknowledge that conflict is inevitable when people work together	Know your style preference
No one is "bad" or "wrong" for having a different point of view or a different work style.	Do you avoid conflict at all costs or do you love to win?
Diverse work groups are strong work groups	Are you a natural compromiser or do you give in to others?
Look for the positive elements, such as creative solutions, that others bring to your group.	Are you skilled in seeking solutions so that all parties get something that they want?
<u>Acknowledge that emotions are neither right nor wrong; they just are valid in and of themselves.</u>	Know your instinctive responses
	Do you have negative associations with the words "conflict" and "anger"?
	Stay centered
	What do you want to have happen?
	Can you use self-discipline to remain focused on your goals?
	Respect the other person
	Do you actively listen to others?

Personality: Personality is a person's unique social, emotional, physical, and behavioral characteristics. Often thought of as a person's emotional make-up, personality determines how a person reacts to change, challenges, how feelings are interpreted, and how conflicts are resolved. When the leader-manager has an awareness of the powerful impact that the emotional environment has on workers productivity, he or she will direct resources into managing this environment. Increasingly, it is accepted that emotional intelligence, EQ, is a key tool for getting along with others, taking control of one's life, thinking clearly, and making decisions (Goleman 1995). Daniel Goleman, a Harvard psychologist and author of Emotional Intelligence, redefined what it means to be smart. He believes that to be successful, the qualities of the mind, once thought of as character, matter more than intelligence.

Personality Type: The successful leader-manager takes personality factors, such as style and temperament, into consideration when organizing and making decisions. Leader-managers who are familiar with various personality types are better prepared to interact with individuals. Many organizations are encouraging managers and staff to learn about the various personality types and the values and challenges that each type has to offer. One testing instrument that has gained wide acceptance is the Myers-Briggs Type Indicator (MBTI) which established eight basic preferences. These preferences, known as Extroversion (E), Introversion (I), Sensory (S), Intuitive (I), Thinking (T), Feeling (F), Judger (J), and Perceiver (P), combine to form sixteen basic personality types.

The MBTI instrument provides a comprehensive understanding of how a person tends to function in daily life. These tendencies are referred to as preferences. For instance, an employee may test as an ISTP, an introvert (I) who spends time reflecting, a sensor (S) who sees the world in terms of practical facts, a thinker (T) who makes decisions after objective analysis, and a perceiver (P) who prefers unscheduled time. Types vary in many ways including how one sets goals, manages time, and resolves conflicts. The Myers-Briggs Type Indicator is especially useful if a team is having trouble communicating or coming together as a cohesive work group. After the test is completed, all members of the team share the results. By understanding a team member's type, communications are generally improved. As organizations learn about personality types and apply that knowledge to the work environment, they tend to improve their interpersonal relationships and productivity while stress and stress-related illnesses decrease (Isachsen and Berens 1988:16).

MANAGING THE PROCESS FOR REACHING AGREEMENT

- Raise the issue: Identify the problem and be willing to "put it on the table" to uncover the root causes of the conflict.
- Discover interests: Don't be afraid to ask about the other parties' real interests - their needs, hopes and concerns. Interests are satisfied in numerous ways
- Generate options: Develop at least five possible solutions to ensure that all alternatives are considered.
- Develop agreements: After reviewing all the options, all parties in conflict work together to develop and endorse an agreement that meets independent standards of fairness.

Source: Managers' Communications Toolkit (U.S. Treasury Department, 1994), p. 8.

Diversity: The workforce of today has changed to become inherently diverse. These shifts have presented a challenge for managers to create an atmosphere that maximizes the richness of diversity and translates the valuable asset of a diverse workforce into increased productivity. Differences in age, gender, ethnicity, and education are greater than they ever have been. In the past, white male employees dominated the parks and recreation and the overall workforce. Changes have occurred rapidly and trends indicate that they will continue. For instance, in 1913 less than 25% of adult women worked outside of the home, and only 3% of married women held jobs. By 2006, women are expected to make up 47% of the workforce, while white males, the traditional source of labor in the United States, will drop to 39.4%. Additionally, in the year 2000, 10% of the nation's workforce was foreign born, but by the end of the 21st century, 50% will be immigrants or descendants of immigrants who arrived after 1980 (Klein 1998). Consider, too, that in 1988, whites made up approximately 80 percent of the overall workforce, and by the year 2050 this will decrease to less than 50 percent (Luthans 1995:53).

Some leading-edge agencies have made unique efforts to institutionalize the value of diversity through their organizational structure. A longitudinal review of diversity research indicates that diverse groups produce a greater number of alternatives in problem solving, generate higher quality ideas, and exhibit a higher level of cooperation in complex tasks (Milliken and Martins 1996:402-433). Harnessing the power of diversity, 70% of Fortune 500 companies, and a growing number of non-profit firms, have adopted diversity initiatives that have prompted organizational change (Digh 1998:117). To be effective, diversity must be related to the organization's strategic vision, and the organization must have a relatively egalitarian non-bureaucratic structure that will promote the exchange of ideas (Thomas and Ely 1999:142). Many organizations have worked to achieve a workforce that mirrors the composition of the customers with the underlying belief that this creates a better understanding of those being served by the organization. This is successful in community recreation programs where the diverse workforces represents the community at large.

Organizational approaches to managing diversity may include mentoring, training, team building, and benefits that respond to an increasingly diverse climate such as flexible work arrangements and child care (Cascio 1995:62). At the foundation of these strategies is the belief that differences should be respected, valued, understood, and appreciated. Managers encourage cooperation, differing opinions, listening, personal reflection, and ongoing interaction. They develop systems and procedures that support diversity, and rewards which are based on results. They prepare by learning as much as possible about diverse individuals.

This will help them to develop appropriate interactions and empathy. Empathy gives the leader-manager a better perspective which improves interaction and decision making. This garners the respect and loyalty of the diverse workforce.

Directing

Even with the most logical organizational plan in place, it will most likely not work out just as the manager anticipates. This leads to the third function of the management process, directing. Directing is a complex process of getting people to work effectively and willingly. Beginning at the top level of the management hierarchy, it works its way to the frontline manager who directs employees by using two different but related processes: guiding and motivating. First, the manager guides employees by demonstrating the task or through example. Leader-managers do not give orders, but, instead, enlist support by requesting and persuading. They recognize and promote human qualities in all individuals (see also Chapter Three). Second, the manager entices the employee into working effectively and willingly through motivation or the use of a stimulus or incentive devised to satisfy an employee's need.

Motivation: Motivation is the inner state that activates or moves a person toward a goal. It refers to forces that energize, direct, and sustain a person's efforts. All effort, except involuntary reflexes, is motivated. In the work organization, a highly motivated person will strive to achieve the leisure service organization's goals (Bateman and Snell 1999:440). Motivation differs from manipulation which usually implies deception. Manipulation, a mechanism used to induce employees by providing a perceived benefit, is rationalized by those managers who assume that employees will not or cannot be inspired for the real reasons. When used as the norm, manipulative actions eventually come to the forefront, resulting in a loss of morale and productivity. Effective management requires a working knowledge of the theories behind motivated behavior and individual needs.

Motivational Theories: Through the early part of the twentieth century, the classical theory of motivation - that money is the sole motivator in the workplace - functioned well. At that time most employees were poor and in need of money for the essentials of life. Though still clearly a major factor, it is no longer the only thing that motivates (Martin and Petty 2000:158). As a result, leader-managers understand the content of motivation through an awareness of differences in people's needs, desires, and goals. They also study the process of motivation or how individual's make choices based on preferences, rewards, and accomplishments.

One of the earliest theorists was psychologist Abraham Maslow who identi-fied a five-level hierarchy of human needs, shown in Figure 4-1. He theorized that most people are driven by several of these needs, not just one, and they move from one need level to the next in a building-block fashion. Maslow's hierarchy of needs became widely accepted in the field of management with managers using a variety of motivational tools to appeal to several motives or energizing forces from within. Once one need was satisfied, managers found it necessary to appeal to another. Consistency of the hierarchy for all individuals caused the theory to be questioned.

FIGURE 4-1

Maslow's Hierarchy of Needs

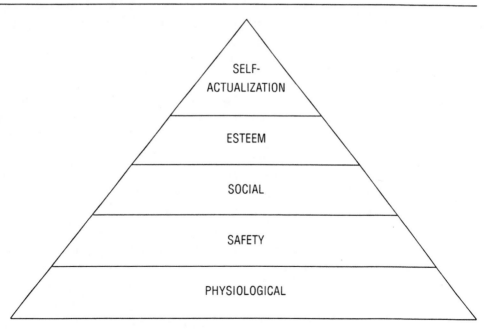

Also falling into the category of content theories with his two-factor theory was Frederick Herzberg, author of The Motivation to Work (1959) and Work and the Nature of Man (1966). His theory is based on job satisfiers (motivators) and dissatisfiers (hygiene factors) shown in Figure 4-2. Believing that people could be motivated by work itself, his research illustrated that extra effort or doing more than normal comes from providing motivators beyond resolution of hygienic problems (note: the motivators are roughly the same as Maslow's esteem and self-actualization needs, whereas the hygienic factors are basically the physical, security, and social needs). His theory showed that motivators alone may not cause satisfaction. Instead, employee satisfaction may also depend on the need to remove dissatisfaction. The two-factor theory has been criticized on the notion that job factors were placed in one category or another. Can it be said, for instance, that salary and status are never motivators or that responsibility and growth potential are always motivators?

In Practice: In dealing with esteem and self- actualization, managers consider that all people are unique. One individual's need for achievement, affiliation, and power is markedly influenced by environment. All subordinates, then, cannot be treated alike although equal treatment and non-bias standards remain essential. While negotiated deadlines may help some employees, it could mean alienation for another. For employees to be satisfied, there may be a need for managers to remove possible sources of dissatisfaction. To test Herzberg's two-factor theory, a survey exploring the motivational devices of coaches in the National Football League was designed. Though player's claimed salary to be their main motivator, it was soon discovered that successful coaches used many of the motivational theories utilized by business management. By using individual psychological motivators to build egos or to reject players by benching them, the survey found that coaches were able to go beyond financial rewards to effectively induce their players to perform better (Waldo and Kerin 1978:15-18).

The process of motivation requires that managers understand how individuals make choices based on preferences, rewards, and accomplishments. Complementing the Content Theories, the Process Theories of Motivation describe, explain, and analyze how behavior is energized, directed, sustained, and stopped. They are, in effect, mechanistic in nature, describing methods of changing behavior without particular regard to an individual's needs.

FIGURE 4-2

Herzberg's Two Factor Theory

Factors Promoting Job Satisfaction (Motivators)	*Factors Promoting Job Dissatisfaction (Hygiene)*
Achievement	Policies and Administration
Recognition	Supervision
The Work Itself	Relationship with Supervisor
Responsibility	Work Conditions
Advancement	Relationship with Peers
Growth	Personal Life

Salary

	Relationship with Subordinates
	Status
	Security

Adapted by Jane Lammers from: Herzberg, Frederick *The Managerial Choice: To Be Efficient or to Be Human* (Salt Lake City: Olympus Publishing Co., 1982), p. 426.

Victor Vroom, author of Work and Motivation (1964), wrote that people determine their behavior on the basis of the probability of various outcomes of that behavior. In other words, employees behave in a manner that maximizes their net outcomes. If an employee, seeking promotion, perceives that politics are more important than performance, performance will become less important in that employee's path for success. Influenced by what they have experienced before, people react according to what they perceive. This would mean that employees anticipate what is in it for them as they work.

Managers must also keep in mind J. Stacy Adams' Equity Theory which states that workers compare their work efforts and rewards with others in similar situations. Employees working for the state park system may seek the benefits of those working for the city park system.

Another theory, so simple that it is easy to overlook, is that of noted psychologist B.F. Skinner who found that positive reinforcement increases the strength of response. Managers also influence a desired response by removing negative or adverse conditions. Consequences, then, can cause behaviors to increase, continue, decrease, or stop. Managers must keep in mind, however, that everyone's behavior makes sense to them. Hence, rewards or positive reinforcement must make sense to the person to whom they are being applied. Interestingly, if a manager does something or does nothing, behavior in the subordinate will change. Whether consequences are reinforcing or punishing is controlled by the receiver, but the manager must be certain that the desired behavior is generated. To be effective, positive reinforcement must be: personal, immediate, specific, sincere, consistent, and not mixed with other messages. Any behavior that is rewarded is likely to be repeated.

Social psychologist Douglas McGregor felt that managers had failed to appreciate the importance of Maslow's work. He grouped several managerial assumptions about workers' motivations together as Theory X. These include: the average person dislikes work and will avoid it if possible; because work is not liked, force, control, direction, or threat of punishment is needed to motivate the worker; workers prefer to be directed, wish to avoid responsibility, lack ambition, and want security above all else.

Wanting to formulate a more contemporary look at working people, he formulated Theory Y which suggested that working is a natural state like rest and play; people work not to avoid something like punishment or security, but also to achieve something that is valuable to them; employees actually seek responsibility to gain control over their efforts and as such do not need to be controlled and dependent upon others. McGregor believed that people will work to satisfy those needs not just their psychological and social needs. The effective organization, then, does not need to create controls and/or penalties as much as it needs to remove obstacles to better performance. People will identify with the goals of the organization if through achieving them they can fulfill their own needs (Quick 1980:26-27).

Developed by William Ouchi, professor at the University of California, Los Angeles, Theory Z is often referred to as Japanese Management. This theory involved a human relations approach which professed treating employees at all levels as if they were one family working together harmoniously to achieve organizational goals. Behind the theory lies the belief that employees with a sense of identity and belonging are more likely to perform their jobs conscientiously and enthusiastically. In this manner, lower-level needs in Maslow's ladder may be satisfied as well as middle-level needs like working in groups and higher-level needs like taking on more responsibility. Theory Z is questioned by those who are not resolved that United States citizens with a tradition of individualism and self-reliance can respond to a system of teamwork versus competition. Teamwork, they point out, has been essential to the Japanese who live in a densely populated, resource-poor land.

Motivation and Organizational Design: Knowing the theories and strategies involved in motivation is one thing, but applying them to the workplace is another. First, the Organizational Development process is not a process designed to do something to people or to organizations, it, instead, uses the energy of the people to transform conditions from "what is" to "what can be." To do this, agencies zero in on what motivates their employees when undertaking organizational design, but how do managers in parks, recreation, and leisure service delivery systems motivate employees? Many of these employees work in government agencies and the nonprofit sector, and tend to be motivated by customer interaction and the mission of the agency. Motivational strategies are designed around personal satisfaction, structure, growth and development, accomplishment, recognition, and fair pay. Collaborative team approaches which engage people in data gathering, feedback, and joint action planning, also motivate employees. Other approaches follow.

Frontline Service: Service industry managers in parks, recreation, and leisure delivery systems are charged with directing their frontline employees to provide excellent service. To maximize service, managers recognize their frontline as a prized resource. They recognize that talented employees must be treated fairly to keep them in a positive frame of mind as they approach the customer on a daily basis. Looking to the East for guidance, managers learned that employees in Japan were promised their position until age 60 or for life for an exchange of loyalty in return. After this basic human need for security is satisfied, employees are further motivated by greater decision making opportunities and tasks are rotated to alleviate boredom, extreme specialization, and rigidity. Though life guaranteeing positions may be difficult to grant in some service industries, some agencies and organizations in the United States are stressing the importance of the employee first and customer second, recognizing that a satisfied employee provides better service to a more satisfied customer.

By promoting advancement opportunities from within the agency or organization, goodwill and long-term commitment is reinforced. Motivational efforts to improve quality in the frontline involve appreciation, training, freedom to do their jobs, fair pay, and recognition for extraordinary service. The Walt Disney Company stresses customer importance and the emotional connection that customers share with employees. To motivate and encourage their frontline, they generally promote from within, have many promotional opportunities, keep wages competitive, and provide favorable benefits.

Marriott Corporation offers strong orientations designed to build pride in their employees and to aid them in establishing direction. Mentors provide them assistance during the early stages of their work. Continued training helps their employees to grow and shows them that they are not forgotten. Once forgotten, morale is lost, and employees can become cynical and apathetic. Those who excel in managing the frontline know that creative, sensitive individuals are hard to come by. If they "burn-out" and leave the agency, the change impacts service and reduces productivity. A major priority of the National Park Service is to upgrade the benefits of its frontline. Recognition goes far in encouraging employees to go the extra mile. When morale is strong, leader-managers observe fewer problems, absences, complaints, injuries, and illness. Service and quality improves with customer satisfaction.

Total Quality Management (TQM): Total quality means understanding the needs and expectations of everyone who is impacted by the mission of the organization, and trying to meet or exceed those needs or expectations. To do so, leader-managers emphasize the humanistic over the technical, thus, bringing out the leadership qualities in the manager rather than the directive. Centered in principles, human relations, consistency, research, improvement, progression, and feedback, total quality encompasses the need for continuous improvement in four dimensions: personal and professional development; interpersonal relations; managerial effectiveness; and organizational productivity (Covey 1991:250-252).

The first, calls for the establishment of strong communications, principles, teamwork, and empowerment. The second, is established through goodwill between leadership, management, and employee. The third, is developed through motivational win-win situations accomplished through empowering rather than dominating situations. The fourth, means producing quality programs or products, either by doing things better or differently; by studying the needs of the customer and getting feedback on services rendered; and by establishing motivation through an award system for cooperation, innovation, and teamwork.

Quality teams are formed to solve systemic problems using systematic problem-solving methods which include identifying problems, selecting problems, analyzing the root cause, identifying possible solutions, selecting solutions, testing solutions, implementing solutions, and tracking effectiveness. In public sector agencies, quality recreation service teams work on problems ranging from reduced waiting time for the tennis courts to expediting payments to contractors. For TQM programs to be successful, leader-managers instill the concepts of a strong work ethic, integrity, and commitment to goals while helping employees grow and develop their skills as professionals. This is encouraged by offering rewards and motivators to those who are cooperative, work toward team unity, provide innovative ideas, and improve in these categories. Individuals also receive immediate satisfaction because they are consulted in the decision making process, thereby, impacting the inner workings of the organization. In other words, they belong. When public service agencies turn to TQM styles, it is important that managers remember the power of motivational devices and remove the adverse or negative. For instance, team assignments cannot be productive if employee workloads are already too full. In addition, when employees are asked to serve on teams, they must receive open communications and necessary information. If not, they become uninspired, recognizing that their work can be of no true value to the organization.

In the Field...

QUALITY PARK SERVICE

FIGURE 4-3

Quality Park Service Structure

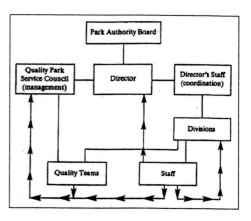

The Fairfax County Park Authority in Virginia created a Quality Park Service Council cooperating on common goals. Though their agency mission - to preserve park land and provide quality facilities and services - remained in tact, a new vision was promoted by the agency's director. It called for the agency to be a pacesetter by providing high quality services that would exceed the public's expectations in response to accusations that upper management was too often competing rather than To accomplish the vision, a new structure was established as here in Figure 4-3. The Council, given the overall responsibility to implement what became known as Quality Park Service (QPS), encouraged employees to participate in a cultural shift. Stressing the positive, they encouraged employees to thank others for their efforts rather than placing blame. The Council also asked employees to raise agency-wide issues that needed resolution. In addition, the Council established Quality Teams to tackle important agency-wide issues and problems, and Project Teams to help plan development projects authorized by the Board. The first challenge of the Capital Projects Team, for example, was to compile a critical needs list and to prioritize what needs the agency should respond to first. They established dollar estimates for each entry and then ranked them according to safety, legal requirements, facility protection, and revenue generation. Teamwork provided the Fairfax County employees with an opportunity to learn new skills and to be directly involved in problem-solving. The decision making process serves as a direct motivator, and further motivational devices are made available by the Council through nine award categories established to recognize employees for their efforts.

Source: Fairfax County Park Authority, "Can We Work Together?" Park Pacesetter Vol. V, No3, August 1993. (Fairfax, VA: Fairfax County Park Authority). p. 4.

Rank Order Competition: Some organizations have large pay raises between employee steps within the hierarchy. The monetary reward is an incentive for employees at lower levels to compete for the prize. Called the rank-order tournament theory, this practice began in the 1980s as a business theory. It rests its case on the "winner takes all" theory used in sports. Studies indicate that professional athletes try much harder to win a tournament if a large purse awaits the winner as opposed to a simple 60-40 split. Economists who tested the theory on the Professional Golf Association found that each player lowered his score by 1.1 strokes over 72 holes (Norton 1994:36).

Although the theory is that the larger the raise the harder each employee will work to reach the prize, this may not be the case. If incentives are not adjusted carefully and the spread is too large, the competition level may be too severe. Team cooperation becomes extremely difficult to obtain and employees may even sabotage each others efforts. In this situation, the theory could lead to lower overall productivity. Additionally, some employees might be inclined to eliminate themselves from the competition, in effect, forfeiting their right to contest the prize but gaining the freedom to do less. Those who remained in the competition but lost, may also lose their drive once the motivator is no longer attainable. Other experts believe that the work environment is more critical to success than compensation (Pfeffer 1999:91).

Flexible Work Arrangements: Flexible work arrangements allow employees to make choices that better suit their individual lives. This flexibility to choose is a powerful motivator and includes flextime, flexiplace, job sharing, and compressed work schedules. Flextime allows employees to arrange their work hours. Flexiplace enables more employees to perform their work at home or other approved locations. Job sharing permits two people to share one full-time position, and compressed work schedules allow employees to work longer workdays and shorter workweeks. Shorter work weeks of 30 hours are now an option in some workplaces, and employees may have the choice to use overtime hours to increase vacation time.

On July 11, 1994, President Clinton signed an executive order urging all federal agencies to create a "family-friendly" work place. The President wrote, "Broad use of flexible work arrangements to enable federal employees to better balance their work and family responsibilities can increase employee effectiveness and job satisfaction, while decreasing turnover rates and absenteeism." By the year 2000, Watson Wyatt, a benefits consulting firm, reports that nearly 43% of large employers let their employees work from home at least a portion of the time and 27% offered a reduced workweek (Ligos 2001:D-1). Employees working for the Forest Service in San Bernardino National Forest, for instance, can select a regular work schedule, a 10-hour workday with Fridays off, or a 9/80 work schedule which includes a nine day work schedule of 80 hours with an extra day off every two weeks, usually a Friday or Monday.

Success depends primarily on the commitment of leader-managers and participating employees. Leader-managers focus more on meeting objectives and less on the daily work processes. Employees stay focused, have clear goals, and know how they will be measured. Completion of work is made through prearranged deadlines and success is measured through quality (Apgar 1999:179). Alternative work schedules offer win/win situations for the employee and the employer. Employees find these schedules rejuvenating and a savings in commuter time and costs. Employers find that the motivated employees increase their productivity (Apgar 1999:187-188). In addition, less driving makes compressed work schedules environmentally sound.

Controlling

A strategic control system is designed to support managers in evaluating the organization's progress with its strategy and, when discrepancies exist, in taking corrective action (Bateman and Snell 1999:143). Control consists of three steps: establishing standards, evaluating performance against standards, and taking corrective action when standards are not met. In short, it is a means of checking whether the situation is "out of control." When managers control, they compare where they have been with where they should be, and make adjustments where they are needed. It should not be thought of as a restrictive action or process, but as a means of monitoring progress toward organizational goals, resetting objectives when change demands it, and establishing corrective deviations if objectives are not being met.

A Complicated Function: A complicated function, control, if not handled properly, can decrease motivation. For example, appropriate control systems must be objective, but they must also allow for the subjective or the human elements of control. The human element balances inadequacies that could arise from unique or unusual circumstances. Too much control is detrimental when a parks, recreation, or leisure service delivery system already enjoys employees who are deeply committed to its success and are fully aware of its objectives, policies, and standards. In these cases, where a high degree of self-control exists, external controls of authoritarian leadership are unwelcome (Williams et.al.1985:431). Nonetheless, employees, charged with responsibilities, must be held accountable to their superiors for the performance of their duties. Negative reactions are less likely to occur when leader-managers communicate the positive relevance of the control process, make the process clear, are fair and realistic, provide prompt feedback, and offer help as needed. Through the controlling function, corrective action is applied only when it is necessary to do so to assure that the organization's objectives are actually being properly fulfilled. Revisions may also be needed to meet changing conditions.

Staying on Track: The controlling function is important to every aspect of the parks, recreation, and leisure service operation. Though many government agencies did not tend to acknowledge this function of the management process until recent years, it is now understood to be especially important to non-profit agencies because they are evaluated on performance rather than a clearly defined profit (Drucker 1990:105). Ultimately, the control function keeps the agency on track, points the way to improvement, helps the agency to recognize when change is imminent, and provides useful information for marketing.

The Control Process: Like directing, controlling is particularly important to frontline and middle managers. Frontline managers work with employees to help strengthen work habits, and they collect information on a regular basis to monitor the work process. This information is available to middle managers who strive to solve routine problems before they develop into bigger ones. Leader-managers use four basic control steps shown in Figure 4-4. The first step involves setting standards of performance based on the agency's objective. The second is the creating a feedback system; the third, a comparison of actual performance with established standards to determine any variations; and fourth, an action if a deviation exists.

The first step sets standards or criteria for measuring the performance of the agency as a whole. These standards are set by top management and are monitored through the establishment of specific goals which can be readily measured, such as units of productivity or amount of profitability. Productivity might be measured through employee turnover while profitability could be monitored through attendance at events. The four common measurements used in standards are time, quality, quantity, and cost. The second step involves the establishment of a feedback system of regular reports for all levels of management. This is an on-going process which generally involves progress reports and monitoring systems. The third step compares actual performance with desired performance by analyzing data from the feedback system. The fourth step requires that either the status quo be maintained, corrective action be taken, or standards be modified. Figure 4-4 shows a practical example of the four step system in action. For more information on the evaluation process see Chapter 16.

FIGURE 4-4
_____

The Control Process in Action
_____

A local YMCA received two complaints that the temperature of the pool was too warm. Lowering the temperature would be a monetary savings. The pool staff decided to experiment with the temperature and lowered it by two degrees. Because they had previously surveyed pool use, they found that the higher temperature was preferable and justified.

- Setting Standards: During February approximately 800 people normally use the pool.
- Establishing a Feedback System: This February only 685 people used the pool.
- Comparing Performance to Standard: This February showed a loss of 115 people when the temperature was lowered.
- Evaluate/Act: Corrective Action was taken: The pool temperature was returned to its normal temperature. Results were compared again the next month.
_____

MANAGING IN THE NONPROFIT SECTOR

The nonprofit sector of park, recreation, and leisure service delivery systems is exceedingly diverse. In its broadest sense, it includes government agencies, art and cultural institutions, youth organizations, colleges and universities, and co-operatives among others. While the fundamentals of management remain the same for the nonprofit and profit sectors, managing in this environment differs in some respects from commercial recreation. First and most importantly, it should be recognized that nonprofit agencies are formed to provide a service rather than to make a profit. Second, they lack a truly direct-line of responsibility because they have no direct owners with the exception of taxpayers and donors whose designation is loosely defined. Third, leader-managers work not only with staff but with volunteers.

The Bottom Line

Because the very existence of the nonprofit agency is steeped in its ability to bring about a change in the individual and society, it is said that these agencies have no bottom line or clearly identifiable measure of performance in terms of profitability. This has left many agencies with the challenging task of measuring

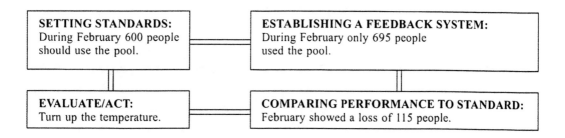

their success through service objectives which can be difficult to analyze because of their long term nature. Even so, leader-managers, are increasingly asked to be answerable to their contributors, taxpayers, customers, and constituencies. They must account for expenses and show results by measuring performance to goals.

As a result, nonprofit managers are increasingly seeking clear strategies for improving productivity by keeping goals that are high but not absurd to meet. They are pressed to place scarce resources into activities which bring results. Yet, they cannot loose site of the moral and charitable obligations of their agency. Because there are, however, more moral causes than funds to back them, their agencies are easily spread too thin. Nonprofit leader-managers, as a result, are forced to find their niche in order to respond to lean financial budgets. They make difficult choices and decisions (Drucker 1990:111-112). To do this, parks, recreation, and leisure service managers turn to their mission and define it into reality. They look outward to research the needs of the community as they relate to the mission and to the strengths of programs offered by other agencies. These managers are actively building partnerships with other organizations in the community so that their agencies can help to meet the needs of the community and avoid duplication. For even though a moral effort may be worthy, it may best be filled by another agency. Likewise, whenever new trends are adapted, old ones are discarded. Never stagnant, nonprofit leader-managers encourage risk, but admit failure if the results do not meet expectations after appropriate time has been given to a new project. This bottom-line orientation is becoming more routine to nonprofit managers in parks, recreation, and leisure services. In sharpening both cooperation and competition through cost effectiveness, moral demands are kept in balance.

Responsibility to the Board

Although owners of nonprofits are loosely defined, managers report to a multiplicity of constituencies who are reflected in the board of directors and commissions. Individuals on boards and commissions are generally deeply committed and are likely to be intensely involved in running the agency or organization. They make sure they have competent management and serve as the guardians of the mission. Management must, therefore, insure that boards and commissions understand the nonprofit's vision and mission, as well as their obligations to the agency.

Keeping the Board Effective: To help them become effective rather than meddlesome, top management assists the board to fuse into a team and points them in the right direction by assisting with setting goals which they too are held accountable for to the nonprofit agency. And because they serve as governors, sponsors, ambassadors, consultants, and fund raisers for the agency, it is up to the leader-manager to keep them fully informed of any positive or negative outcomes (Drucker 1990:173). In addition, they need to understand how their endeavors improve the quality of life of the individuals who are served, and how they may best serve in their leadership roles within the agency and to the community at large. To help them serve the agency in their strongest capacity, management can aid the process by establishing an orientation for new members and by providing ongoing training sessions through conferences and other programs.

Working with Volunteers

Fifty percent of all Americans are now active volunteers (O'Connell 1998:1). Each year, for example, more than 120,000 volunteers donate over 4 million hours of service in the national parks (Pietschmann 2000:1). Volunteers teach, lead, officiate, assist, write, build, and help in various ways. Representing a diverse group of individuals of all ages, cultures, talents, and abilities, they have one thing in common - they make a difference. Managing volunteers appropriately is important to nonprofits and park, recreation, and leisure service agencies because volunteers are often the life-blood of the agency. Without them, many agencies would not be the same and others would become extinct. Volunteers, with their own needs including social and developmental opportunities, challenge the leader-manager to keep the spark alive by avoiding the situation where the work becomes a job. Managers let volunteers know that they depend on them for their meaningful work. They treat volunteers with respect and provide a flexible environment. Common sense guidelines and managerial practices serve to minimize problems that can be associated with volunteers such as short-term commitments, high turnover, potential liabilities, and poor work (Scott 1996:53). At the same time, management has a duty to maintain responsible and representative volunteers. This requires an investment of time, one of the manager's and staffs' most limited resources.

Volunteer Structures: Various structures are used when managing volunteers. For instance, four structures in Therapeutic Recreation are described by Henderson and Bedini (1991:50). Each is designed around funding, responsibility, and time. In the Individual Specialist structure, staff specialists recruit their own volunteer force, develop job descriptions, interview potential candidates, and train them for the position. They also supervise, evaluate, and recognize their recruits. This structure, more likely to be used in smaller settings, has the disadvantage of producing an additional time demand on specialists. The second or Volunteer Coordinator structure makes use of one specialist who takes on the responsibility of coordinating the entire volunteer program. More popular in moderately-sized recreation programs, this method ensures that all volunteers are managed in the same manner. Additionally, individual specialist duties are not compromised by their involvement in the training process. The disadvantage is that one person coordinates the program rather than providing services. The third or Agency Volunteer Coordinator structure is used by a number of larger organizations which can afford to support a department to administer the volunteer program for all units. Finally the Outside Agency Coordination structure looks to another agency to manage the volunteer program. Voluntary Action Centers, available in many communities, function like employment agencies by matching volunteers with community needs. In some situations, more than one structure is used within one setting because the different approaches may better suit the diverse functions. Though volunteers require time, energy, and special funding their value to the organization, when properly managed, is returned in service and political support. Chapter Five includes more information about managing volunteers.

SUMMARY

- The skills of both the leader and manager can and should be developed by an individual manager.

- Eliciting results, managers focus on efficiency, logistics, methods, policies, procedures, and the bottom-line whether it is customer service or the financial status of an organization.

- In general, there are three levels of management with each level relying on three basic types of managerial skills: conceptual, human relations, and technical.

- Managers perform the four basic functions of management: planning, organizing, directing, and controlling.

- Planning is a process in which managers set objectives and develop a course of action to accomplish them. Plans begin with goals and objectives and take into consideration budgets, schedules, data, the organization's existing resources, and the general economy.

- Organizing is the process of using available resources in the most efficient manner to accomplish the goals and objectives. Through the process of organizing, managers determine the tasks that their employees are to do.

- Organizational development, referred to as OD, is a planned approach to the growth and management of organizational change. This includes developing into a more productive agency in which all of the parts are integrated into an effectively functioning whole.

- Directing is a complex process of getting people to work effectively and willingly. Beginning at the top level of management, it works its way to the frontline leader-manager who directs the employee by using two different but related processes: guiding and motivating.

- Control consists of three steps: establishing standards, evaluating performance against standards, and taking corrective action when standards are not met. In short, it is a means of checking whether the situation is "out of control."

• Managing in the nonprofit sector differs in some respects from commercial recreation. First, nonprofit agencies are formed to provide a service rather than to make a profit. Second, they lack a truly direct-line of responsibility because they have no owners with the exception of taxpayers and donors whose designation is loosely defined. Third, managers work not only with employees but with volunteers.

LEARNING ACTIVITIES

1. You were recently selected to manage the volunteer program for your organization. Please describe how you would plan, organize, direct and control this valuable resource. How do volunteers differ from employees? How are they similar?

2. The community's managers in the parks, recreation, and leisure service delivery system have decided to meet each quarter to network and establish partnerships to meet the community's recreational needs. A) Why would it be important to understand the mission of each entity? B) Give an example of how this understanding could facilitate the group's interaction. C) Do private providers have a role in community organizing? Why or why not?

3. There are three basic types of managerial skills: conceptual, human relations, and technical. Identify a recreational organization in the community and describe three typical events that would emphasize the use of each one of the three skills.

4. Keeping employees involved in their work and interested in contributing to the success of the organization is a challenging task. Describe what techniques you would use to promote or maintain this type of positive environment.

5. Identify an organization in your community that has a reputation for excellent management. Do you know why they have this reputation?

REFERENCES

Apgar, M. (1999) "The Alternative Workplace" **Harvard Business Review On Managing People.** Boston: Harvard Business School Press.

Bateman, T. and Snell, S. (1999) **Management Building Competitive Advantage.** New York: Irwin McGraw-Hill.

Cascio, W.F. (1995) **Managing Human Resources.** New York: McGraw-Hill Inc.

Cook, M. (1999) **Time Management Holbrook.** MA: Adams Media Corp.

Digh, P. (1998) "Coming to Terms with Diversity," **HR Magazine** November.

Drucker, P. (1992) **Managing for the Future.** New York: Penguin Books USA, Inc.

Drucker, P. (1990) **Managing the Non-Profit Organization.** New York: Harper Collins Publishers.

Goleman, D. (1995) **Emotional Intelligence.** New York: Bantam.

Hammer, M. and Champy, J. (1993) **Reengineering the Corporation.** New York: Harper Collins Publishers.

Heller, R. (1998) **Making Decisions.** New York: D.K. Publishing, Inc.

Henderson, K. & Bedini, L. (1991) "Using Volunteers in Therapeutic Recreation" **Journal of Physical Education, Recreation, and Dance (JOPERD).** Vol 62, No 4. April issue. Reston, VA: American Alliance for Health, Physical Education, Recreation, and Dance.

Isachsen, O. and Berens, L. (1988) **Coronado.** New World Management Press.

Klein, M. (1998) 21st Century Jobs, and The Way We Were" **American Demographics.** February http://www.demographics.com /publicantions/fc/ 98_FC/9802F12.htm.

Knight, R.M (1995) "Reengineering: The Business Buzzword" **Sky.** Vol 24, No.1, Fort Lauderdale: Halsey Publishing Co.

Ligos, M. (2001) "For Some Workers, Flextime Beats Out Fulltime" **The San Diego Union-Tribune** January 29.

Luthans, F. (1995) **Organizational Behavior.** New York: McGraw-Hill, Inc.

Martin, J. and Petty, J. (2000) **Value Based Management.** Boston: Harvard Business School Press.

Milliken, F. and Martins, L. (1996) "Searching for Common Threads: Understanding the Multiple Effects of Diversity in Organizational Groups" **Academy of Management Review.** Vol 21 No 2 April.

Norton, R. "Making Sense of the Boss's Pay" **Fortune.** Vol 130, No.7 October 3 issue New York: Time Inc.

O'Connell, B. (1998) "American's Voluntary Spirit U.S. Society & Values" **USIA Electronic Journal.** Vol. 3, No. 2, September

Overin, F. (1994) **Dealing With Conflict.** San Diego: Continuing Education Centers.

Pfeffer, J. (1999) "Six Dangerous Myths About Pay" **Harvard Business Review On Managing People.** Boston: Harvard Business School Press.

Pietschmann, J.(2000) "About Our Volunteers" **Volunteers-In-Parks.** December. http://www.nps.gov/volunteer/index.htm

Quick, T. (1980) **The Quick Motivation Method.** New York: Martin's Press.

Scott, J. (1996) "Volunteers" **Parks&Recreation.** Vol 31 No 1, November. Arlington, VA: National Recreation and Park Association.

Thomas, D. and Ely, R. (1999) "Making Differences Matter" **Harvard Business Review On Managing People.** Boston: Harvard Business School Press.

Waldo, C. and Kerin, K. (1978) "NFL Coaches and Motivation Theory" **MSU Business Topics.** Autumn Issue, Lansing: Michigan State University.

Williams, J.C., Dubrin, A., Sisk, H. (1985) **Management and Organization.** Cincinnati: South-Western Publishing Co.

Wisinski, J. (1993) **Resolving Conflicts on the Job.** New York: AMOCOM American Management Association The Work Smart Series.

CHAPTER 5

PERSONNEL MANAGEMENT

Learning Objectives

After studying this chapter, you should be able to do the following:

1. Appreciate current and future expansion in leisure services.

2. State the causes and consequences of the change that has taken place in leisure services.

3. Differentiate among the positions available in the fields of recreation, parks, and leisure services.

4. Understand how the hiring process takes place for the type of work performed in leisure service.

5. Compare job satisfaction to negative elements such as burnout in the fields of recreation, parks, and leisure services.

6. Understand the roles played by consultants, contractors, and volunteers in leisure services.

In discussing personnel management in recreation, parks and leisure services, two factors must be considered. First, in the last few years, the employment possibilities in these fields have expanded beyond the professional training in public recreation which began over seventy years ago. Second, personnel management has gone through important changes in the last few decades.

LEISURE SERVICES: EXPANSION AND CHANGE

Employment opportunities in the agencies dealing with parks, recreation, and leisure services have not only expanded in the past few years, but they have also become subject to the same change affecting other employment opportunities. Expansion came on the heels of a growing American economy, which became increasingly service oriented after World War II. Although at certain times the economy slowed down and impacted employment, on the whole, the American service sector economy was, and still is, expanding at a rate faster than that of the manufacturing sector. There are expanding opportunities today in parks, recreation, and leisure services, particularly in non-governmental agencies, and the future looks bright for opportunities in these areas. "Traditional" jobs were once provided through local communities for graduates under the traditional recreation curriculum. Today these represent only a small part of the expanding possibilities for recent graduates, who are now professionally educated under a different type of recreation curriculum.

Expanding Opportunities

The United States Department of Commerce reports that over 241,000 persons are working in the "expanded" leisure services in 1998 (*Statistical Abstracts, 1999*). The expansion has gone beyond the provision of public recreational services at the local; state; and federal levels, to semi-public/nonprofit, and commercial recreational offerings.

Local Government Positions: Local government positions were the "traditional" positions around when the recreation movement began early last century. In a 1940 publication, the list of positions dealing with municipal recreation service included superintendent, general supervisor, supervisor of special activities, director of recreation center, play leader, and specialist (Butler, 1940:95). Over half a century later, the positions provided through the local government positions have been given new titles, but the responsibilities have remained very similar to the earlier ones. Today, openings in public agencies are for administrators or executives, supervisors of districts and specialties, directors of centers and special facilities, and direct leaders (Jensen and Naylor, 1994: 85-106). Some positions in these local governments fall under civil service procedures.

State Government Positions: Most of the positions in state governments concern outdoor recreation. This is due to the fact that, together, the states own about 78 million acres of land and water, which have outdoor recreational potential. These resources are classified roughly into 26.5 million acres in state forests; 9 million acres in fish and wildlife areas; 5.5 million acres in state parks; 500,000 acres in school land, and 36.5 million acres in unclassified land (Ibrahim & Cordes, 1993:160). Additionally, most states have tourist information and promotion offices that employ persons with backgrounds in parks, recreation, and leisure studies. As is the case with the local governments, positions in state government are subject to civil service procedures.

Federal Government Positions: Most position at the Federal level deal with outdoor recreation. The National Park Service employs close to 7,000 people working in about 340 areas. A limited number of positions can be found in the United States Forest Service, the United States Fish and Wildlife Service, the Bureau of Reclamation, the United States Army Corps of Engineers, the Bureau of Land Management, and the Tennessee Valley Authority. Other positions in the United States Government include opportunities for recreation and creative art therapists within the Veterans Administration. Now and then the Armed Forces of the United States announces civilian position openings in all three branches for recreation specialists to serve either in this country or abroad. Most positions in the federal government fall under the civil service category.

Youth Organizations: Employment opportunities are available with youth organizations such as the YMCA, YWCA, the Boy and Girl Scouts, and the Boys' and Girls' Clubs. Worldwide the YMCA employs close to 6,000 serving in 9,000 units. While the number of YWCA employees is not as high, this youth organization hires persons with backgrounds in parks, recreation, or leisure services. The Boy Scouts have close to 60,000 scout troops in the United States. With access to around 600 camps, professionals are needed to run and maintain them.

The Camp Fire Organization, which caters to the needs of about half a million young men and women, also needs highly qualified personnel. The same can be said about the Boys' and Girls' Clubs, which caters to the needs of millions of America's youth living in low-income communities.

Therapeutic Recreation: Many hospitals of different sizes and specializations have therapeutic recreation positions. Mental, veterans', and children's hospitals,

particularly, are interested in providing recreational activities and related thera-
pies. For example, the Veterans Administration has entry-level positions in recreation therapy as well as in creative art therapy (art, dance, music, or drama).
In the case of federal and state hospitals, the positions are subject to civil service
regulations. There are a number of hospitals of different affiliations and or private
which also have positions in therapeutic recreation.

Commercial Recreation: There are opportunities for employment in commercial recreation enterprises, companies, and establishments that sell recreational
products and provide leisure pursuits. For example, campgrounds might be
managed by larger corporations but on the other hand could be run as a small
business. Both entrepreneurial and commercial recreation are profit-motivated.
The entrepreneurial service describes the efforts of one individual or a small
group beginning a business that offers a service or provide a product in recreation, parks, or leisure fields. The business may continue on a small scale. On
the other hand, commercial recreation is a large-scale enterprise that may have
been operating for a while. Management style and orientation for each of these
two types of operations must be distinguished. The management of a campground run by a large corporation differs from one run by an individual or a very
small company. Most of the positions in the commercial recreation sector are in
travel and hospitality industries; sports and recreation products and manufacturing; contractual services; and employee recreation services. These are the positions that represent future employment in the fields of parks, recreation, and
leisure services.

A Changing Scene

Three important factors—changes in employment practices, restructuring of the
workforce, and the electronic revolution have led to the changes in the employment scene in general. Although the first and the second factors—changes in
employment practices and restructuring of the workforce—may have affected
employment in only the United States, the third factor—the electronic revolution— has affected employment in the United States as well as in other industrial
nations such as Canada, Germany, and Japan.

Workers' Civil Rights: The Civil Rights Act of 1964 required public, semi-
public, and private agencies dealing with parks, recreation, and leisure services

to change many of their employment practices. The changes brought about the concept of the "Equal Opportunity Employer" which increased the efforts of employers' to recruit and hire more minorities and women. Accordingly, another important change resulted from the civil rights movement: Women and minorities began to develop expectations of leadership roles in the workplace.

On the heels of these two changes came an alteration of the established practice of "Employment at Will". Based on English Common Law, this practice in the United States gave employers the absolute right to terminate an employee. Challenged in American courts, this practice was overturned thus discontinuing "Employment at Will." This means that the management of an agency dealing with parks, recreation, or leisure service must be very careful in its hiring decisions, since the firing of an "unproductive" employee is not as easy as it used to be.

Restructuring and Downsizing: About two decades ago, a number of factors helped to restructure the workforce. The first to affect employment in the United States and other industrial nations was the introduction of and the improvement in electronic devices. Today, some positions in both industry and services have become obsolete due to the introduction of electronic devices. The second and more important factor is the general decline in the economic growth both in the United States and abroad. The early years of the 1980s witnessed a reduction in the workforce in many industries and services in order to cut cost.

For the United States, the end of the Cold War brought about the closure of many defense industries due to the low demand of military equipment. The closing of numerous military bases in many communities followed, and the services provided in these communities, including the public services in parks, recreation, and leisure were also impacted. Loss of revenue led to reduction of the tax base on which federal, state, and local governments depended in order to provide services in all fields, including parks, recreation, and leisure services.

By the mid 1990s the employment picture began to improve, but most of the new positions were low paying service jobs. Paucity of high-paying service jobs may have led to the increase in entrepreneurial businesses, started by beginners in businesses. For instance, there has been a phenomenal increase in the number of small specialty cafes in Southern California, leisure establishments mostly during free time in activities which are meaningful in themselves, such as socializing with friends, listening to music, and readings in poetry. A phenomenon witnessed in the Northwest is the increase in the number of coffee- serving drive-ins. In many areas of the country, adventure recreation businesses are booming.

The Electronic Revolution: With the 20th century at an end, another crucial factor affecting personnel management is at play. An electronic revolution is taking place. For example, the computer is blamed for many lost jobs as in the computerized answering service that replaced the telephone operators. In general, these losses are seen in the employment market, but how do electronic devices affect employment in parks, recreation, and leisure services?

A number of questions may shed light on the possible relationship between electronics and personnel in these fields. For instance, how much does watching television take away from the time that could have otherwise been spent attending a concert or play? Do more children stay at home to play electronic games than spend their free time playing baseball in the local park? Are aerobics done at home following televised instruction as good as the aerobics done in a gymnasium?

If this is the case, the impact on the personnel in parks, recreation, and leisure services would be felt in each instance. For example, the need for a music specialist would be reduced in the first case, for a sports leader in the second case, and for an aerobic instructor in the third case.

POSITIONS: STRUCTURES AND FUNCTIONS

Despite downsizing and restructuring and the electronic revolution notwithstanding, the number of jobs in parks, recreation, and leisure services has increased. A job indicates the tasks and duties required from a person at his or her work. On the other hand, the term position indicates not only the role one plays in the workplace for which one is rewarded by a salary, benefits, and other compensations but also the elements that make the tasks performed easier and their outcomes rewarding. Elements such as promotion, evaluation, burnout, and satisfaction are important aspects of every position.

There are various positions in parks, recreation, and leisure services. As previously stated, a position includes a title as well as a group of tasks assigned to one or more persons. On the other hand, a job describes the tasks done by one or more persons. For instance, the job of a supervisor in recreation, parks, and leisure services is different from the job of a community center director, yet the agency may have two directors doing similar jobs. A particular job in two different agencies may be done by people in two different positions. Specifying the nature of each job to pinpoint the job's responsibilities and expectations is necessary, but the essential qualifications of the person who performs the job's tasks is also important. The employment function, an important element of employment, also needs discussion.

The Employment Function

The purpose of employment function is the effective and efficient performance of the agency. The agency's performance requires more than the mere recruitment and selection of the right persons in the right positions. The agency must make a concerted effort to develop a workforce that is both capable and willing to fulfill its mission (Heisler and et al., 1988:99). A clear vision by both the management and the workforce must be emphasized where the mission is concerned. The term mission may appear to connote a service-oriented, nonprofit organization. In fact, profit-making agencies have missions as well.

The Mission: As mentioned in Chapter Three, the mission of an agency, whether public; semi-public/nonprofit; or commercial, is crucial to the agency's smooth functioning. Accordingly, the leadership/management of the agency should see that its mission is observed in the recruitment, selection, and development of its workforce. The agencies with which this text is concerned vary in affiliation and orientation, yet all of them should ask an important question in defining their mission: Who is the customer? Although most of the agencies in parks, recreation, and leisure area are service-oriented, some are product-oriented. In both cases, the customer is the user of the service and purchaser of the product. This means that the agency's number one task is to identify its customer.

Another important question can impact an agency's mission: What is value to the customer? Contrary to the common belief that value resides in the product or service, it, in fact, resides in the satisfaction of the consumer. To the alert management, this means that ultimately its own performance and that of its workforce will be judged, exclusively, by the degree of satisfaction of the consumers of the agency's service or product.

Among the many tools suggested to improve a service or product and to enhance the possibility of customer satisfaction is the process known as job analysis, through which the duties and responsibilities that comprise a job are determined. Successful recruiting, staffing, and selecting of personnel depend on this process. For a job to be done well, certain qualifications on the part of the person who performs its tasks are required. These factors are prerequisites for consumer satisfaction.

Job Analysis: In order for an agency to fulfill its mission, a number of tasks must be performed by the staff. Once an agency's mission has been identified, the tasks needed to fulfill the mission are also identified. A number of tasks put together form a job. In analyzing a job, Caruth, Noe, and Mondy suggest that job analysis should consist of four major components (1988):85-103):

1. Job Identification: A list of all jobs is compiled. In large organizations, the list could be done by departments and in small organizations by all staff members. The tasks in these positions are analyzed, and if there is a need to form a new cluster of tasks, these are identified to form the core of the new job to be announced.

2. Duties and Conditions of the Job: This is the major task of job analysis. The data collected for this phase could be collected through questionnaires, interviews, or observation. What will an occupant of this position do and under what conditions? This question will be answered from the data collected.

3. Needed Qualifications: What skills, abilities, and experiences are needed to perform the tasks of this particular job? This is a difficult determination since this step requires skill, ability, and experience on the part of the job analyst.

4. Job Description and Specification: A written document containing the duties and responsibilities of the job is prepared specifying the skills, abilities, and experiences needed from the person hired for the job.

The Hiring Process

The hiring of new employees should be thought of as a first step in creating a type of an investment portfolio. Odiorne suggests a number of rules for hiring employees, six of which are applicable to parks, recreation, or leisure services agencies (1987:24-30).

1. Diversify the Portfolio: As an investment, the employee's portfolio should be treated wisely. Also with investments, it is advisable not to place all funds in one type of stock. The same should be applied to employee's portfolio. With a mix of experienced and new professionals, a variety of ages, and different backgrounds, the employees will be an asset to the agency.

2. Concentrate on Workhorses: Although hotshots and stars are needed in many agencies, wise management should concentrate on workhorses, the employees who will actually do the job.

3. Avoid Mass Hiring: Hiring should be spread over a long period. Management should be deliberate with each hiring. Experience shows that mass hiring has often led to disastrous inefficiency.

4. Promote from Within: Although controversial, it may be necessary to promote from within the agency. This not only will cut hiring cost but will also raise morale. However, hiring from outside is a good practice for entry- level positions.

5. Take Chances: Now and then and particularly for higher positions, management is encouraged to take chances—to bring in fresh ideas and new blood into the agency. This practice corresponds with rule number one: a mix of employees is desirable.

6. Follow One's Own System: Wise management understands that there is no infallible system; following a system that has been successful in another agency will not guarantee success. Also, it goes without saying that the hiring process should be in compliance with federal and state laws.

It is important to remember that Title VII of the Civil Rights Act of 1964 prohibits public agencies as well as unions, employment agencies or any similar groups from discriminating against employees or potential employees on the basis of race, color, religion, sex or national origin. This law was amended in 1972 when the Equal Employment Opportunity Act was passed extending the above provisions to educational institution and private companies with more than 15 employees. Despite the recent backlash against these provisions, they are still intact.

Recruitment: A well-designed procedure should be followed in the recruitment of new personnel. Two internal factors should be taken into consideration before recruitment takes place. The first factor is a human resource plan that delineates the options available for "good" applicants. The second factor is promotion from within. Once management arrives at a conclusion concerning the aforementioned two factors, a number of steps should be taken when recruiting persons to fill the vacancy. One essential step is the position description which is followed by the announcement of the vacancy.

Position Description: Although there is relative freedom among smaller agencies dealing with parks, recreation, and leisure services, a standard description of the vacant positions has evolved over the years. Typically a written announcement is either distributed or published and includes the following information: title of the position, qualifications, responsibilities, fringe benefits, salary range, deadline for application, and procedure and date of filling the position. In agencies affiliated with large systems such as county, state, and federal governments or the armed forces, standardized hiring policies and procedures should be followed, using the established forms.

Announcement Of The Position: If a decision is made to promote from within, a written announcement should be placed on the agency's bulletin board to notify the current employees of that job opening. If the vacancy is announced to a wider audience, the announcement could be placed in the publications of professional organizations or through the career placement offices in colleges and universities. A good way of announcing vacancies is in the placement sections of regional and national conventions.

Employment Application: An application form which will be filled out by the applicant should include the needed information such as personal data, education, employment history, references, and special skills. A sample of an application is given in Figure 5-1. The application should be filled out by the applicant and returned along with a resume and letters of recommendation. All these documents should be analyzed in light of the following criteria (Caruth, Noe, and Mondy, 1988:159).

- Is the resume well written?
- Is the resume presented well and logically?
- Is a positive image conveyed from the recommendations?
- Is there evidence of contributions by the applicant?
- Are there specific examples given by the recommender?

FIGURE 5-1

Page 1—Employee Application

EMPLOYMENT APPLICATION
FOR THE POSITION
OF: _____

APPLICANT INSTRUCTIONS: Please read the recruitment announcement for the position desired. If you possess the qualifications for the job, show clearly on this application all previous education, training and work experience which qualify you for this position. Print, using ink or typewriter. Answer all questions accurately and completely. All statements in your application are subject to verification and incorrect or incomplete statements may bar or remove you from employment. Read the Certificate of Applicant in Section 6 carefully before signing.

1. PERSONAL DATA

NAME (Last)	(First)	(Middle)	Area Code	Home Telephone
Home Address (Number and Street)			Area Code	Work Telephone
City	State	Zip Code	Social Security Number	
Do you have a valid Driver's License? Yes ☐ No ☐			Are you at least 18 years of age? YES ☐ NO ☐	
State Number Class Expiration Date			If no, can you submit a valid work permit? YES ☐ NO ☐	

2. EDUCATION AND TRAINING (Attach additional sheets if necessary)

Circle Highest Grade Completed	Name and Location of Last Grade or High School Attended		Did you graduate? YES ☐ NO ☐	Do you have a GED Certificate? YES ☐ NO ☐
1 2 3 4 5 6 7 8 9 10 11 12				

Name and location of Colleges, Universities, Business or Trade Schools Attended	Number of Units Completed	Sem.	Qtr.	Major Subjects	Title of Degree or Certificate	Dates Received or Expected

Please describe additional course work or training (including military) which would qualify you for this position.

Please list certificates or licenses of professional or vocational competence you possess which relate to this position.

Please describe any pertinent skills you have such as typing, shorthand, computer (hardware and software), machine or equipment operation, or foreign language skills.

3. A "YES" ANSWER TO ANY OF THE NEXT 3 QUESTIONS REQUIRES AN EXPLANATION UNDER SECTION 4.

A. Have you ever been employed by the City of Whistler? Yes ☐ No ☐ From _____ To _____ Department _____
B. Are you related to anyone currently employed by the City of Whistler? Yes ☐ No ☐ Name _____ Department _____
C. Have you ever been convicted or forfeited bail in any criminal matter? Yes ☐ No ☐
(You may omit minor traffic violations.) Indicate below for each offense the (1) Date, (2) Offense, (3) Place, (4) Action taken.
PLEASE NOTE: A conviction is not an automatic bar to employment. The offense for which you were convicted, when it occurred, and your conduct since the offense will be considered in terms of the job for which you are applying.

4. ADDITIONAL INFORMATION

Use this space to provide additional information as required by this application, or to describe in greater detail any aspects of your experience or activities that are pertinent to the job you are seeking.

_____
_____
_____
_____
_____

FOR HUMAN RESOURCES DEPT. USE ONLY

Accept: _____ Reject: _____ Reason: ☐ Education ☐ Experience ☐ License ☐ Other _____

AN EQUAL OPPORTUNITY EMPLOYER

FIGURE 5-1 *(continued)*

Page 2—Employee Application

Name of Supervisor _____

Reason for Leaving _____

No. Supervised (if any) ____ No. Of Hrs. Per Week ____ Salary $ ____ Hr. ☐ Wk. ☐ Mo. ☐

From ____ To ____
    Mo. Yr. Mo. Yr.

Name and Address of Employer

Title of Your Position _____

Duties You Performed _____

Name of Supervisor _____

Reason for Leaving _____

No. Supervised (if any) ____ No. Of Hrs. Per Week ____ Salary $ ____ Hr. ☐ Wk. ☐ Mo. ☐

From ____ To ____
    Mo. Yr. Mo. Yr.

Name and Address of Employer

Title of Your Position _____

Duties You Performed _____

Name of Supervisor _____

Reason for Leaving _____

No. Supervised (if any) ____ No. Of Hrs. Per Week ____ Salary $ ____ Hr. ☐ Wk. ☐ Mo. ☐

From ____ To ____
    Mo. Yr. Mo. Yr.

Name and Address of Employer

Title of Your Position _____

Duties You Performed _____

Name of Supervisor _____

Reason for Leaving _____

No. Supervised (if any) ____ No. Of Hrs. Per Week ____ Salary $ ____ Hr. ☐ Wk. ☐ Mo. ☐

From ____ To ____
    Mo. Yr. Mo. Yr.

Name and Address of Employer

Title of Your Position _____

Duties You Performed _____

Name of Supervisor _____

Reason for Leaving _____

No. Supervised (if any) ____ No. Of Hrs. Per Week ____ Salary $ ____ Hr. ☐ Wk. ☐ Mo. ☐

6. CERTIFICATE OF APPLICANT - PLEASE READ CAREFULLY

I have read and understand all the information contained in this application. I authorize the release of information concerning my qualifications, character, or prior employment record to the City of Whittier through inquiries to any sources, except as noted under Section 5. I certify that all statements in this application are true and complete; that there are no misrepresentations, falsifications, or omissions of material fact and I am aware that any misstatements or omissions of material fact may cause rejection of my application, disqualification from competing for, or discharge from any employment in this jurisdiction. Furthermore, I may be required to submit verification of any information provided on this application. I understand that as a condition of employment I may be required to take and pass medical and psychological tests including drug and alcohol screens, background and reference checks.

Signature _____   Date _____
                                              Month   Day   Year

A process for ranking the applicants should be established. The elements to be taken into consideration are qualification, experience and skills of the applicant.

The Screening Interview: A preliminary screening process should be established to rank the applicants. The elements to be taken into consideration are qualifications, experience and skills of the applicant. A selection committee or a person charged with hiring of a new person reviews resumes and letters of recommendation received for the open position, resulting in the elimination of many applications. The remaining candidates are then invited to the agency for screening interviews. In the meantime, the agency can conduct reference checks on these individuals; Sometimes the information given on the application is exaggerated or the recommendation letters may not contain enough detailed information.

One of the difficulties employers face is that both letters of recommendation and reference checks are under the aegis of the Privacy Act of 1975. This act gives job applicants the legal right to review reference checks and recommendation letters that are made concerning his or her employment. In this case the telephone is much more useful. Also, by visiting the applicant's current place of employment and by visiting his or her co-workers, one may get a better picture of the applicant's skills, abilities, and personal qualities.

Selection Of Candidates: The selection of candidates to fill a vacancy is a risky process since it is shrouded in legalism as it requires judgments about people and their abilities; therefore, it is subject to discrimination charges and lawsuits. Caruth, Noe, and Mondy suggest that the diagram in Figure 5-2 be used as a model of the selecting process.

A number of factors affect the selection of candidates and eventually the choice of a finalist. For instance, the higher the position in the agency, the more sensitivity, complication, and involvement in the decision process should be expected. In addition, How fast should the decision be made? And how many candidates should be interviewed may play an important role in the selection process.

FIGURE 5-2

A Model of the Employee Selection Process

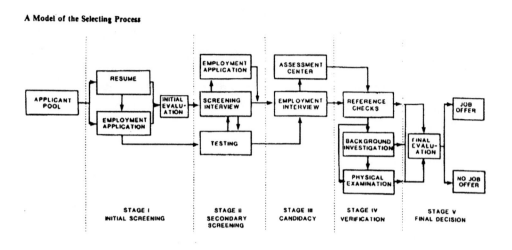

A Model of the Selecting Process

ON THE JOB

Once hired, an employee performs his or her tasks under the supervision of a superior. However, if he or she is a highest-ranking member of the working team, he or she will be under the watchful eyes of a board or council. In either case, a certain performance level is expected from the new employee, and his or her performance will be evaluated by the supervisor or the council. In the meantime, hopefully the employee will find his or her job satisfactory and so he or she will not suffer from a phenomenon that plagues the workplace now and then known as burnout.

Quality of Service

Whether serving at the front desk in the local recreation center, or enforcing the regulations in a state park, or giving a talk about the flora and fauna in the national park, Quality of service is expected. MaKay and Crompton (1990) advocate that the quality of any service is reached when each of the following is in place.

1) Reliability—The ability to perform the service independently

2) Assurance—Treatment of consumers insipires confidence

3) Tangibles—Quality of apperance of personnel, facilities, and equiptment.

4) Empathy—Individualized attention to consumers.

5) Responsiveness—Willingness to help consumers.

Job Satisfaction

It is important that the management of an agency dealing with parks, recreation, and leisure services be aware of the degree of satisfaction employees derive from their jobs in the agency. Many employees spend long hours at work thus making it their second home. Since work plays a very important role in their lives, it is crucial that management finds out the degree of satisfaction among the work force.

At the core of employee satisfaction is his or her attitude toward a particular object or subject. One's attitude is revealed through one's reaction to the object or subject. According to Baron and Greenberg (1990:154), one's reaction seems to revolve around three major components: an evaluative aspect of the object or subject, a cognitive component leading to belief or disbelief in it, and a behavioral component revolving around the intention to act toward it in a certain way. For instance, one's attitude toward physical activity includes an evaluation of its worth, and the belief in its value, and if the person sees physical activity as beneficial then he or she will behave accordingly by exercising daily. It is clear that in order to ensure effective organizational behavior, an employee's attitude toward his or her job should be such that he or she values it, believes in its importance, and reacts positively toward it. This may be a reasonable way of concluding that the employee is satisfied with his or her job.

Causes of Job Satisfaction

Efforts to formulate comprehensive theories about job satisfaction have yielded mixed results. According to Baron and Greenberg (1990:164), most of the factors of job satisfaction fall into three major categories.

1. Factors Related to Policy: For instance, the agency's employee reward system could make a difference in employee satisfaction. If the employees view the reward system as being fair, job satisfaction is enhanced. Also, does the agency's decision-making process include input from the employees? A third element related to the policy of the agency, entails the employees' perception of the quality of supervision. If the employees view their supervisors as fair and competent, the employees' level of satisfaction is higher.

2. Work Conditions: While most people like to have challenging jobs, not boring, and non-challenging, the reverse may occur. The job could be become so exhausting that it leads to job dissatisfaction. It is also reported that jobs that have varied tasks seem to be more satisfying than the jobs that have limited or repetitive tasks. Moreover, jobs that have a pleasant environment and some social interaction are more satisfying than others.

3. Personal Characteristics: Interestingly, persons with high self- esteem tend to report satisfaction with their jobs more often than do others. Similarly, people with the ability to withstand stress tend to be more satisfied with their jobs. Also, people in higher positions and seniority tend to be more satisfied with their jobs than people in lower positions and with less seniority. In addition, research reveals that a person who is generally satisfied with his or her life is more satisfied at work as well.

Supervision and Evaluation

Supervision is a task or series of tasks given to an experienced person to oversee the productivity of subordinate workers and to ensure the quality of the service or product they render. The workforce in parks, recreation, and leisure services can be divided into order givers and order takers. As such orders flow downward and reports flow upward. In most agencies dealing with recreation, parks and leisure services, those who supervise give orders and receive reports while those are supervised receive orders and give reports.

While the above may be true as predicated by the organizational chart of the agency, research shows that the supervisor is "a master and a victim of double talk." The double talk results from subordinates' demands to participate in decision making and management's pressure to increase productivity and ensure quality (Odrione, 1987:19). Supervision in parks, recreation, and leisure services is not easy because it requires a number of personal qualities and acquired skills.

In order to fulfill his or her supervisory capacity well, the person charged with supervision in these fields should master certain skills which can be divided roughly into three categories.

Technical Skills: Hands-on experience with the skills that the person is supervising is useful. It is rather difficult to appoint someone as supervisor in an activity without his or her knowledge of the technical skills required for this activity. Prior experience or knowledge of the activity should be required of the person charged with supervision. For example, the director of aquatics should have experience in either coaching or teaching swimming.

Administrative Skills: Technical skills alone do not make a good supervisor. Administrative skills are needed for a number of supervisory functions such as quality control, cost constraints, and achievable objectives. Although management by objectives seems to be an important administrative tool for supervisors, supervisors should be ready for management by anticipation—being prepared to tackle and solve problems. Continual inspection that ensures quality control and cost constraints must be practiced by the supervisor. By knowing what is going on at work, an important tool of good supervision is being utilized.

Interpersonal Skills: Studies show that the lack of interpersonal skills is a common thread in supervisory failures. Odrione believes that three basic interpersonal skills should be mastered by the supervisor. First an understanding of human behavior is required. One must know what motivates people and what frustrates them. Secondly, communication skills such as listening, talking, writing, and conducting meetings are important in supervision. Finally, value clarification skills help reveal what others value, and help one understanding how this process can be used as a source of motivation (1987:21).

Rules Of Supervision

In order to be fair to the supervisor and the supervised, management in parks, recreation, and leisure services should be sure that rules are followed in the supervisory process. Supervisors need to ask questions such as, do workers go through an adequate orientation period upon joining the agency? Are there enough in-service training sessions provided so they can master their tasks? Are there adequate feedback mechanisms provided periodically by the agency?

Orientation: An orientation program should be developed to welcome new arrivals and to acquaint them with an agency's policies, practices, and procedures. Although formal orientation sessions may be short-term, in time and scope, the supervisors should be alert to the fact that absorbing an agency's policies, practices, and procedures within a few hours or one day is difficult. Orientation sessions should last a few hours to one day. Some orientation programs are planned in phases to cover the employee's probation period. The content of orientation will dictate the time needed. Accordingly, it is incumbent upon the supervisor to continue to orient the new worker for a few days or even weeks after the new employee's arrival.

Baron and Greenberg suggest that the success of an orientation program depends on the observation of certain principles (1990:308-9) outlined in the following:

1. Avoid information overload. New employees cannot absorb all that is relayed to them in a short period.

2. Do not emphasize paper work. The new worker will not be able to gain an accurate picture of the agency by filling out forms.

3. Avoid scare tactics. The session should emphasize the positive not the negative aspects of the agency.

4. Provide relevant information. During the orientation session provide only relevant concise information.

5. Build a two-way communication. An opportunity to raise questions and seek clarification should be provided during the session.

In-Service Training: The parks, recreation, and leisure agency may have been very careful in finding a well-qualified person for the vacancy. Nonetheless, in-service training is needed to further his or her knowledge of the policies, practices, and procedures of the agency. Moreover, in-service training is needed to acquaint the new arrival, as well as others, with new techniques and operations that appear on an almost daily basis in this era of technological advances. To insure the success of in service training, Baron and Greenberg suggest the following principles (1990:308):

1. Determine the precise skills to be learned. Professional preparation does not provide many of the social and technical skills needed.

2. Provide the workers with feedback on their performance. The in-service training is provided to enhance their performance. Did it?

3. Tailor the in-service program to the need of the job. Generic training does not yield good results.

4. Evaluate the in-service programs on a regular basis. Do not assume that the program is automatically successful.

Meetings and Conferences: According to Brief and Tomlinson (1987: 126), weighty volumes have been written on how to conduct meetings. All these books admit that this is a difficult task. The three general guidelines for managers and supervisors to follow in conducting productive meetings are given below:

1. Take Charge. Before calling the meeting, the chairperson should formulate a plan on how to meet the objectives.

2. How these objectives can be met and the criteria to evaluate the outcome should be communicated.

3. Exercise Control. The chairperson should be sure that the group adheres to the plan as   formulated. He or she should avoid digressing and keep the group on track without being intimidating.

4. Encourage Quality Participation. The group should be directed in a pleasant and non-threatening place. The chairperson should ask for opinions and direct the discussion without overly dominating the meeting. The chairperson should use breaks or jokes as mechanisms of reducing tension.

Performance Appraisal: Among the many tasks of supervision is appraising the performance of subordinates. Despite the advances made in the science of management and the emphasis given to the role of appraisal in improving quality of service or product, 70 percent or 4,000 employees in 190 firms reported that their bosses did not give them a clear picture of what is expected of them. Odrione suggests the following for reviewing performance of subordinates by supervisors (1987:30):

1. Review the performance of everyone periodically. An employee is not motivated unless he knows how well he is doing.

2. Develop an agency-wide review system. A common format should be used by all units in the agency.

3. Obtain approval by superiors. In the case of a larger system, bosses should approve the process in principle.

4. Train supervisors in conducting of reviews. The review process should be consistently applied otherwise legal complications may follow.

5. Conduct objectives-centered performance review. The review should revolve around an individual's job objectives.

6. Conduct reviews periodically and continually. Supervisors should provide feedback to subordinates on their performance.

7. Plan your reviews carefully. Supervisors should be aware of the objectives agreed upon and the results expected from the performance.

8. Schedule individual sessions carefully. No subordinates should be missed. Careful planning and appointments must be well thought out.

9. Focus the discussion on goals and results. The review session should not deviate into topics unrelated to goals and results.

10. Take as much time as necessary. Typically reviews take more time than what is allotted, but the review must be complete.

11. Do more listening than talking. Since the subordinate is being reviewed, he or she should be given ample time to react.

12. Seek consensus. Allow the subordinate to arrive at a conclusion about his or her performance.

13. Focus on the future. The purpose of the review is to go over past performance for the purpose of improving future performance.

14. Make notes during the session. It is hard to remember everything, particularly, if there are many review sessions.

15. Ask supportive questions. Questions such as "What can be done to help you achieve your goals?" show support.

16. Confirm agreement in writing. When the review is completed, all agreements should be confirmed in writing. They can be used for future reference.

17. Builds self esteem and increase motivation. The purpose of the review is to improve performance which can be done by enhancing self-esteem.

Coping With Poor Performance: Poor performance is situational in many cases. Accordingly, failure at work may be the outcome of a mismatch between the job and the person. According to Odrione (1987:142), there are many kinds of performance failures such as:

1. Former stars whose performances slipped over the years.

2. Workhorses whose skills have eroded.

3. Difficult workers whose problems have resisted any correction.

4. Dead wood who show no promise.

Odrione (1987) suggests six steps in analyzing poor performance:

1. Advance specifications of performance: Employees should be aware of what is expected of them apriori. Left to their own devices, employees may develop their own ideas of what is expected.

2. Removal of obstacles to success: A supportive manager produces successful performance in the workforce while the punitive manager does not produce success.

3. Access to training: Managers should not assume that their subordinates are well prepared for all the tasks required of them. During this time of rapid change, the need for in-service training is paramount.

4. Favorable consequences: Unfavorable consequences for doing the expected task may be followed by wrong behavior. Workers should be encouraged when doing the things right.

5. Feedback of results: Workers should not be allowed to proceed assuming that they are doing well. They should be apprised continually of their performance.

6. The personal factor: Low performance may be due to health and/or emotional problems, stress, and work habits. A close look at the person will help to understand the causes of his or her low performance.

A number of remedies have been suggested, including redesigning the job and training sessions. Other suggestions include flexible time or carpooling for the tardy. If all attempts to improve performance fail, the management should take the following necessary steps:

1. The worker should be notified of his or her low performance and made aware of the available mechanisms to remedy the situation. Report of the action should be recorded in the employee's personnel file.

2. If the performance continues to be below expectation, the worker should be notified, issued a reprimand, and informed that a third offense will result in suspension.

3. The supervisor should consult with his or her superior concerning the third offense. The employee should be laid off for a few days with a warning that a repeat of the offense may result in discharge.

4. If after the third warning, the employee still has not met expectations, he or she should be discharged. This is done with the knowledge and approval of superiors and the personnel department.

Odrione suggests that in addition to the steps in disciplinary action, supervisors should observe a number of rules to avoid a reversal in any decision. The supervisor should be certain that the employees know a rule on hand that clearly outlines the dismissal process. Generally speaking there is a twelve months statute of limitation for minor incidents and three years for layoff reports. The supervisor should avoid verbal or physical behavior that may create future animosity. When a laid-off employee returns to work, he should be treated like any other employee (1987:157-59).

Termination Of An Employee: In order to avoid a condition that may lead to a tedous, long, and unpleasant legal battle, the management should be aware of the steps to be taken in order to avoid it. Termination of an employee's service should not come as a surprise to him or her. The employee will likely be surprised if the aforementioned steps on poor performance are not followed. Clear warnings are important not only in notifying the employee of his or her performance but also to the judge and the jury in litigations. "You should be prepared to articulate the legitimate, performance-based reasons for any termination before acting," (Mickey, 1994:58).

It is suggested that management consider asking for a resignation if such a request might minimize the employee's anger. But such a resignation should not be construed as being submitted under pressure. Moreover, it is important to explain to the employee that, upon resignation, the agency is not going to oppose his or her application for unemployment benefits.

In general, the person conveying the news of termination should be sympathetic, although too much sympathy may backfire. A discussion of future plans is advisable including options for health insurance and re-training, remaining leave, and severance pay. If the employee has shown a tendency toward violent reactions, the local police should be notified of the termination. These forms (Figure 5-3 and 5-4) are used in a park and recreation department, entitled Employee Separation Report and checklist, when an employee is terminated, laid-off, or is quitting on his or her own.

Burnout and Stress

Burnout describes the process in which the worker's attitude and behavior changes to negatively affect his or her job performance. Stress, on the other hand, refers to the unpleasant subjective state accompanied by high levels of emotional arousal. Stress is only one of many factors that could lead to burnout.

Burnout and stress are experienced among professionals and staff in most workplaces, but Trice and Beyer believe that stress and burnout in many human service occupations is somewhat exaggerated. They report that nearly ten times as many articles deal with job stress in police and nursing periodicals as appear

FIGURE 5-3

Employee Seperation Report

EMPLOYEE SEPARATION REPORT

EMPLOYER: _____ EMPLOYEE: _____ S.S. NO.: ____ – __ – ___

UNIT/DEPT: _____ WORKED IN STATE OF: _____

DATE HIRED: _____ LAST DAY WORKED: ___/___/___ EFF. DATE OF TERM: ___/___/___

POSITION: _____ SUPERVISOR: _____ RATE OF PAY: $ _____

TERMINATION PAY: FROM ___/___/___ TO ___/___/___ VACATION $ _____ IN LIEU OF NOTICE $ _____ SEVERANCE $ _____

REASON FOR SEPARATION

LAYOFF (Lack of Work):   LEAVE OF ABSENCE From ___/___/___ to ___/___/___   SUSPENDED From ___/___/___ to ___/___/___
( ) Permanent
( ) Temporary   Reason: _____   Reason: _____
( ) On Call - Completed Last Assignment? Yes ( ) No ( )   STRIKE – Notify Gibbens of All Labor Disputes

EXPLANATION (Use Reverse Side, if necessary): _____

_____

_____

DISCHARGE:

Dates of Relevant Warnings: _____
( ) Absenteeism (Explain Reason for Last Absence Above)
( ) Tardiness (Reason Given for Final Tardiness Above)
( ) Rule Violation (Rule No. _____)
( ) Insubordination (Explain Above)
( ) Physically Unable to Work (Leave or Transfer Offered?)
( ) No Show, No Call (Number of Days _____)
( ) Dishonesty (Admission? Conviction? Witness? Proof?)
( ) Negligence (Explain Above)
( ) Intoxicated (Drug Test? Behavior Observed? Witness?)
( ) Inability or Not Qualified (No Misconduct Alleged)
( ) Failed to Meet Standards During Evaluation Period
( ) OTHER (Explain Above)

VOLUNTARY QUIT:

Was Prior Notice Given? Yes ( ) No ( )
( ) Personal Reasons (Explain Above)
( ) Illness - Injury (Leave of Absence Offered?)
( ) To Leave the Area (Where? Why, Reason?)
( ) Other Employment (Where? When? With Whom?)
( ) To Attend School
( ) Dissatisfied with Job (Show Reason Above)
( ) Never Returned - Job Abandonment
( ) Family Obligations (Leave of Absence Offered?)
( ) Voluntary Layoff (Job still available?)
( ) Refused to Discuss Reason
( ) Retired (Show Amount and % Financed by Employer)
( ) OTHER (Explain Above)

Was separation suggested or requested by management? Yes ( ) No ( )   Will employee be replaced? Yes ( ) No ( ) Unknown ( )

Signed: _____ Date ___/___/___   Employee Signature: _____

Exit Interview Witness: _____   ( ) Employee Refused to Sign

G90-ESEP   Important: All Employee Separation Reports sent to   should include copies of relevant warnings.

FIGURE 5-4

Page 1—Separation Checklist

Submit Checklist and Personal Action Form
Together to Controller's Department

EMPLOYEE SEPARATION CHECKLIST

Employee's Name_____

Termination Date
(i.e. last day on City Payroll)_____

Position_____

Last Scheduled Day to Work _____

Department_____

	Service	Disability		
_____ Resignation;	_____ Retirement;	_____ Retirement;	_____ Dismissal; Other: _____

Instructions: The purpose of this checklist is to ensure that personnel leaving the City's employ return all City property, receive required information, and complete the necessary forms prior to their separation and issuance of their final paycheck. Each department head should designate an employee, preferably at a management level, to complete Step I below. The person who processes each item should sign and date the form on the appropriate line.

Distribution: Employee's department should submit the checklist and the Personnel Action Form together to the Payroll Staff in the Controller's Department who, in turn, will return the form to the Human Resources Department.

Checklist Update: Please notify the Human Resources Department of items to be added or deleted on this checklist may be applicable.

STEP I - To Be Completed By Employee's Department

	Processed By (Signature)	Date Processed
1. Personnel Action Form	_____	_____
2. Employee Separation Report (Re: Unemployment Ins.)	_____	_____
3. Badge	_____	_____
4. I.D. Card(s)	_____	_____
5. Uniform(s)	_____	_____
6. Equipment and Tools	_____	_____
7. Locker Key	_____	_____
8. Office/Building Key	_____	_____
9. Vehicle Key	_____	_____
10. Parking Permit	_____	_____
11. Other (Specify)	_____	_____
_____	_____	_____

FIGURE 5-4 *(continued)*

Page 2—Separation Checklist

---

12. Compensation Due Employee	Balance to be Paid Upon Separation	Processed by (Signature)	Date Processed
a. Straight Time Worked	_____ hrs.		
b. Overtime Worked	_____ hrs.		
c. Vacation Accrued	_____ hrs*		
d. Sick Leave Accrued	_____ hrs*		
e. Comp. Time Accrued	_____ hrs		
f. Uniform Allowance Due Employee	$ _____		
g. Uniform Reimbursement Due Within 2 Yr. of Hire Date	$ _____		
H. Investigator Pager Pay- Police Only	$ _____		

* To be calculated by the Controller's Department

	Processed By (Signature)	Date Processed
13. Final Paycheck Disposition		
a. Advise employee final check to be mailed		
b. Complete if employee will pick up final paycheck from their department		
14. Return Departmental and Supervisor(s) Personnel File(s) to Human Resources (except Community Services & Library)		

STEP II - To Be Completed By Controller's Department: ATTENTION PAYROLL

	Processed By (Signature)	Date Processed
1. PERS Disposition		
2. a. Insurance Continuation --Retiree		
b. Insurance Continuation --Cobra		
3. Deferred Compensation		
4. Tuition Reimbursement Due City Within 48 Months of Separation (See SOP #19)		
5. Payroll Deduction (e.g. Credit Union, Flex-RAP, etc.)		
6. Previous Payroll Adjustments (e.g. payroll discrepancy, vacation advancement, etc.)		

STEP III - To Be Completed By Human Resources Department

	Processed By (Signature)	Date Processed
1. Exit Interview		
2. Conflict of Interest Form (upon Separation) Call City Clerk's Office		
3. Notify employee's department when form completed that final paycheck can be released		
4. File this form in employee's personnel folder		

in comparative periodicals in law and medicine (1993:199). Nevertheless, human service professionals do suffer from burnout and stress.

Burnout in Service Organizations

Although stress on the job may lead to burnout, it is not the only factor that leads to such a state. A number of other factors may lead to burnout among professionals working in human service agencies as shown below.

Causes Of Burnout: Cherniss (1980) suggests that the following factors could lead to burnout among human services professionals, including those who serve in recreation, parks, and leisure service agencies:

1. The Myth of Professional Competence: Although the concern about competence can be felt any worker in a new job, novice human serviceprofessionals are the most vunerable to the crisis of competency. The myth that credentials automatically prepare one to enter a profession may dissipate within the first few months on the job. Even when a feeling of cometence is gained after a few successful months on the job, a lingering sense of inadequacy may remain.

2. Strained Consumer-Professional Relations: Typically a young professional working in an entry-level job will have to deal with the public. In human services agencies that require motivating others, the novice-and at times, the experienced-professional may find it difficult to motivated his or her group members. After years of studies on human behavior with perhaps unrealistic expectations, the novice professional's lack of success may end in frustration, and eventual burnout.

3. Bureaucracy: New professionals,working under the influence of the idealized portrayl of professional work from college years, often wake up to face a bureaucratic structure that may have rules and policies that are frustrating to them. Moreover, due to their shorter tenure in the agency, these novice professionals encounter limitations in their autonomy, and this limitation, coupled with a lingering feeling of incompetence, may lead to greater frustration and potential burnout.

4. Professional and Social Isolation: The number of new professionals hired   into a recreation, parks, and leisure service agency is usually very limited. While in college, the young professional usually interacted with people of his or her own age. But upon entering the field, he or she may find himself or herself isolated professionally and sometimes socially, having lost contact with his previous peers and not having adequate time to established new friendships. Although the situation may change eventually, the feeling of isolation may lead to burnout.

Nature and Causes of Stress: According to Baron and Greenberg (1990), the basic nature of stress revolves around three aspects. The first is the physiological aspect in which one experiences a feeling of alarm, followed by a resistance to such feeling. As a result, the person is in a state of exhaustion. The second aspect concerns the nature of the stressors such as the events or objects that lead to these physiological reactions. While it is hard to pinpoint why certain events and objects lead to stress, they seem to share certain properites: these stressors are intensely experienced and are seen as uncontrollable by an individual. The third aspect of stress revolves around the recognition of the cause of stress. This occurs when an individual percives a situation that is not only threatening to his or her impor- tant goals but also as insurmountable. How does this occur in the workplace, particularly in the workplace of recreation, parks and lesiure services?

Stress in Lesiure Services: There are a number of factors that could lead to stress among professionals and staff in a recreation, parks, and lesiure service agency. It is important that management and immediate supervisors of these workers be sensitive to these factors.

1. Occupational Demands: Some jobs are more stressful than others, because they require making decisions, monitoring others or devices, performing   unstructured tasks, working in unpleasant physical conditions, or having   continual exchanges with others.

2. Role Conflict: Role conflict could lead to conflicting demands which may ead to stress. For example, when a person is put in charge of two jobs with little time to do either one, such a conflict would lead to stress.

3. Role Ambiguity: Uncertainty often leads to stress especially when a person is given undefined tasks for which he or she is not prepared. Managers and supervisors should be aware of this potential problem.

4. Overload: Stress may result from both quantitative and qualitative overloads. The quantitative overload occurs when the person is asked to do more work than he or she can complete in a specific period. On the other hand, qualitative overload occurs when the person is asked to do work which is not within his or her ability.

5. Underload: The same priniciples applied to overload is applied here. A quantitative underload means to little work for the time allotted, and qualitative underload means easy work which can be done quickly. In both cases, boredom may result with stress as a possible consequence.

6. Responsibility for Others: Persons who are in charge of others must communicate with them, motivate, reward, and punish them. Research reveals that these tasks are more stressful than dealing with the physical side of things such as equiptment, supplies, or products, or with the financial aspects,such as bookkeeping. This means leaders, supervisors, and managers in recreation, parks, and leisure services are working under potentially stressful conditions.

7. Lack of Social Support: Isolation has been mentioned before as an important factor in burnout among human services professionals. When dealing with this problem, managers and supervisors could use several different mechanisms. Among these are social gatherings that include members of the agency, such as sports, meetings and other activities.

8. Lack of participation in Decision Making: The feeling of helplessness leads to stress. Most people feel that they know a lot about their work, and would like to be asked for input. Staff input on the work enviornment is a wise strategy on the part of the management of a recreation parks or lesiure service.

9. Worthless Output: Baron and Greenberg (1990:241) state that one of the causes of burnout occurs when job conditions imply that one's efforts are useless, ineffective, or unappriciated by the management.

10. Leadership Style: Leadership style seems to play an important role in causing burnout. When a supervisor demonstrates less

consideration toward his or here employees, a high level of burnout often occur (Baron and Greenberg 1990:241).

11. Sexual Harassment: This term refers to the unsolicited contact or communication of a sexual nature whether directed towards men or women. Physical contact, propositions, offensive remarks, and nonverbal attention are forms of sexual harassment. More importantly, these actions are illegal, and the management of a recreation, parks, or lesiure service would be well advised to take action to reduce and eliminate the possibility of such occurances.

Coping With Stress: According to Shank (1983), there is no magic cure for stress as the emphasis is on survival. Soul searching and self-confrontation should be used to arrive at the cause of burnout. The process of self-diagnosis is usually lonely and painful: however it is essential if the cure is to come from within. Shank suggests that in the early stages of burnout a growing state of fatigue, increased irritability, and loss of enthusiasm set in. Eventually feelings of fear, anxiety and helplessness occur. Somatic signs follow such as continuous colds, shortness of breath, and weight gain or loss. Since this is a gradual process, these signs should be heeded and changes affected. Attempts to discover the stressorsare important at the early stages of burnout. Perhaps the need for private time should be considered, such as a long vacation at this point. Another approach would be to change jobs or tasks. Shank concludes by stating that burnout is highly individualistic and so too are the remedies.

Sexual Harassment and Lesiure Services

In light of the most recent studies on sexual harassment, Baron and Greenberg suggest the following recommendations be used to combat it in the workplace (1990:232).

1. Developing a Formal Policy. The policy should specify very clearly behaviors that constitute sexual harassment, and management should communicate it to all employees in the agency.

2. Providing a Mechanism for Complaints. The workers should be aware that there is a mechanism avaliable to them prior to taking legal action.

3. Witnessing Sexual Harassment. All workers should be encouraged to serve as witnesses to instances of sexual harassment. Efforts should be made to overcome the natural reluctance of becoming a witness.

Terpstra and Baker (1987) indicate that courts rule in favor of the complainant under the following conditions:

1. When the complainant is subjected to serious forms of harassment such as physical contact and propositions linked to promotion;

2. When the occurrence is witnessed by others; and

3. When the complainant has informed the management of the harassment prior to taking legal action.

CONSULTANTS, CONTRACTORS AND VOLUNTEERS

Most agencies dealing with recreation, parks, and leisure services, regardless of size of their staff, may seek outside help. Consultants and contractors provide services paid by the agency. On the other hand, volunteers who are not paid, should also be allowed to serve as long as certain stipulations are stated in the agency's policy on volunteers. Other policies, procedures, and practices should be developed by the agency concerning consultants and contractors.

Consultants and Leisure Services

Although consulting is a very old practice, only recently did it become a profession and acquire a definition. According to Gallessich (1982:6), professional consultation is advice given by an occupational expert who has specialized training. The consultant is a specialized professional who interacts with the consultee—the agency employees—concerning work-related activities.

The Need for Consultation: When should an agency in recreation, parks, and leisure services hire a consultant? The overall goal of consultation is to improve the delivery of the service. For instance, the agency should decide whether its goals are attainable or need some modifications. Perhaps a consultant at this point could help the agency clarify and/or modify its goals. Also, consultants are needed in planning, a process discussed in Chapter Four. Consultants may be needed for smaller projects such as in collecting data on public opinion concerning a particular project as well as many other activities that do not fall within the functions of the permanent staff.

Types of Consultants: A consultant who claims to be knowledgable in all aspects of recreation, parks, and leisure services should be viewed with scrutiny. According to Patton et al. (1989:79), today's consultants usually specialize in one of these areas: program, management, facility, and/or space.

Selection of a Consultant: The consultant should be a person with vast expertise in one of the areas listed above. Since the goals of the recreation, parks, and lesiure services vary widely from those of the services dealing with commercial recreation to the ones dealing with public recreation and from those of small agencies to very large ones the consultant should be selected with great care. The consultant should be objective and be able to handle delicate issues. He or she should have no interest in the agency or the community in which it is located.

Compensation for consultation vary according to the type of services renered and the method of payment. According to Patton and others, consultation fees may range from $500 to $2,000 per day (1989:81). Sometimes payment to a consultant could be based on a fixed fee or a percentage of the construction cost. Some consultants prefer a retainer.

Contractors and Leisure Services

An agency dealing with recreation, parks, or leisure services may also need the assistance and or the services of independent contractors. Many of these agency contract out some of their functions in order to cut cost. Some of these contracted functions include, but are not limited to, the following categories:

1. Maintenance of facilities, fields, and resources.

2. Planning and constructing new facilities, fields, and resources.

3. Purchase of equiptment, materials, and supplies.

4. Management of concessions and facilities.

5. Providing specialized programs.

Since the passage of Proposition 13 in California, which reduced the amount of money allocated to public parks and recreation departments (particularly the ones dealing with local offerings), the utilization of private contracting has increased at a phenomenal rate. The assumption is that private contracting is not as expensive as the public sector. Nonetheless, before hiring a private contractor for a job, some factors should be considered.

1. The private contractor should equal or exceed the agency's own workers' technical abilities or skills.

2. The marketplace should have enough private firms to do the job to ensure competitive prices.

3. The contract should be written in such a way as to ensure quanity, quality, and price of work as shown in the following section.

Elements of A Contractual Agreement: A contract should include the following elements:

1. Party identification: Names of the client and the contractor.

2. Purpose of the Contract: Terms and conditions under which the servicewill be provided.

3. Provision of Service: Specification of the type of service provided.

4. Compensation for Service: Statement of the rate of compensation for service provided.

5. Terms of Agreement: Duration of the agreement and conditions for its termination.

6. Other provisions: This could include the exculsivity concerning the degree of independence to subcontract and confidentiality concerning the work to be done. (see Figure 5-5)

FIGURE 5-5

Independent Contractual Agreement

AGREEMENT FOR PERFORMANCE OF
SERVICES BY INDEPENDENT CONTRACTOR

The City of ____ , hereinafter referred to as "CITY", finds it necessary and desirable to allow for the use of City facilities for recreational classes by persons who will conduct _____; therefore this agreement is made this _____ day of _____, 19____, between the CITY and

Name _____   SS# _____

ADDRESS _____   PHONE _____

CITY _____   ZIP CODE _____

hereinafter referred to as INSTRUCTOR hereby agrees to the following:

The INSTRUCTOR agrees to be compensated for all services at the rate of _____% of the total registration fee. The total registration fee will be based on the total number of participants enrolled in said class.

1. The INSTRUCTOR shall organize, supervise, prepare, conduct, and complete the course of instruction.

2. It is understood and agreed upon between the CITY and the INSTRUCTOR that the INSTRUCTOR is not an employee of the City and the CITY is in no way associated with the actual performance of the services rendered under this Agreement; that the INSTRUCTOR is an independent CONTRACTOR solely responsible for his/her performance of the services hereunder, compliance with all City Ordinances, and solely liable for all labor and expenses in connection therewith, and for all damages which may be occasioned on account of the conduct and operation of the services rendered, whether the same be for personal injuries or damages. It is further understood that the CITY is interested only in the results obtained and that the instructor shall perform as an independent CONTRACTOR with sole control of the manner and means of performing under this Agreement.

3. INSTRUCTOR agrees fully to exonerate, indemnify, and hold harmless the CITY from and against all claims or actions, and all expenses incidental to the defense of any claims or actions, based upon or arising out of damages or injury to persons or property caused by or sustained in connection with the performance under this Agreement.

4. It is specifically understood between the parties hereto that the CITY shall not be required to provide for Worker's Compensation Benefit Insurance for the INSTRUCTOR, and INSTRUCTOR hereby specifically waives any claims or demands for such benefits.

5. All instructors will attend the first class meeting regardless of the number registered unless previously excused by the Director of Community Services or his/her designee.

6. This Agreement may be terminated by either party for any reason, and at any time. Notice to terminate this agreement shall be given in writing.

CITY OF

_____   _____
INSTRUCTOR'S SIGNATURE   Director of Community Services

_____   _____
Print Name   Director of Human Resources

                                            _____
                                                      City Manager

Distribution: White-City Clerk; Pink-Human Resources Dept.; Blue-Controllers Dept.; Green-Hiring Department; Yellow-Contractor

Volunteers and Leisure Services

Volunteers' involvement in the recreation movement has been documented in many history books. With the professionalization of the recreation movement, the question is what role should the volunteer play in today's recreation, parks, and leisure services?

A volunteer offers his or her services free of charge, not expecting remuneration. However, there are expectations required of a volunteer, and recently, certain procedures and expectations have become clarified. For instance, volunteers will be recruited as needed and will be placed according to need, and performances will be periodically assessed.

Reasons for Using Volunteers: Some reasons for using volunteers include their help to expand services that otherwise could not be offered. Also, volunteers can provide certain talents and skills not found among the staff of an agency, and volunteers contribute to good public relations, particularly those who are influential members of the community. Finally, volunteers may bring enthusiasm and new perspectives to an agency. (See Figures 5-6, 5-7.)

FIGURE 5-6

Volunteer Application

PARENT PERMISSION FOR VOLUNTEERS UNDER 18

I hereby allow _____, my son/daughter, to participate in the City of Whittier Community Services Volunteer Program.

_____   _____
Signature of Parent   Date

_____
Signature of Volunteer
                        FOR OFFICE USE ONLY _____
                              ASSIGNMENT
WYN site_____
Leisure classes_____
Therapeutic Recreation Program_____
Theatre_____
Clerical_____
Community Center_____
Sports_____
Maintenance_____
Senior Center_____
Information & Referral_____

Recruitment of Volunteers: The following are some suggestions for the recruitment of volunteers (MacLean, Peterson, and Martin: 1985:305).

1. Survey interests in clubs, church groups, schools, neighborhood centers, and service organizations.

2. Investigate rosters of retirees from business, industry, or the professions.

3. Peruse newspapers to get names of hobbyists.

4. Establish a volunteers' bureau.

5. Contact advisory councils of other human service agencies.

Performance of Volunteers: The type and caliber of volunteers needed and the standards for fulfilling the mission are set by the agency, and the agency should have complete control over these standards, clearly conveying them to every volunteer. Evaluation of the role and performance of each volunteer should be done periodically.

CIVIL SERVICE

Civil service encompasses positions held by civilian workers in the federal, state, and local governments. As noted from records of ancient civilizations, civilians have worked for governments early on in the organization of human society. The practice has continued in various types and at different levels of societies.

Historical Background

Records of those who served in the government showed that it was an ancient practice and one which was continued through the days of the Roman Empire, until its collapse. The practice was revived with the rise of nation states in Western Europe.

While the idea behind the revival of civil service in Europe was to provide a cadre of public servants, the drive behind its introduction in the Unites States was different. Civil service began in the U.S. as an attempt to prevent the use

FIGURE 5-7

Medical History

MEDICAL HISTORY- Note: All information given on this form is CONFIDENTIAL

Personal Physician:_____Address:_____
Medical Insurance:_____

Have you ever had or have you now:

Check Each Item	Yes	No	Check Each Item	Yes	No
Asthma			Loss of Appetite, Nausea,		
Back Trouble			Vomiting		
Bones or Joint Deformity			Malaria		
Broken Bones or Bone Disease			Nervosa Breakdown		
Cancer, Cyst, Growth or Tumor			Neutitis		
Change in Bowel Habits			Numbness or Weakness		
Chest Pain or Pressure			Operations		
Chills, Fever, or Night Sweats			Pain in Shoulder, Arm		
Chronic Cough			or Hands		
Chronic or Frequent Colds			Palpitation or Pounding Heart		
Coughing or Vomiting Blood			Diabetes		
Recent Gain or Loss of Weight			Difficulty in Hearing		
Difficulty in Sleeping			Rheumatic Fever		
Dizziness			Rheumation or Arthritis		
Double Vision or Blindness			Running Ears		
Epilepsy			Rapture		
Excessive Worry or Depression			Scarlett Fever		
Foot Trouble			Severe Ear, Nose or Throat		
Frequent or Severe Headaches			Troubles		
Frequent or Severe Indigestion			Shortness of Breathe		
Hay Fever			Sinus Trouble		
Head Injury			Skin Trouble, Rash or		
Heart Trouble			Disease		
Heat or Sun Stroke			Swelling Ankles or Feet		
High Blood Pressure			Swollen or Painful Joints		

FIGURE 5-7 *(continued)*

Medical History

<u>Ill Effects from Medicine</u>	<u>"Trick" or "Locked" Knee</u>
<u>Kidney Stones or Blood in Urine</u>	<u>Tuberculosis</u>
<u>Liver Disease or Jaundies</u>	<u>Ulcers</u>
<u>Have you ever had any illness/injury</u>	<u>Varicose Veins</u>
<u>Other than those listed above</u>	<u>Venereal Diseases</u>

If yes, describe and give age at   Weakness or Fatigue

Which occurred?

Have you ever been a patient at a hospital?

If yes specify when, where and why.

Certificate of Applicant, Read Carefully Before Signing
I hereby certify that all statements and this Medical Form are true and complete to the best of
my knowledge.

SIGNATURE   <u>DATE</u>

---

of federal jobs as a payoff to someone for services rendered. A policy to this effect began in 1828 under President Andrew Jackson's administration. Nonetheless, job seekers continued to put pressure on subsequent administrations until it became necessary to take further action in the years following the Civil War. President Ulysses Grant asked Congress for legislation that governs appointments.

In 1871, a rider on a bill authorized the president to prescribe regulations for admission to civil service. President Grant appointed the first civil service commission, and the first competitive examination was held under its auspices in April, 1872. But the actual legislation establishing a civil service commission passed in 1883. This act reestablished the Civil Service Commission, created a modern merit system for many offices, and authorized the president to expand this system. Behind the reforms of late 19th century lay the efforts of the National Civil Service League, supported by public reaction against the corruption of the times. By 1900 the proportion of the federal civil service under merit system reached nearly 60 percent; by 1930 it had exceeded 80 percent.

The Depression period of the 1930's saw both a near doubling of the federal civil service and some renaissance of patronage politics especially in the administration of work relief. Congress extended a version of the merit system to first-, second- and third-class postmasters; federal agencies were all required to have personnel offices; the Tennessee Valley Authority, under a special merit system statute, commenced to pioneer in government-employee labor relations; and pay and position-classification systems were improving.

Beginning in the late 19th century, civil service reform came also to many state and local governments, although relatively more slowly and less completely. By 1940 one-third of the states had comprehensive merit system. Most cities act under their own statues, but in New York, Ohio, and New Jersey there is general coverage of local jurisdictions by state constitutional or other state legal provisions. In one-quarter of the states, notable among which is California, the state personnel agencies may perform technical services for localities on a reimbursement basis.

Employment: According to the **Occupational Outlook Handbook**, published by the U.S. Department of Labor, there were 241,000 jobs in 1998 in the field of recreation, and many additional workers held summer jobs as recreation workers, about half worked in park and recreation departments of municipal and county governments. Nearly 1 in 4 worked in membership organizations, such as the Boy or Girl Scouts, the YMCA, and Red Cross, or worked for programs run by social service organizations, including senior centers; adult daycare programs, or residential care facilities like halfway houses; group homes; and institutions for delinquent youth. Another 1 out of 10 worked for nursing and other personal care facilities.

Other employers of recreation workers included commercial recreation establishment, amusement parks, sports and entertainment centers, wilderness and survival enterprises, tourist attractions, vacation excursion companies, hotels and resorts, summer camps, health and athletic clubs, and apartment complexes.

According to the **Handbook**, overall growth in employment in the recreation field is expected through the year 2005. But growth in local hiring is expected to slow due to budget constraints. While the local sectors' share of employment will shrink, other opportunities will be available in part-time and seasonal jobs (1999:159).

SUMMARY

- Changes in leisure services have occurred in the last few decades due to workers' civil rights, restructuring of the workforce, and the electronic revolution. Expected expansion in these services will be seen more in the semi-public/nonprofit and commercial sectors than in the public one.

- The hiring and recruitment of personnel in leisure services, whether public, semi-public, or commercial, follows certain procedures that are now standardized on the basis of past experiences.

- Today, leisure services, regardless of their level or type, seek a professional who can become involved in the creation of a vision and the promotion of a mission for his or her agency.

- Policy, work conditions, and personal characteristics are important factors leading to job satisfaction. Nonetheless, burnout and stress are seen in the workplace, including leisure service agencies, resulting from a number of factors such as strained relationships, bureaucracy, isolation, role conflict or ambiguity, and inadequate workload.

- Formal policy on how to handle sexual harassment should be adopted by leisure service agencies along with the mechanisms to handle complaints.

- Leisure service agencies are becoming increasingly dependent on the services of a new line of ancillary personnel such as consultants, contractors, and volunteers. Accordingly, policies and practices should be developed for them.

LEARNING ACTIVITIES

1. Go to the closest public library and check out the most recent edition of **The Occupational Outlook Handbook**, which is published by the United States Department of Labor. Check the outlook for recreation, parks, and leisure services. (Also available on-line www.bls.gov/ocohome.htm)

2. Call the local parks and recreation department and make an appointment with one of the professionals working in that department. Interview the professional about the different tasks that he or she performs as part of the job.

3. Make a list of the factors that may lead to burnout or stress. During your interview with the professional from above (Learning Activity 2), ask about these factors being present in his or her job.

4. Call a semi-public/nonprofit agency dealing with recreation, parks, and leisure service. Ask if you can volunteer your services. Find out how the volunteers are selected and evaluated.

REFERENCES

Baron, R.A. and J. Greenberg (1990). **Behavior in Organizations: Understanding and Managing the Human Side of Work.** Boston: Alyn and Bacon.

Brief, A. and G. Tomlinson (1987). **Managing Smart: A No-Gimmick Handbook of Management Techniques that Work.** Lexington,

MA: Lexington Books.

Butler, G. (1940). **Introduction to Community Recreation**. New York: McGraw-Hill.

Caruth, D. L., R. M. Noe III and R. W. Mondy (1988**). Staffing the Contemporary Organization.** New York: Quorum Books.

Cherniss, Cary (1980). **Professional Burnout in Human Service Organizations**. New York: Praeger.

Department of Labor (1994**) Occupational Outlook Handbook.** Washington, D.C.: Department of Labor.

Harvey, Donald (1970). **The Civil Service Commission.** New York: Praeger Publishers.

Heisler, Wm., D. Jones and Ph. Benham Jr. (1988). **Managing Human Resources Issues.** San Francisco: Jossey-Bass Publishers.

Ibrahim, H and K. Cordes (1993). **Outdoor Recreation.** Dubuque, IA: Wm. C. Brown.

Jensen, C. and J. Naylor (1994). **Opportunities in Recreation and Leisure Careers.** Lincolnwood, IL: VGM Career Horizons.

McKay, K.L. and J.L. Crompton (1990) Measuring the Quality of Recreation Services. **Journal of Park and Recreation Administration.** 8(3):47-56.

Maclean, J. and J. Peterson and W.D. Martin (1985). **Recreation and Leisure: The Changing Scene.** New York: Macmillan.

Mickey, Jr., Paul (1994) "Tips for Handing Terminations," **Nation's Business**, V. 82 July:58-60.

Odrione, G. (1987). **The Human Side of Management: Management by Integration and Self-Control.** Lexington, MA: Lexington Books.

Shank, Patricia Ann (1983) "Anatomy of Burnout," **Parks and Recreation,** March 52-58 71.

Statistical Abstracts of the United States (1999). Washington, D.C.: Bureau of the Census.

Terpestra, D.E. and D.D. Barker (1987). "Outcomes of Sexual Harassment Charges," **Academy of Management Journal** 31, 185-194.

U.S. Department of Labor (1999) **Occupational Outlook Handbook.** Washington D.C.: U.S. Printing Office.

CHAPTER 6
FACILITIES AND EQUIPMENT

Learning Objectives

After studying this chapter, you should be able to do the following:

1. Understand that planning and designing a facility is a long process that is composed of many stages.

2. Appreciate the complexity in providing facilities for recreation, parks, and leisure offerings on both the national, regional and local levels.

3. Take into consideration the needs of handicapped persons when it comes to designing recreational and sporting facilities

4. Maintain recreational and sporting facilities, equipment, and supplies. In addition understand the purchasing procedures for leisure services.

5. Understand the types and causes of vandalism and the steps needed in its management.

The agencies of parks, recreation, and leisure services build their programs based on the facilities and equipment provided. Accordingly, designing and managing facilities; along with maintaining safe equipment are important aspects of management in these fields.

PLANNING AND DESIGNING FACILITIES

Planning is an important step which determines how to proceed from one level to another. Planning in recreation, parks, and leisure services should be inclusive of all aspects of the service. This section will be limited to the planning of the facilities as a process through which the need for acquiring new facilities or improving existing facilities is determined.

Stages In Planning Facilities

1. Form a committee that represents the widest possible audience and participants in the program. The committee should determine the guiding principles for designing the facility, i.e., relation to the master plan, current and future needs, and realistic cost.

2. Seek the services of a consultant. Funds should be allocated for that purpose. Services of a consultant may prove to be very beneficial. Qualifications of the consultant are of prime importance.

3. Collect data which supports the need for acquiring new facilities and or improving existing ones. Data on enrollment trends, demographic changes, and new standards should be included.

4. Survey existing facilities as to size, features, conditions, and current standards. These data should be compared to currently acceptable practices.

5. Calculate the cost of the facility. The input by the consultant is useful at this point or a visit to nearby facility may help in this endeavor.

6. Prepare a document that describes the steps taken and includes the data collected. The document should be widely distributed and feedback required.

A survey of recent research on planning and designing recreation areas and facilities shows that professional who are involved in these processes such as architects, landscape architects, and parks and recreation administrators feel that spatial distance between recreation facilities is important. About one third of them tend to prefer the inclusion of amenities such as ponds, pools, and running trails as part of the design (Rogers 1993).

Facility Planning Consultant: Managers should realize that consultants who claim to be able to do everything from program and marketing to facilities and business management should be viewed with suspicion. As discussed in Chapter Five, some consultants specialize in facility planning and construction. These specialists will try to find answers to the following questions (Patton and others 1989:80):

1. What are the specific program requirements? Types of activities? Number of participants to be served? Peak usage?

2. What are the specific space requirements for the activities? Administration? Storage?

3. What are the interrelationships of various spaces? Offices? Activity? Lockers?

4. What are the best resources for architects? Trade journals? Professional associations?

The aforementioned document should be prepared containing not only the data collected and the answers to the above questions, but also should discuss the selection of the site, cost analysis, and feasibility study. The feasibility study answers a very important question for the agency: Is it feasible to achieve maximum use by building this type of facility? The document should be distributed widely and discussed by members of the staff and representatives of the users, if possible. Eventually the document will be submitted to the decision maker or makers.

Selecting an Architect: Development of the design requires the hiring of an architect in case of an indoor facility, a landscape architect for an outdoor facility or both. The qualifications to look for before hiring these professionals includes items such as: membership in professional organizations, license to practice in the state, access to qualified contractors and subcontractors, and provision of references on previous work on similar projects (Resnick, 1992). The architect or the landscape specialist will be responsible for designing the facility, providing construction documents and supervising construction.

Designing the Facility: The planning committee should include a pre-design phase so the very important element of space allocation can be discussed thoroughly with the architect. Agencies should look for consultants who specialize in space planning. The allocation of certain areas within the facility to particular activities should be the goal of the agency and the purpose behind erecting the facility. For instance multifunctional space planning is cost effective in that, besides multiple use, it is both labor and energy efficient. A decision has to be made on multifunctional space during the pre-design phase.

The second phase following the pre-design phase is the schematic design which involves the introduction of rough drawings of the interrelationships of space allocations within the facility. This is done by the architect or landscape architect based on the goals of the agency and the purpose for erecting the facility. At this stage, the drawings can be modified in light of staff and others input. Also a preliminary estimation of cost should be available at this point. Attention should be given at this stage to the building code, and a visit to city hall is advisable at this point. Traffic flow and crowd control should be discussed during this phase.

Another important element in designing a facility is ambiance. Attention should be given to both the exterior and the interior of an indoor facility and to the landscaping of an outdoor facility. Sometimes an interior designer may be hired to select the proper textures, materials and colors needed for the interior of a facility.

In the design development phase, which follows the approval of the schematics, detailed sketches are provided which include floor plans, or ground plans in the case of an outdoor facility, building elevations, and equipment and furniture arrangements.

Once the final design is approved, a contractor is selected. Competitive bidding seems to be the best method of choosing a contractor. Before deciding on the contractor, his previous work on similar projects, whether public, semi-public or private should be checked along with the degree of satisfaction owners have with the performance of the contractor. The hiring of a construction manager who provides expertise on proper building materials, and electrical and mechanical systems is rather popular today (Hunsaker, 1992).

OUTDOOR FACILITIES AND OPEN SPACE

In this section a number of facilities will be described. These facilities serve a myriad of agencies dealing with parks, recreation, and leisure service. The intention here is not to indicate that each of these facilities should be included in each agency dealing with these fields, but that each facilities developed by an agency is dependent on its own philosophy, goals, and mission. These are mere examples of what facilities can provide to consumers and participants along with the standards that have evolved over the years that lend them both safe and effective.

Typical Outdoor Facilities

Following are typical facilities that are provided by public, semi-public, and private recreation agencies. Some of the features mentioned herein will be elaborated on in another section.

Playlots These are small areas provided basically for preschoolers either in a public park or in a housing development. If erected by itself, a playlot serves best in high density areas. Usually a playlot is part of a larger outdoor recreational facility. Its area should be surrounded by a low fence or shrubs and provide benches for adults who accompany the youngsters. Play equipment such as gliders, swings, six-foot slides, and a small merry-go- round is adequate for the activities of this age group.

Playgrounds These areas provide activities for an older age group. Some equipment help the psychomotor aspects of the growing child through the use of somewhat larger equipment than the ones described in the playlot. Modular equipment is used to enhance the affective domain of the child. This equipment, when painted with bright colors, increases emotional responses. The cognitive domain of the child is enhanced with equipment that stimulates curiosity, imagination and exploration.

Small Games Courts These are multipurpose areas which are developed in conjunction with the playlot or the playground. Among the many activities that appeal to the young people is hopscotch which can be done there.

The Neighborhood Park These facilities require 3 to 5 acres of land and may incorporate some of the features of the previous facilities. The rest of the land should emphasize horticultural features such as floral arrangements, turf areas, shrubs, and trees. A small picnic area is desirable in these facilities.

Community Park In addition to the play and horticultural features of a neighborhood park, a community park should include facilities that cater to many age groups such as adolescents, adults and seniors. Playfields are included for baseball, football and basketball. A small community center that offers a variety of indoor activities is a desirable feature of this facility.

City-wide Park Ideally a park that serve a population of 50,000 to 100,000 will have additional features such as an aquatic center, a community center, an outdoor theater, a nature trail, a winter sport facility and a day camp.

Regional Park These are facilities that could be developed through the cooperation of two cities or through the county to provide additional recreational features such as a lake, a golf course, a bridle path and a skating rink, or any of the features mentioned in the following section.

Special Outdoor Areas

Besides the facilities listed above, a number of outdoor recreational facilities are worth mentioning as follows.

Alpine Slide This is a facility used by commercial ski operator. The participants are lifted up to the top of the skiing area then slide downhill on plastic sleds through dual cement flumes. This is a family activity since people of all ages participate in it.

Archery Range Adequate space should be provided for this popular sport. The shooting distance could reach 100 yards and additional space is needed as a safety measure. The end of the area should be provided with an earth bunker or bales of hay piled up to the top of the target.

Bridle Path and Ring A minimum of a 10 feet width is recommended for a bridle path to allow for two way traffic. The length of the path will vary according to availability of a trail that is free of large boulders and low hanging branches. While there is no need for a special surface, boggy areas should be covered with cinder or similar materials. A stable, a riding ring, feeding, and hitching racks should be provided at a reasonable distance from public use areas.

Bicycle Pathway This is both an expensive and extensive undertaking which may require the cooperation of many agencies. The idea is to create a circular route. Mapping of the existing routes that are not heavily used by regular traffic may lead to the development of a bicycle pathway that is usable.

Community Gardens There are different ways of providing the community with a garden. Some are tract gardens in which a piece of property is divided into small plots of 20 square feet each and are allocated to families and groups to tend. Others are display gardens that are composed of one plant such as roses and are taken care of by a local public agency, an association or a business.

Curling Area Curling is a popular sport which is played on natural or artificial ice on a flat area approximately 200 feet long and 40 feet wide.

Exercise Trails These facilities are still popular with many people. Parcourses, as they are sometimes called, are typically a mile and half long and include about 15 stations. Each station provides a form of exercise which collectively help in enhancing and maintaining physical fitness.

Golf Courses Golf is a popular sport and it is estimated that there are 20 million golfers in the United States today. The National Golf Foundation expects the number to reach 30 million soon. The building of a golf course is also an extensive and an expensive undertaking. A minimum of 70 acres is needed for a standard 9-hole par three course, and a minimum of 120 acres is needed for a standard 18- hole course. Helmick suggests that informality should be the name of the game in designing the clubhouse. It needs a small locker room since most golfers bring their clubs and come dressed for golf. A snack bar area for 30 or 40 persons is recommended since golfers tend to socialize after a game. The atmosphere there should be homelike and friendly (1992:32).

Ice Rinks Both natural and artificial ice rinks are now used in many communities. While the size of the facility will depend on the type of activities to be conducted, the ice surface itself should be 85 by 200 feet. The size of the facility itself will depend on the features included such as seating capacity, offices, dressing rooms and the refrigeration room.

Marinas The number of slips to be provided and the types of boats to be served by this facility will determine its size. The most critical issue in marina development is the site selection. The factors to be considered in the selection include environmental features, distance to deep water, impact on traffic, and contamination problems. The types of dock, fixed or floating should be determined as soon as possible. Amenities should include a restroom with showers, slips, a parking lot, a fuel dock, boat and food service area, a fishing pier with a fish cleaning station, and an administrative office (Jensen, 1992).

Nature Center These facilities could be provided in conjunction with a larger recreational or educational facility or by itself. A building of 2500 square feet is adequate which includes, other than the museum area, office space, a classroom, a small library, a science laboratory, toilet facilities, and storage area.

Outdoor Amphitheater The size of these facilities will be determined by the purpose behind them and the availability of usable area. A natural bowl or depression with a 10 to 20 degree slope is ideal for an amphitheater. The stage should be at least 30 by 50 feet, have storage space and have adequate seating.

Picnic area Picnicking is a very popular recreational activity and an area for it could be incorporated in all types of parks. Sometimes a picnic area is established by itself. Douglass suggests that a picnic area should be established within 25 miles from the home of the persons for whom it is planned (1993:174). A picnic unit should have 200 square feet. The tables should have the benches attached to them and be made of durable material. It may be necessary to fasten down the tables. Other than the tables, some picnic unit should have a fireplace or fire pit and a refuse container. If the tables are clustered, every four or five tables should have a fireplace and a large refuse container.

Roller Skating Rink An area of about 100 by 200 feet is adequate for a skating rink. A track for speed skating could be added which encircles the ring, but its boundaries must be marked and its curves banked for safety purposes. The surface of both the rink and the track should be smooth and sprinkled with rosin.

Skiing course A skiing course should include various slopes for beginning as well as advanced skiers. It also should have a building, a refractor and a ski tow. Slopes will vary from 100 feet with a drop ratio of 4:1 for beginners to 250 and a drop ratio of 3:1 for advanced skiers.

Sleighing and Natural slopes can be used for these popular winter sporting
Tobogganing Areas activities. The slope should be free from obstruction, wide
enough to accommodate sleds, and away from regular traffic.
The hillside should have a long bottom run-off for safety
purposes.

Nature Trails These facilities can be provided for hiking, horseback riding,
bicycling, snowmobiling, cross country skiing, off-road motorcycling and all terrain vehicle riding (Douglass, 1992:188). For
hiking trails a 5-8 feet width and an 8 feet height is recommended. The trail should run along ridges and high grounds as
much as possible. The width for horseback riding trails is 10
feet with a clearance of 10 feet also. While bicycle trails should
have level grades as much as possible, mountain bicycle trails
should.have good drainage. Both trails should be 8 feet wide for
one way traffic. Snowmobile trails should be between 15 and 30
miles long and 15 feet wide. Cross-country skiing trails should
have no more than a 12 percent grade with a turning radius of
25 feet. Old logging roads are recommended for motorcycling
and ATV trails and should have between 80 and 250 acres of
land. Nature trails should have enough bends and curves to give
the feeling of isolation. Enough areas should be provided on the
trail to allow for group gatherings.

Field and Court Sport

This section concerns outdoor facilities that are commonly built to accommodate
sport activities as shown below. Many sport activities that take place indoors, and
will be covered in another section.

Baseball field A square area of about 400X400 feet is needed for a baseball
field. A 20-feet high backstop should be placed 60 feet behind
the home plate. For regulation baseball, the diamond is 90 feet a
side, which makes the line across 127 feet, 3 and 3/8 inches.
The two foul lines should extend 350 feet for regular play and

300 for seniors. The length of the diamond's sides will vary according to the league, 60 for little league, 80 for pony league and 90 for Babe Ruth League.

Football field This field should be laid in a north and south direction to avoid the sun shining directly unto the players. The field should be level, 360 feet long, and 160 feet wide. The two goals placed at the two ends of the field should be 120 yards apart. The goal posts are 20 feet high with a cross bar 10 feet above the ground. The width of the goal varies from 18' 6" to 23" 4". The field itself is 100 yards long with two end zones extending 10 yards behind the goal line. Yard lines are at 10-yard intervals from the goal line to the center of the field.

Handball courts Outdoor handball courts can be either one wall or three wall courts, 12 inches thick. The one wall should be 16 feet high and 20 feet wide. The three walls should be 20 feet high and 22 feet wide. For the court itself, the front walls should be 34 feet long for the one wall and 40 feet long for the three walls. The width also varies from 8' 6" to 10' respectively.

Lacrosse field The Lacrosse field extends 330 feet in length and 160 feet in width. Two goals are placed at the end of the field at 270 feet. The goals are 6x6 feet with a net securely placed seven feet behind the center of the goal.

Soccer field The maximum length of a soccer field is 120 yards and the minimum is 100 yards. The width is no more than 75 yards and no less than 65 yards. A center line divides the field and a circle of 10 yard radius is drawn in the middle of that line. Two goals 8 yards wide and 8 feet high are placed at each end line with a box 44 by 18 yards drawn in front of each one. This box is known as the penalty area. A small box 12 by 6 yards is drawn in front of the goal. This is known as the goal area. A penalty kick mark is placed 12 yards away from the center of the goal. An arch is drawn above the penalty box to ensure a 10 yard distance from the penalty mark.

Shuffleboard A smooth pavement is recommended for this court. The playing area itself is only 39 feet long and 6 feet wide, yet at few extra feet should be allowed on all sides of the court. The playing area could be marked off by paint.

Tennis Courts Although the playing area is only 78 by 36 feet, an area approximately 120 by 60 feet is needed for each court, There are many surfaces from which to choose for a tennis court. Pervious surfaces include clay and fast dry while impervious surfaces include concrete, asphalt and synthetics.

Track and Field The area needed for a track and field event is approximately 600 by 276 feet. The track should shed water to the inside. Material for the track varies significantly from cinder to synthetics. Inside areas are used for jumping and throwing events. The high jump area could be made of the same surface as the track and should provide a minimum of 25 yards with an arc of 150 degrees. The long and triple jump should have a runway of 60-yards ending in a landing pit 12X4 yards. The elevation is identical to the take-off board dimensions, are 4'X4' and is immovable. Pole vaulting requires a pit 5 yards wide and 4 yards deep. It should be made of sponge and rubber and should be 36" high. The runway should be about 50 yard long. The throwing circles could be made of cement with a band of steel placed flush on the outside. The shot put and hammer circles are a bit smaller than the circle for discus throwing.

Swimming Pools

The shells of most large pools are made of gunite which is a form of concrete applied by pneumatic pressure. Small pools are sometimes made of fiberglass or vinyl. Vinyl is suggested for pools that have extensive use or are expected to last five years. The inside finish of the pool is done with plaster, tile, or painting. The overflow system should be designed so that it would accept displaced water through an open gutter or a rim flow. A hydraulic system will allow for circulation and filtration of the water. A pump will bring the water from the pool, pass it through a filtering system, and return it back to the pool. There are basically three types of filtering systems. The sand filter system holds the impurities within the media bed and is cleaned through backwashing. The cartridge type system traps the residues through permeable cylinders of fibrous material. These cylinders are cleaned by backwashing. The diatomaceous earth filters includes a thin layer of diatomite slurry which is held against a thin woven mesh. The system is cleaned by backwashing and additional diatomite slurry is added at this point.

Factors to Consider: These factors should be considered when designing a swimming pool:

- The manager's office is facing the pool.
- A toilet-shower facility is adjacent to the office.
- Separate storage space is allocated.
- Use of metric measurement is needed for competitive pools.
- The filtering area is easy to access.
- An area for sunbathing is provided.
- An area for lounging is included.
- An area for eating is set aside.
- Diving boards should face north or east.
- Adequate overhead is required for diving in indoor pools.
- Depth of the pool is 12 feet for one meter, 13 for 3 and 17 for 10-meter boards.
- Adequate provision of life saving equipment is on hand.
- Underwater light is 12-volt type.
- Automatic control of pool chemicals is installed.
- Proper temperature controls are provided.
- Pool is fenced according to regulations.
- Warning signs are properly placed.
- A telephone is provided in pool area.
- First aid station and equipment are available.
- Water slides of non-slippery material are placed 8 feet into pool.

New Approaches and Designs: The typical swimming pool design is now being supplemented with ideas that help in both the design and utilization of a very popular recreational facility. A number of rules should be observed in designing a swimming pool:

> **Rule #1:** Since participants spend more time on the deck than in the water, a pleasant environment should be provided.
>
> **Rule #2:** The overwhelming majority of the public enjoys participatory aquatic entertainment for the whole family.
>
> **Rule #3:** Management must be well educated, entrepreneurial, and innovative.

Carl Fuerst (1993) suggests that in lieu of a swimming pool, a family aquatic center should be built which provides new and exciting aquatic opportunities for families, adults and children; provides an increase in participation with revenue sufficient to meet operating expenses, is appropriate for use by all ages and includes facilities for those with disabilities. In addition it should provide an attractive, exciting, safe quality aquatic experiences on a year- round basis, and have additional bather capacity for the high-use summer month.

Evidence to the success of these new approaches and designs can be seen in the combined aquatic and fitness center of Prince William County, Virginia. Although initially the project was met with some resistance, it is now very well attended. Its success is attributed to the fact that the project endeavored to meet the needs of as many members of the community as possible. The facility has adequate access, building services, youth lounge, weight room, and numerous locker rooms.

Other Aquatic Facilities

Though swimming pools have always been popular, interest is growing in other aquatic facilities as well.

Waterparks: Despite the expense, water parks are becoming very popular features in recreation, be it public, semi-public or commercial. In all these cases, the first step in the development of a waterpark is the feasibility study. Typically a water park area should be at least 60 acres in size and should include, among other things, a large swimming lake (about six acres), a sandy beach, a diving dock, a boat dock, a bathhouse/restroom facility, a playlot, and a nature trail (Design 1994).

In selecting the site for a waterpark, four utilities are essential: electricity of three phase-12, 500 volt, potable water from an eight- inch-main with adequate pressure, natural gas for heating the water, and adequate sewerage and/or disposal system (Waterpark 1993). The design of the park should follow the steps provided at the beginning of this chapter.

Camps

Organized camping refers to recreational and educational programs that take place in a natural setting. This can vary according to the type of camp. The following are the camp types that have been suggested by McLean and others (1985:261):

Day Camp	This is the simplest form of camp since the camper sleeps at home. Since the day activities are conducted in a natural setting and for the whole day, this program is known as a day camp. This activity is usually directed to the very young, and takes place in a somewhat isolated open space. It includes physical features that allow for different and unique educational and recreational opportunities such as water.
Group Camp	When a preexisting group, such as the Boy or Girl Scouts, camps out overnight, such an activity is classified as group camping. Usually the group brings simple equipment such as sleeping bags and cooking utensils. In many parts of the country, an open space with minimum facilities is provided for group camps.
Resident Camp	This is the most elaborate of camps and the facilities could vary from a simple building to an elaborate labyrinth of structures. A large dinning hall with a modern kitchen, tents or cabins, central lodges, infirmaries, campfire circles, laundries, docks, beaches, stables, craft shop, nature center, playing fields, and a recreation hall are some of the facilities found in resident camps.

Campgrounds

Hultsman and others (1998:176), suggest that a minimum of three hundred camp-sites in either public or private campgrounds is required to break-even. They suggest that the cost of operation and maintenance should be offset by fees in the case of a public campground. Private campgrounds charge higher fees to offset capital outlay and to realize some profit.

Control is an important problem that the managers of campgrounds face is control. Since most campgrounds are located away from the most traveled paths, control over who enters the campground is essential. Cooper (1992: 56) suggests three preliminary steps to be taken prior to designing and constructing of a campground:

1. Research: This phase should be directed toward collected quality and quantity information that will help in the analysis. Most of such information is found in government offices, ergo research is essential.

2. Site selection: This is the next step to be taken prior to embarking on building a campground. Location, accessibility and an attractive natural setting should be emphasized. If the land is already owned by the agency, the same factors should receive careful consideration.

3. Site Analysis: This step should take into consideration the location of the site and accessibility as well as its physical aspects such as soil, topography, drainage, water availability and vegetation. Other factors to be taken into consideration in the analysis of the site are the cultural and environmental elements such as building, utilities, noise and pollution resources and environmental hazards.

INDOOR FACILITIES

While most recreational activities take place outdoors, a number practiced indoor due to inclement weather or as a matter of tradition. Following are some of the indoor facilities with which the manager should be acquainted.

Neighborhood Center As the name indicates, the purpose of this center is to serve a neighborhood, a part of city that may vary from a population of ten to twenty thousand persons. The size of the facility varies according to need and availability of space and funds. The minimum that is expected in such a facility is a multipurpose room, a room that can be used in many different activities. Some neighborhood centers include, in addition to the multipurpose room or rooms, a gymnasium, shower and locker rooms, and a kitchen.

Community Center This facility should be designed to serve more than one neighborhood. In addition to the facilities listed in the neighborhood center, it should also have an auditorium, a small/library/reading room and meeting rooms.

Field house Commonly seen in northern latitudes, this is a facility which includes a large enclosed area for physical activities This is usually a low cost facility where a less expensive fabric structure is sometimes used. Some field houses are built as air-supported structures while others use wooden domes. The floor should be made of heavy-duty material to withstand the weather and heavy use.

Gymnasium An important question should be asked before designing the gymnasium: Is it intended for multiple use? In other words, is the gymnasium limited to basketball or will it include other activities such as volleyball, badminton, and or other activities? A minimum of 125 square feet of usable space should be allowed per person at peak load. The ceiling of a gymnasium varies in height from 12 to 24 feet. The higher ceiling is recommended for basketball and volleyball, while the lower one is sufficient for activities such as wrestling and badminton. The walls should be made of sturdy material to withstand heavy use. Windows are not recommended for gymnasiums, and the lower parts of the walls should be coated in such a way as to allow for easy cleaning. All corners on the walls should be rounded. The floor should be made of a durable material, either hard wood or synthetics. Lighting varies from 50 to 200 foot-candles depending on the type of use.

Dance Facility This facility should have a high ceiling of at least 20 feet and floor space of at least 100 feet per person. The floor should have a smooth, but not slippery, surface. The walls should have no protruding structures. Windows should be provided above 10 feet to allow for natural lighting. Otherwise, adequate lighting should be provided.

Multipurpose areas This facility could be used in the many activities that allow for street shoes such as social dancing, table games, and simple get- togethers. The room should be large enough to accommodate a reasonable number of participants. Square footage should vary from 60 to 100 per participant. The floor should be made of durable material such as concrete or heavy vinyl. The ceiling should not exceed 12 feet.

Clubhouse As previously mentioned under the golf course section, the clubhouse should provide an atmosphere that is homelike and friendly. The clubhouse should take advantage of golf course views, and should allow for the gathering of 30 to 40 people around a drink and snack bar area.

Health Spas Health spas vary according to setting. Patton and others suggest four possible settings as follows (1989:3-16). In the corporate setting, a program is planned for the employees. In the community setting health spas are provided by public agencies such as the local recreation department or semi-private agencies such as the YMCA. The commercial setting provides service to the public for profit, and finally, the clinical setting offers health spas geared toward treatment.

PLANNING FOR THE HANDICAPPED

The general idea behind the planning for the handicapped is to make the recreational facilities easily accessible and usable by members of special populations. These are the populations that include the physically and mentally challenged as well others who need special attention.

General Standards

These general standards are recommended in designing facilities and areas for the handicapped:

- Extra large parking spaces should be allocated for vans.
- Ramps and turns should allow for all types of wheelchairs.
- Restrooms should be large enough for wheel chair access and the facilities should have grab bars and accessible sinks and mirrors.
- Telephones and drinking fountains should meet adequate heights requirements.
- Doors should be at least 32 inches wide with thresholds flush with the floor.
- Emergency signs should be conveyed graphically and should have flashing lights.
- Braille markers should be used wherever possible
- Interpreters should be provided for the hard of hearing.

Specific Modifications

While the above general standards should be applied across the board, all facilities should be subject to modifications to suit the needs and abilities of the different special populations. According to Kidd and Clark (1982), the range of activities in which the handicapped could participate is limitless. The publication list 46 activities in which they could participate. The publication suggests the following modification of recreational activities to suit the handicapped.

Swimming Pools: There are a number of ways to prepare or modify a swimming pool for use by disabled persons. A ramp four feet wide and equipped with handrails could slope down to the shallow end of the pool. Another way of equipping a pool for handicapped persons is to mount a winch which could be attached to chair to lower the participant into the pool.

Parks: When a park is equipped to receive disabled persons, some information on the type of facilities provided should be made available to them. The most important step to accommodate the disabled is to make the approaches and entries to the park free from barriers such as steps and protruding walls. The walkways should be made of stable and firm material and should not contain excessive slopes.

Picnic tables in the park should be placed in such a way that a person in a wheelchair can use them effectively. A space should be provided at the end of the table for a person in a wheelchair. Also park benches should be located adjacent to the walkway, and the walkway surface should be firm. Space should be allowed next to the bench for the person using a wheelchair.

The area around the barbecue grill should also be made amenable to use by a person in a wheelchair. The surface should be firm and designed in such a way as to allow for maneuverability around the grill. The campfire circle could be raised to allow a person in a wheelchair to join in. The fountains in the park should not be recessed into the wall, as a person in a wheelchair would have difficulty reaching it. If the park has an amphitheater, access to it should be graded. If gardening is one of the activities provided, some garden beds could be raised to allow wheelchair users to participate.

Sport Facilities: Handicapped persons could be both spectators of, and or participants in, sports events. In both cases the management of a recreation, parks or leisure service agency should be able to modify the facility to suit a handicapped person. Whether it is a seat in the stadium or the locker room, the handicapped should have a barrier free route from the parking lot and bus stop, or to the place to which he or she is heading. Toilet facilities should be prepared for handicapped persons. He or she should not only have access to the locker room, but should also have a special change room in which assistance can be given, if need be.

MANAGEMENT & MAINTENANCE OF FACILITIES

The maintenance of a facility or an area is one of the most important aspects of management in parks, recreation, and leisure services. A well maintained place gives the feeling that it is well run. Therefore, maintenance is an important public relations tool. Moreover, well maintained facilities and areas are attractive to the users and to the workers themselves. Well managed and maintained facilities and areas are tools of economic efficiency in that they reduce deterioration and decrease frequent replacement of equipment. Since maintenance is so important in the management of facilities and areas in parks, recreation, and leisure services, it should be taken into account from the very beginning.

Maintenance and the Planning Process

Also crucial to the planning is the future maintenance of the facility. Accordingly, a member or a representative of the staff, who will eventually run the facility, should be included in the planning process. If such persons are not available, an expert, who has management experience in a similar facility, should be included from the pre-design phase on.

According to Sharpe and others, planners could be too far removed from the day-to-day operation of a facility and may unintentionally design areas and facilities that produce unnecessary problems for the maintenance staff later (1994:250). Moreover, there may be a tendency on their part to reduce the cost of building the facility at the expense of good maintenance practices. Therefore a checklist should be prepared for use during the design phase. For instance the checklist should include locations and numbers of electrical outlets and plumbing facilities. The checklist should also include inadequate surface finishes and inappropriate building material. While good materials may be costly, they will reduce future spending on maintenance. According to Bitner, maintenance cost could amount up to 70% of the operating budget (1991).

Management of Facilities

For the facility to operate smoothly, an important question must be answered: For whose usage and for what purpose is the facility provided? A system of priorities should be developed and adhered to when considering the facility's usage. For instance does an activity of an organized group have priority over a drop-in activity. Do scheduled classes have priority over adult activities? Once the list of priorities is completed it should be made known to all concerned so scheduling can take place.

Users of the facility should be apprised on how the facility is utilized. Where reservations are required, the users should be informed of the process for reserving the facility. Since ample time is needed to prepare the master calendar. It is suggested that a schedule be posted at the entry of the facility, say a week ahead. In many instances a reservation form should be developed to help alleviate any misunderstandings and future conflicts.

Rules Concerning Use of Facilities: The person or group requesting the use of the facility must abide by the rules and regulations set forth by the agency. It is advisable that the users sign an agreement to this effect.

Maintenance of Facilities

In parks, recreation, and leisure services, a well-versed maintenance crew is a must. Many maintenance positions are entry-level positions which pay only minimum wage. Some of these positions should be allocated to highly skilled laborers such as mechanics, electricians and plumbers. In large leisure delivery systems, the skilled staff could be centralized and then called when emergencies arise. If these skilled workers are not found among the maintenance personnel, contracting out is suggested.

Since the work of the maintenance staff takes place behind the scenes, and often when no one is there, it is important that the manager, or a designate, uses motivational techniques to achieve the best possible results from the maintenance staff.

When establishing a maintenance program for parks, recreation, and leisure services, the following guidelines have been suggested (Sternloff and Warren 1993:7-18):

1. Maintenance objectives and standards must be established. For example the facilities should be clean and orderly at all times. The facility should also be aesthetically pleasing, and should provide a safe and healthy environment.

2. Maintenance should use personnel, equipment and material efficiently. Work should be done as soon as possible with an optimum number of workers and with proper and adequate equipment and material.

3. Maintenance should be based on a sound written plan as suggested at the beginning of this section. The plan should be the result of the collective efforts of all the people involved in maintenance.

4. Maintenance scheduling should be based on sound decisions by the people involved be they maintenance staff or other personnel. Priority should be given to urgent cases.

5. Preventive maintenance should be emphasized so that the optimum life of the facilities and equipment, particularly the ones that are inconstant use, can be realized. The maintenance program should be designed to protect the natural environment.

6. The maintenance department or unit within the agency must be well organized, adequately staffed and financially supported so that it may be able to do the needed tasks.

7. Safety of the public and the employees must receive primary consideration in the planning and scheduling of the maintenance program.

8. The maintenance staff should be trained to report any hazardous conditions as soon as possible.

Maintenance Organization

There are a number of ways to organize the maintenance staff in a parks, recreation, or leisure service agency. Centralized organization relies on one central location from which the crews are dispatched to keep the facilities and equipment in proper shape. The decentralized organization works on the idea of dividing the premises up into smaller zones each having its own crew. The functional organization divides the crew up into units so that each one is in charge of certain functions such as preventive maintenance, alteration, installation, etc. Although the centralized organization is most popular, the other two should be tried by the agency's management and the one most suitable for the agency should be chosen. This decision depends on many factors such as the layout of the premises, conditions of facilities and equipment, skill of personnel, and location of special use equipment.

Preventive Maintenance: According to Evans (1984:III-102), this kind of maintenance involves a planned and controlled program of systematic inspection, adjustment, and replacement as well testing and analysis. A record should be kept for this kind of maintenance.

Deferred Maintenance: Whether due to tight budgets or through lack of awareness and neglect, maintenance of facilities and equipment are often postponed to the extent that their effectiveness and value to the agency are often in doubt. A detailed inspection is needed to detect the presence of deferred maintenance and its impact on the agency's mission. If found, the impact is easier to correct.

Daily Maintenance Schedule

Although many daily tasks will be routinely followed, it is suggested that a daily schedule be prepared the day before and that the last task listed should be underscored for easy identification of possible additional tasks that may be added after appraisal (Sternloff and Warren, 1993:47).

The priority of certain tasks will determine the daily planning of the maintenance schedule. Other than the typical preventive maintenance, Sternloff and Warren suggested that there are three classes of priorities when it comes to maintenance: emergency, routine, and standing. Emergency maintenance is needed when a problem occurs that may threaten the safety of the operation or causes serious disruption in it. Routine maintenance concerns less disruptive problems which may be somewhat delayed and standing maintenance refers to the recurring tasks (1993:46).

EQUIPMENT AND SUPPLIES

Equipment and supplies used in the activities of a parks, recreation, and leisure service must be stored or kept in a place that prevents their easy deterioration. For instance computer and typewriters should be covered in the evening. Also the management should keep at hand an inventory of the number and conditions of the equipment whether durable such as a trampoline or perishable such as coloring crayons. The same should be applied to materials such as chlorine and fertilizers.

The management of equipment and supplies requires that three types of requisition be prepared. One requisition for request, the second for damage, and the third for repair.

Purchase of Equipment and Supplies

Once the management determines that the equipment or material requested is not available on the premises, purchasing it becomes necessary. The agency is well advised to designate a person as a purchasing agent. The person could assume this task for the whole agency or for a unit therein. This does not mean that this person will be buying everything for the agency. Rather, he or she will be charged with the mechanism of purchasing. The policy on purchasing should be made clear to all concerned. For instance, items that cost under a certain amount can be bought directly without the need for sending bids out to merchants.

A purchase requisition should be used by the person who is asking for equipment or supplies. The request should be checked against the inventory which is kept by the agency. Once it is agreed that the purchase is necessary, a purchase order is prepared. A purchase order is an indication that the agency is in need of the particular equipment and supplies. However, the mere provision of a purchase order to a merchant does not mean that it will be processed. A prior agreement between the agency and the merchant who is receiving the purchase order must be concluded. Otherwise the amount to cover the purchase should be prepared in the form of a check or cash. Upon paying in cash, a receipt should be acquired for record keeping.

Specifications and Bids

Today there are so many brands of equipment and supplies that specifications of the exact type of equipment and supplies should be made clear in the purchase order or in the bids sent to merchants. The bid is a good way of acquiring equipment and supplies at reduced prices. By lowering their prices for the same item or equivalent items, merchants compete for a company's business.

The bid is a list that gives the quantity need of a particular item with its specifications provided. The column on unit price is left blank for the merchant to fill in. A deadline for the bid should be given in a cover letter that accompanies the list or lists to the specialized merchants.

In the presence of a designated committee, it is advisable that a specified day to established for the opening of all bids. This is important to protect the single buyer from possible future complications.

Maintenance of Equipment and Supplies

Maintenance of equipment begins with an inventory which shows the name, cost, date of purchase, serial number, model number, specific conditions, warranty data, storage location, and maintenance record. Initially, every piece of equipment is covered by a warranty for a certain period of time after which the agency should continue the needed maintenance. The management of the agency should keep the maintenance manual which is provided by the manufacturer for all the equipment on hand.

Special Considerations: Sharpe et al suggest that there are two special considerations that should be taken seriously by the management of the agency dealing with parks, recreation, or leisure pursuits. The first is solid waste management, and the second is the idea of recycling. In-service training of the staff as well as informing the users of the service are two effective means in maintenance (1994).

Safety: The safety of both staff and visitors is another important factor in the use of equipment and facilities in the agency. Continual inspection by the management or by a standing committee on safety is suggested. Another aspect to consider is the disposal of infectious waste, particularly in resident camps. Recent regulations of the Occupational Safety and Health Administration (OSHA) concerning exposure to blood-borne pathogens should be heeded. In general, disposable gloves should be used and a container should be provided for the disposal of infectious waste. Tin cans or rigid plastic containers should be used to dispose of this material (Erceg 1993).

Another very important safety factor to consider is the management of chemicals in a recreation, parks, or leisure service agency. In response to state and federal "Right-to-Know" laws, manufacturers of chemical supplies provide purchasers with Material Safety Data Sheets (MSDS). These sheets should be used as guidelines for health, safety, and storage procedure in the agency (Glancy and Donnelly 1988).

VANDALISM

According to Sharpe et al, vandalism is a term used by the establishment, owners, managers and taxpayers of recreation places, and describes the wanton acts that lead to the destruction and defacing of property. Attempts at understanding this phenomenon are still incomplete (1994:327).

Types and Causes of Vandalism

The term itself is derived from the Vandals, the Germanic people, who in 455 of the Common Era, attacked Rome and destroyed its public buildings, thus vandalism. Although the phenomenon of vandalism is old, attempts at understanding it are relatively new. In an attempt to understand the wanton destruction of property, research looks at the underpinning motivational factor or factors to find the reason behind these acts. The motives behind the types of destruction are varied and are usually classified into different categories. For instance, Sharpe et al describe these six types as follows.

1. Acquisitive vandalism occurs in the process of illegally obtaining money.

2. Playful vandalism is the outgrowth of group activity and accounts from a large percentage of vandalism.

3. Malicious vandalism such as plugging a sink in a community center comes from the enjoyment of destroying the property of others.

4. Erosive vandalism such as cutting trails in a park results from the ignorance and disregard to public property

5. Tactical vandalism such as setting incendiary fire is premeditated for the purpose of attracting attention

6. Vindictive vandalism is motivated by the desire for revenge and takes many forms.

Clearly the motivational factors behind some of the vandals' acts include the possibility of neglect and or irresponsibility. Interested scholars have tried to emphasize these elements in understanding the phenomenon of vandalism in recreation, parks and leisure services. For instance, Knudson suggests other motives as seen in the ten types of vandalism he suggested (1984: 500-501).

1. Overuse destruction which may appear as vandalism yet it is intentional.

2. Conflict vandalism when a user moves a park bench thus altering the designer' plan.

3. "No other way vandalism" when a particular object is used for something for which it is not intended or designed.

4. Inventive vandalism as in bouncing a ball against the wall, an activity for which the wall is not designed.

5. Curiosity vandalism as driving a motorcycle up and down a fragile hillside.

6. Self expression vandalism as is seen in carving one's name on a tree or engaging in graffiti.

7. Spin off vandalism in which an act lead to another destructive act as a fighting groups begin to destroy park equipment.

8. Slovenly vandalism which reflects bad manners such as littering and similar careless acts.

9. Malicious vandalism in the wanton destruction of the city property in light of perceived mistreatment.

10. Thrill or dare vandalism which represents danger to self and others.

Management of Vandalism

Vandalism is not a phenomenon from which only recreation, parks, and leisure agencies suffer. Many other agencies such as schools suffer from this undesirable phenomenon. The management of an agency dealing with parks, recreation, and leisure service should do as much as it can to reduce the occurrence of these destructive acts on its premises. Whether these acts could be completely eliminated is moot. But there are means through which they could be drastically reduced. The following steps have been suggested by a number of writers (Mathews, 1970; Grosvenor, 1976; and Sharpe et al, 1994).

Awareness of the Problem of Vandalism: The first and most important step in combating vandalism is to raise awareness of the staff and members of the community of the existence of the problem. Facts about the different acts taken against the agency's property should be gathered and made public. Briefings about these acts along with some explanation of the phenomenon should be conducted for both staff and members of the community with special attention given to the youth of the community. Youth, particularly gang members if they exist, should be made cognizant of the consequence that may result from the perpetrators of these acts.

Design of the Facilities: Although the initial cost of a well designed facility, which could be vandalism proof, may be high, it could be justified in the long run. Better designs, stronger materials, and pleasant looks are usually deterrents to vandalism. Brick, concrete blocks, and rock are suggested for outside walls, and smooth nonporous material such as tile is recommended for inside walls.

Restrooms are most vulnerable to vandalism. A number of changes in design could help in its reduction. For instance, drain pipes could be easily hidden. The mirrors could be made of metal and electric hand dryers could be installed in lieu of towels. All fixtures in the restroom should protrude as little as possible. Heavy polyester resin could be used on sinks and bowls. Bathroom stalls could have doors removed, and windows in the restrooms should be as high as possible.

Tables and benches made of polyvinyl chloride plastics are vandalism proof to some extent and should be used. Simply designed concrete fireplaces and rings in a simple design are best against vandalism as would drinking fountains made of masonry structure.

Elevated signs are harder to vandalize than the ones at a regular height while high density discharge lighting (HID) seem to be working in reducing incidents of vandalism. Thorny plants, when not forbidden, keep people on the right path and also decrease the possibility of being picked or stolen all together. Among the other suggestions to combat vandalism is the idea of a movable feed kiosk. This kiosk has been successful at Cape Cod National Seashore. The fee kiosk which is removed from its site at the end of the day, lifted by a fork life and stored in convenient compound.

Security and Law Enforcement: Surveillance over recreation and park facilities is an important deterrent to vandalism. The use of night guards is useful in curbing vandalism as well as monitoring certain areas of the facility with either a closed circuit TV or an alarm system. In large parks, patrolling during known problem hours is suggested. To avoid detection by the determined vandals, the patrol schedule and travel pattern should be varied along with the use of unidentified vehicles now and then.

Although the apprehension of a vandal is the first step in applying the law to such illegal behavior, there is no guarantee that the person will be convicted. Yet this should not deter the management of a recreation, parks or leisure service agency from doing its best to capture the culprit. Apprehension should be followed by prosecution. At this point a close working relationship with the local police is important. In many instances the management of an agency dealing with recreation, parks, or leisure services is reluctant to prosecute. This may be due to fear of reprisal, uncertainty about the outcome and the fear of creating a negative public relation.

Information, Education and Awareness: An important aspect in combating vandalism is related to public and personal knowledge and awareness. These will come with education both formal and informal. While the recreation, parks, and leisure service agency has little to do with the educational curriculum of the local schools, an attempt to engage the school in making the young people aware of the seriousness of vandalism in the local community may pay off in the long run.

Involving the parents in the attempt to solve this problem is also suggested. Parents need to understand that they are legally responsible for damages incurred by their offspring. Visitors to the recreation area, whether it is a parks or a sport facility, need to know how vandalism impacts their enjoyment of the leisure experience. The California Department of Parks and Recreation uses signs to this effect as does the National Park Service.

SUMMARY

- In planning and designing facilities, a number of steps should be taken including forming a committee, selecting an architect and conducting a feasibility study.

- A number of outdoor facilities should be considered in planning and designing facilities including the typical ones such as playlots and parks and special outdoor areas such as alpine slides and nature centers.

- Field and court sports are important ingredients of any recreational activities. A number of these facilities should be included in designing a recreational program.

- With the popularity of aquatic activities on the rise, attempts should be made to enhance existing pools with new ideas for better utilization. Another popular aquatic facility is the waterpark.

- A recreational program could be enhanced by providing camping possibilities, the simplest of which could take place in a day camp.

- When designing recreational facilities and areas, handicapped persons should be taken into consideration. A number of modifications can be utilized to this end.

- The management and maintenance of recreational facilities and areas should be based on the most up-to-date concepts and procedures. Efficiency and safety should be kept in mind at all times.

- Vandalism of leisure area is increasing and is becoming a major problem for management. There are many types of vandalism, ergo as many types in managing and controlling it.

LEARNING ACTIVITIES

1. Visit your local recreation center. Make a sketch of all the facilities and areas in the center. Gather a group of five people of both genders and of different ages. Show them the sketch as ask them to modify it so that it serves their needs. Can their suggestions be reconciled?

2. Make a list of the items which have been suggested in this Chapter concerning the needs of the handicapped. During your visit to the aforementioned center, check if these suggestions are taken into consideration.

3. Visit a neighborhood park. Find out if it is, in your opinion, well maintained. If not, what are your suggestions?

4. Take a drive around your city, try to locate the most extensive area hit by graffiti. What are your suggestion to alleviate this problem?

REFERENCES

Bitner, Dick and May Bitner (1991) "Automating P&R Operations," **Parks and Recreation** Jun40-43.

Bronzan, Robert (1974) **New Concepts in Planning and Funding Athletic, Physical Education and Recreation Facilities**.St. Paul, MN: Phoenix Intermedia.

Cooper, Rollin (1992) **Campground Management: How to Establish and Operate Your Campground.** Champaign, Ill:Sagamore Publishing.

Design (Summer 1994) **Twin Lakes Recreation Area:Water Play Area.** Washington, D.C. National Park Service.

Design (Spring 1993) **Combating Vandalism.** Washington, D.D. National Park Service.

Douglass, Robert (1993) **Forest Recreation.** Prospect Heights, Ill: Waveland Press.

Erceg, Linda Ebner (1993) "Infectious Waste in Camp," **Camping Magazine,** January/February:35-37

Evans, Teresa B. (1984) **Facilities Management: A Manual For Plant Administration.** Washington D.C.: The Association of Physical Plant Administrators.

Flynn, R.(Editor) (1985) **Planning Facilities for Athletics, Physical Education and Recreation.** Reston, VA: AAHPERD.

Fuerst, Carl (1993) "The Family Aquatic Center," **Parks and Recreation,** July:34-37

Glancy, Maureen and Grace Donnelly (1988) "How to Manage Chemicals in Your Department",**Parks and Recreation** March:34-37.

Grosvenor, John (1976). "Control of Vandalism-An Architectural Design Approach," **Vandalism and Outdoor Recreation: Symposium Proceedings.** Berkely: CA USDA General

Technical Report PSW-17. Pacific Southwest Station Experiemental Station

Helmick, Wil (1992) "Clubhouse Design: Getting a Bang for Your Buck", **Parks and Recreation**, May:30.

Hultsman, J., R. Cottrell and W. Hultsman (1998) **Planning Parks for People.** State College, PA: Venture Publishing.

Hunsaker, D.J. (1992) "What you should know Before You Build," **Parks and Recreation**, July: 52.

Jensen, Clayne (1992) **Administrative Management of Physical Education and Athletic Programs.** Malvern, PA: Lea and Febiger.

Jensen, William (1992) "Marina Development in the Public Sector," **Parks and Recreation,** November: 46.

Kaiser, R and J. Mertes (1986) **Acquiring Parks and Recreation Facilities Through Mandatory Dedication.** State College, PA; Venture Publishing.

Kidd, Brian and Ross Clark (1982) "Outdoor Access for All," **A Guide to Designing Accessible Outdoor Recreation Facilities.** Department of Youth, Sport and Recreation. Victoria, Australia.

Knudson, D. (1982) **Outdoor Recreation.** New York: Mac Millan

Mathews, Robert P. (1970) "Theft and Vandalism in Western Washington Forest," **Journal of Forestry** 68(7):415- 416.

Parks, J and B. Zanger (Editors) (1990) **Sport and Fitness Management.** Champaign, Il: Human Kinetics.

Patton, R. and Others (1989) **Developing and Managing Health/Fitness Facilities.** Champaign,II: Human Kinetics.

Resick, M., B. Seidel and J. Mason (1970) **Modern Administrative Practices in Physical Education and Athletics.** Reading,MA: Addison-Wessley Publishing.

Resnick, Alan (1992)"The Architect's Story," **Parks and Recreation**, July:40.

Rogers, S. Elaine (1993) "Current Research in Areas and Facilities," **Parks and Recreation.** December:22

Sharpe, G., Ch. Odegaard and W. Sharpe (1994) **A Comprehensive Introduction to Park Management.** Champaign, Il: Sagamore Publishing.

Sternloff, Robert E. and Roger Warren (1993) **Park and Recreation: Maintenance Management.** Scottsdale, AZ: Publishing Horizons.

Turner, Al (1991) "Public Pool 2000," **Parks and Recreation,** November: 45-49.

U.S. Architectural and Transportation Barriers Compliance Board (1994). **Recommendations for Accessibility Guidelines: Recreational Facilities and Outdoor Developed Areas.** Washington, D.C.: U.S. Government Printing Office.

Waterpark (1993). "Developer's Reference. Lenexa," KS: **Splash Magazine**

White, Sue, W. and Larry M. Landis (1992) "Is Your Aquatic Facility People-Friendly?" **Parks and Recreation,** July: 60.

Wood, A.J.(1990) "Golf and Government: A Partner That Works," **Parks and Recreation,** May:48-51 (V 15:5)

CHAPTER 7

MANAGEMENT AND NATURAL RESOURCES

Learning Objectives

After studying this chapter, you should be able to do the following:

1. Understand the importance of managing natural resources.
2. Define the concept of preservation.
3. Define the concept of multiple-use.
4. List the principles that guide ecosystem management.
5. Understand collaborative resource management.
6. Describe techniques for managing visitor impact.

The country's natural resources, including the rich open stretches of land with mountains, deserts and prairies, lakes and wetlands, rivers and streams, offer a vast playground for the recreation enthusiast. A number of federal, state, and local agencies protect these natural resources and provide recreational opportunities where people and wildlife compete for space. Private rural lands are also open for recreation, and more than 10,000 miles of rivers have been designated for inclusion in the National Wild and Scenic Rivers System (Cordell *et. al.* 1999:86). Other water based recreation abounds. Many of these lands and water systems are jointly managed. Non-profits are becoming increasingly involved in natural resource partnerships as managers of land and water systems seek out creative solutions for funding (Sansom 2000:110) that will help them keep pace with the public demand for outdoor programs and resource protection.

Because more and more park, recreation, and leisure service delivery system managers are becoming directly or indirectly involved with resource management and since all such managers are called upon to be stewards of nature, natural resource management is defined in this chapter. Additionally, the two basic management principles of preservation and multiple-use are presented along with a brief familiarization of the federal agencies that practice these principles. The history, purpose, objectives and laws that steer these federal agencies are explored, as are guiding concepts such as biodiversity, conservation, threatened and endangered species, and ecosystems. Rapport and unity are discussed along with controversies that affect participation in natural resource management.

All managers will strive to achieve balance between preservation, alternate uses, and enjoyment; use their knowledge to consider the environmental impact of facility development; make recommendations to support environmental decisions that bring about a better future for all species; teach others to tread lightly on the land and encourage them to pursue recreational activities that do not place an undue burden on the natural environment; help find appropriate locations for all activities including those that have a more detrimental environmental impact; and protect popular parks and recreation sites by encouraging use during off-peak seasons.

A DEFINITION

The National Recreation and Park Association (NRPA) defines *natural resource management* as "the art of making land and water produce adequate yields of products and services for social and economic use (NRPA:1)." Because a diverse range of employment opportunities deal directly and indirectly with the natural resources and park management industry, we address this subject. These positions include but are not limited to adventure travel coordinators, campground directors, environment interpreters, fish and game wardens, interpretive specialists, museum directors, natural resource planners, outdoor recreation managers, park maintenance directors, park managers, range managers, recreation planners, soil conservationists, watershed managers, and wildlife managers. Many park, recreation, and leisure service delivery system managers who are directly involved in natural resource management are employees of national, state, county, or municipal parks. On-the-other-hand, private and corporate landowners, including owners of coal and timberland, are developing a heightened interest in environmental protection and land management due to increased public interest.

In The Field...

Conservation

Gifford Pinchot, known as the Father of the National Forest, said "*Conservation* is the foresighted utilization, preservation, and/or renewal of forests, waters, lands, and minerals, for the greatest good of the greatest number for the longest time." This 19th century description is still used today.

Increasingly private lands are opening to the public for recreation, thereby, improving public relations and creating new job opportunities. Corporate landowners in eight West Virginia counties are offering hundreds of thousands of acres of land, for example, for the development of a new multiple-use trail system that will be professionally managed for public use (Hatfield-McCoy Recreation Development Coalition, Inc. 1998:1,12). Likewise, the Environmental Protection Agency is developing recreational sites on lands that are being reclaimed. Conservation efforts play a key role as managers plan the most appropriate use for these and other specified natural areas.

MANAGEMENT POLICY

Natural resources possess inherent value, but they are also assigned value by groups of people. In other words, the same resource may share different values to different people. Sometimes these values are complimentary, but at other times, they create tensions and win/loss situations. A forest, for instance, can be revered by an environmentalist and a hiker for different reasons, yet, their coexistence can be complimentary. The forest could also be prized for its economic benefits such as lumber. This use, however, can spark opposition from the environmentalist and the hiker who find their resource under threat. If the forest is over-logged for lumber then the environmentalist and hiker will eventually lose their resource. So, too, will the group who uses the lumber for profit if proper resource management techniques are not employed. On the other hand, if no lumber can be cut or if restrictions are too severe then the lumber industry is harmed along with the people it serves. Society, which is in part composed of environmentalists, hikers, and lumber company employees, ultimately decides the way the forest will be used through public law. In the United States, different forms of natural resource management have developed.

By the late nineteenth century, timber and minerals were being stripped from the nation's land. Rivers were diverted and dammed, and the landscape left behind was burned, scarred, and eroded. Americans with forsight called upon Congress and the President to act and to limit the abuse. In response, the first national park was established in 1872, the first national monuments in 1906, and the National Park System in 1916. In 1891 major forests were set aside as preserves, and in 1905 the U.S. Forest Service was created to manage 85 million acres of forest preserves. Most of the remaining public land, referred to as the public domain, was managed by the predecessor to today's Bureau of Land Management. Some other sections of the public domain later became national wildlife refuges.

Largely due to these Congressional acts, two management policies emerged that govern the management of the natural areas used for recreation: the principle of preservation and the principle of multiple-use. Under both principles, managers examine the consequences of certain actions, formulate necessary trade-offs, and project probable future impact (Becker 1993:93). The discussion of each of these management principles is accompanied by a brief background on the federal land management agencies that follow the particular principle. They serve as models for various state and local land management practices.

Preservation Policy: The *preservation policy* is a single-use or restricted use concept which is generally followed in most of America's federal parks and to some extent in state and local parks. Resources, under this concept, are not available for exploitation. Only three percent of the world's land area is now devoted to the preservation of nature. While some countries have set aside as much as 38 percent of their territory, a few have set no land aside. By the early 1990's, the United States had set aside approximately 8% of its land under this policy (National Park Service 1993). These parks and reserves are vital but by themselves are not likely to be decisive in the quest to sustain natural resources and biological diversity. If this quest is to succeed, much of the preservation of biological diversity must come about on lands used for many purposes.

NATIONAL PARK SERVICE

The National Park Service (NPS) is designed to manage the natural resources of the national park system according to the single-use policy in order to maintain, rehabilitate, and perpetuate their inherent integrity. The Service's natural resource policies are aimed at providing the American people with the opportunity to enjoy and benefit from natural environments that are evolving naturally with minimal influence from human actions. In a global context, the National Park Service is seen as a model of preservation and conservation management - one that offers valuable lessons to a world that is increasingly concerned with environmental degradation, threats to wilderness, and rapid cultural and historical change. To perform capably under these kinds of pressures, however, the Service itself must be innovative, well-managed, and guided by wise public policies. This is especially true as an ever-growing population impacts park units, often bringing traces of economic and social activities that are inimical to the purposes that the parks are designed to foster. An examination of the development of the preservation policy as established through this agency follows.

National Parks: When Yellowstone, the world's first national park, was created in 1872, Congress set aside more than 2 million acres as "a public park or pleasuring-ground for the benefit and enjoyment of the people." The legislation assigned the new park to the control of the Secretary of the Interior, who would be responsible for issuing regulations to provide for the "preservation, from injury or spoilation, of all timber, mineral deposits, natural curiosities, or wonders within said park, and their retention in their natural condition (16 USC 21-22)." Other park management functions were to include the development of visitor accommodations, the construction of roads and bridle paths, the removal of trespassers from the park, and protection "against the wanton destruction of fish and game (16 USC 21-22)." This idea of a national park was an American invention of historic consequences, marking the beginning of a worldwide movement that influenced a management style (Ibrahim and Cordes 1993:133; National Park Service 1997:6-7).

In The Field...

Biological Diversity and Preservation

Land and recreation managers have an important role to play in maintaining biological diversity through coordinated planning. In California, for example, a Memorandum of Understanding was signed to conserve the state's biological resources while maintaining the state's social and economic viability. As a result, major public agencies and private groups coordinate resource management efforts and environmental protection activities to emphasize regional solutions to regional issues that will help to conserve the full range of biological diversity within each planning area.

When scientists speak of *biological diversity*, they simply mean variety of life: variety of species and their genetic variation and variety of communities of plants and animals. For billions of years an abundance of life forms have enriched the earth. As these different forms of life evolved, others died out and became extinct. Sometimes cataclysmic events, like abrupt climate changes, caused mass extinctions and new species evolved. Managers of natural resources are witnessing another extinction of unprecedented proportions. People are rapidly altering and destroying environments that have fostered a diversity of organisms.

The current rate of extinction is about a thousand times higher than it was before humans appeared on earth. Some scientists estimate that this rate may multiply by ten over the next one hundred years, largely because of modern human activity. In fact, since the pilgrims arrived at Plymouth Rock in 1620, biologists believe that more than 500 species, subspecies, and varieties of our nation's plants and animals have become extinct.

Source: Bureau of Land Management. *Rare Plants and Natural Plant Communities: A Strategy for the Future.* GPO 1992—018-6850, p. 9-10; National Park Service *Biological Diversity* GPO 1993-342-398/600138; U.S. Fish and Wildlife Service *Why Save Endangered Species* Arlington, VA: Division of Endangered Species, April 2000.

In The Field...

Canada's National Parks

Canada's national parks and park reserves protect some of the most precious natural resources in Canada. The stated goal of the park system is:

To protect for all time representative natural areas of Canadian significance in a system of National Parks, and to encourage public understanding, appreciation, and enjoyment of this natural heritage so as to leave it unimpaired for future generations (Stephenson 1991).

In the Canadian system, preservation was not strictly adhered to, however, for decades the Canadian national park system allowed hunting, mining, and logging. Though commercial development still remains a major feature of a number of the parks today, a shift gradually took place to balance the protection of natural resources from commercial exploitation for their own inherent value.

Today the primary rationale for establishing parks is to set aside forever at least one significant segment of each of the country's specific types of natural resources. Grasslands National Park in Saskatchewan is just one example. Created in 1981, it preserves Canada's true short-grass prairie.

National Monuments: At the same time that interest was growing in preserving the great scenic wonders of the West, efforts were underway to protect and preserve the sites and structures associated with early native American culture. In 1906 the Antiquities Act authorized the President "to declare by public proclamation (as national monuments) historic landmarks, historic and prehistoric structures, and other objects of historic or scientific interest (16 USC 431-33)." These set-asides have become known as national monuments, and have set a standard for other historic preservation societies to follow.

The National Park System: In 1916, Congress created the National Park Service in the Department of the Interior to:

> promote and regulate the use of the Federal areas known as national parks, monuments, and reservations...by such means and measures as conform to the fundamental purpose of said parks, monuments, and reservations, which purpose is to conserve the scenery and the natural and historic objects and the wildlife therein and to provide for the enjoyment of the same in such manner and by such means as will leave them unimpaired for the enjoyment of future generations (NPS Organic Act, 16 USC 1).

This language lies at the heart of national park system management philosophy and single-use policy. To achieve this congressional mandate, managers are required to apply policies in a consistent and professional manner. With more than 360 park areas to manage, this is not a task. The individual parks contain various tangible natural and cultural features such as animals, plants, waters, geologic features, archeological sites, and historic buildings and monuments that must be preserved. They also have intangible features such as natural quiet, solitude, space, scenery, a sense of history, sounds of nature, and clear night skies that have received congressional recognition, and are important components of peoples' enjoyment of parks. In the NPS *Management Policies,* the terms *resources* and *values* mean the full spectrum of tangible and intangible attributes for which parks have been established and are managed. These policies recognize that all parks are complex mixtures of values and resources, each with its own unique qualities and purposes, and each requiring specific treatment in the development and implementation of management strategies and operational plans.

Future Plans: To address critical issues, the Service initiated an intensive review of its responsibilities and prospects at a special symposium entitled *Our National Parks: Challenges and Strategies for the 21st Century*. At the symposium, the NPS reaffirmed its fundamental elements, and created a vision composed of six strategic objectives that influence all park, recreation, and leisure service delivery system managers to approach preservation and the single-use policy. They are listed in Table 7-1.

Six critical issues face the National Park Service as it enters the 21st century: (1) their ability to protect resources from external threats and to positively influence compatible land uses and resource management within regional ecosystems and the historic context of parks; (2) the protection, restoration, and maintenance of park resources; (3) strengthening the parks' abilities to identify and evaluate their resources; (4) the stature and professionalism of research and resource management and their integration into park management; (5) public support for resource stewardship programs; and (6) the processes governing the addition of new areas and the expansion of additional areas to the national park system (National Park Service 1991:123-124).

Multi-Use Policy: The primary challenge of the *multiple-use* policy is to balance economic use with conservation. This is accomplished by providing opportunity for the development of needed resources while protecting other resource values from inadvertent damage or destruction.

TABLE 7-1
___

Six Strategic NPS Objectives
___

1. *Resource Stewardship and Protection.* The primary responsibility of the National Park Service must be the protection of park resources.

2. *Access and Enjoyment.* Each park unit should be managed to provide the nation's diverse public with access to, and recreational and educational enjoyment of the lessons contained in that unit, while maintaining unimpaired those unique attributes that are its contribution to the national park system.

3. *Education and Interpretation.* It should be the responsibility of the National Park Service to interpret and convey each park unit's and the park system's contributions to the nation's values, character, and experience.

4. *Proactive Leadership.* The National Park Service must be a leader in local, national, and international park affairs, actively pursuing the mission of the national park system and assisting others in managing their park resources and values.

5. *Science and Research.* The National Park Service must engage in a sustained and integrated program of natural, cultural, and social science resource management and research aimed at acquiring and using the information needed to manage and protect park resources.

6. *Professional.* The National Park Service must create and maintain a highly professional organization and work force.

Source: National Park Service *The Vail Agenda* (Washington, D.C.: U.S. Government Printing Office, 1991), pp. 3, 123-124.

In the Field...

Preservation of Threatened and Endangered Species

In 1973 the Endangered Species Act was designed in an effort to preserve and restore all federally listed endangered and threatened species to the point where they are again viable, self-sustaining members of their ecological communities. By granting these species legal protection and by requiring a recovery plan for each listed species, managers may select captive propagation and reestablishment as well as protection and management of habitat as methods of recovery. Conservation actions have successfully protected 99 percent (U.S. Fish and Wildlife 2000) of the species listed as endangered or threatened from becoming extinct, but management of endangered species often requires cooperative ventures.

In Florida, for example, the National Park Service, the U.S. Fish and Wildlife Service (which leads the Federal effort to protect and restore animals and plants that are in danger of extinction), and the Florida Game and Fresh Water Fish Commission work together cooperatively to protect Florida panthers living in Everglades National Park, Big Cypress National Preserve, and state and private lands. Likewise, the USDA Forest Service, other federal and state agencies, and non-profit organizations are currently engaged in several thousand cooperative wildlife habitat enhancement projects. In 1998, the Forest Service restored over 167,000 (Williams 2000:151) acres of terrestrial habitat.

Source: National Park Service *Endangered Species in the National Parks.* (Washington, DC: National Park Foundation); U.S. Fish and Wildlife Service *Why Save Endangered Species* (Arlington, VA: Division of Endangered Species, April 2000); Williams, Gerald *The USDA Forest Service.* (Washington, D.C.: USDA Forest Service, July 2000), pp. 137,151.

Often these multiple uses are compatible with or even dependent upon one another. For example, roads built for logging provide access to the forest for recreation, including hiking, camping, cross-country skiing, and hunting. The same watersheds that provide cities and towns with drinking water are also used for fishing, rafting, and boating. Harvested areas provide forage for various forms of wildlife, as well as space for cross-country skiing, snowmobiling, and other types of recreation. Private lands like those which are managed primarily for timber offer a variety of recreational uses to the public, particularly fishing and hunting. They also allow access for fish and wildlife study and watershed management. Many landowners conduct programs to improve fish and wildlife habitat on their lands.

Through a process that balances alternative uses and involves the public at all steps, multiple-use management permits agencies, such as the USDA Forest Service and the Bureau of Land Management, allow for the many different uses of public lands while ensuring that their various resources will remain available for the future. To better understand multiple-use management, the policies and the development of the multiple-use concept within these two agencies follows.

THE UNITED STATES FOREST SERVICE

The USDA Forest Service: A Multiple-use Agency: The National Forest System was born over 100 years ago with the passage of the *Creative Act* or Forest Service Act of 1891 (16 USC 471) and the designation of the first Forest Reserves by President Benjamin Harrison. At the time of passage, many Americans believed their country was headed for a shortage of both timber and clean water if some land were not protected from exploitation. As a result, Yellowstone Park Timberland Reserve was established (now part of the Shoshone and Teton National Forests). Other Americans, convinced that timber and water were unlimited, were opposed to bringing large tracts of land under federal management. By 1911, the Weeks Act was passed and the Federal Government was permitted to buy back lands in the East to form national forests that were designed primarily to protect the watersheds of navigable rivers and streams (Ibrahim and Cordes 1993:118-119; Williams 2000:5, 26, 38).

Protection: The first challenge to national forest and national grassland managers was the protection of forests and grasslands from fire. Today the Forest Service is the largest wildland fire management agency in the Nation. Working with federal, state, and local agencies, the Forest Service plays a leading role in training, development, mobilization, and support of wildland fire managers and firefighting personnel throughout the United States and in several large foreign countries.

Restoring Watershed and Grazing Lands: With the transfer of the national forests to the Department of Agriculture's newly formed Forest Service in 1905 (16 USC 472, 524, 554), attention was also given to mapping these lands, managing grazing use to protect watersheds, and developing a transportation system. Lands that had been abused by timbering, cropping, and grazing and then abandoned were purchased under authority granted by the Weeks Act and restored to productivity. In cooperation with the States, the reintroduction of deer, elk, and turkey in areas where they had not been seen for generations and the restoration of overgrazed mountain watersheds were early successes.

Multiple Use Sustained Yield Act: In 1960, Congress enacted the first of the environmental protection laws. The Multiple Use Sustained Yield Act (16 USC 528-531) which asserted that "national forests are established and shall be administered for outdoor recreation, range, timber, watershed, and wildlife and fish purposes." That Act defined multiple-use as "the management of all the various renewable surface resources of the national forests so that they are utilized in the combination that will best meet the needs of the American people (16 U.S.C. 528-531)." In applying the principles of multiple-use management to actual activities, the Forest Service relies on the joint professional judgment of foresters, range conservationists, wildlife and fisheries biologists, and sociologists working in concert and responding to the input of public interest groups and individuals. After the Act was signed, the Forest Service was active in managing the national forests where all resources were treated equally (Williams 2000:102,105-106).

Balancing Resources: The primary focus of the multiple-use role is to balance the resources that are provided from forests and rangelands through Forest Service programs. Because the resource base is biologically capable of producing a broad array of resources, the Forest Service has a significant opportunity to manage and reduce conflict among resource users and to meet competing resource demands. Resource investments can further enhance productivity of the resource, allowing higher levels of multiple-use.

Management: The premise underlying the agency's role is that typical areas of forest or rangeland can compatibly produce multiple resources and that the productivity of these resources can be enhanced by careful management. Finding the most compatible blend of resource uses is central to the Forest Service's management philosophy. Sometimes resource uses are incompatible in the same areas, as in the case of timber, harvesting, and providing habitat for threatened or endangered species like the Spotted Owl. Although multiple-use management may not overcome conflicts between mutually exclusive resource uses, it can be used to lessen incompatibilities by promoting compatibility rather than competition. When possible, increased resource investments and new scientific management information are used and applied to ease tensions.

Long-term strategic planning is done under the authority of the Forest and Rangeland Renewable Resources Planning Act (RPA) of 1974 (16 USC 1600-1614) which began in 1976 (Williams 2000:122). This Act directs the Forest Service to develop two documents: a comprehensive assessment every 10 years and a recommended Forest Service programs response to the assessment every five years.

The 1990 RPA long-term strategic plan called for an ecological approach to the implementation of multiple-use management as the most important management policy for natural resource management of the national forests and grasslands. By embracing ecosystem management (see Table 7-2) and ensuring environmentally acceptable commodity production as a working philosophy, the Forest Service changed its management style from short-term to long-term efforts that would ensure a healthy productive environment for years to come. Other major objectives included improved scientific knowledge about natural resources; responding to global resource issues; and recreation, wildlife, and fisheries resource enhancement (Forest Service 1994:1;Williams 2000:142).

Future Management: Increasing demands will be placed on the Forest Service as the public's expectations and visitations continue to grow. How well these resources will be managed will require continual adjustment to the population's needs, values, and understanding. This will require the Forest Service to embark on a national marketing strategy to create a supportive and knowledgeable constituency into the 21st century. To accommodate increasing demands on its outdoor resources, the Forest Service will develop a wide range of management tools that will be used to improve permit systems, increase public/private sector investments, enhance site development, advance the efficient use of fee systems, and increase partnerships and volunteerism (Cordell *et. al.*1999:49).

TABLE 7-2

Ten Elements of Ecosystem Management

By the late 1980's, many researchers and public land managers were convinced that an ecosystem approach to manage public lands was the only logical way to proceed in the future. Today, it is the driving force behind current policy of the Forest Service and Bureau of Land Management, and other Interior agencies. The following 10 elements contain what ecosystems management means for public and private land management:

1. Multiple Analysis Levels - Use different levels of analysis, from the site specific location to the broad watershed perspective or even larger.

2. Ecological Boundaries - Define ecosystems by analyzing and managing them across political and administrative boundaries.

3. Ecological Integrity - Protect the total natural diversity, ecological patterns, and processes. Keep all the pieces.

4. Data Collection and Data Management - Require more research, better data collection methods, and up-to-date information.

5. Monitoring - Track results of management actions. Learn from mistakes. Take pride in successes.

6. Adaptive Management - Use adaptive management, a process of taking risks, trying new methods and processes, experimentation, and most of all remaining flexible to changing conditions or results. Encourage better public participation and involvement in planning, decision-making, implementation, and monitoring.

7. Interagency Cooperation - Work with agencies at the federal, state, and local levels, as well as the private sector, to integrate and cooperate over large land areas to benefit the ecosystems.

8. Organizational Change - Change how the various agencies work internally and with partners to encourage cooperation and understanding, as well as advance training for on-the-ground employees. Expand partnerships and cooperation with other agencies and the public.

9. Humans Are Part of Ecosystems - People are a fundamental part of ecosystems, both affecting them and affected by them. Involve people at all stages in the analysis and decisionmaking phases.

10. Human Values - The human attitudes, beliefs, and values that people hold are significant in determining the future of ecosystems as well as the global environment. Seek balance and harmony between people and the land with equity across regions and through generations by maintaining options for the future.

Source: Williams, Gerald The USDA Forest Service. (Washington, D.C.: USDA Forest Service, July 2000), pp . 144-145.

OTHER SERVICES

The Bureau of Land Management

A Multiple-use Agency: Approximately 268 million acres, more than any other federal agency, are managed by the Bureau of Land Management (BLM) (Cordell *et. al.* 1999:49). Most of this acreage is located in the Western United States, including Alaska, although small parcels are scattered across the Eastern United States. These lands offer endless recreational opportunities and settings that include desert, mountain ranges, alpine tundra, evergreen forests, expanses of sage brush, and red rock canyons that were once called "the land nobody wanted."

Creation: In 1812 Congress established the General Land Office (GLO) to administer the public lands with the primary purpose of passing public lands to private ownership. In the west, a controversy developed over the appropriate size of a homestead, but initially no increases in the standard 160 acre plot occurred. As a result, many of the less fertile lands in the west could not support a home-stead. Instead, they were used by nearby homesteaders to graze cattle. In part, as a result of this condition and practice, a patchwork of western lands remained in the public trust. Left primarily to private management, no systematic land management program was underway. Finally, the passage of the Taylor Grazing Act in 1934 and the establishment of the United States Grazing Service provided for active range management on the public lands, but this was seen as interim management pending final disposal into non-Federal ownership. In 1946, the Grazing Service was merged with the GLO to create the Bureau of Land Management within the Department of the Interior. The BLM became responsible for managing all the resources on the nation's remaining public lands that were not previously assigned to other agencies. Straddled with more than 2,000 unrelated and often conflicting laws pertaining to the public lands, the BLM had no unified legislative authority to manage these lands (Muhn and Stuart 1988:23-58).

Multiple-use: When Congress enacted the Federal Land Policy and Management Act of 1976 (FLPMA), it finally gave the BLM a legislative mandate and made the BLM a true multiple-use agency. The law recognized public land as a national asset that could provide goods, services, and vast natural resources for millions of Americans. Today the BLM manages recreational areas, wildlife habitat, wilderness, rangelands, wetlands, forests, mineral, land resources, archaeological and historic sites, fishable streams, oil resources, natural gas reserves, coal, geothermal energy, and wild horse and burros. To manage these resources the BLM turned from traditional multiple-use management toward the end of the 20th century to ecosystem management (see Table 7-3), finding that traditional management decisions were sometimes made on the basis of maximizing short-term production of the land. This often led to degraded streams and streamside areas; unhealthy rangelands; degraded plant, animal, and fish habitats; and unhealthy forests. Additionally human population growth, increased use, fire exclusion, flood control, and other factors were contributing to the degradation of the public lands, thereby, causing significant declines in the number and range of many plants and animals. If this decline was to continue it was realized that further generations of Americans would not have been able to benefit from their public lands.

In the Field...

Ecosystems and Ecosystem Management

An *ecosystem* is a community of plants and animals (including humans) that function together in their environment. Small ecosystems fit into larger ecosystems. Very large ecosystems are sometimes called *ecoregions*. When healthy, ecosystems provide clean, clear water; furnish habitat for fish, wildlife, and plants; offer way stations for migratory birds; help purify the air and prevent soil erosion; supply rich, fertile, and productive soils; turn over higher water tables; afford greener streamside area; allow for more songbirds; clean streambanks; create buffers for flooding; present better fishing and hunting; result in a more resilient mix of native plants; effect increased productivity; produce healthier livestock; and encourage disease-free forests. Healthy ecosystems also help to ensure that future generations will have the opportunity to draw social, aesthetic, and spiritual benefits from the land. Since ecosystems do not stop at traditional boundary lines, active partnerships between federal agencies and private industry is extremely important.

Ecosystem management (EM) is an environmentally sensitive, socially responsible, and scientifically sound way to manage the nation's multiple-use lands so that the environment will be healthy, diverse, and productive year after year. EM also means trying to restore damaged resources to a healthy condition. In recent years, policymakers have become more aware of the importance of preserving the natural diversity in our physical environments. The following principles guide ecosystem management:

* Learning to live within nature's limits.

* Knowing the condition of the land.

* Using science to make informed decisions.

* Minimizing impacts to the land and repairing damage.

* Thinking in terms of the long-range benefits to society rather than short-term gains.

* Working with the public to develop common goals to maintain healthy lands.

* Using teams with a variety of skills to manage the land.

* Being flexible.

* Working with local communities to find solutions and resolve differences.

Source: Cordell, H. Ken *et. al. Outdoor Recreation in American Life: A National Assessment of Demand and Supply Trends* (Champaign, IL: Sagamore Publishing, 1999); Bureau of Land Management *Ecosystem Management in the BLM.* (GPO, 1994 - 573-183/84016), p. 2; Haynes, Richard W. "Frameworks for Ecosystem Management," *Natural Resource News* Winter 1994 Vol 4 No 1 (La Grande, OR: Pacific Northwest Region, Forest Service), pp. 1-2.

TABLE 7-3

Strategic Goals of the Bureau of Land Management

In its *Blueprint for the Future*, the BLM plans to restore and maintain healthy ecosystems by:

* improving existing inventory and monitoring procedures.

* conducting ecological and socioeconomic assessments.

* enhancing their ability to manage, exchange, and use automated spatial and land record data.

* developing ecological and social indicators that measure the health of the land and the sustainability of local communities.

* revising planning procedures to reflect ecosystem management principles.

* providing inventory of significant natural, cultural, historical, and recreation resource values on the public lands and initiating protective measures where appropriate.

* identifying degraded ecosystems that should be restoration priorities.

* documenting and sharing successes in implementing ecosystem based management approaches.

Source: Bureau of Land Management *Blueprint for the Future.* (GPO: 1995 0-162-301, 1995), p. 7; Forest Service *Ecosystem Management.* (Washington, D.C.: GPO R6 EM TP 045, 1993).

Future Management: The BLM's new focus entails managing on a broader "big picture" scale which will require working more closely with private and state land-owners, and measuring progress based on the health of the land. For example, the BLM and the Forest Service began working together to forge a comprehensive ecosystem approach for restoring and managing aquatic habitat and associated watersheds on Federal lands in the West. The effort called PACFISH was designed to benefit Pacific salmon, steelhead, and sea-run cutthroat trout, whose populations have declined dramatically in recent years. In fact, since this approach addresses an entire watershed, it will benefit many other species as well. Additionally, in *Recreation 2000: A Strategic Plan* and *Recreation 2000 Update*, recreation was recognized as a major component of the multiple-use mandate. The goal, to provide quality adventure outdoor recreation opportunities for all people, including hiking, rock climbing, canoeing, fishing, hunting, horseback riding, cross country skiing, mountain biking, and four-wheel driving while maintaining a healthy ecosystem, will call for continued development of partnerships, grants, and alternative funding (Cordell *et. al.* 1999:54).

Different Management Styles: While the Forest Service and the Bureau of Land Management represent the multiple-use policy with many similarities, there are differences between the agencies which have affected the management of resources through the years. The National Forests, which generally came to the Forest Service unencumbered, were reserved from the public domain prior to occupancy. The BLM, for diverse reasons, has always been more responsive to its local, commodity oriented constituents. In part this is because it did not, until recently, have authority to meet other demands. As such, the BLM manages land which had a long history of private use prior to the belated assertion of federal authority in the 1930s.

Further, the Taylor Grazing Act dedicated the lands to a single, specific use - grazing, rather than to multiple-use. Note the difference - the National Forests are not called *National Timber Lands*. In the courts, it was not until the 1960s that grazing permits were consistently recognized as a privilege that the BLM could modify, rather than a right of the ranchers. The result of this distinction in the origin of the lands is that the Forest Service has been able to manage "its" lands and resources, while the BLM has been obliged to conserve their lands by trying to regulate the private ranching practices of the permittees. That necessity and provisions specifically added to the Taylor Grazing Act resulted in a significantly different labor force between the two. While the Forest Service was drawing employees from newly developed forestry schools, BLM was required to hire ranchers from the state in which they would be working. This orientation toward local operators was intensified in the early 1950s when Congress cut the Bureau's budget and most BLM employees either lost their jobs or were paid by the local Grazing Advisory Boards (Fairfax 1988:226). When the BLM began hiring again in the 1960's, graduates from the east and west were hired which signaled a departure from its regional orientation that had been attached to the agency.

By structure, the BLM is basically a western operation organized on a state-by-state basis which maximizes the influence of the state congressional delegation in BLM matters; whereas, the Forest Service's early and successful efforts to obtain sufficient eastern land led to its national orientation and minimization of western domination. Its mid-level management through its regional organization, put it out of direct reach of the states' congressional delegation. Although the FLPMA of 1976 did not specifically repeal the Taylor Grazing Act, it finally gave the Bureau a firm and continuing basis for exerting comprehensive management authority and to impose diverse multiple-use management programs which it had been fabricating for nearly two decades. Because in the 1980s, it had four times the land to manage but only one seventh the personnel and one third the budget, the BLM pulled far ahead in its ability to involve private enterprise in public resource management and partnership endeavors (Fairfax 1988:226). Its move, however, to ecosystem management is sorely met by some ranchers whose immediate single-use needs clash with monitored procedures.

COLLABORATION AND SHARING

While agency missions vary, some distinctions between the agencies have narrowed. For example, public demand for more hotels, lodges, restaurants, and other services in remote areas of the national parks, puts preservation into a back seat at times. At the same time, public pleas for preservation and environmental protection within the nation's multiple-use agencies has caused these agencies to look to new management styles which are more harmonious with nature. In all cases, the nation's public agencies have entered new arenas which cater more to recreational interests. Tourists, backpackers, snowmobilers, rock climbers, boaters, air-tour operators, hunters, and many other groups are asserting their rights to use all public lands, crying foul at any suggestion that their pursuits need to be regulated or prohibited. Hunting, generally not permitted in national parks, is now allowed in one national park, along several national riverways, seashores, trails, and on all national preserves (Craig 1991:43). In the meantime, multiple-use agencies strive to create boundaries that are more congenial with preservation efforts. Agencies have successfully established various approaches to collaborative resource management and partnerships with a variety of interest groups (Attarian 1999:75). They cooperate when managing special resources like wilderness, national rivers, and national trails. And they share ideas and research to solve problems.

Collaborative Efforts and Partnerships: In order to manage for sustainable ecosystems, managers must plan over the long-term for ecosystem integrity and for the benefit of multiple generations of people. Efforts to develop greater clarity and specificity about the values that society assigns to ecosystems are being undertaken by various agencies and interests groups through collaborative efforts. A few examples follow:

Forest Service: The Forest Service established the *Every Species Counts* program to bring together the resources and commitment of its agency with other federal and state agencies, private organizations, and individuals to ensure that the habitats of threatened, endangered, and sensitive species on national forest lands are properly managed to enhance species recovery and conservation, such as the rehabilitation of the Puerto Rican parrot in the Caribbean National Forest.

National Oceanic and Atmospheric Administration: Through its marine sanctuary program, the National Oceanic and Atmospheric Administration (NOAA) has partnered with others, including Native American Indian tribes - the Makah, Quinault, Hoh, and Quileute - to protect and preserve the great resources that the ocean holds. In this partnership, the Olympic Coast National Marine Sanctuary is working to preserve these coastal tribes' traditional rights to resources in a manner compatible with resource protection.

Tennessee Valley Authority: The Tennessee Valley Authority (TVA) uses species diversity information to target its efforts to protect and improve water quality in the river system. Many of these efforts are aimed at helping communities manage sources of pollution which are a major threat to biological diversity.

In the Field...

Collaboration Management in Action

In Colorado, a climbing advisory group, the Action Committee for Eldorado, was established to assist park managers at Eldorado Canyon State Park with fixed hardware management, Leave No Trace climbing education, fund raising for education and natural resource protection, and development of management strategies for addressing climbing-related impacts. Since 1993 they have raised more than $70,000 for trail maintenance, construction, and resource restoration projects.

Source: Aram Attarian. "A Collaboration in Resource Management: The Stone Mountain Project." Parks & Recreation Vol 34, No 7 (Ashburn, VA: NRPA, July 1999), p. 75.

Coordinating Efforts

The wilderness movement originated in the late 1800's, after much of what had recently been wilderness in eastern North America had been cut, mined, cleared, plowed, or roaded. Within the Forest Service, the preservation of roadless areas helped to establish the first wilderness areas on the Gila National Forest in New Mexico and Superior National Forest in Minnesota in 1924 and 1926. Forest Service researcher and wilderness advocate, Bob Marshall, developed the first set of regulations for creating wilderness areas, and by the early 1960's, the Forest Service had established 80 wilderness areas. Marshall's regulations evolved into the basis for the Wilderness Act of 1964, which gave legal protection to wilderness areas for the first time (Forest Service 1998:54).

Upon passage, all National Forest wilderness areas became part of the National Wilderness Preservation System, and the Forest Service was directed to study all of its remaining "primitive" areas to determine which of these should be preserved as wilderness areas. The National Park Service and the Fish and Wildlife Service were to do the same. With the 1976 passage of the Federal Land Policy and Management Act (FLPMA), the BLM was given its wilderness mandate. Figure 7-1 shows the distribution of wilderness lands among the four federal land management agencies.

Managing the Wilderness Preservation System: To protect wilderness lands for future generations, wilderness land managers from preservation and multi-use agencies are guided by the definition of Wilderness as articulated in Sec.2(c) of the Wilderness Act (Cordell *et. al.* 1999:388):

> ...area where the earth and its community of life are untrammeled by man, where man himself is a visitor who does not remain; land retaining it primeval character and influence, without permanent improvement or human habitation, which is protected and managed so as to preserve its natural conditions; and which generally appears to be primarily affected by the forces of nature, with the imprint of man's work substantially unnoticeable.

FIGURE 7-1

Designated Wilderness on Federal Lands

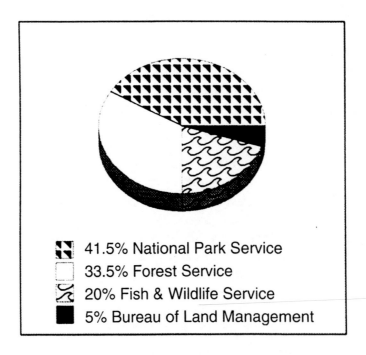

41.5% National Park Service
33.5% Forest Service
20% Fish & Wildlife Service
5% Bureau of Land Management

Source: USDA Forest Service *Charting our Future...A Nation's Natural Resource Legacy* FS-630 (Washington D.C.: United States Department of Agriculture Forest Service, October 1998), p 54.

Many assumed that the designations would assure preservation. In fact, the idea of managing naturalness and solitude was seen as a paradox. As pressures of wilderness use and recreation's impact increased, it became paramount that wilderness land needed to be managed or it would be lost. When the first textbook on Wilderness Management came out, the authors (Hendee, Stankey, and Lucas 1978:6) explained that wilderness management was not the control of nature, but the management of "human use and influence so that natural processes are not altered (Hendee, Stankey, and Lucas 1978:7)." They stressed that Federal agencies should develop policies that would not significantly deviate from place to place, but would allow for flexibility in order for managers to respond to their own unique conditions (Hendee, Stankey, and Lucas 1978:15). As recreational pressures continued to increase, managers developed the following general wilderness management guidelines (Departments of Agriculture and Interior 1989):

- Provide public education on wilderness values and methods to minimize user impacts.
- Favor wilderness-dependent activities in management decisions.
- Generally do not allow permanent structures or installations, such as campgrounds, buildings, or radio antennas.
- Manage visitor use to protect the wilderness resource.
- Prohibit the use of motor vehicles, mechanical transport, and motorized equipment except in emergencies, and permanent or temporary roads.
- Exclude timber harvesting.
- Allow fires to burn under preplanned prescribed conditions to include both naturally occurring fires and those ignited by wilderness managers.

Future Management: The greatest challenges facing wilderness preservation will be an increased population that will encroach upon surrounding areas, changing wilderness values, human impact, technology, and a growing pressure for uses that are not compatible with wilderness(Cordell *et. al.* 1999:384; Wilkinson 1999:23-25).

Managers will be challenged to constantly evaluate requests for exceptions to the wilderness definition and to keep the ecological integrity of wilderness in tact through *direct* and *indirect* management techniques (see Carrying Capacity in this chapter). The future of strong wilderness management requires good information from specialized wilderness research. True success stories in wilderness management, such as use regulations, visitor education, and the development of limits, have been based on scientific research. Research done on or in the wilderness will be dependent upon the managing agency, and the managing agency will depend upon research to improve its management decisions.

A Shared Concern- Management Visitor Impact: Because visitor increases in recreational use have the potential to adversely affect the ecological integrity of natural resources, managing their impact has become an increasingly important managerial duty. Managing the impact of visitors involves development of structural solutions, including paving areas and redirecting activity; persuasive education programs, including brochures and interpretive programs that describe low impact use; and alternative appropriate means to achieve a reasonable distribution of use over recreational areas and sites.

Carrying Capacity: One of the most important responsibilities of management is determining the resource's carrying capacity. The concept of *carrying capacity* is a simple one: it is a resource's capacity to sustain recreation without deterioration to the resource. The carrying capacity of a resource depends on several factors such as type of activity, seasonality, habitat, general attractiveness of the areas, and the site in relationship to population distribution. To determine carrying capacity, both the ecological resources and the attitudes of the users are considered along with management's objectives (Ford and Blanchard 1993:57).

The concept of carrying capacity emerged in the 1950s and 1960s when the demand on outdoor recreation resources reached new levels. Today new and more active pursuits place additional stress on land and water. Ultimately, the public must either accept the changes that those activities cause or accept limitations - even prevention. Limiting impact is highly dependent on a sense of stewardship or commitment of those who use the resource including leader-managers of outfitters and those who manage the resource. Other trends also impact management decisions. These include the uneven distribution of visitors during peak time periods and heavier use of areas close to population centers. A study by

Wahburne and Cole (1995) found that two-thirds of the managers in wilderness areas believe that use exceeds capacity. Hendee, Stankey, and Lucas (1978:171) proposed caveats for managers when evaluating carrying capacity:

1. The determination of carrying capacity is ultimately a judgmental decision.
2. Carrying capacity decisions depend on clearly defined objectives.
3. The range of available alternative opportunities must be taken into consideration.
4. Carrying capacity is a probabilistic concept and not an absolute measure.

Carrying capacities, then, are not necessarily permanent, but fluctuate according to the mix of relevant factors. Various approaches must be devised to influence the visitor's impact on the resource.

Direct and Indirect Management Techniques: Two generally accepted principles have been used by wilderness managers to control or deter overuse. *Direct management techniques* ration or limit use through regulatory measures, like issuing a limited number of permits through a mail-in reservation system. Twenty percent of the National Forest campground capacity is managed under special-use permit. *Indirect management techniques* are manipulative techniques used to deter overuse such as entry fees. Which of these techniques is more acceptable is debatable. The first is criticized because it is authoritarian and restrictive of freedoms. The second, is often seen as too light-handed at a time when the environment is endangered (Cole 1995:6-7).

Estimating Use Rates: Over the next 50 years, the Forest Service expects demand to increase from 800 million to 1.2 billion visits to the national forests per year (Forest Service 1998:53). A *recreation visit* is the arrival of any person at a site, area of land, or body of water for recreation purposes. These visits can be measured by either the recreation visitor-hour or the activity-hour. An activity hour measures a specific recreation activity at a site for continuous, intermittent, or simultaneous periods of time aggregating 60 minutes. Another unit of measurement is the *activity day* or *recreation day*. One "day" represents the average number of hours of participation per day in a given activity. When it is not feasible to make an actual count, alternatives include estimates based on observations, the manager's judgment, or sampling.

Future Projections: The way in which recreational users enjoy the outdoors changes. Estimated rates depict current trends, and current trends help managers to project future use of resources. For instance, non-consumptive and wildlife activities are expected to increase 61 percent nationally to 2050, while hunting will decline by 11 percent (Cordell *et. al.*334-335). Technology will continue to influence recreation through the development of new activities. Researchers anticipate the emergence of jet-pack backcountry camping, jet snow skis, night activity with special night-vision binoculars, and personal all-terrain hovercraft. In the meantime, other technological advances such as cellular phones and geographic positioning systems (GPS) are expected to improve safety and communications. This added sense of security also presents complications, including overconfidence, increased risk-taking, and the destruction of peace and quiet. The type of activity will be just as critical as the number of users (Ewert 1999:61). Many activities are likely to place additional burdens on resources, thereby, affecting the carrying capacity and perhaps calling for more direct rather than indirect management techniques. When used properly, management tools are powerful forces for mitigating negative aspects of recreation in natural areas (Ewert 1999:61-63).

SUMMARY

- The National Recreation and Park Association defines the expansive area of *natural resource management* as "the art of making land and water produce adequate yields of products and services for social and economic use."

- In 1916, Congress consolidated the management of various parks by creating the National Park Service (NPS) in the Department of the Interior through the Organic Act. The National Park Service practices preservation and is designed to manage the natural resources in order to maintain, rehabilitate, and perpetuate their inherent integrity.

- In 1905 the U.S. Forest Service was established to manage 85 million acres of forest preserves. This agency practices multiple-use, a policy that balances economic use with conservation by providing opportunity for the development of needed resources while protecting other resource values from inadvertent damage or destruction.

- Approximately one-eighth of the Nation is managed by the Secretary of the Interior through the Bureau of Land Management (BLM) founded in 1946. The Federal Land Policy and Management Act of 1976 (FLPMA) made the BLM a true multiple-use agency.

- Known as the father of conservation, Gifford Pinchot, defined conservation as the foresighted utilization, preservation, and/or renewal of forests, waters, lands, and minerals for the greatest good of the greatest number for the longest time.

- An *ecosystem* is a community of plants and animals (including humans) that function together in their environment. Very large ecosystems are sometimes called *ecoregions*. Ecosystem management means keeping the environment healthy, diverse, and productive so people can benefit year after year.

- Agencies have successfully established various approaches to collaborative resource management and partnerships with a variety of interest groups. They cooperate when managing special resources like wilderness, national rivers, and national trails.

- When a resource encounters heavy use, its capacity to sustain recreation without deterioration to the resource should be determined. The ecological resources, the attitudes of the users, and management's objectives need to be weighed in arriving at the resource's carrying capacity.

LEARNING ACTIVITIES

1. You are attempting to explain the basic difference in National Park Service and Forest Service resource management. What would you say to your friend from Germany about the differences between the two agencies.

2. Research a wildlife refuge in your area.. Describe the refuge, include suggested times to visit, and define its purpose. Consider visitor impact.

3. Is there an ecosystem or ecoregion that is of special interest to you? Tell us about the management of it. Is its integrity protected? Did this occur naturally or did an agency or organization work to keep it in balance? Are efforts underway now to ensure its future?

4. As a future leader in recreation, you will need to stay informed about your local land environment. What trends and issues exist today in the management of natural resources? Your source might be the newspaper, periodicals or an interview with a natural resource manager. Describe the major points of both sides of the issue, or the positive and negative aspect of the trend.

REFERENCES

Adams, J. (1995) **National Resources Defense Council Letter.** New York.

Attarian, A. (1999). "A Collaboration in Resource Management: The Stone Mountain Project," **Parks & Recreation** July 1999 Vol 34, No 7. Ashburn, VA: NRPA.

Becker, R. (1993) "Assessing Impacts in the Real World Outdoor," **Recreation Management** edited by Jubenville, A. and Dwight, B., State College: Venture Publishing, Inc.

Bureau of Land Management (1993) **Managing The Nation's Public Lands.** Washington D.C.: U.S. Government Printing Office

Cole, D. (1995) ";Wilderness Management Principles: Science, Logical Thinking or Personal Opinion," **Trends.** Vol. 32 No. 1. Arlington: U.S. Department of the Interior National Park Service and National Recreation and Park Association.

Cordell, H.K., Bergstrom, J.C., Hartmann, L.A., English, B.K. (1990) "An Analysis of the Outdoor Recreation and Wilderness Situation in the United States: 1989-2040," **Forest Service RM-189 April**, Washington, D.C.: U.S. Government Printing Office.

Craig, B. (1991) "Diamonds and Rust," **National Parks** Vol. 65 No. 5-6, May/June 1991 Washington: National Parks and Conservation Association.

Department of Agriculture and Department of the Interior (1989) "Wilderness Values and History and An Enduring" **Resource of Wilderness GPO 1989 238-913** Washington: Department of Agriculture and Department of the Interior.

Ewert, A. (1999) "Outdoor Recreation and Natural Resource Management: An Uneasy Alliance," **Parks & Recreation.** July 1999 Vol 34, No 7. Ashburn, VA: NRPA.

Fairfax, S.K. (1988) **The Differences Between BLM and the Forest Service Opportunity and Challenge: The Story of BLM.** Washington, D.C.: U.S. Government Printing Office.

Ford, P. and Blanchard, J. (1993) **Leadership and Administration of Outdoor Pursuits.** State College, PA: Venture Publishing, Inc.

Hendee, J., Stankey, G., and Lucas, R. (1978) **Wilderness Management.** Washington D.C.: USDA Forest Service.

Ibrahim, H. and Cordes, K. (1993) **Outdoor Recreation.** Dubuque: Brown and Benchmark.

National Park Service (1993) **Biological Diversity GPO.** 342-398/600138. U.S. Government Printing Office.

National Park Service (1990) **Management Policies GPO.** 773-038/20013. U.S. Government Printing Office.

National Park Service (1997) **The National Parks: Index GPO: 1997- 417-646/ 40003.** U.S. Government Printing Office.

National Park Service (1991) **The Vail Agenda.** Washington D.C.: U.S. Government Printing Office.

National Recreation and Park Association **National Resource and Park Management.** Arlington: National Recreation and Park Association.

Stephenson, M. (1991) **Canada's National Parks.** Scarborough, Ontario: Prentice-Hall.

U.S. Fish & Wildlife Service (2000) **Why Save Endangered Species?** Arlington, VA: U.S. Fish & Wildlife Service, April 2000. U.S. Forest Service (1998) **Charting our Future...A Nation's Natural Resource Legacy.** October 1998 FS-630, Washington D.C.: United States   Department of Agriculture Forest Service.

U.S. Forest Service (1994) **Highlights Report of the Forest Service 1993. 300-094/ 00220.** Washington, D.C.: U.S. Government Printing Office.

U.S. Forest Service (1986) **What The Forest Service Does FS-20.** Washington, D.C.: U.S. Government Printing Office.

U.S. Forest Service (1990) **National Forest 1891-1991 FS469 December.** Washington: U.S. Government Printing Office.

U.S. Forest Service (1991) **The National Forest - Ending Their First Century FS-495 May.** Washington: U.S. Government Printing Office.

U.S. Forest Service (1994) **Report of the Forest Service: Fiscal Year 1993 300-094/00220.** Washington D.C.: U.S. Government Printing Office.

Wilkinson, Todd (1999) "Promised Land National Parks," **National Parks.** October 1999 Vol. 73, No. 9-10,

Washington D.C.: National Parks and Conservation Association.

CHAPTER 8

MANAGING IN THE TECHNOLOGICAL ENVIRONMENT

Learning Objectives

After studying this chapter, you should be able to do the following:

1. Understand the need to manage the technological environment.
2. Describe applications used in recreation.
3. Discuss the stages of change when adopting new technology.
4. Understand the need for clear policies and procedures.

In today's challenging environment, the recreation manager has the responsibility to utilize technology to meet the demands of the public for efficient service. This mandate requires that managers include the wise utilization of technology in accomplishing the mission of their agency or organization. Although it is not wise to apply technological solutions to every problem, the manager needs to be well informed in order to consider these options in decision making. If leader-managers of park, recreation, and leisure service delivery systems are informed, creative, and prudent in their selection of applications and their utilization of resources, the world of recreation and leisure can be enhanced by this fast paced changing world of technology.

Management of the technological change process to new technology is discussed. And the managers responsibility to set policies and procedures for the protection of hardware and software, computerized information, and individual privacy is addressed.

Trends in organizations indicate that managers are responsible for bigger staffs, more assets, and larger volumes of transactions. Technology can help the manager with these responsibilities through information systems and software packages that provide informative reports that facilitate decision making.

ORIENTATION TO TECHNOLOGY

The technology explosion is not only expected to continue but to accelerate. The psychological and social impact will be enormous as society becomes more individualized and dependent upon technology. Advancements in information and information technology will continue to drive dramatic changes in the way that we learn, work, and conduct our business. Office buildings, for instance, are much less relevant today since technology allows many office workers to accomplish their tasks at home. Likewise, services provided by people continue to be replaced by technological applications. From 1978 to 1997 it is estimated that 43 million jobs were lost to technology (Hill and McLean 1999:15).

Increasing the ability of the workforce to utilize emerging technologies effectively will determine the competitive position of the recreation industry. Those who keep up with and utilize the technological advances will grow and prosper, while those who do not or cannot keep up will suffer losses. The key for the American workforce over the next several years is to enhance their skills to use technology creatively, solve problems, communicate solutions, improve productivity, and establish values related to the impact of technology.

In the Field...

Notebooks in the Woods

Ann Kreik, the founder of the Salt Lake based speakers bureau and agency for athletes, *Extreme Connections*, totes her notebook computer along on rock climbs and trips into the back country. She types her E-mail correspondence and proposals in the woods or on a climb emerging periodically to plug into a phone line at a lodge. There she checks her America Online account, and sends faxes and e-mail messages to her business contacts. Thanks to technology, she can work in the outdoors and still run her business.

Threefold Task

When approaching technology, the manager in recreation has a threefold task (Alden 1992: 41-44). First, managers should be capable of applying existing mature recreation technology to improve quality or productivity. Second, managers need to look for innovative ways to use technology. This involves observing technological applications in agencies other than recreation, and then creatively thinking of similar applications for recreation programs. Third, managers must stay abreast of developing technologies. Increasingly, larger organizations are creating a position of Chief Technology Officer (CTO) with whom managers interact with to meet their technological needs.

Even though most recreation agencies cannot afford to be on the cutting-edge of technology, managers should still watch new emerging technology and anticipate that in about three years or less, the cost will drop significantly making it feasible to implement. Experimenting with *bleeding edge* technology costs are extremely high with budget over-runs expected, and many of the *bugs* or problems with the technology have not been identified yet. Technology leadership is attractive to those seeking high profits from successful innovative changes. Simply watching this zone for new applications, gives the manager time to consider creative options and to make plans for the future. Individuals that adopt technology after the bleeding edge period do not have to deal with as many risks.

Adopters: Adopters of new technology generally fall into five groups. These groups are called *innovators*, *early adopters*, *early majority*, *late majority*, and *laggards* (Bateman and Snell 1999: 579). First to accept new technology are the adventurous *innovators*. Some are even considered extreme. Following the first group are the *early adopters,* who others generally look to for leadership. The third group to respond are called the *early majority*. They are generally not community or industry leaders, and tend to study new technology before implementing it. The *late majority* eventually follows, but often only because of social pressure to do so. *Laggards* or the final group are typically suspicious of change and innovation (see Table 8-1 and Figure 8-1).

TABLE 8-1

Five Groups of Adopters

Innovators	Risk-takers who some consider extreme.
Early Adopters	Leaders who others look to for ideas.
Early Majority	Important members of the community who take longer before trying a new innovation.
Late Majority	Followers who often adopt only out of necessity and pressure.
Laggards	Individuals who are suspicious of change.

Source: Design by Jane Lammers based on data from Bateman, Thomas and Snell, Scott *Management Building Competitive Advantage (* Boston, MA: Irwin/McGraw-Hill 1999), p.579

FIGURE 8-1

Percentage of Adopters by Type

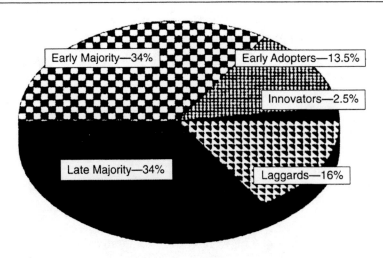

Source: See Table 8-1.

MANAGING THE TECHNOLOGICAL CHANGE PROCESS

One of the most significant developments effecting change today is advanced technology. Many organizations are redesigning the way that they deliver services and run operations. For example, e-commerce is rapidly and unexpectedly changing the economy, society, and politics much like the railroad did 170 years ago (Drucker 1999: 50). In fact, the Information Revolution is just beginning to be felt as new technologies like e-trade develop and lead to major new industries (Drucker 1999: 47).

TABLE 8-2

Suggested Steps in the Technological Change Process

- Inform the users during all stages of development and implementation.
- Involve executives, users, and external stakeholders in planning.
- Have a model available for inspection and experimentation.
- Allow for suggestions and questions about the technology.
- Address fears and concerns such as job security as early as possible.
- Test systems with actual users prior to implementation.
- Conduct hands-on technological training for all users and managers.
- Have manuals and reference materials easily accessible.
- Set-up a feedback system so problem areas can be addressed.
- Allow for continuous improvement of the system if possible.

The Human Factor

When any significant part of an organization undergoes a change, especially one associated with technology, many dynamics are taking place. This includes the human factor. The manager cannot afford to ignore human reactions to change caused by technology. Accepting or embracing technological change occurs at different times depending upon the individual's personality type and the organization's ability to facilitate the change process. Professional planners generally advise manager's to keep employees and users informed throughout the planning and implementation process. In addition, when models of the technology are available for inspection and comment, it helps everyone adapt better. By opening channels of communication, fears can be addressed and suggestions considered. Table 8-2 shows suggests steps that park, recreation, and leisure service delivery system managers can use when planning an organizational change to new technology.

Job Security: Employee fears of technological change frequently center around job security. This issue needs to be addressed in an honest fashion. If the issue is not addressed, hidden resistance will accumulate which could result in employee sabotage. Ideally, management will anticipate when a new system will mean job eliminations. Plans should include attrition through natural departures and retirements to accommodate any reduction in personnel when possible. The leader-manager may also be able to pledge to reassign displaced personnel to areas of expansion and growth or plan retraining. When this commitment is possible, transitions due to technological change will be smoother and even energizing for the organization. And the earlier these assurances are made, the more successful the entire outcome will be.

Stages in the Change Process

When an agency decides to design and implement a system that uses new technology, the significant undertaking demands a step by step approach. Generally, the process of adopting to change includes five steps: planning, design, test/ implement, monitor, and improve (Baird et al 1987).

Plan → Design → Test/Implement → Monitor → Improve

The Planning Stage: *Planning* is often conducted by technical experts with little or no management experience. Far preferable, is the practice of including the actual users of the system, i.e. customers, operators, front-line managers, and executives along with the technical experts. At this stage, an assessment of the needs, goals, and objectives of the entity is necessary. Reference to the mission statement, the current plan, discussions with the executive-in-charge, and actual observations of operations are considered. Constraints, or items that limit the process, such as funding, the degree of commitment of upper management, organizational culture, logistical challenges, personnel readiness, public needs, adaptability of existing systems, and legislative environment are all considered. The planning stage is critical because it lays the foundation for change.

The Design Stage: The *design* stage includes the selection of the appropriate hardware, software, reference documentation (manuals), networking requirements, location, and personnel. Procedures are also designed to inform personnel and the public of the new technology. Public relations personnel can be very useful in publicizing these procedures. The later stages of the design process include rigorous testing and the preparation for training employees. After all, new technology is worthless without employees who are properly trained to apply it (Ross and Sharpless: 1999:29).

The Implementation Stage: The *implementation* stage starts with more elaborate testing of the system to determine its reliability and fitness for use. To create an effective and efficient system, tests are designed around the actual users during a typical day. Results of these tests may require that the system be returned to the design stage. Once the system is ready for adoption, several methods of introduction are available. These include the *crash, parallel, pilot*, or *phased-in* methods (Baird et al 1987).

Methods of Introduction: With the *crash* method, the old system is set aside and the new system is implemented all at once. As the term implies, the risks involved are significant because the entire system could fail leaving the organization paralyzed. Not only is service interrupted, credibility can be lost. *Parallel* implementation involves operating both the old and new systems simultaneously. This is preferable in terms of risk but it may not be feasible in terms of cost and personnel availability. A *pilot* implementation, calls for only one portion of the organization to adopt the system. If it fails, damage is limited to the individual unit or segment. *Phased* implementation permits portions of the old system to be substituted by the new process. Because the old and new segments need to be compatible, this is generally not practical. Table 8-3 provides a brief description of these methods along with an advisory of the primary disadvantage of each that must be considered before a selection is made.

TABLE 8-3

Four Implementation Strategies

TYPE	DESCRIPTION	ADVISORY
Crash	New system is implemented all at once.	System could crash with no back-up in place.
Parallel	Both old and new systems operate at once.	Expensive to run two systems simultaneously.
Pilot	Only part of the agency uses the new system.	Problems that develop with full scale operation are not apparent.
Phased	Substitutes parts of the new into the old system.	Often the old and the new systems are incompatible.

Continuous Improvement: Once the system is functioning, it needs to be continuously monitored for effectiveness. Feedback is obtained through observation, questionnaires, suggestion forms, discussion topics, and actual requests for assistance. Depending on the size of the system, technical personnel may even be needed to maintain the system and support the employees. These individuals serve as ideal sources of feedback and evaluation. Complaints, in the meantime, are viewed as excellent indicators of the need for more training or modifications.

The Technology Life Cycle

Managers should keep in mind that technology has a generally predictable life cycle. New technology begins with an idea that will satisfy a recognized need that culminates in a technological innovation. Early progress tends to be slow as experiments with design and operational techniques are improved, but innovation is at its highest when improvements are continued as the innovation is refined. Then costs become more competitive until the technology is widely used and reaches a higher performance level. During this mature stage, there are fewer new customers, refinements lag, and the price decreases. Technology can remain in this stage until a new idea creates another economic or performance advantage, or until the old technology is replaced by the new.

POLICIES AND PROCEDURES

Along with the design of a methodical approach to the actual adoption of a new system of technology, consideration is needed for the subsequent impact that the new operating environment will have on the work environment. Logical policies and procedures keep the computerized environment functioning properly and protect the work of the organization.

Like any other asset, policies and procedures need to be set for the security of computer hardware and software. This is a function of management. Locking the door at the end of the day is not enough. Additional precautions and security steps are necessary because much of what is valuable about a computer system is the software and information stored inside. Data can be lost due to computer glitches, power outages, and unexpected events. This makes back-up procedures for data critical. Steps also need to be taken to protect against unauthorized access, disclosure of private information, and copyright infringements.

Protecting Against Damage

Management establishes policies which encourage work habits that include timely back-ups of computer files. When back-ups are routinely made, the organization's work is safe-guarded and damages due to malfunction are limited. Back-up copies are the organization's best insurance against intentional and unintentional damage.

Even with back-up copies, the manager insures that each department, computer system, and individual has a contingency plan in the event of an interruption such as a power shortage or computer crash. Preventative hardware is available to minimize the damage due to power shortages. Routine checks for computer viruses that attack programs, destroy data, or reduce the computer's memory capacity are conducted to reduce crashes.

Protecting the Information

Managers help safeguard computer systems from unwelcome invaders by arranging for security programs that limit access to sensitive computer information. These programs help to minimize unauthorized disclosure of information, mischief, and costly thefts to park, recreation, and leisure service delivery systems.

To protect the integrity of the security system, managers instruct personnel about steps that they can take to help safeguard the system. Without the security steps, invaders, known as computer hackers, are more likely to cause damage, confusion, and embarrassment by accessing and even changing computerized records, for instance, assets, reservations, or payments. Table 8-4 provides some suggestions for managers to share with employees.

TABLE 8-4

Tips for Safeguarding Data When Using Networked Computers

- Computers are not left on while unprotected by passwords.
- Passwords consist of a combination of letters and numbers that are not easily guessed.
- Passwords are memorized, not written down.
- Strange activity on the computer screen, unusual files on the hard drive, or an unusual shortage of memory are warning flags that a computer virus may have invaded the computer's memory.
- Duplicate servers and memory devices are considered.
- Data files should be backed-up often.
- Back-up copies are stored in a safe place
- Experts are consulted for current secure procedures.

Protecting the Individual

Parks, recreation, and leisure service delivery systems store information about the organization's personnel and members. Leader-managers stay current regarding ethical and legal responsibilities to safeguard this information from improper disclosure. Resulting privacy policies are clearly stated and distributed to all employees. Leader-managers also make sure that employees are not privy to information about members or other individuals except on a need-to-know basis. *Need-to-know* means that the information is provided to personnel only if it is needed to carry-out job responsibilities. Likewise, leader-managers have ethical and legal responsibilities to their own employees regarding electronic information. Access guidelines for electronic personnel records and requirements to notify when electronic work environments are monitored are just two examples. Legal advisors may be consulted about these duties, especially as the organization's capacity to store and analyze personal information increases.

Protecting Intellectual Rights

Since some employees do not realize that copyright laws may prohibit the copying of computer software, it is critical for leader-managers to establish clear policies and procedures that prohibit illegal copying. Employees need to understand that copyright laws generally permit only legal copying of software for back-up purposes or for installation onto machines that are authorized by the vendor. Software purchased for the office computers cannot be installed at home for either business or personal use. Federal laws are sometimes enforced through surprise inspection of business premises for illegally copied, or *boot-legged* copies of software. Fines for violations are very substantial and must be paid by the employer. Employers and employees alike have an ethical and legal responsibility to abide by these rules that protect the intellectual property of the programmers who created the software.

SOFTWARE OPTIONS

Recreation managers plan and approve the appropriate use of software in order to achieve the mission of the organization. While specialists in the organization may be more familiar with the latest technological applications, the manager needs to maintain an overview of what is available for effective planning and control. The National Recreation and Park Association (NRPA) Oglebay Computer Use Institute offers sessions each year that feature hands-on computer classroom sessions taught by park and recreation practitioners, top professors, and park and recreation commercial vendors. There are also hands-on try-before-you-buy sessions offered by the commercial vendors. Students of varying levels of computer knowledge attend the sessions to gain knowledge about trends in recreation technology.

Recreation tasks that can be accomplished more efficiently with the use of computer software programs include registration for camp, aquatic programs, or other activities; league scheduling and standings; facility reservations; facility and equipment rentals; facility maintenance; facility use statistics; questionnaires; accident reporting; newsletters; membership databases; mailing labels and mailing letters; poster preparation; demographic analysis; tracking activity revenue; expense analysis; budget preparation and monitoring; graphic analysis of revenue, expense, budget; registration analysis; membership pass with bar codes;

and interactive edutainment. Several groupings of software programs that facilitate effective management are described in the sections that follow.

Office Productivity and Scheduling Software

Office productivity software automates everyday tasks and includes scheduling, project management, personal information managers called PIMs, and other convenient devices. Custom recreational software saves time, thereby increasing the productivity of employees. Facility scheduling software provides all personnel with updated availability information and management reports that help staff prepare for scheduled events. Several vendors specialize in meeting the needs of park, recreation, and leisure service delivery systems, and new products are continually developed and introduced by them and others to increase efficiency and effectiveness.

In The Field...

An Online Park and Recreation Resource

NRPAnet (www.NRPA.org) is an interactive electronic recreation network sponsored by the National Recreation and Park Association (NRPA). Information is available about the association as well as the overall park, recreation, and leisure services community. The research network provides reference to thousands of citations and abstracts of professional journals and recreation libraries including *Parks & Recreation* Magazine, *Journal of Leisure Research, Therapeutic Recreation Journal, Recreation & Parks Law Reporter*, and the Park Practice Program's *Trends, Design and Grist*. In addition, subscribers have a "hot button" to query NRPA's Information Resources Office with additional research questions. Network features include:

- Listserve: a powerful networking tool
- Research Database
- National Job Bulletins
- Discussion Forums
- Legislation & Public Policy Information
- Conferences and Workshop Listings
- NRPA Marketplace
- Announcements

Management Software

Management's responsibility to plan, organize, direct, and control is enhanced through effective software information systems that combine the features of database, spreadsheets, word processing, and communications programs into integrated software packages. Large organizations typically have elaborate customized computer systems that track, measure, and report on all aspects of an organization's performance. Smaller organizations may select software packages that are more generic in nature, although still very powerful in providing useful information for the manager.

In the Field...

Paperless

The Indianapolis City government, which includes the Indianapolis Department of Parks and Recreation has committed to a paperless environment by using electronic data, such as e-mail, Internet, Intranet (a local version of Internet) and other forms of cyberspeak to save trees and their printing budget.

Source: Ross, C. and Sharpless, D. *Innovative Information Technology and Its Impact on Recreation and Sport Programming* <u>The Journal of Physical Education, Recreation and Dance</u> Vol. 70 No. 9, December 1999, p. 28.

Accounting software, whether elaborate or simple, is designed to record daily transactions, and to summarize weekly, monthly, quarterly, and yearly activity. This software allows annual budgets to be closely monitored by showing monies spent to date, funds that have been allocated by purchase orders, and any other funds remaining. In addition, revenues from fees for the use of facilities can be tracked and compared to amounts collected in the prior year.

Comparisons of budgeted amounts and actual amounts, with prior periods of time, such as last year or last month, are easily made. Managers can plan ahead by projecting the next year's income and by making modifications as needed. Reports may show, for example, receipts from user fees or the number of visitors who entered the park. Table 8-5 is a management report submitted to Congress showing an analysis of fees received from various federal recreation sites. Integrated management software assists in the compilation of data from operations that can be displayed in reports like the elaborate example seen in Table 8-5.

TABLE 8-5

III. Recreation Fee Revenues ($millions)

Gross Revenues Under the Recreational Fee Demonstration Program					
	Before Demonstration			**During Demonstration**		
Bureau/Receipt Category	**FY 1994**	**FY 1995**	**FY 1996**	**FY 1997**	**FY 1998**	**FY 1999**
National Park Service						
Non-fee demo receipts	75.7	80.5	77.8	77.2	7.5	9.5
Fee demo receipts	0.0	0.0	0.0	45.1	136.8	141.4
NPS Totals	75.7	80.5	77.8	122.2	144.3	150.8
U.S. Fish and Wildlife Service						
Non-fee demo receipts	2.2	2.3	2.2	2.3	0.4	0.3
Fee demo receipts	0.0	0.0	0.0	0.6	3.1	3.4
FWS Totals	2.2	2.3	2.2	2.9	3.5	3.6[a]
Bureau of Land Management						
Non-fee demo receipts	1.8	2.6	3.3	3.2	2.6	1.5
Fee demo receipts	0.0	0.0	0.0	0.4	3.5	5.2
BLM Totals	1.8	2.6	3.3	3.7	6.1	6.7
USDA Forest Service						
Non-fee demo receipts	10.9	9.5	10.0	9.0	5.5	5.5[c]
Fee demo receipts	0.0	0.0	0.043[b]	9.3	20.8	26.5
USFS Totals	10.9	9.5	10.0	18.3	26.3	32.0
Total, All Four Agencies						
Non-fee demo receipts	90.6	94.9	93.2	91.8	15.9	16.7
Fee demo receipts	0.0	0.0	0.043	55.4	164.2	176.4
Totals For All Agencies	90.6	94.9	93.3	147.2	180.2	193.2

[a]Does not total precisely due to rounding error.
[b]The USDA Forest Service implemented the Recreational Fee Demonstration Program in FY 1996 with four small projects that generated $43,000 in revenues during the year.
[c]An estimate based on FY 1998 receipts.

Source: *Recreational Fee Demonstration Program Annual Report to Congress Fiscal Year 1999.* U.S. Department of the Interior: www.doi.gov/nrl/Recfees/2000R/2000Report.htm

Asset Management Programs

Asset Management Programs help track inventory and other assets, and they assist the manager with arranging proper maintenance. For instance, museum accession records can be computerized with each item in a museum's collection entered into the asset system. Specific information such as the tracking number, the estimated value, the original donor, the basic description, the country of origin, the category of art, the date created, the storage location, the events in which it has been displayed, and care and maintenance requirements is entered. When a new exhibit is planned, a convenient list of items relating to the exhibit's theme can readily be identified. In addition, maintenance schedules can automatically be generated from these systems, such as a chronological list of the service dates for the care and upkeep of the museum pieces.

These asset management systems are useful in providing inventories of facilities, flora, fauna, land areas, equipment, and supplies. The Forest Service's TRIS, or Trail Information System, is a prominent example of an elaborate system. Trail users benefit from TRIS at Forest Service visitor centers or at participating local outfitter stores to research trail locations, length, difficulty, conditions, restrictions, camping availability, etc.

Personnel and Payroll Systems

Personnel and Payroll Systems database software facilitate detailed record-keeping tasks. Payroll checks and other related accounting, including deductions for health care, taxes, and retirement are automatically calculated by the programs after basic information is entered. Personnel records such as anniversary dates, salaries, position classification, and training can all be tracked and monitored. Systems to assist with legal record-keeping requirements for safety such as injury and incident reports or for other legal requirements are also available.

SUMMARY

- Management includes overseeing the effective application of technology to achieve an efficient and effective organization.

- Adopters of new technology generally fall into five groups. These groups are called innovators, early adopters, early majority, late majority, and laggards.

- If an agency decides to design and implement a system that uses new technology, it is a significant undertaking that needs to be approached on a step by step basis. Generally, the five stages of adopting a change include: planning, design, test/implement, monitor, and improve.

- Policies and procedures need to be set for the security of the computer system. These policies focus on the valuable information and programs stored on the system and seek to protect the integrity of the information, the privacy of the individual, and the intellectual rights of the programmers.

- Powerful software programs allow the manager to be well informed, maintain control, and to run an efficient operation.

LEARNING ACTIVITIES

1. Take note of the technological applications that you observe in the normal course of your day. Are any of these applications adaptable to the recreation industry? Please explain.

2. Imagine that you have joined the management staff of a recreation organization that has not utilized computer technology. You would like to encourage its adoption. What types of resistance can you anticipate? What technology would you advocate and how would you go about it? Why?

3. Why might a park, recreation, and leisure service delivery system choose to follow rather than lead technological innovations?

4. Do you know anyone that has been impacted by technological changes on the job? Interview them about their involvement in the change process and their reaction to it. Do they believe the technological change was beneficial to the organization, to the customers, to the employees? Were the steps suggested for the implementation of technological change followed? What suggestions do they have to improve the change process?

5. As a new manager in city recreation you observe that the staff has settled into a habit of buying one software program and copying it onto all the computers. Most of the staff is not aware that this is a problem. The budget has been so tight in recent years that the former manager did not take any action to correct the situation. First, what is the problem with this behavior? Second, what steps could you take to resolve this situation? Please discuss your approach.

6. Sign-on to the website of two public recreation agencies. Describe your on-line experience at each site. Then compare your two experiences. Make at least three suggestions for improvement.

REFERENCES

Alden, J. (1992) **Readings in Management 21st-Century Management: New Dimensions of Leadership For the New Century.** Department of the Treasury U.S. Government Printing.

Baird, L.S., Post, J.E., Mahon, J.F. (1987) **Management Functions.** New York: Harper & Row, Publishers.

Bateman, T. and Snell, S. (1999) **Management Building Competitive Advantage.** Boston: Irwin/McGraw-Hill.

Drucker, P. (1999) "Beyond the Information Revolution" **The Atlantic Monthly** Vol. 284 No. 4 October p. 47-57.

Hill, J. and McLean, D. (1999) " Introduction: Possible, Probable, or Preferable Future?" **The Journal of Physical Education, Recreation & Dance** Vol. 70 No. 9 Dec. p. 15-17

Ross, C. and Sharpless, D.(1999) "Innovative Information Technology and Its Impact on Recreation and Sport Programming" **The Journal of Physical Education, Recreation & Dance** Vol. 70 No. 9 Dec. p. 26-30.

CHAPTER 9

FISCAL MANAGEMENT

Learning Objectives

After studying this Chapter, the student should be able to do the following:

1. Identify the sources of revenues for recreation, parks and leisure agencies, regardless of affiliation or size.

2. Describe some of the innovative methods of fundraising which are now being used to supplement the revenues of both public and semi-public /nonprofit agencies.

3. Understand how a budget is developed in an agency dealing with recreation, parks and leisure services as well as the mechanisms used for controlling it.

4. Appreciate and be able to identify the new trends in fiscal management that are utilized today in the leisure service sector.

5. Comprehend how expenditures are itemized in the agencies dealing with recreation, parks and leisure services.

While the program is the core of what a parks, recreation, or leisure service agency is all about, finances are the agency's prime mover. Therefore the fiscal aspects of the agency must receive considerable attention from the management. Fiscal responsibility revolves around the money that is coming in; and the money that is going out. Whether the agency is public, semi- public or private, finances play an important role in helping it achieve its goals.

All three types of agencies, public, semi-public and private, must exercise prudence in matters of finance. While a private, profit-making agency can always use profit as its criterion of success, the public and semi-public agencies will find it difficult to measure their success in dollars and cents.

Since the public and semi-public agencies are non-profit organizations, the use of dollars and cents as criterion of success may not be totally reliable, even if profits were realized. Nonetheless, all three types of agencies share an element in common which could be used as a criterion of success: satisfaction of the consumer/ participant. How can such satisfaction be measured? A reasonable measure of satisfaction is enrollment in the program. In the case of a private agency, satisfaction, as reflected in the increase in enrollment, would yield more income. In the case of the public and semi-public agencies, the increase in enrollment, in itself, could be used as sign of success. When fees are charged by these two types of agencies, some profits may be realized. But the sources of income for the public and semi-public agencies are not limited to the fees collected upon enrollment, other sources of revenue are available as discussed in the next section.

REVENUE AND THE LEISURE SERVICE AGENCY

Sources of revenue for an agency dealing with recreation, park or leisure services vary according to its type, affiliation and location. While the public agency providing these services depends on taxation as its basic source of revenue, the semi-public agency depends on membership and contributions and the private agency depends on membership and fees as its sources of revenue.

Revenue and the Public Agency

While taxation is the main source of funds for a public agency such as a municipal department of recreation or a special park district, other sources are available for financing a public agency. Following are these resources:

General Taxation: There are more than one type of taxes that are used in funding public service in recreation, parks, and leisure pursuits. General taxes are the most common method of funding these services. General taxation, in turn, can be divided into three categories, income, sales and property taxes. Funds acquired from property taxes are the main source of revenue used to support local services including recreation, park or leisure service. The other two types of taxes, income and sales taxes, which are usually collected by federal and state governments, may be used indirectly in supporting these services as will be seen later.

Special Taxation: There are provisions in some states that special districts be established to provide special services such as park and recreation. Special taxes are levied on particular items such as amusement admissions or liquor for the purpose of supporting these services. In other instances, special taxes are levied on the properties which will benefit from the service and not on all the properties within the municipality. According to Kraus and Curtis (1990:286) a recent trend is to impose special assessment taxes on residential developers, the revenue from which would be used to finance capital outlays for recreation and parks.

Bonds: Municipal and other bonds are used by governments as a method of raising money that would be repaid within a specific period of time. The monies acquired from the sale of the bonds are usually used in financing major capital projects such as land acquisition and the building of large facilities. There are many types of bonds with which the management of a public agency offering recreation, park or leisure services should be acquainted. For example a **term bond** is paid at the end of the specific period for which it is issued usually between ten and thirty years. Since the interest paid on the term bond remains the same, the **callable bond** allows for the repayment at any time. In such case the bond can be reissued at a lower rate of interest, if such a possibility exists. A serial bond allows for an annual repayment of a portion of the principal plus interest. While a **general obligation bond** is repaid from the general tax revenue, an **assessment bond** is repaid from a special tax levied on those who benefit from the use of the land acquired or the facility provided through the bond.

Government Grants: While most government grants come from the federal government, smaller grants can be acquired for recreation, parks and leisure services from state governments and private foundations. In the last three decades since the passage of numerous benchmark forms of legislation, billions of dollars have been allocated to the improvement in the services with which this volume is concerned. The great beneficiaries of these grants were open space and park development. A number of acts provided funds that were given to local and state government that helped to improve conditions in outdoor pursuits as well other recreational pursuits. The Land and Water Conservation Funds, the Community Development Block Grants, the Comprehensive Employment and Training Act and the General Revenue Sharing provided about $1.2 billion to local and state agencies dealing with recreation, park and leisure services in the 1970's alone (Benedict 1978:39). These funds are not readily available now.

Foundation Grants: The idea of reducing the role of the government in public services along with the tendency to reduce its budget mande the public monies that were once available to recreation, parks and leisure services scarce beginning at the mid 1980's. The public agencies dealing with these activities shifted their attempts in acquiring funds to private sources. According to Kraus and Curtis (2000:165) there are four types of foundations which may be approached by the management of an agency in recreation, parks or leisure services. The company foundation is created by the mother company for the purpose of corporate giving. The family foundation is created by a family for the purpose of reducing taxation by giving grants to deserving projects. The community foundation is created for the purpose of helping a particular community, be it residential such as a city, or spiritual such as a religious community. The special purpose foundation is created to meet a special need. Recreation, parks and sports are sometimes included by some foundations. Kraus and Curtis suggested the following strategy for the development of grant proposals (2000:167):

1. Establishment of a foundations' committee that is composed of well qualified, enthusiastic persons.

2. Preparation of a list of the foundations that are believed to have interest in recreation, parks or leisure services in general.

3. Development of a proposal concept by the committee and the sounding off of a foundation or two before developing the final draft of the proposal.

4. Preparation of a formal grant proposal which should follow the proposed outlines found in the literature on grant writing.

5. Presentation of the proposal with a cover letter preferably delivered by hand, if not, by mail.

6. Follow-up process in which a meeting could be requested for the purpose of explaining the project further.

Fees and Charges: With the decline of revenues from governmental grants, public agencies providing recreation, parks or leisure services began to depend on fees and charges as important sources of revenue. According to Warren (1986:F5), there are seven types of fees and charges in the fields of recreation, parks and leisure services in general:

1. Entrance Fees are collected upon the entrance into certain recreational areas such as zoos and botanical gardens.

2. Admission Fees are collected upon being admitted to a theatre, museum or theme park.

3. Rental Fees are charged for the use of a nonconsummable property such as bicycles and boats,

4. Users Fees are charged for participation in an activity such as golfing, skiing or swimming.

5. Permit Fees are collected to be allowed the right to hunt, fish or camp.

6. Special Service Fees are charged to cover certain events such as day camp or class instruction.

7. Concession Fees are obtained for the operation of a gift shop, a restaurant or a store on the premises of the agency.

As public monies dry up, the dependence on fees and charges as a source of revenue in public recreation is increasing. While this may cause concern for the agency, a recent study shows that a slight increase in user fees has not affected visitations to public recreation sites (Schroeder and Louviere, 1999).

Concessions: Concessions are a good source of revenue for a department of recreation, parks or leisure services. The concession allows a private person or a business to provide a service to the public who use the facility. The department charges a certain amount of money usually on a monthly basis or a percentage of the gross income of the concession. Concessions are used for rental and food services more than any other type of service. Concession could be a very good source of income for a recreation, parks or leisure agency.

Other Sources of Revenue: With the sources of funding from public monies drying up fast, public agencies dealing with recreation, parks and leisure services reverted to methods of fundraising that were at one point conducted by semi-public and private agencies. These are innovative methods where the public agencies are concerned. A section in this chapter will be devoted to these new methods.

Revenues and the Semi-Public Agency

The term semi-public refers to the agencies that, although not affiliated or ad-ministered by a public entity, do not depend on profits as the main source of revenue. Good examples of agencies that are listed under this category would be the YMCA, the Boy Scouts and the Girls Club. All these agencies seek both public and private support in their endeavors. Still other sources of revenue are used by these agencies.

Membership Dues: While the revenues from membership are not substantial, membership plays an important role in allowing the use of facilities or the joining in activities in the semi-public agencies. Membership dues in these organizations vary according to age and to the type of membership. For instance, membership rates per month in the YMCA in a town of 70,000 persons are $15 for young adults (14-20 years of age),$35 for adults (21-62 years of age), $30 (62 and older) $55 for family with children up to 17 years of age, and $40 for a single parent family with children up to 17 years of age.

Fees and Charges: In a fashion similar to what is done by the public agencies in recreation, parks or leisure services do, the semi-public agencies also collect fees and charges for certain activities that are not included in the membership. For instance enrollment in the day camp of the above mentioned YMCA costs about $80 for one week. That YMCA operates a camp in the nearby mountains and a stay of one week costs about $120.

The United Way: The concept of having an organization collecting donations within the community is a uniquely American invention, which, according to

Drucker, is a response to the discovery that people got tired of being asked for donations by so many non-profit organizations and became suspicious of where their donations were going. The United Way is the organization that helps in the efforts of the non-profit organizations to raise funds through donations. Drucker suggested that a semi-public agency is better off joining it since the ones "who don't, who think they can rely on high pressure selling, just don't do very well" (1992:51).

Donations: Other than the revenues from the United Way, donations from individuals and foundations are sought by semi-public agencies. Fund development campaigns, particularly for capital outlay projects, are very a effective means of revenue. The "term fundraising" is being replaced by the term "fund development" because the idea today is to build up a constituency of donors in order to have a broad, sound, solid advocacy base (Drucker, 1992: 85).

Gifts and Bequests: Corporate giving to public and semi-public agencies is rather impressive. On average it takes almost two months between the time an application is submitted and a final answer is given. Four hundred twenty companies that participated in a questionnaire ranked fourteen criteria as shown in Table 9-1.

TABLE 9-1

Evaluation Criteria

	Rated one or two	
Criteria	No. Companies	% Companies
Impact on Local Community	423	87.6
Geographic Location	419	86.7
Management Capability	326	67.5
Artistic Merit	287	59.5
Employees Involvement	265	54.9
Quality of Application	209	43.3
Board of Directors	186	38.5
Size of Audience	165	34.1
Support by Other Firms	133	27.5
Coordination with Similar Groups	113	23.4
Support by Foundations /Government	75	15.6
Publicity Value	72	14.9
Matching Grants	60	12.4
Gifts from Individuals	39	8.1

It is clear from the table that the impact on the local community is an important criterion in corporate gifts. This should be a good omen for agencies providing local parks, recreation, and leisure services.

Where open space and parks are concerned, land is often given as a gift or as a bequest by corporations and individuals to agencies, both public and semi-public, that are dealing with recreation, parks, or leisure services. For instance between 1975 and 1981, the Nature Conservancy received close to 140,000 acres of land.

Revenues of the Private Agency

There is a wide range of private agencies dealing with recreation, parks and leisure service, and the sources of their revenues will vary accordingly. Although service-oriented, money making is the private agency's *raison detre*. Of these agencies, according to Scott (1998:132) a common theme throughout most companies in financial distress is a lack of financial control and discipline. Companies that enter the leisure business are in this business to make a profit. Profit refers to the money left over after all expenses of the agency have been paid. Since their services vary significantly so will their sources of revenue. Some revenue is provided by activities through membership as in the case of health spas. Others rent out equipment such as boating outlets. Still others will grant a user permit as in the case of skiing resorts. The following are the sources of revenues of these private, profit- making enterprises.

Membership Dues: The most commonly used membership dues structure is the initiation fee and monthly dues system. Sometimes annual membership dues are collected along with usage fee. In all these cases, it is important that an adequate dues structure be established on sound bases. If the dues are set too high, the prospective member may be reluctant to join. However, if the dues are too low, he or she may question the quality of the service.

Patton and his colleagues suggest that a segmented dues structure be adopted, which means that certain dues will be collected for more than one type of service. The dues structure should take into consideration the possibility of a renewal term membership.

Sales: Many private enterprises in recreation and leisure pursuits deal with the sale of both goods and services. Pricing these goods and services, as well as forecasting their sales, are crucial to the success of the enterprise. Pricing strategy and policy should determine the base prices as well as the schedules of discounts and price differentials between products.

Forecasting is also important to sales. There are a number of ways to accomplish this task. The management may use a jury of experts to determine the volume of its expected sales. Sometimes the customers themselves may help in forecasting sales. Statistical methods are sometimes used to forecast sales as well as the deductive method. A combination of these method yield reliable results.

Fees and Charges: Fees and charges are collected on the basis of use. For both public and semi public leisure service agencies, the types of fees and charges are listed as revenues. Many of these types apply also to private agencies. In fact, they are important sources of revenue for such an agency. The same cautions listed under membership dues and sales of a private agency dealing with recreation, parks, or leisure services must be heeded here under fees and charges. If too high, the prospective users may shy away from the agency, if too low, they may question the quality of the service. To determine reasonable fees and charges, the management of the agency could consult some experts in the field, ask the customers themselves, use a statistical method, or better yet use a combination of these three approaches.

Consultation and Contracting Fees: The role of the consultant and the subcontractor in recreation, parks, and leisure services is discussed in an earlier chapter. The number of consultants in these fields is increasing as the jobs in the public sector are declining. Subcontracting, which is also increasing, is looked upon as a means of reducing cost for public agencies. Both the consultants and subcontractors are independent, private agents who charge fees for their work. Their revenues come from fees which are paid according to prior agreements as shown in the section on consultants and subcontractors in Chapter Five.

INNOVATIVE METHODS OF FUNDRAISING

Many forms of fundraising have been used over the years not only by recreation, parks, and leisure services but also by public, semi-public, and private agencies dealing with services in general. Some of the fundraising experiences of W. Grant

Brownrigg, who served as the executive director of a nonprofit organization, follow. From his experiences in fundraising Brownrigg states that there are four fundamental principles in the process which should be kept in mind at all times (1982):

1. **People give to other people.** Regardless of the effectiveness of the program for which the funds are requested, fundraising is a personal experience, and people will give to other individuals.

2. **Volunteers solicit and the staff does the work.** In other words while the volunteers make contacts, staff members take care of the fundraising mechanics and details.

3. **Fundraising is the board's responsibility and the staff's job.** While the board may be helpful, the management should realize that fundraising is its job.

4. **Nothing is easy and fundraising is no exception.** This process requires careful attention to every detail such as, names correctly spelled, deadlines met, and contributions matched with interest.

On the other hand, Hay, who suggests 534 ways to raise money, provides five guidelines for successful fundraising (1983):

1. **The Alternative:** A good look at the agency's fundraising history, which is now being called fund development, will reveal both successful and failed events.

2. **The Audience:** The larger the number benefitting from the funds raised, the greater the base of support will be. Yet the fundraising events could still be new.

3. **The People:** They are the ones who will participate in the campaign. How much energy and what skills do they bring with them? The selection of the campaign leader is very important.

4. **The Goal:** Without a goal, it would be hard to determine if the project is on target. The goal should be challenging but also attainable.

5. **The Doubts:** To avoid feeling uncertain about the details and problems of the project, a consultant should be hired.

Hay classifies the ways an agency raises money into a number of categories such as:

- Amusements
- Auctions
- Awards and ceremonials
- Bazaars
- Carnivals and circuses
- Coupons and premiums
- Dances
- Donations
- Drawings
- Endorsements

- Endowments
- Entertainment
- Excursions
- Exhibits
- Fairs and Festivals
- Family Events
- Fashion Shows
- Meals
- Parties
- Publications

- Sales
- Service
- Speakers
- Swap Meets
- Telethons
- Thrift Shops
- Tours
- Workshops

Granted some of this activities may not be suitable for raising money for a recreation, parks, or leisure services, but many could be useful in this endeavor. Fundraising activities are expected to increase in such agencies, be they public or semi-public. The reason for this is the decline in public funds which is expected to affect the revenues of both public and semi-public agencies. Fundraising from individuals and foundations is the wave of the future on the local, regional, national, and in fact, international level, a trend which must be faced by recreation, parks, and leisure service agencies.

According to Kraus and Curtis (2000:172), colleges and universities have recently developed a strategy in which they urge their alumni to name the institutions in their wills. Perhaps the aficionados of recreation and sport in the community could follow suit.

THE BUDGET AND THE LEISURE SERVICE AGENCY

The budget of a recreation, parks, or leisure service agency revolves around the formulation of future plans through the use of financial figures. Both revenues and expenses are delineated. The budgetary process represents the "dollarization" of future plans. Through it, a sense of orderliness is established as future plans are reduced into definite numbers, thus allowing the management to see clearly how revenues are derived and where expenses are going. The management of a recreation, parks, or leisure service agency must become familiar with the budgetary process and the amount of energy and time that should be allocated for it.

The Budgetary Process

All leisure service agencies, whether public, semi-public, or private must concern themselves with the budgetary process which should end with a well-developed budget. Such a budget, if constantly monitored and adequately controlled through a well-disciplined reporting process, should give the management the opportunity to steer the agency along a well-charted course. While this statement is intended for the management of profit- oriented businesses, nonetheless, the alert management in recreation, parks, or leisure service agencies, which are generally not-for-profit, should adhere to this principle in order that a well-developed budget may be produced. Many of the techniques originally developed for business have been borrowed for application in the budgeting process in nonprofit organizations. Birkofer, et al list these five tools, borrowed from business, as being useful in the budgetary process (1987:639):

1. Responsibility Center Accounting: This fundamental budgeting tool assigns individuals the responsibility for preparing and managing individual portions of the budget, which are some sometimes called units.

2. Variable Costing and Flexible Budgeting: This practice is useful for nonprofit organizations, which experience measurable variations in their level of activity and can isolate cost or revenues that vary directly with the activity level. The leisure service agency falls under this category.

3. Standards for Cost and Performance: Developing variable cost setting methods can eventually be used to establish standards for cost; and for individual performance. In providing a certain activity, for example a tennis tournament, the current cost can be compared against its previous cost.

4. Work Measurement: In repeated activities such as the preparation for a baseball tournament, it is possible to go a step further by performing a study on the time it took to complete the tasks needed

in this job. This can be used, in turn, to develop what is known as the "relative value units", i.e. how long it will take to prepare a tournament in basketball.

5. Time Reporting: Personnel costs form a large part of the nonprofit agency 's budget. Thus the budgeting of the time of the professionals who work in the agency is important in evaluating their performance.

6. The authors stated that the last three tools, standards for cost and performance, work measurement, and time reporting are met with great resistance in nonprofit organizations because they measure individual performance very explicitly.

Regardless of the tools used, each service agency has its own unique character which influences its budgetary process, i.e. the character of a small municipal park and recreation department varies from the character of a large park district. Nonetheless, the following steps are recommended in preparing budgets regardless of the character, size, and or affiliation of the agency.

Early Preparation: Any budget must be considered at least several months in advance, if not an entire year. Budget preparation is a very involved procedure and a schedule for the preparation of a budget for a municipal park and recreation department was suggested over two decades ago. The authors proposed a four period-schedule in preparing that budget, each period lasting three months (Hjelte and Shivers, 1972: 344). So, if the fiscal year begins in July, next year's budget preparation should begin the following July.

In the first three-month of preparing the budget, preliminary estimates are made for the coming year. The most important determinant of the new budget is the previous year's budget. A tentative ceiling for the current year's expenditure is agreed upon in this first period. During the second period, the managers of the various budgets are asked to adapt their estimates to the ceiling figure. If the unit managers are requesting more funds than allowed to them, their request will be considered during the third period. A preliminary budget is developed in light of the input of the budget managers who are asked to justify their estimates for extra funds. The final draft of the proposed budget is worked out in the fourth and last period of preparation.

The preparation of the budget should be looked upon as an opportunity to examine the agency's program. Undoubtedly, fiscal decisions have program implications and visa-versa. Also, program decisions have fiscal implications.

Perhaps a session, or even a retreat, should be planned to reflect on the mission of the agency and its relationship to the budget.

Types Of Budgets

In every day living, one talks about allocating part of his or her income for different purposes. A sum of money is allocated for food, another for recreation and a third for medical expenses, and so on. The same idea could be applied to the budgeting process of an agency. A certain fund will be allocated for a particular purpose and another for second purpose, etc.

These allocations are called budgets and are given different names, e.g. capital budget, operating budget, and auxiliary budget. Another method of describing budgets in a recreation, parks, and leisure services could be either flexible or inflexible budgets. The details of each of these budgets are provided below.

Capital budget: Capital budget designates the funds to be spent on improvements such as the building of a new facilities and the purchase of new equipment and tools. The cost of a new facility has skyrocketed in recent years and the need for justifying it should be given considerable attention by the management in order to gain the support of the powers to be. Capital budget also includes the cost of purchasing new and improved equipment and tools. Granted the new technological advances have saved both time and energy, yet their prices have also increased. Accordingly, the justification for their purchase must be stated during the presentation of the budget.

Operating Budget: In this budget funds are allocated for the daily operation of the agency. Items such as salaries, fringe benefits, travel and conferences, contractual services, public relations, utilities, supplies, maintenance, repairs, communications, rentals, commodities, interests, and debt payments are examples of what an operating budget includes.

Flexible and Inflexible Budgets: The budget typically attempts to plan expenditures and forecast income. Yet such plans and forecasts cannot anticipate future events. Emergencies and unforeseen circumstances dictate the need for flexibility in budgeting. For instance, the expected income from fees which was included in the budget may not be realized due to, let us say, a long period of inclement weather. How could such slack in income be accounted for in the budgetary process?

In some circles the notion of flexibility has a negative connotation as being a sign of inefficiency. "Slack" is sometimes equated with "fat". In fact "the most effective organizations tend to be those in which resources can be marshaled as necessary to meet contingencies" (Meisnger and Dubeck, 1984:100). If the budgeters call these "slacks" reserves, they may be met with their unfortunate absorption. Most budget managers are reluctant to call them reserves for fear that they may lose the "reserve". When things are tight, "reserves" usually are out the window. Regardless of the name, flexibility for some budgetary items is needed.

In the meantime there are a number of fixed expenses that, by the very nature of their allocation, will have to be somewhat inflexible. Utilities such as electricity, gas, and telephone would fall into this category. Other categories should be looked upon as flexible and can be manipulated so as to achieve the needed result of a balanced budget at the end of the fiscal year. But flexibility and inflexibility are not the actual method of classifying budgets. The typical method is described below.

Budget Classification

Over the years a system of classifying budget, both capital and operating, has been adopted by most agencies. A recreation, parks, or leisure service agency that is affiliated with a main agency, such as a city or a county, should use the classification system of the main agency. Otherwise a budget classification system should be adopted along the general lines commonly used by parks, recreation, and leisure service agencies. Kraus and Curtis, (1990:250) suggestions are given below.

Budget Authorization and Approval

Once the proposed budget is ready, it is usually presented in a formal way to either a group of people or to a person who is in charge of the agency. In some cases a public agency dealing with municipal recreation, parks, or leisure services has an elected or selected board or commission which reviews the proposed budget. The same applies in the case of a semi-public agency. In the private sector, a top administrator may be the one to whom the budget should be presented.

Kraus and Curtis suggest that the following four elements be observed during the presentation of the proposed budget (1990:259):

1. Careful preparation: Whoever is presenting the proposed budget must be thoroughly familiar with it. He or she must be able to justify each and every item listed in the budget.

2. Opening statement: A brief opening statement should describe the main thrust of the proposed budget giving a short description of any new directions as well as the priorities adhered to in formulating the proposed budget.

3. Response to questions: The presenter must anticipate and be ready to answer questions raised during the presentation of the proposed budget. The responses should be short and factual.

4. Demeanor of the Presenter: The presenter should give an aura of confidence. This means avoiding vacillation under fire, remaining in control, and showing no anger or frustration during the presentation.

Budget Execution

Budget execution revolves around the disbursements of funds as authorized by the budget. The execution must abide by both the law of the land and the regulations of the agency and its main affiliate. Accordingly effective budgetary controls must be in place during the whole period of budget execution. Two methods are used as means of controlling the budget, periodic checks, and purchasing procedures.

Periodic Checks: It is suggested that budget control reporting in nonprofit agencies be very similar to the one used in profit-oriented organizations. Unit managers should receive monthly reports on the units' performance versus their budget (Birkofer and others, 1987:634). This periodic check is intended to compare the actual amount spent on an item, and the budgeted amount for that item. The difference between the two figures is called the variance, which is estimated in either dollar amounts or percentages. The variance is calculated by subtracting the actual amount spent from the amount budgeted. If the budgeted amount is greater than the actual spending, the variance is positive. If the actual amount spent is greater than the amount budgeted, the variance is negative. This is shown in the following Figure 9-1.

FIGURE 9-1

Budget Classification

1000. Services, Personal
    1100. Salaries and Wages, Regular
    1200. Salaries and Wages, Temporary
    1300. Other compensations
2000. Service, Contractual
    2100. Communication and Transportation
        2110. Postage
        2120. Telephone and Telegraph
        2130. Freight and Express
        2140. Traveling Expenses
        2150. Hired Vehicles
    2200. Subsistence, Care, and Support
        2210. Subsistence and Support of Persons
        2220. Subsistence and Care of Animals
        2230. Storage and Care of Vehicles
    2300. Printing, Binding, and Public Relations
        2310. Printing
        2320. Typing and Mimeographing
        2330. Binding
        2340. Public Relations
        2350. Engraving and Stamping
        2360. Lithographing
        2370. Photographing and Blue-Printing
        2380. Publication of Notices
    2400. Heat, Light, Power, and Water
        2410. Furnishing Heat
        2420. Furnishing Light and Power
        2430. Furnishing Water
    2500. Repairs
        2510. Repairs to Equipment
        2520. Repairs to Buildings and Other Structures
    2600. Custodial, Cleaning, and Other Services
        2610. Custodial Supplies
3000. Commodities
    3110. Office
    3120. Food
        3121. Food for Persons
        3122. Food for Animals
    3130. Fuels and Lubricants
        3131. Coals
        3132. Oil, Gas, and Other Fuels
        3133. Lubricating Oils
    3140. Institutional
        3141. Clothing and Household
        3142. Laundry and Cleaning
        3143. Refrigeration
        3144. Surgical and Medical
        3145. General

    3150. Park and Recreational
    3160. Horticultural and Zoological
    3170. Playgrounds and Centers
    3180. Beaches and Camps
    3190. General
    3200. Materials
        3210. Building
        3220. Road
        3230. General
    3300. Repairs
        3310. Parts of Equipment
        3320. Parts of Structures
4000. Current Charges
    4100. Rents
        4110. Buildings and Offices
        4120. Equipment
    4200. Insurance
        4210. Buildings and Structures
        4220. Stores
        4230. Equipment and Apparatus
        4240. Official Bonds
        4250. Employees' Liability
    4300. Refunds, Awards, Indemnities
    4400. Registrations and Subscriptions
    4500. Taxes
5000. Current Obligations
    5100. Interest
    5200. Pensions and Retirement
    5300. Grants and Subsidies
6000. Properties
    6100. Equipment
        6110. Office
        6120. Furniture and Fixtures
        6130. Instruments and Apparatus
        6140. Tools
        6150. Recreational and Park
        6160. Motor Vehicles
        6170. Nursery
        6180. Animals
        6190. General
    6200. Buildings and Improvements
        6210. Buildings and Fixed Equipment
        6220. Walks and Pavements
        6230. Sewers and Drains
        6240. Roads
        6250. Bridges
        6260. Trees and Shrubs
    6300. Land
7000. Debt Payments
    7100. Serial Bonds
    7200. Sinking Fund Installments

Since a variance amount is expressed in a dollar amount, it does not give a total picture. Percentage is a better indicator of the fiscal picture of the item being examined. The percentage is calculated by dividing the dollar variance by the budgeted dollars x 100. The resulting percentage, either positive or negative, would be a good indicator of the fiscal position of the item at hand. For example, as shown in Figure 9-2, $1,000 was allocated for that item in the budget of which $500 was spend half way through the fiscal year. The equation would be 500 over 1000 multiplied by 100= 50%. This means that the agency spent fifty percent of the funds allocated for this item at that particular time. If this happen to be in the middle of the fiscal year, then the fund is being spent at a reasonable rate.

Some funds will be spent early in the fiscal year and others will be spent towards the end. Periodic checks will help both the general management and the unit managers to know their budgetary situation. This process is also useful in preparing future budgets in that it will give an accurate picture of where an increase in allocation is needed. For instance, the items that have negative variables towards at the end of the fiscal year need to be examined as to the possibility of increasing their allocations.

Bookkeeping: The accounting equation shows that an increase or decrease in income is very much dependent on expenditures. The best method for keeping track of this process is double-entry bookkeeping in which each transaction is recorded as a debit entry in one account and a credit in another.

ACCOUNTING AND AUDITING SYSTEMS

The simplest form of accounting is the cash system which reports revenue and cost as the actual cash is received and spent. The personal check is the most commonly used record keeping system. The current balance reflects the financial status of the individual. A very small agency or department dealing with recreation, parks, or leisure services may be able to function with this very simple system. The next accounting system is known as the accrual system.

FIGURE 9-2

Periodic Check Chart

TRANS DATE	TRAN TYPE	DOCUMENT NUMBER	DOCUMENT REF #	DESCRIPTION	ACCOUNT/ FUND	BUDGET ACTIVITY	TRANSACTION ACTIVITY	ENCUMBRANCE ACTIVITY	BALANCE AVAILABLE
				Current Unrestricted Fund	100000				
				BEGINNING BALANCE: Printing and Duplicating	8120	.00	.60	.00	
				ENDING BALANCE: Printing and Duplicating	8120	.00	.60	.00	-.60
				BEGINNING BALANCE: Professional Services	8140	200.00	.00	.00	
				ENDING BALANCE: Professional Services	8140	200.00	.00	.00	200.00
				BEGINNING BALANCE: Other Services	8190	.00	.00	.00	
05/15/2000	INN1	I0036560		Other Services Bon Appetit	8190		97.43		
				ENDING BALANCE: Other Services	8190	.00	97.43	.00	-97.43
				BEGINNING BALANCE: Office & Instruction Supplies	8210	50.00	.00	.00	
				ENDING BALANCE: Office & Instruction Supplies	8210	50.00	.00	.00	50.00
				BEGINNING BALANCE: Entertainment	8325	250.00	.00	.00	
				ENDING BALANCE: Entertainment	8325	250.00	.00	.00	250.00
				TOTAL ORGANIZATION:					
				Operational Costs	07	500.00	98.03	.00	401.97
				Net Balance Available		500.00	98.03	.00	401.97

The Accrual System: In this system, revenue is listed when earned, whether it is actually received or not. Costs occurred or not are also listed. This system is widely used because it gives the management an accurate picture of all disbursement, obligations, and the current status of a particular fund. For instance, the fund allocated for a line item, such as maintenance, is listed along with the amount spent on that item as of that day. The computer is used to facilitate the process by producing monthly reports for each unit in the agency, by showing the amounts allocated for each item, by displaying the amount spent, and by showing the balance remaining.

Cost Accounting: This system of accounting requires that the activities and the functions of a recreation, parks, or leisure agency be separated into individual units. Separate accounts are kept for each activity and each function within a unit, such as special events and facilities. These accounts are used to measure the cost of each of these activities and functions. This method is useful in evaluating efficiency and performance, as well as the feasibility of future expansion.

The Balance Sheet: On the last day of the fiscal year, the balance sheet provides a picture of the agency's financial picture. It is more or less a snap shot and not the total picture of the fiscal status of the agency. The financial statement provides the total picture since it requires more detailed information than the balance sheet does. The balance sheet is divided into two parts: the top shows the assets (income) and the bottom shows the liabilities (debts), with both parts being equal. In the case of a private leisure service agency, the income, hopefully, includes some profit.

The Auditing Process

Another effective tool of control over fiscal matters is the audit. Audits are performed either internally within the agency or they are performed by an external service. The idea behind auditing is to verify that the transaction has taken place and that it has been accurately recorded and carried out.

Internal Audits: It is recommended that an internal audit be conducted on a continual basis by an experienced staff member or by members who are knowledgeable of the accounting and fiscal operation of the agency. Sharpe and others suggest that an internal auditor service must be on hand continuously concurrent with reports filed regularly. The internal auditor or editors should be responsible to and report to one of the top administrator in the agency (1994:133). Granted, the internal auditor or auditors will neither eliminate the abuse of fiscal procedures nor prevent misappropriation of funds, but the fiscal management procedure may be modified in such a way that these mishaps will not occur again.

External Audits: Sometimes it is necessary to seek an external service to do the auditing. This may be due to the lack of qualified personnel who can do the auditing, or because the management feels that such an audit is needed. These types of audits are also known as post-audits since they take place some time after the transactions have taken place. Many of the recreation, parks, and leisure services agencies are audited by designated authorities within the states or provinces in which they are operating. When federal funds are appropriated, federal authorities conduct the audits. These "official" audits usually take place a year or more after the end of the fiscal period being audited. The management of a recreation, parks , or leisure service agency must be aware of this possibility and be prepared to assist the team doing the auditing.

An auditing may also be requested by the foundation which is supporting an agency's project through a grant. Some foundations reserve the right to audit the project or require that an audit be conducted by a certified public accountant. In this case Lefferts (1983: 172-202) suggests that it may be useful to separate the project funds, from the general funds and develop a Project Line Item Budget. The items to be included represent the different activities of the project.

TRENDS IN FISCAL MANAGEMENT

New realities are challenging the fiscal management of a recreation, parks, or leisure service agency. These new realities are faced not only by the public or semi-public agencies but also by private agencies.

Cutbacks, sometimes called downsizing or retrenchment, are a reality which all three types of agencies face. Moreover, the public agency providing recreation, parks, or leisure service, which has been shielded from "marketing" its services since the park and recreation movement began a century ago, has to be concerned with this element in its financial management.

With the increased competition among different agencies that are providing recreation, parks, or leisure services, pricing of their services, whether subsidized by public monies or not, must receive considerable attention from the management.

The realities of current economics, the trends in public opinion, and the new political orientation necessitates that the management of recreation, parks, and leisure service agencies consider the following practices.

Cutbacks and Downsizing

Cutting back programs and personnel is a painful process not only for those doing it but also for those affected by it. It is particularly painful when permanent staff is affected. Not only will those released suffer, but also those who remain on the job are known to suffer from very low morale. When termination must take place, unless the management is very careful, an unpleasant situation could occur.

Paul F. Mickey Jr. offers the following as the best possible method of handling termination. The person delivering the unpleasant news must deliver it simply, concisely and sympathetically. However, too much sympathy is counter-productive. The news should be offered early in the conversation. The person delivering the news should not create a false aura of hope, particularly if it is unlikely to occur. The manager, or whoever was designated to deliver the news, should help the employee concentrate on the future. Topics such as health insurance options, remaining leave, severance pay, and the like should be discussed (1994).

Marketing and Leisure Service

The term marketing may seem to be applicable to commercial recreation only. In fact the meaning behind the term, although only recently introduced in public and semi-public agencies dealing with recreation, parks, and leisure services, could be very useful. Simply put, marketing is the process through which one shows others what is being offered.

While Kraus and Curtis (2000: 184) suggest that this process entails four "p"s, Scott (1998:137) suggests an additional three are necessary. For both authors, the first "p", stands for program or product. Although most agencies dealing with recreation, parks, and leisure services deal with programs, some commercial enterprises in these fields deal with products. The second stands for the place where the program or the product is offered. While the third "p" stands for price, the importance of the fourth "p" lies in the fact that it represents the heart of the marketing process, promotion. Scott adds three more "p"s as essential for the success of marketing: people, physical environment, and process. People dealing with the service or product must be neat and presentable. Additionally, the facility where the product is sold or the service is provided must be safe and tidy. Also throughout the marketing process, every step must be directed toward targeting and satisfying the customer, client, or user.

It is evident that the need to promote the program of a public agency dealing with recreation, parks, and or leisure service is of paramount importance in this period of declining public fiscal support. Promotion of the program may lead to increased participation which, in itself, is a factor in gaining the needed support. Also if fees are charged, an increased participation means a welcome increase in income.

A number of steps are suggested in the promotion of the program and or the product of recreation, parks and leisure service agencies (O'Sullivan, 1991).

1. **Target Marketing:** This step is needed not only to identify the potential users/consumers of the service but also to determine their needs, interests and general characteristics.

2. **Marketing Strategies:** The next step is used to identify and to select specific segments in the market that are promising and are suitable for marketing. Approaches to these segments should be agreed upon in this step.

3. **Marketing Mix:** In this step the management of a recreation, parks, or leisure service should attempt to offer a mix among the first three "p"s, program (or product), place, and price. The mix should appeal to the user/consumer.

4. **Promotion:** This is the fourth step, per Kraus and Curtis, in marketing the program (or product) of the agency. The most effective means of communication should be used in this step.

In the execution of these four steps, the utilization of the additional three elements suggested by Scott would be indeed very beneficial.

Although, some concerns have been raised about the current emphasis on marketing as a technique to be used in public and semi-public leisure service agencies suffering from lack of public support, these concerns will be discussed in detail in Chapter Seventeen on "Current Issues and Future Trends."

Pricing and the Leisure Service Agency

Pricing of a commodity or a service requires careful analysis. While this may be true for a business that functions in a competitive environment, pricing of a public service is also crucial to its success. Since a public service does not operate in a vacuum, it is also subject to some of the same elements that are at work in the "market place." A public agency dealing with recreation, parks and leisure services is subject to the same factors that affect the marketing of a commodity or a service provided by a business albeit in a subtle way. For instance, a public agency may have a competitor in a semi-public agency or even, in some instances, a private agency. Even though the services provided by a public agency are subsidized by public funds which help to reduce its price, the important factor of quality of the service should be taken into consideration. The quality of the service or commodity should be such that the customer may not be enticed to seek the service from a semi-public or private agency.

It is clear from the foregoing that pricing of a service or a commodity is much more complicated than may be assumed. Undoubtedly, there is more than one dimension to the pricing of a commodity or service provided in the fields of recreation and parks. Crompton and Lamb (1986:136) suggest that two important dimensions to pricing should be considered when making decisions on pricing: monetary dimension and nonmonetary dimension.

The Monetary Dimension: This dimension of pricing a service or a commodity utilizes the actual dollar amount which it will cost the participant or consumer. Yet, as previously stated, the pricing of a commodity or a service involves more than just mere dollars and cents. For example, in providing tennis lessons to a group of beginners in the local park and recreation department, the price should not be limited to the salary and fringe benefits of the instructor and the administrative cost. The dollar amount derived from these two elements should not be the only factor that enters into the price determination of the tennis lessons. Other hidden, indirect nonmonetary factors should also be taken into consideration when determining the price of the tennis lessons.

The Nonmonetary Dimension: As O'Sullivan (1991: 98) suggests there are three factors related to the pricing of a program or a service: time, association, and effort on part of the participant not the provider. For example, the price of a service should take into consideration the amount of time that the prospective participant or buyer is willing to spend to participate in the program or purchase of the commodity. In the example above, when determining the cost of the tennis lessons, the amount of time the participant or the adult, who may be accompanying him or her, has to spend waiting his or her turn should be taken into consideration. If the number of tennis courts in the department is ample, the price could be set at a particular level. Otherwise the pricing should be adjusted so as to entice participation despite some waiting time on the part of the users.

The same is applied to the effort factor on the part of the participant or participants. If and when the user finds himself or herself having to use extra effort to participate in the program, its attractiveness is reduced. Accordingly, the price should be lowered as an enticement for participation.

The social factor with which the user or users will be associated upon joining the service should be taken into consideration in pricing. For example, when organizing a trip, the group with which the person is travelling may determine the volume of participation. The mixing or separating of age groups may be an important element in the volume of participation, an important element in pricing the service.

Pricing Objectives: Pricing objectives will vary according to the type of agencies providing recreation, parks, and leisure services. The public, semi- public, and private agencies have different objectives which impact their pricing objectives. Still each of these agencies, regardless of affiliation, should develop enough flexible pricing objectives to allow for proper functioning. For example, does the agency seek to increase participation? Or does it seek to increase revenue? Furthermore, can the agency achieve either of these objectives?

Price Determination: A number of methods are used to determine the price of a service or a commodity. Bullaro and Edginton(1986:229-30) suggest these four methods:

1. Going rate pricing: The assumption here is that the market has already established the price of the commodity or service.

2. Demand-oriented pricing: Typically this pricing is used by both semi-public and public leisure services.

3. Segmented-differentiated pricing: This type provides for more than one price which allows certain users the ability to pay.

4. Cost oriented pricing: This method takes into consideration the actual cost of the service or commodity.

EXPENDITURE OF A LEISURE SERVICE AGENCY

Since leisure service agencies vary from public, semi-public, to commercial, expenditures will vary significantly. The following is a list of the possible expenditure of a leisure agency. Other items under each of the main categories may be added according to the type and size of the agency.

Salaries and Wages

This very important expenditure category should be monitored by all types and sizes of agencies. In some cases, this category may be included under the expenditure of the main headquarters. Nonetheless, it is important to keep track of the expenses encountered. Subheadings used in this category are as follows:

Full-time administrators
Full-time staff
Part-time staff
Full-time hourly staff
Part-time hourly staff
Payment in lieu of notice (severance pay)
Retroactive Pay
Overtime wages
Temporary Employment
Other pay

Fringe Benefits

Although fringe benefits will vary from one agency to another, the following represents a general idea of the fringe benefits practices in most places of employment in the United States:

FICA Taxes

Retirement or pension cost

Health Insurance

Workman's Compensation Insurance

Unemployment Insurance

Dental Insurance

Life Insurance

Earned Time (vacation and or sick leaves)

Services

Under this category, expenses that are encountered in providing for the smooth operation of the agency are listed. Most agencies, regardless of their affiliations, follow a comparable listing.

Communication and Information

Postage and Shipping

Printing and Duplicating

Conferences and Conventions

Travel and Transportation

Professional Services

Maintenance and Repair Services

Other Contract Services (e.g. pest control)

Utilities

All recreation, parks, and leisure service agencies use the following utilities, the costs of which are not within the control of the management. These items are necessary for the adequate functioning of any modern service agency.

> Telephone/Fax/Telegraph
>
> Electricity
>
> Natural Gas
>
> Water
>
> Trash and solid waste disposal

Equipment and Supplies

Items listed below are becoming increasingly costly, and the management usually tries to control these expenditure. Nonetheless, equipment and supplies are needed in all operations.

> New Equipment (over $1000)
>
> Minor Equipment (under $1000)
>
> Equipment Replacement
>
> Furnishing (over $1000)
>
> Minor Furnishing (under $1000)
>
> Land Improvement
>
> Buildings Improvement
>
> Other Improvements
>
> Office Supplies
>
> Maintenance and Repair Supplies
>
> Custodial and Cleaning Supplies
>
> Computer supplies
>
> Chemicals for plants and pools)
>
> Paint
>
> Park Signs
>
> Apparel

Dues and Publications

All recreation, parks and leisure service agencies should become members in the different professional organizations that have some bearing on their functions. This section of expenditure is spent on the following activities:

Dues and Memberships

Publications

Subscriptions

Miscellaneous Costs

Other costs will be encountered by the recreation, parks and leisure agencies. The following list represents some of these possible expenditures.

Rental and Leases

Protection Insurance

Liability Insurance

Debt Expenses

Charge Card Expenses

Auto Allowance

Irrigation Service

Taxes and assessments

PRIVATIZATION

Privatization is a fiscal tool in management and could be applied in two different ways. Outsourcing or contracting out entails the use of an outside contact or contractors, to perform a function or a service, the outcome of which is cost effective. Other than saving money, this arrangement could allow for flexibility. Also, the outside contractor may be able to provide a better service than would the agency. Moreover, liability is shifted from the agency to the contractor. The idea of outsourcing was tried in the golf services of three cities. These cities were able to attain goals which were unattainable with regular delivery system (Gustafson and McLean 1999).

Glover argues that privatizing leisure services is more efficient than direct provision because it 1) reduces the cost of delivery, 2) introduces competition and consumer' choice, 3) avoids the oversupply of services, 4) displaces inefficient personnel, and 5) stimulates greater measurement (1999).

The disadvantages of outsourcing include loss of control over programs, potential of conflict, and possible lack of response on part of the contractor to the needs and interests of the citizens (Crompton, 1998).

Another form of privatization is *divestiture*. This takes place when control of certain assets are given to private parties. A good example of divestiture occurs when the federal government puts a non-profit or for-profit organization in charge of camps within its jurisdiction. As is the case with outsourcing, the ultimate test here is an economic one. Also the advantage and the disadvantages of such an arrangement are similar to the ones listed under outsourcing. Also the advantage and the disadvantages of such an arrangement are similar to the ones listed under outsourcing.

SUMMARY

- Revenues of a public agency providing recreation, parks or leisure service come mainly form taxes. While bonds and grants are sometimes used, many public agencies are beginning to depend on fees and charges as important sources of revenues.

- Semi-public/nonprofit agencies depend on membership, fees, and the community chest as their sources of revenue. Donations and gifts are becoming increasingly important in the smooth functioning of nonprofits.

- Membership and sales are the major revenue sources in commercial enterprises offering recreation, parks or leisure services. Consultation fees are also a good source of income for some of these agencies.

- Many innovative methods of fundraising are used by all three types of agencies. This revenue form is particularly important to semi-public/nonprofit agencies.

- Budgeting for the agency offering recreation, parks, or leisure service has become both an art and a science. Certain rules are now followed in the preparation and execution of the budget.

- Another important aspect of fiscal management in an agency is accounting and auditing. Both are important processes that help in the smooth functioning of the agency.

- Funds have been drying up for most agencies dealing with recreation, parks and leisure services and among the most recent trends in fiscal management is how to downsize the agency without causing too much damage. Other trends include marketing and pricing.

LEARNING ACTIVITIES

1. Visit your local park and recreation department. Write down the charges collected for participating in certain activities. Visit the local YMCA and find out the same. Compare the charges of a public agency to the charges of a semi-public/nonprofit agency. What generalizations can you make based on your findings?

2. Call City Hall in your hometown. Find out when the City Council will be discussing the City Budget. Attend the meeting and write a report on your observations.

3. Attend a meeting of the local board or commission of parks and recreation. Try to find out the sources of funding and the classification of expenses in the city's department of parks and recreation.

4. Visit a commercial enterprise dealing with some recreation, parks or leisure service or one that is providing recreational goods such as sporting equipment, records and tapes, or a travel agency. Describe how it is operating.

REFERENCES

Baumback, Clifford M.(1983) **Basic Small Business Management.** Englewood Cliffs, NJ: Prentice-Hall inc.

Benedict, Ruth (1978). "Federal Support for Local Park and Recreation Systems," **Trends.** Fall.

Birkofer, John R. , Richard S. Wasch and Clifford Kramer (1987)"Budgeting in Nonprofit Organizations," in Sweeny, H.W. Allen and Robert Rachlin, **Handbook Of Budgeting.** New York: Wiley.

Bullaro, John and Christopher Edginton (1986) **Commercial Leisure Services: Managing for Profit, Service and Personal Satisfaction.** New York: Macmillan.

Crompton, J.L. (1998) "Forces Underlying the Emergency of Privatization in Parks and Recreation." **Journal of Park and Recreation Administration** 16 (2):88-10.

Glover, T.D. (1999) "Propositions Addressing the Privatization of Public Leisure Services: Implications for Efficiency, Effectiveness, and Equity." **Journal of Park and Recreation Administration** 17(2):1-27.

Gustafson, T.F. and D.D. McLean (1999) "The Operating Structure of Privatized Golf Services." **Journal of Park and Recreation Administration** 17(4):39-55.

Hay, J. Thomas (1983). **534 Ways to Raise Money.** New York: Simon and Schuster.

Ibrahim, Hilmi and Kathleen Cordes (1993). **Outdoor Recreation.** Madison: Brown and Benchmark.

Kraus, Richard and Joseph Curtis (1990). **Creative Management in Recreation, Parks and Leisure Service.** St. Louis: Mosby.

Kraus, Richard and Joseph Curtis (2000) **Creative Management in Recreation, parks and Leisure Services.** St. Louis: McGraw-Hill.

Lefferts, Robert (1983) **The Basic Handbook of Grant Management.** New York: Basic Books.

Mickey, Jr., Paul (1994) "Tips for Handling Terminations," **Nation's Business.** V. 82, July:58-60. Washington, D.C.: U.S. Chamber of Commerce.

Meisinger, Richard J. and Leroy W. Dubeck (1984) **College and University Budgeting.** Washington, D.C. the National Association of Business Officers.

O'Sullivan, Ellen L.(1991). **Marketing for Parks, Recreation and Leisure.** State College, PA: Venture Publishing, Inc.

Schroeder, Herbert and Jordan Louviere (1999) "Stated Choice Models for Predicting the Impact of User Fees at Public Recreation Sites," **Journal of Leisure Research.** 31:(3), p.300-24.

Scott, Jonathan T. (1998) **Fundamentals of Leisure Business Success.** New York: The Hathorn Press.

Sellers, J.R. N.J. Gladwell and M.S. Pope (1999) Fiscal Management in B.Van der Smissen et al., **Management of Park and Recreation Agencies.** Ashburn, VA: NRPA.

Sharpe, G. Ch. Odegaard and W. Sharpe (1994) **A Comprehensive Introduction to Park Management.** Champaign, IL: Sagamore Publishing.

Whitmyer, Claude, Salli Rasberry and Michael Phillips (1989). **Running a One-person Business.** Berkely, CA: Ten Speed Press.

CHAPTER 10
MARKETING

Learning Objectives

After studying this chapter you should be able to do the following:

1. Describe the concept of marketing.
2. Describe the three stages of the evolution of marketing.
3. Understand market segmentation and market research.
4. List and describe the four Ps of the marketing mix.
5. Understand the elements necessary in a strategic marketing plan.
6. Describe differences between the service and product orientations.
7. Understand the various aspects of the marketing environment.

Even though recreation is a basic human need, when and how it is engaged in are still voluntary choices. How people choose to spend their discretionary time and money is a decision that only they can make. Play to one person may be work to another, and what is risky and recreationally exciting to one person may be commonplace to another. While people are seeking escape and relaxation, whereas others are looking for adventure and socialization. The unique complexities of this broad concept of recreation and leisure can be addressed through the marketing process. Whether the emphasis is on serving the homeless or competing with the finest spas, marketing for park, recreation, and leisure service delivery systems has become an integral part of the operation.

As one expert suggests, recognizing the needs and desires of consumer groups and then instituting programs and services to meet those needs reflect the real mission of leisure delivery systems (O'Sullivan 1991:14). In fact, marketing is so important that the manager should make every effort to encourage the agency or organization to employ a marketing expert or turn to a professional marketing agency for assistance. Within smaller organizations, the leader-manager will often lead the charge. In either case, marketing has become an important management tool because it facilitates the use and delivery of leisure services. And, in today's information-based society, market research will provide information that will ultimately result in enlightened decision-making (Riddick and Russell 1999:vi,367).

THE BASICS OF MARKETING

Marketing encompasses the sum total of everything that an agency or organization does to promote its service or product. The process begins at the moment the service or product is conceived (Levinson 1998:8), and is the major force that keeps the organization focused on meeting customer demand. Marketing influences the lives of most people in society. Market researchers study our lives, our patterns and activities, as well as our needs and desires.

From all of this study, a plan emerges that results in action. This *marketing strategic plan* reflects the choices that the organization makes based on its knowledge of the market. The plan serves as a tool that helps the entire organization focus its resources towards meeting the needs of its selected market. With this expansive approach, it is not at all surprising that most new significant directions in management are oriented around marketing strategies.

Marketing: A Definition

Marketing is an essential management function that is needed in order to create or identify customer demand followed by an exchange of that entity's product or service. It was not always thought of in this way though. Over a century ago, it was believed that bringing a quality product to the market would attract plenty of customers in and of itself. Marketing later evolved into a second phase, which was focused on promoting existing products. Now, in a later stage, by studying the market first, marketing seeks to identify the products and services that are needed or desired. From this research phase, the organization formulates a marketing plan that directs the organization toward meeting the needs and desires of its customers - a vital concern of parks, recreation, and leisure service delivery systems.

The American Marketing Association officially defines *marketing* as the process of planning and executing the conception, pricing, promotion, and distribution of ideas, goods, and services to create exchanges that satisfy individual and organizational objectives. At the core of this concept is the exchange of value that takes place between a buyer and a seller. This means that in market planning, the recreation agency will be challenged to identify the needs of its market (customers), select and develop the appropriate service or product, develop communications to get the service or product to the customer, and follow-through to ensure satisfaction.

Identifying Customers' Needs: To understand the needs and desires of present and potential customers, the agency looks at what the customer really wants. This is accomplished through market research. Market research takes some of the risk out of deciding what recreation and leisure services and products should be presented. When a marketing approach is used, the agency will not push a service or product that is not wanted. In other words, effective marketing is user, not seller, oriented. This realization is the foundation of the *marketing concept* (Sawyer and Smith 1999:176) in which operations are oriented around customer relations and satisfaction while a reasonable profit is made (or a recovery of costs as the case may be with public agencies and nonprofits). Today's customers are increasingly more demanding and are often not satisfied with a service or product that simply meets their needs. They also want to satisfy their imagination and dreams (Gianlugi and Longinotti-Buitoni 1999: 300). Market research, as a result, seeks to identify and encompass these high expectations.

The Selection of a Market: It is often difficult for recreation agencies to realize that they cannot be all things to all people. Sometimes they spread themselves too thin. Once the needs and characteristics of several markets have been identified, the agency must decide which markets it can serve. This is defined by keeping the agency's mission, goals, and available resources in mind. Nonprofit agencies need to consider the needs of those who cannot always pay, and government agencies must wrestle with opposing public viewpoints. The Bureau of Land Management serves markets interested in outdoor recreation and cattle grazing. Sometimes the needs of its separate market segments clash, but the agency must define how it can potentially reach each market segment in a fair and beneficial manner as defined by the market and the agency's mission.

Communications: After the agency has developed the appropriate service and products for the park, recreation, and leisure service market, the benefits of the service or product need to be communicated. An agency might choose to use public relations, publicity, sales promotion, advertising, or personal selling. The public image influences not only the specific market segment served, but also the community that funds or sponsors a government agency.

Making the Service or Product Available: Availability means making it easy for the customer to participate in the service or to buy the product. The offering has to take place at the right time and at the right price. For instance, a survey taken by a community senior center showed that seniors taking a popular water aerobics class at 6:00 A.M. actually preferred a 10:00 A.M slot. The time was shifted, and the director learned that 22 more individuals enrolled.

The Evolution of Marketing

To grasp the growing significance of marketing, the evolution of marketing needs to be understood. Marketing evolved through three specific orientations (O'Sullivan 1991:3-4): product orientation, sales orientation, and customer orientation.

Product Orientation: Marketing's first orientation, *product orientation*, began over one hundred years ago and dominated marketing for years. Dealing specifically with the manufacture of products, it was believed that a quality product could sell itself. This orientation influenced the service market. Under this philosophy, for example, a park, recreation, and leisure service delivery system created the best services possible and waited for the customers to arrive. Problems with this method arose when a quality service or product was created, but the customers were not aware of its attributes. This led to the second, more sophisticated orientation.

Sales Organization: S*ales orientation* uses advertising and personal selling to overcome consumer resistance and to convince consumers to buy the service or product. This orientation was designed to awaken public interest, but it meant that marketing was still subservient to the service or product. Both profit and nonprofit agencies used promotional means to spark consumer and public interest in the organization's existing service or product. Some recreation agencies have been reluctant to leave this orientation.

Consumer Orientation: The emerging *consumer orientation* arrived when it became clear that an organization's survival demanded that managers pay more attention to the potential customers who would use or buy the services and products. In some organizations, the customer is now referred to as a *guest* to emphasize respect for that person. Under this consumer orientation, target markets are studied in order to understand and anticipate the customer's needs and desires. Marketing efforts begin to play a key role in the overall planning process of the organization. In addition, studies now influence what types of services are offered and the design and manufacture of a product. Because all organizations - profit and nonprofit - wish to satisfy the customer, this orientation has influenced the approach of most organizations. Park, recreation, and leisure service delivery systems have learned that the customers' needs must be satisfied. When a study commissioned by the International Health, Racquet and Sports Club Association found that non-exercisers believed that health spas did not pay attention to their difficulties, the results had definite implications for marketing (Dreyfus 1997:20).

Customer preference not only emerged at the core of marketing, but it also became a key consideration at all levels of an organization. Even the manner of billing a customer is adapted to the needs of the individual. Previously, it was only during the actual sale or exchange that the customer was central; otherwise, the internal operations of the organization took priority. This change in orientation has been embraced by many organizations.

Market Segmentation

Market *segmentation* is the process by which a market is divided into groups of consumers who have similar desires and needs and who tend to respond to certain offerings in similar ways. Though no single variable such as marital status can fully describe a *target* group, segmentation of the market can be used effectively to determine the services and products that certain groups seek. When a group is identified with similar preferences that match the services of the organization, it is referred to as a target group. For a recreation organization, these are the people who are likely to desire certain programs or services, and are potential participants. If a health spa advertises with young body beautiful athletes in tight, skimpy workout clothes, it is targeting its audience and should not expect to attract overweight adults who may be intimidated (Riddick and Russell 1999:368).

In The Field...

BLM's Customer Commitment Pledge

The mission of the Bureau of Land Management is to sustain the health of the public lands for present and future generations. In carrying out that mission, the Bureau has made a firm commitment to serve its customers, the citizens of the country. In doing so, it pledges the following to its customers:

- We will listen to the customer and respond to suggestions.
- We will incorporate customer service performance standards into management reviews and performance rating systems.
- We will educate ourselves about customer service concepts and techniques.
- We will use our experiences with customers to improve the way we do business.
- We will seek out the best business practices, measure our performance against them, and continually improve our performance.
- We will always treat customers in a courteous, efficient, and professional manner every time we are contacted.
- We will work with customers to meet their needs while complying with laws and regulations.
- We will advise customers if their request cannot be filled in their initial contact with us, tell them who will respond to their request and when to expect that response.

Source: Bureau of Land Management *Our Commitment to Customer Service* (Washington D.C.: U.S. Government Printing Office).

Target markets are most often identified on the basis of common descriptors. Some of the variables considered for market segmentation include social class, sex, life-style, age, and usage rate. For most park and recreation organizations, these descriptors include leisure needs and interests and other factors (O'Sullivan 1991:8) such as geographic (location of home and work), sociodemographic (age, gender, marital status), behavioral (activities engaged in), and synchrongraphic (time preferences and time constraints). For example, an Adventure Ecotourism Travel Outfitter has learned that seniors enjoy educational cruises. This is a start, but the outfitter will need to narrow its target market by identifying seniors with sufficient income, interest, independence, and health to make the trip. By targeting a narrower potential market, a more focused and efficient approach to marketing is possible.

The target market is identified and selected in light of the organization's mission. Once market segments are selected, the organization decides how to *position* its service or product so that it becomes distinguishable from the competition. This effort is based on the organization's ability to provide benefits that are distinct or of high quality. For instance, the YMCA is well known for its excellent swimming programs which creates distinction. How any organization is presented can be tailored to the target market's values, emotions, and self-image.

Market Research

Market research is undertaken to help managers gain information regarding the market that they wish to serve. Research provides the agency with critical strategic information. Market researchers study our lives, our patterns and activities, and our wants and desires. They identify needs and determine whether these needs have been met. They study how people are exposed to new information, how they process it, and what actions they are likely to take as a result. They study population trends, and what customers think that they want and what they actually want. They analyze what triggers a person to move from a passive interest to an actual exchange of money. And once an exchange occurs, market researchers study *customer loyalty*, and why the customer returning for more.

Depending on the type of information sought, the process of collecting it can be time-consuming and expensive. The cost, however, is usually balanced with potential losses from poor decisions. Research areas include the identity of the market, the size of the market, the location of the market, and the reasons why that the market will want the service or product. Other information, including information about consumer preferences and the competition, can also be obtained. Various marketing research methods, including analyses of primary and secondary data, can provide answers.

Primary Data: *Primary data* is collected by the recreation agency or business directly from the source. It is used when detailed and specific information is necessary. A park, recreation, or leisure service delivery system can pursue this information by hiring a marketing research firm or by conducting research itself. Research is usually conducted by observation or through surveys. The *observation* method includes actual observation of customers or participants. The *survey* method is usually accomplished through telephone, mail, the web, or personal interviews.

Table 10-1 presents comparative information about these four basic delivery methods. Organization utilize a variety of methods that range from on-site personal interviews at the time of actual use to electronic surveys completed by visitors at park kiosks. With no paper or mailing costs needed, the latter is considered environmentally friendly. Another promising innovation for parks, recreation, and leisure delivery systems is the use of electronic forums to identify a group's consensus opinion on a surveyed topic (Young and Jamieson 2001:42-58).

Secondary Data: *Secondary data* is data that has already been collected, compiled, and published. It is collected from various sources including the federal, state, and local governments; trade, professional, and business associations; colleges and universities; research organizations; libraries; marketing firms; and private consultants or government-sponsored consulting assistance programs, such as the Small Business Administration (SBA) in the United States and the Federal Business Development Bank (FBDB) in Canada. A vast amount of data can be collected from the Federal Government, marketing researchers often purchase publications such as the *Monthly Catalog of the United States Government Publications*. Additional sources include the *Statistical Abstract of the United States*, the *Marketing Information Guide*, the *Survey of Current Business*, the *Census of Population*, and the *County and City Data Book*.

TABLE 10-1

Comparison of Survey Delivery: Telephone, Mail, Web, and Personal Interviews.

	Telephone	*Mail*	*Web/E-mail*	*Personal Interview*
Speed	fast	slow	fast	slow
Cost	inexpensive	inexpensive	inexpensive	expensive
Type of Questions	simple, direct	simple, direct	simple, direct, sophisticated	sophisticated, detailed
Caveat	Tele-surveys are viewed as a nuisance by many. They may impact public relations.	Procrastination and distractions deter responses. The group that does respond may be biased.	Cyber-privacy deters some responses. The group that does respond may be biased	Detailed responses can be difficult to quantify, analyze, and describe.
Tip to improve response	Use newsletters or mail to notify members ahead of time so call is anticipated	Design a short questionnaire. Offer a gift for responding.	Offer free web registration for responding to a short survey	Interview 6 to 12 responders at once to speed the process and create synergy.
Best Use/ Advantage	allows for quick turn-around on specific topic	best for broad nationwide surveys	fast processing; low risk of data entry errors	to solicit in-depth, honest, and sincere answers

THE MARKETING MIX

There are many possible ways to satisfy target markets and to make a service or product appealing through the use of options such as color, brand, cost and method of advertising. These options are referred to as *controlled options*, and there are hundreds of combinations. These options are conveniently packaged into four adjustable strategies or interrelated variables known as the "four Ps"— product, place, promotion, and price. Various combinations of the options are referred to as the *marketing mix*. The decisions that make up the marketing mix, once implemented, become the basis for providing customer satisfaction and determining marketing success. The objective of satisfying the customer is achieved when each party involved in the exchange takes on a greater satisfaction from what is received than from what is given up. The four P's must find balance in the marketing mix to effect the exchange. In this way, the resources of the agency are used efficiently, and the consumer's needs are met, resulting in a successful operation and a successful relationship.

Product: A product or offering includes all aspects of the physical product or the service being offered. Product strategy includes making decisions about quality, uses, features, assortment, style, design, warranty, guarantee, service, brand, and other options that help to make the product or service more appealing based on market research. Park, recreation, and leisure entities are dominated by service providers.

Considering Service and Product Differentiation: Although service marketing and product marketing have much in common, certain strategies are not the same. A fundamental difference exists because services are performed and consumed, whereas products are manufactured and processed. These fundamental differences should be considered when planning a park, recreation, and leisure service delivery system's marketing strategy. Service sector attributes that are different from those of the product industry are shown in Table 10-2.

TABLE 10-2

Service Sector Attributes

1. *Services are intangible.* Because services are intangible, it is complicated for consumers to inspect them before purchasing. Compared to a product, services are difficult to display, physically demonstrate, and illustrate. When purchasing a tennis racket, the consumer can see it, handle it, and swing it before purchasing. A resident of Houston, Texas does not, generally, have the opportunity to visit the Rogue River in Oregon before rafting in the summer months. This creates a greater risk for the potential customer. For these customers, other familiarization options are possible such as video tapes and brochures.

2. *Services are simultaneously consumed and produced.* The service operation is limited by the simultaneous availability of qualified staff and willing customers. Though the Grand Canyon National Park encompasses a large area, only a limited number of visitors can be accommodated on the mule trip to the canyon's depth at any one time. On the other hand, the number of swim goggles produced or purchased during the year is not affected by a similar timing constraint. Goggles can be produced ahead of time, and then distributed as the market demands.

3. *The quality of the service is affected by the client's input.* Service quality depends on genuine communication from the clients about their needs in order to make effective and useful modifications to a service. Effective open listening and communicating consistently about the customer's needs is essential (Geraghty 1998: 199). A program designed for teenagers requires the adolescent advice to reach its fullest potential. Many organizations are adding members from all target markets, including adolescents, to advisory boards.

4. *Services are not standardized.* The quality of service varies depending on where and when the service is performed and who performs it. A kayaking trip on a wild and scenic river will likely be more successful than a kayaking experience in a polluted lake. An aerobic dance instructor may be more energetic in the morning than at the end of the day. A state park may offer fewer services during the winter, but the summer may have fewer camping opportunities because of crowds. A ranger with a background in botany might offer a more interesting forest walk than a ranger with a anthropological background who wishes to tour ruins.

Source: Cyr, D. and Gray, D. *Marketing Your Product* (British Columbia: International Self-Counsel Press Ltd,, 1994), 3.

Place: Placing a product means providing it at the right place at the right time. Distribution strategies include decisions on such things as service outlet location, shelf location, time of year, type of shipment, convenience, design, and facility. When marketing for recreation, place refers to a number of factors including the actual location of the program or service, accessibility, parking availability, season, and time offered. Many parks, for example, have different recreational opportunities during the off-season to expand accessibility.

Promotion: Promotion is informing and persuading the target market about the value of the service or product. The major promotional tools are public relations, publicity, sales promotion, personal selling, and advertising. Which tool is used is important to the success of the campaign. Often perceived as the entire marketing process, promotion is a critical element of the marketing mix and is described in detail in next chapter. To attract clients, promotion programs may influence potential consumers as they go through various stages before making their final decisions. These consumer stages are described in Table 10-3.

TABLE 10-3
_____

Consumer Stages
_____

RECOGNITION: The first stage in selecting a service or purchasing a product occurs once the potential customer recognizes a need. This could be brought about by a desire to socialize, to lose weight, to be active, to be more physically fit, etc. Potential customers may be prompted through promotional programs designed to help them recognize needs. The leader-manager as a marketer recognizes cues that trigger interest. For example, exercise programs appeal to individuals right after the holidays or just before swimsuit season. The garden club will attract new members during the first warm days of spring.

INFORMATION: With the need recognized, potential customers usually research various services or products. Leader-managers make information available, calling attention to the organization's service or product. This requires an understanding of where customers look for information - brochures, displays, salespeople, other customers, or advertisements. Because dissatisfaction can produce poor public relations, every effort is made to portray the service or product as realistically as possible.

EVALUATION: After this information is processed, the customer makes the decision. If two agency's offer similar programs, the program is selected that places more emphasis on areas valued by the potential customer. For instance, the individual may value the security provided at one location. Advertising campaigns can even cater to target audiences by emphasizing these attributes. A fitness spa can stress a play area for children.

CHOICE: At this point, a customer usually makes a decision. The exchange may be postponed, however, if the individual is not certain that the time or financial cost is worth it. A customer might consider any physical harm that could be sustained or question whether the service or product will really work. A potential kayaker, for instance, may decide that the river is too dangerous, or a person seeking to lose twenty pounds before summer may decide that the goal is impossible. If leader-managers understand the potential risks, they can help alleviate these anxieties by providing safeguards, guarantees, opportunities to test, names of customers to contact, testimonials in brochures, and staff to answer questions.

POST-PURCHASE BLUES: After participation in a program or purchase of a product, the customer evaluates the experience based on prior expectations. The leader-manager uses this opportunity to obtain honest information through customer evaluations and suggestion forms.

Source: Cyr, D. and Gray, D. *Marketing Your Product* (British Columbia: International Self-Counsel Press Ltd.,1994), 36-37.
_____

Price: Price is the amount of money given in exchange for a service or product. Price greatly influences the image of the product or service and whether or not it will be purchased. The established price takes into consideration the three C's - cost, competition, and the consumer (Hisrich 1990:5). It involves management policies on discounts, payment periods, and credit terms which are often referred to with words such as *premium, tuition, rate, fee, retainer, honorarium, fare, interest* and *charge* (Johnson, Scheuing, & Gaida 1986:11). The pricing policy of public agencies and nonprofits may be based on the need to recover costs or to support other programs.

If the buyer perceives the price to be greater than the benefits received, the sale or exchange will usually not take place. The price paid by the buyer must be equal to or less than the total satisfaction acquired from the cluster of benefits received (Hiam and Schewe 1992:20). This is formulated in the equation seen in Figure 10-1.

FIGURE 10-1

The Benefit Equation

Price $\$\$ \quad \leq \quad$ | — Product = attributes of the product or service

Price $\$\$ \quad \leq$ | — Place = right place at the right time

| — Promotion = informing and persuading
the target market

THE STRATEGIC MARKETING PLAN

The *strategic marketing plan* defines the organization's objectives and states how to attain them. It is the big picture of what the agency or organization will do in the market, and is a blueprint for matching its mission, resources, and market opportunities. Usually devised by top management, the plan sets the tone for the entire organization. With it, the organization has a vision to pursue. Without a plan, marketing efforts tend to be reactive and inefficient rather than pro-active. Jay Conrad Levinson (1998:54-56), author of the *Guerrilla Marketing* and *Guerrilla Marketing Attack,* believes that through competitive marketing an entity can take the lead in developing creative strategies within its own market. This marketing edge forces other organizations to react rather than lead.

Creating the Plan: Creating a vital strategic plan is not a simple matter. It requires that the leader-manager identify the organization's current position; recognize its relationship to other organizations and the community in general; assess the organization's resources; and understand its customers, their needs, and how they perceive the organization's service or product. This information is matched with the organization's internal operations which include staff qualifications, technological readiness, financial strength, and appropriateness of facilities. Future problems must be identified and opportunities anticipated. Strengths must be developed and weaknesses understood and addressed. Sometimes it is even necessary to relinquish certain services or products to another organization or competitor that has a better handle on the particular area.

To succeed at designing a plan, leader-managers undertake three processes discussed earlier in this chapter. First, they divide the market into segments and target their market (market segmentation). Second, data and information about the target market is studied and analyzed (market research). Finally, an appropriate mix of communication tools is selected to reach these potential customers (marketing mix). Philip Koter, author of *Strategic Marketing for Non-Profit Institutions*, criticizes many nonprofit organizations for marketing their services in the wrong order. He believes that too many nonprofits communicate and advertise their service before planning their strategy through the use of market segmentation and research. Table 10-4 presents several reasons for a leader-manager to design market plans.

TABLE 10-4

Reasons To Design a Market Plan

Leader-managers design market plans for a number of reasons:

- To introduce new services or products
- To expand into new markets
- To revitalize services, products, or markets
- To respond to a drop in participation, sales, or profits
- To respond to competition
- To motivate employees
- To enhance the organization's reputation

Source: Dirks, L. and Daniel, S. *Marketing Without Mystery* (New York: American Management Association, 1991), PP. 3-4.

The Continuous Process: After the leader-manager designs the plan based on the marketing research and the recreation entity's vision, the guidelines for implementation are designed, communicated, and launched. With goals clearly defined, the leader-manager monitors and evaluates the marketing process. Feedback often leads directly to new plans, rendering it a continuous process because the needs of the customer, the environment, and the organization are always changing.

The Advantage: Whenever a leader-manager is capable of adapting strategic marketing to the decision making process, the park, recreation, and leisure service delivery system has an advantage because its ultimate goal is to satisfy the customer by providing the best possible service or product. When marketing strategies are implemented, demand intensifies. As customers learn that the recreation entity is striving to meet their needs, this piques public awareness and attracts a larger market. This increase in customers can only be sustained if the service or product is as good or better than portrayed in the marketing tools.

In The Field...

FAIRFAX COUNTY PARK AUTHORITY'S STRATEGIC PLAN

The strategic plan of Virginia's Fairfax County Park Authority identified the need for a comprehensive marketing program that would continuously analyze the marketing environment and recommend actions that could better respond to the needs of their target markets. In moving forward, the park authority established a philosophy that the agency existed to satisfy its customers. At an earlier date, however, the county, which had worked to establish appropriate facilities, had mistakenly designed programs around the convenience of instructors. This typical mistake resulted in a substantial fiscal deficit, and the county responded by revising its approach.

An aggressive marketing plan was established that recognized the needs, wants, and interests of the market, and a balance between the county's needs and the needs of the customers was created. To achieve their goal, a study was undertaken that divided the market into subdivisions. Computer models were used to predict buyer behavior based on customer demographics and their markets were segmented accordingly. Each segment's different demands were met through programs designed to attract that particular audience. Then, their own records that were developed from admissions, program registration data, usage patterns, fees collected, and sales receipts were used to help them develop additional information for their market strategy. This transformed their programming philosophy which resulted in benefits to their participants and to their own attendance rates.

Attention was not only focused on attracting new customers, but in retaining them as well. Statistics showed that attracting new customers actually cost five times more than keeping an existing one. This concept influenced their marketing strategy. Statistics from their own research also influenced their strategy. Management had suspected that customer service was a critical weakness, but statistics showed that custodial maintenance and equipment availability and breakdown were actually their greatest service liabilities. Corrective actions intensified; they responded to customer requests to improve the entertainment value of the swimming pools by including water play features; and classes were selectively advertised in their quarterly magazine as a result of a readership profile. Computer technology enhances their ability to analyze future information and tabulate results of their marketing program. By understanding the needs of their market, the Fairfax County delivery services have been improved, thus, allowing the agency to "do the right thing rather than doing things right."

Source: Tadlock, Lynn. "Marketing Starts with Information." *Parks & Recreation*. Vol 28 No. 5, (Ashburn, VA: National Recreation and Park Association. May 1993).

Quality and Service: The recreation leader-manager's understanding of the unique characteristics of the service industry is essential to the integration of marketing concepts into the total organization. The service industry differs from manufacturing primarily because the service product is intangible and quality is difficult to predict. These characteristics require a strategic marketing response to service consumers. The well- managed park, recreation, and leisure service delivery system stabilizes the quality of service, and emphasizes its reputation for quality. And when results support it, an effective strategy emphasizes predictable satisfaction rates. These techniques build the prospective consumer's confidence in the service quality and reduces the fear of disappointment. Techniques to standardize service programs as much as possible increase reliability which ultimately increases consumer satisfaction. In other words, what the customer expects is the service that will be delivered (Geraghty 1998: 29).

Techniques to develop and maintain a quality program are necessary to meet the customers' expectations. As such, the leader-manager knows that outstanding performance by service employees is central to quality and the consumer-demand it stimulates. Thus, development of well-trained personnel who are rewarded for excellence is an integral part of achieving service quality. The use of high quality equipment also reflects positively on the intangible experience. It not only impresses guests that the intangible service is of similar high quality, but it also inspires employees to be their best as well. It is also helpful to introduce a tangible element to associate with the quality of the intangible service experience, such as a quality piece of clothing or a hat sporting an emblem.

THE MARKETING ENVIRONMENT

Park, recreation, and leisure delivery systems do not operate in a vacuum. They must interact with the world. Leader-managers are continually confronted with a number of environmental forces that cannot necessarily be controlled, but must be considered when planning marketing strategies. These environmental considerations fall into the following major categories: demographics, culture, technology, economy, and law and politics. Each varies in importance, depending upon the nature of the service or the product offered, and each area affects the recreation entity in its ability to operate effectively. Obstacles and opportunities need to be responded to in a responsible and ethical way. Too often, the well-intentioned manager has been thwarted because the organization is not truly committed to achieving superior relationships with their customer (Day 1999: ix). Because the marketing environment undergoes continual change, managers are encouraged to periodically assess each category to determine current situations and future trends. Healthy organizations do this on a continuous basis.

Demographics

Demographics are the statistical characteristics of a market. Demographics include, for example, *population, age distribution, family composition, ethnic mix, mobility, geographical location,* and *education.* These characteristics need to be monitored and factored into the marketing effort. The cruise industry, for instance, is already planning ahead to the year 2010 to 2030 when the remaining baby boomers enter the 65-and-over age group. Statistics such as those offered in Figures 10-2 and 10-3 can be a valuable source of information when planning ahead and setting goals.

FIGURE 10-2

Percentage of U.S. Population by Age in Years 2050 and 2000

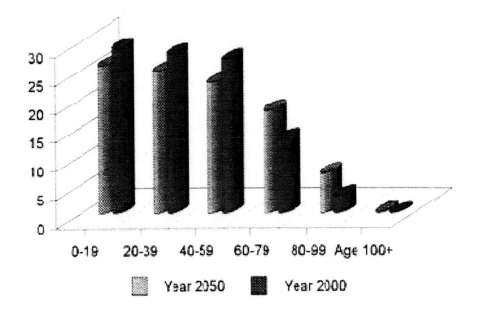

Source: Day, Jennifer Cheeseman, *Population Projection of the United States, by Age, Sex, Race, and Hispanic Origin: 1992 to 2050* P25-1092. Washington, D.C: U.S. Department of Commerce. pp. xvi-xvii.

FIGURE 10-3

Percentage of U.S. Population by Race or Ethnic Origin in Years 2050 and 2000

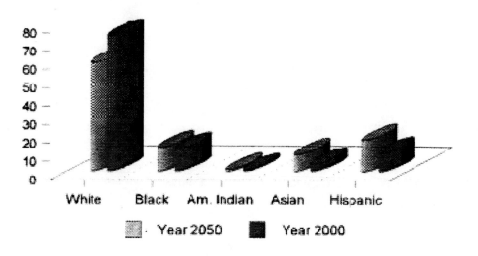

Source: See Figure 10-2

Culture

The social environment includes the attitudes, values, and behavior patterns of society. Many North Americans value freedom, individuality, practicality, achievement, progress, humanitarianism, comfort, and youthfulness (Cyr & Gray 1994:25). These values produce unique individuals who function in a blended society that is subject to particular patterns. These social patterns affect marketing in a number of ways, which are always subject to change and the need for more study. Today's consumer, for example, tends to appreciate durable goods and luxury services that save time and promote personal health, fitness, and care. They appreciate security, travel, culture, and higher education. Services and products must adapt to these changing needs, but values can vary according to geographic area, age, and ethnic and religious background.

Technology

Technological developments affect marketing in many ways. Telecommunications make mass promotion possible through radio, television, and telephone. Computers allow for greater sophistication and increased communications through websites. Technologically advanced equipment helps service workers do their job efficiently or eliminates the need for them completely.

Because the customer's loyalty goes to the best service or product available at the right price, technological demands and adaptations are a must. Management, as a result, keeps track of innovations that complement the service offered, increase efficiency, and ultimately lower costs. The leader-manager, as we have noted in Chapter Nine, will also be required to prepare the workforce for change and to arrange for necessary training. But from a marketing standpoint, technology should always be used to improve customer service and never to detract from it. This means that human contact and public relations cannot be forgotten.

Economy

The health of the economy directly impacts the ability of the park, recreation, and leisure delivery services to expand and upgrade their technology and services. The economy also impacts the market's ability to use these services. Because the economy can and does change rapidly with far reaching effects, managers are subject to respond to economic conditions and make appropriate changes in market strategy.

Over one hundred years ago, economist Ernest Engle presented an economic concept that remains in effect today. Called Engle's Law, the concept states that as people's earning power increases, the percentage of income spent on food, housing, and household operation remains constant, but the percentage spent on clothing, education, health care, recreation, entertainment, and transportation increases (Cyr & Gray 1994: 28). After World War II, for instance, service expenditures accounted for approximately one-third of personal consumption expenditures, but by the mid-1980s they accounted for one-half (Johnson, Scheuing & Gaida 1986:27). The recession in the early 1990s, with its high unemployment and decrease in the number of middle income earners, hurt sales and travel. This fluctuation aroused a greater need for home based recreation facilities and programs that could cater to the unemployed.

As a rule, the demand for services, in contrast to sales of goods, tends to fluctuate less during economic cycles. Even so, park, recreation, and leisure service managers recognize that the service industry includes nondiscretionary services such as medical care and haircuts. Recreation and travel, on the other hand, is considered discretionary spending, which can be curtailed (Johnson, Scheuing & Gaida 1986:30).

Politics and Law

Attitudes and reactions of people and government affect the political environment. And changes in the political environment often lead to alterations to the legal environment and the way in which existing laws are enforced. Nonprofit agencies respond formally to legal mandates of consumers through their board of directors and businesses respond through consumer boards.

Although laws bind managers to certain acts and contracts, leader-managers develop market strategies by staying alert to political opportunities and studying changing tides. As a preemptive measure, many agencies and businesses hire lobbyists or governmental representatives to monitor and influence the political and legal environments. As a marketer, the leader-manager needs to keep up with and understand major laws and regulations relative to the leisure market. Compliance nurtures and protects a strong public relations effort, makes good economic sense, and defines the organization as a desirable and trusted member of society.

SUMMARY

- Management has taken a leadership role in integrating key marketing concepts into the mainstream of operations. Central to this integration has been the adoption of the orientation toward customer needs at all levels of the organization, and at all stages of the transaction with the customer.

- Marketing evolved from three specific orientations: product orientation, sales orientation, and customer orientation.

- Market *segmentation* is the process by which markets are divided into groups of consumers who have similar desires and needs, and tend to respond to certain offerings in similar ways. Though no single variable can fully describe a *target* group, segmentation can be used effectively to determine the services and products that certain target groups seek.

- *Market research* helps managers gain information regarding the market to which they want to serve. Research provides the agency with critical strategic information. Areas of research include who makes up the market , the size of the market, where the market is located, and why the market will want the leisure service or product. Both primary and secondary data can be useful.

- Four adjustable strategies, known as the "four Ps" - product, place, promotion and price - make up the *marketing mix*.

- The *marketing strategic plan* is the managerial process of developing and maintaining a match between an organization's mission, resources, and market opportunities. Usually devised by top management, the marketing plan sets the tone for the entire organization. Without a plan, marketing efforts tend to be reactive rather than proactive.

- Fundamental differences between services and products should be considered when planning a park, recreation, and delivery system's marketing strategy. Services are performed and consumed, while products are manufactured and processed. Recreation services are intangible and simultaneously consumed and produced. Quality is determined by the client's input and the delivery is not standardized.

- The well-managed park, recreation, and leisure service delivery system can emphasize a quality image and fine reputation. When results support it, an effective strategy is to emphasize predictable satisfaction rates.

- Managers are continually confronted with a number of environmental forces that cannot be controlled but must be considered when planning marketing strategies. These environmental considerations fall into the following major categories: demographics, culture, technology, economy, and law and politics.

LEARNING ACTIVITIES

1. Your city research department recently released a report that indicates retirement age individuals are attracted to your community. This is supported by an analysis of population trends which show a significant increase in immigration of age 65 and over to the area. As the director of parks and recreation, you have decided to draft a marketing strategic plan to address this market segment. What is your plan?

2. In another community the city research department identified a trend showing a shift in the population from seniors to generation X individuals. What is your plan? What else do you need to know?

3. You hired a consultant to help with the marketing of your recreation services. After contracting with them, you realized that the firm's expertise is in product marketing, not service marketing. To make the best of the situation, you join the team and try to explain the needs of the potential consumer of services. What would you tell the consultants?

4. You are walking over to a meeting with the Board of Directors to present your proposal to fund a marketing strategic plan. On the way, you run into the Chairperson and begin to walk together. He explains to you that he will probably not fund your proposal because a good solid program sells itself and marketing is only useful if the program is marginal. What do you say?

REFERENCES

Bureau of Land Management (no date) **Our Commitment to Customer Service.** Washington D.C.: U.S. Government Printing Office.

Cyr, D. and Gray, D. (1994) **Marketing Your Product .** British Columbia: International Self-Counsel Press Ltd.

Day, G. (1999) **The Market Driven Organization.** New York: The Free Press.

Day, J. (1992) **Population Projections of the United States, by Age, Sex, Race, and Hispanic Origin: 1992-2030.** Washington D.C.: U.S. Department of Commerce.

Dreyfus, I. (1997). **Shyness Keeps Sedentary Out of Health Clubs.** The Washington Post Feb 18.

Drucker P. (1990) **Managing the Non-Profit Agency.** New York: Harper Collins.

Geraghty, B. (1998) **Visionary Selling.** New York: Simon & Schuster.

Hiam, A. and Schewe, C. (1992) **The Portable MBA in Marketing.** New York: John Wiley and Sons, Inc.

Hisrich, R. (1990) **Marketing.** New York: Barron's Educational Service, Inc.

Johnson, E., Scheuing, E., and Gaida, K. (1986) **Profitable Service Marketing .** Homewood, Ill: Dow Jones-Irwin.

Levinson, J. (1998) **Guerrilla Marketing.** Boston: Houghton Mifflin.

Longinotti-Buitoni, G. (1999) **Selling Dreams.** New York: Simon & Schuster.

O'Sullivan, E. (1991) **Marketing for Parks, Recreation, and Leisure.** State College, PA: Venture Publishing, Inc.

Riddick, C. and Russell, R. (1999) **Evaluative Research in Recreation, Park, and Sport Settings: Searching for Useful Information.** Champaign, IL: Sagamore Publishing.

Sawyer, T. and Smith, O. (1999) **The Management of Clubs, Recreation, and Sport: Concepts and Applications.** Champaign, IL: Sagamore Publishing.

Young, S.J. and Jamieson, L.M. (2001) "Delivery Methodology of the Delphi: A Comparison of Two Approaches." **Journal of Park and Recreation Administration** Vol. 19 (1) 42-58.

CHAPTER 11

PROMOTING PARKS, RECREATION, AND LEISURE SERVICES

Learning Objectives

After studying this chapter you should be able to do the following:

1. Understand the concept and importance of promotion.
2. Define public relations.
3. Recognize publicity tools such as news releases, fact sheets, media kits, news conferences, public service announcements, and speeches.
4. Understand sales promotion including demonstrations, contests, and bonuses.
5. Be familiar with the techniques used in personal selling.
6. Define advertising and its key objectives.
7. Understand that the promotional mix will vary between agencies.

Leader-managers in the outgoing fields of park, recreation, and leisure delivery systems benefit from an interest in, an understanding of, and a talent for promotion. They have key roles in the direction of this vital and complex component of the traditional marketing mix. Leader-managers utilize promotion to inform and persuade the target market about the value of a service or product. Sometimes, promotion is simply used to remind, familiarize, overcome inertia, or add a perceived value to an offering (O'Sullivan 1991:114). When a service or product is already established, promotional efforts are designed to merely remind the target market of the existing service or product. If new programs or products are being offered, the audience needs to be familiarized with it. Guest passes serve as a means to familiarize a target market with a new service or product. They help potential customers get started or overcome inertia. Promotion is also used as a device to add value or status to a service, program, idea, facility, product, agency, or business. Potential clients rely on various promotional messages to learn about specific offerings, their advantages, and other significant details. Though the specific purposes of the promotion campaign may vary, its message must be compelling. This means that the promotional message has to gain the attention of the target market, address its needs and desires, and show that the offering can satisfy. Promotion is explored in this chapter through its five major communication tools: public relations, publicity, sales promotion, personal selling, and advertising.

PUBLIC RELATIONS

Public relations is a promotional activity that makes use of strategic opportunities to favorably influence the opinion of the public or a target market about a service, product, idea, individual, or institution. Traditionally, the effort, done without any tricks, is based on mutually satisfactory two-way communication (Seacord 1999:2). One expert (Larkin 1992:177) takes the communication a step further, describing it as the fine art of getting three audiences to know and love the organization. The three audiences that he refers to include the customers who must get to know the service or product; the community who provides the agency or business with the customers and staff; and the media whose attention can give the agency or business instant credibility. While the public relations effort may go back as far as human communication, its modern beginnings are traced to World War I when Walter Lippmann laid down the basics of the field and the profession in his book entitled Public Opinion. When the first specialists evolved, they referred to themselves as "counselors" because they advised others about improving their public image.

In today's world, no one is immune to the intense scrutiny of the media which may mean that public relations departments or agencies must sometimes move from pro-active support to pre-emptive and reactive public relations. These efforts are designed more to limit damage than to support values. More specifically, pre-emptive public relations is used after an attack to protect and boost key values. Reactive public relations responds to requests or makes refusals in a tactful way (Wiley 1999: 190-191). Increasingly, then, public relations leads the total communication effort, and organizations rely on it to unite their objectives with the public. Professionals even specialize in finance, product publicity, media placement, technical writing, and hundreds of other areas.

Managers of park, recreation, and leisure service delivery systems generally lead the public relations effort by acquiring an intimate knowledge of how the field functions. Equipped with this understanding, they may elect to subcontract their organization's public relations program to a specialized firm that will embrace the agency's values and needs. Talented managers may, instead, choose to hire in-house officers or even assign tasks to employees with special talents. In any case, the leader-managers direct involvement in the promotion effort enhances the organization's prospects for success, and lends support to sales promotion, the sales force, and the advertising campaign. Likewise, the positive public image tends to boost confidence in the service or product itself by closing the credibility gap with a message that is more likely to be believed, thus, absorbed (Harris 1998: 5-6). As Abraham Lincoln once said, "Public sentiment is everything. With public sentiment, nothing can fail. Without it, nothing can succeed."

The Public Relations Effort

The public relations effort is broken into direct and indirect forms. Direct public relations involves one-on-one contact. This occurs when a parking attendant makes contact with the public or when the community is greeted by the staff when entering the facility. Indirect forms of public relations involve publicity or forms of promotional communication for which the media are not paid.

The Direct Effort: The park, recreation, and leisure service delivery system's positive image can never be assumed. It requires the constant effort of every employee. Each member of the staff contributes to the overall image via their relationships with members and others. The friendliness of the administrative assistant's voice when responding to calls, the maintenance and appearance of the facility, and the ski instructor's response to a complaint will all persuade public opinion toward a positive or negative image. The public relations effort, then, does not simply come about from an external effort. It requires an internal effort that grows through relationships that are developed through actions that begin with the leader-manager. By instilling acceptable performance and social responsiveness among staff, leader-managers promote goodwill and an effort to create a favorable image.

Indirect forms of Public Relations: Leader-managers also support outgoing, intelligent representatives from within the agency or organization who are willing to make presentations, participate in interviews, serve on civic boards, or make public appearances. By promoting participation in community events, the recreation agency or business is able to meet its many publics. Publics include the individuals who are drawn together through common interests, such as occupation, religion, geographic location, hobbies, race or nationality, profession, sex, or fraternal interests. Each public should be understood by the representative to a certain degree. This includes knowledge of the organization, the profession, the specific hobby, the health, or recreational interests of the group. Understanding builds rapport and helps in the early establishment of a positive public relations effort (see Publicity in this chapter also).

Developing a Public Relations Plan: Because public relations is a continuous and cooperative effort of the entire staff, including part-time employees and volunteer staff, leader-managers keep all individuals within the agency informed of and included in the strategic planning process. Strategic communications planning helps each member to understand the goals, direction, strategies, and tactics that guide the communications effort. In every case, the public relations plan is devised to strengthen the mission and goals of the entity. The next step is to define the target audience or those who have a stake in the service or product rendered. Once these initial steps have been accomplished, a plan will be devised that is mutually satisfying to the delivery system and the customer. Customers, in this case, can be internal or external to include members or prospective new members outside of the agency or organization.

Before the message is delivered, it will be necessary to consider what actions are needed to accomplish the desired outcome. This requires identification of the services products, and programs that should be defined and developed to produce the end results or greatest dividends. It is also possible that other factors may also need to be overcome, eliminated, or minimized in order to make the goal a reality. Objectives can then be established for measuring success against the goal. To do so, the leader-manager will establish realistic and fair assessments of the time and resources that are needed to complete the objective. If the objective is justifiable, a time line for implementation is set. Finally a comprehensive plan is developed by and distributed to the full team of communicators. This allows each person (and unit) to understand their role as well as the role of their colleagues in the total plan. An evaluation process for the plan is also established.

Updating the Plan should take place throughout the public relations campaign. The managers should provide the entire staff with information about the agency or organization's services, new developments, and the target market. A newsletter, for example, helps to keep the staff well-informed and abreast of inside accomplishments. Likewise, an informed staff can contribute information about the target market by providing input from customers or potential clients. Strategic planning meetings offer other opportunities to improve communications, to discuss current observations, and to share suggestions for improvement. A step-by-step approach to a public relations program is shown in Table 11-1.

TABLE 11-1

Developing The Public Relations Program

- Time and funds are available for the public relations effort.
- The program is developed internally with representation from the entire staff.
- The public relations program is grounded in quality service and performance.
- The needs of the park, recreation, and leisure service delivery system must be understood and translated into communication goals that represent the overall mission and the public relations program.
- The target market or various publics will be defined.
- The public relations staff is selected or staff members with special talents are recruited.
- The public is given open, honest communications.
- The public is given a means to communicate concerns that are evaluated by the staff.
- Every member of the staff is given a written copy of the public relations program and a public relations tool kit.
- A close working relationship is established with the media and others.
- The staff will be informed and updated on current events and agency progressions.
- The public relations program will be evaluated on a regular basis.

In the Field...

DRAFTING THE PLAN

The new director of Cabrillo Sea Kayaking Expeditions was asked to draft a public relations plan for the organization. Before she could begin, however, she determined that she first would need to know if:

- there is a handbook, manual of guidelines, newsletter, or other internal communication to keep members and customers informed?

- there is a system for disseminating information to the media?

- there is a web home-page?

- here is a booklet, flyer, or printed material that tells the story of the organization?

- the members (customers/clients) and staff participate in community activities?

- the organization holds open houses, clinics, seminars, or workshops?

- there are provisions for a speakers' bureau so that civic and service clubs, schools, and other organizations may obtain someone to speak on various topics relating to the organization's services (products), or programs?

- he organization has an information video?

- has inter- and intra-organizational electronic mail utilized to its fullest capacity?

Source: Parkhouse, B. *The Management of Sport: Its Foundation and Application* (2nd ed.). (St. Louis, MO: C.V. Mosby Year Book, 1996).

PUBLICITY

Publicity, an indirect form of public relations, is a method of attaining free communication through a statement of facts that are both interesting and newsworthy (Yale 1993:2). This information can be directed to the general public or to targeted publics so that they will know what is being done, who is doing it, or any other information that the park, recreation, and leisure service delivery system would like for them to know. Publicity is generated through traditional news stories in newspapers, radio, and television; articles in magazines and other publications; appearances on talk and public service shows or other special events; and through websites and other electronic sources. Because paid advertising can be very expensive, this type of promotional activity is especially important to public and nonprofit agencies as well as small businesses whose budgets are limited.

This does not mean that these entities do not advertise or that the larger businesses and corporations with larger pockets do not take advantage of free publicity. Consider the major state tourism office that expends most of its promotional budget on publicity rather than on advertising. By writing their own releases and bringing in travel writers and editors for "familiarization" tours, they can originate numerous articles and feature stories about the attractions in their state. In fact, records show that state tourism offices experience a four to one benefit to cost ratio (Ramacitti 1994:8). In other words, if they had paid for the editorial space and air-time received, i.e. advertising, it would have cost them four times as much as it did to spend a major portion of their budget on news releases, media kits, and "fam" tours.

In addition to being free, publicity has many other advantages. It can create goodwill, one of the major objectives of the public relations effort. The public often sees publicity as more credible than advertising. It also keeps the recreation agency or business in the public eye, aids management in the successful recruitment of employees, and functions to make the agency legitimate within the community. Finally, free publicity is easier for the manager to accomplish than the advertising campaign which requires a great deal of sophistication and/or professional expertise (Ramacitti 1994:12). Even though some park, recreation, and leisure service delivery systems can afford a staff professional who can help direct the publicity program, many proceed without a professional. They depend, instead, on their managers to develop ideas and techniques. There are many ways for managers to generate free publicity.

The News Release

This convenient means for media personnel to attain fresh stories is one of the most important and effective promotional tools used because the news release keeps the park, recreation, and leisure service delivery system in front of the public. Competition can be fierce for space, but every agency or organization has a right to try for coverage since they interact with the community. The manager who knows how to present and write a release has the edge on others. In this case, the release can mean reaching potentially thousands of individuals. Nonetheless, far too many managers shy away from them because they are not acquainted with the necessary features. The mechanics are really not that difficult, but the topic and timing are paramount.

The Topic and Timing: The news release covers a noteworthy subject or topic with universal appeal that is generally uncommon, funny, emotional, nostalgic, or informative. They tell about new events or the traditional, like the annual charity dinner at the community center. Some announce the addition of new board members or a celebrity's appearance at a golf tournament. Staff promotions, retirements, and new officers are newsworthy, as are the details about plans for a renovation. The recent purchase of equipment might catch the media's attention if it is designed to eliminate adverse environmental impacts or some other impact on the community.

Releases may even play off of recent news reports. For instance, if crime is reported to have increased, the YMCA might announce what it is doing to keep youth off the streets. Opportunities are endless and news can also be created by running an opinion poll on the community's reaction to physical fitness, for example. A story that announces plans for an opinion poll could be followed by another that tallies the results. News releases can acknowledge individuals, including an employee or board member who is scheduled to present a lecture. And if the lecture has universal appeal, a follow-up release can share the content. Tournaments, activities, and special events are newsworthy, and they, too, present opportunities for follow-up stories with the results as seen in Table 11-2.

Responding media might opt to use the release in part, in total, or not at all. On the other hand, they could select to contact the source named on the release for more information resulting in a more elaborate story. Timing can mean everything toward obtaining coverage. The best timing usually occurs just before an event, during media downtime (summer for sports), or around holidays if the topic is timely.

TABLE 11-2

Types of Releases

Releases focus on the positive aspects of the park, recreation, and leisure service delivery system whenever possible, and fall into one of four major categories:

The Advance or Announcement:
The advance or announcement is the most prevalent release and provides notification to the public or the target audience of an event or activity before it occurs. They inform the public of openings, free trials, or other special offerings. They are used to announce the organization's positions or roles, for instance, support of a ballot proposition or their sponsorship of a local camp for children. Routine events require a lead time of five to 14 days, whereas, larger events call for 30 days to four months.

The Backgrounder:
The backgrounder gives thorough details on an issue, service or product, or the agency itself. With a more businesslike inflection, it is less time-sensitive than the advance. Although it is often longer in length, it never exceeds two pages. They always include a statement which emphasizes why the story is important. Backgrounders provide the background about a new service or product, or they provide information about a special event, such as an anniversary like the Lewis and Clark Bicentennial. Backgrounders offer a local angle on a national event. This could include the YWCA's Assistant Director's recollection of her participation in the Winter Olympics just before the opening day ceremonies; or the Boston Bicycle Club's viewpoint on the importance of helmets before the staging of the Tour de France. When spring approaches the local garden club may offer tips on spring planting. Some of these releases even lead to a regular series.

The Feature:
Features are like backgrounders with a people-oriented approach. They tend to be lighter and more entertaining through the use of humor or a more dramatic approach. A feature could focus on the retirement of the founder of a local trail club or an employee who climbs mountains on vacation. They sometimes focus on mascots and pets, or the response of working parents to the playground at the new child-care center.

The Follow-up:
Follow-ups provide the public with additional information after a tournament, activity, or event. They announce the results of recent elections, or advise the public of newly appointed members on the agency's Board of Directors. Follow-ups are used to defend the agency's position if it has been attacked for its recent action. In these cases, the news release is not designed to accentuate the positive as much as it attempts to remove the negative. Additionally, they might explain a recent settlement in a lawsuit, or the agency's position on a pending environmental issue. Follow-ups are received by the media within two days of the event.

Source: Ramacitti, D. *Do-It-Yourself Publicity.* (New York: AMACOM, a division of American Management Association, 1994), pp. 24-30.

Preparation: Even if the timing is right, releases will end up in the "circular file" if they do not contain the appropriate information or are poorly written. To begin the writing process, it is helpful to establish a Fact Sheet that provides answers to journalism's five famous questions: who, what, where, when, and why (and sometimes how much). Unless these five questions are answered, the odds of getting media coverage are limited. The "why" question should be answered with the reason the event or story is newsworthy or important. Fact Sheets are also helpful when preparing posters, brochures, and flyers announcing events. These sheets can even accompany the news release to assist the journalists. A sample Fact Sheet is seen in Figure 11-1.

FIGURE 11-1

Sample Facts Sheet

NATIONAL AQUARIUM IN BALTIMORE
Pier 3/501 East Pratt Street
Baltimore, Maryland 21202-3194
410 576-3800
410 576-8238 FAX

Amazon River Forest
Amazing Facts

The Amazon River is more than 4292 miles long - the distance from New York to Berlin.

The Amazon River basin is approximately the size of the United States. It carries the greatest volume of any river in the world and has a network of 500 tributaries and sub-streams. The tides surge as much as 500 miles inland.

The Amazon region contains more than 40,000 species of plants and trees and more than 500 species of moths and butterflies.

More than 300,000 species of insects have been classified in just one half-mile of the Amazon rain forest.

The rainy season in the Amazon produces 80 to 120 inches of rain from January to June. The dry season has a minimum of four inches per month.

The flow of the Amazon contains more water than the Mississippi, Nile, and Yangtze rivers combined.

The Amazon river basin encompasses two million square miles, holding 25% of the Earth's fresh water supply.

More than 20 million live ornamental fishes are sold each year from the Amazon River Basin for the home Aquarium trade.

Forwarding the Release: Once the facts have been prepared into written form in a clear, precise, and reliable manner, it works well to set the draft aside for 24 hours before doing the final editing. Upon completion, the release is forwarded to the Managing Editor(s) of print media and to the News Director(s) of electronic media. They are not addressed to named individuals. See Figures 11-1 and 11-2 for sample news releases. If there are two local papers, the release is sent to both. No newspaper appreciates being "scooped" by the other. In general, editors resent calls designed to follow up the release unless there is some special angle. They are on deadlines that makes them far too busy to follow up each news release with the author. It is equally unwise to ask journalists for clippings of articles. Not only do they not have time, this implies to the editor of the local paper that the author of the news release does not read the paper!

FIGURE 11-2

Sample News Release

American Alliance for Health, Physical Education, Recreation and Dance

1900 Association Drive · Reston, VA 20191-1599
Telephone (703) 476-3400 · (800) 213-7193 · FAX (703) 476-9527
e-mail: info@aahperd.org · http://www.aahperd.org

FOR IMMEDIATE RELEASE:	CONTACT:
March 20, 2000	For information call: Steven Forest 407-352-9700 Brigid Sanner 214 553-0621

American Alliance for Health, Physical Education, Recreation and Dance Convention and Exposition

Community Millennium Trails Project Announced

ORLANDO: – Millennium Trails Program Director Jeff Olson, Office of the Secretary at the U.S. Department of Transportation, will announce the initiation of Community Millennium Trails, the final leg in a three-part national initiative of trail development aimed at recognizing, promoting and supporting trails that preserve open spaces, interpret history and culture, and enhance recreation and tourism.

His announcement will be made during the opening general session of the American Alliance for Health, Physical Education, Recreation and Dance (AAHPERD) Convention and Exposition, March 22, 8:30 - 10:15 a.m.

The 2000 Community Millennium Trails will join a select group of 16 National Millennium Trails and 50 Millennium Legacy Trails designated by First Lady Hillary Rodham Clinton and Secretary of Transportation Rodney Slater.

Florida Governor Jed Bush has selected the Florida National Scenic Trail as Florida's Millennium Legacy Trail.

Olson will also announce the development of a partnership between Millennium Trails and the American Association for Leisure and Recreation (AALR), one of AAHPERD's national association's. As part of the partnership, Kathleen Cordes, AALR Interim Executive Director, will be authoring a book about the trails.

Millennium Trails is a joint project of the White House Millennium Council, the U.S. Department of Transportation, Rails-to-Trails Conservancy, the American Hiking Society and AALR.

For more information visit www.millenniumtrails.org or call 1-877-MIL-TRLS.

In the Field...

Facts about News Releases

The first paragraph of the news release begins with a teaser or catchy phrase and states the most important facts. The following paragraphs include interesting points and more minor facts. This order helps to assure that the most important facts will not be deleted if the editor decides to shorten the release.

The double-spaced releases normally run around two pages in length with one inch margins on all sides. Centered at the top of the first page is a suggested headline followed with triple-spacing to give the editor room for a likely change to the headline. The first page carries a date of release in the upper right corner and ends with the centered word -more- at the bottom of the page if a second page follows. If the article ends with the first page the symbol ### or the number -30- is shown to signal the end of the release. A second page should be numbered, and it is wise to give it a heading in case the pages become detached. Either the start of the first page or the end of the last will give the name, address, and telephone number, FAX, and e-mail of the contact if it is not already included on the letterhead. The last page will indicate if the release will be accompanied "with art." These attachments or photos will accompany the release.

Using E-mail: News releases attract media through the use of e-mail. In fact, reporters receiving electronic communications benefit by not having to re-key the contact's words, and they can easily save or discard the entire document or portions of it. Additionally, if the reporter would like to retain the news release for future use, it is easier to save and to retrieve from the computer's hard drive than a file drawer. Publicists benefit as well because they can send their release directly to the reporter. Likewise, because there is no need to re-key material, it is less likely that a re-keying error will appear in the published article. With these benefits in mind, it stands to reason that the e-mailed story would win out in the end if a journalist had two equally interesting stories to chose from.

The Broadcast News Release

The much shorter broadcast news release is written in present tense. If it cannot be read in 20 to 90 seconds, it is too long (Yale 1993:184). Some news directors prefer an outlined release. The manager of a park, recreation, and leisure service delivery system can benefit by taking note of the media's objectives. Table 11-3 offers some insight.

TABLE 11-3
___

Guidelines for Radio News
___

These guidelines, outlined by management to radio news media, offer inside tips on the criteria for the selection of stories:

1. Who Cares?

   This rules out stories of limited interest, or only those that are used to fill time for the sake of doing a news cast. There should almost always be something going on that is worth talking about. Do not do stories that do not interest the majority of your listeners. On the other hand, make sure you do stories that will interest your target audience. On a rock station, do stories that interest young people: education, substance abuse, or news about rock artists.

2. How Many People Does It Affect?

   A wreck that jams up traffic on the freeway for hours affects many more people than say, a public hearing on tearing down that ugly nuisance in the middle of town. Make your story order and coverage priorities reflect the number of people affected by a given story. There is an exception. Crime, fire and disasters rarely affect more than a few people directly, but everybody is interested.

3. Does My Audience Need to Know?

   Certain issues may not personally impact every listener, but the issue may be significant. The newscast can help in educating the public about significant issues. If a change in school policy is controversial or perhaps unfair, it should be brought to light even if it affects only a few listeners.

4. Did the Competition Have this Story?

   This is a lesser concern, but still significant. You don't want to sound like a complete goofball out in space somewhere because a listener picked up a story on the competition that you don't have. Use the competitors for tips only. If the competitor has a story that is not relevant to your audience, ignore it. One thing you must not do is let the wire service set your agenda. We're doing our own news, and we are in control. Be in charge.

Source: Bammes, Dan. *News Standards and Policy Manual.* (Salt Lake City, Utah: Carlson Communications International).

THE PUBLIC-SERVICE ANNOUNCEMENT

The broadcast industry prides itself in taking an interest in community needs and offering its services to nonprofit groups in the form of a free announcement. Television and radio stations frequently broadcast public service announcements, better known as the PSA. All PSA's are sent to the station's public service director who reviews them frequently so that every worthy group in the community has an opportunity to be heard. If the PSA deals with an issue of local controversy, the station should be given the issue and its background so that they can identify opposing viewpoints to minimize the Fairness Doctrine impact. Whenever the PSA is aired, a thank-you note is appreciated and placed in the station's information files. Not only is this appropriate, it promotes good will for future requests.

Before writing a PSA for radio, the manager should consider the radio station's audience and its format. Certain stations may reflect the target market that the agency is seeking, and the PSA should be written for that audience. Television, with the exceptions of cable and educational television, is not as discerning as radio though different programs tend to attract different audiences. When the PSA is given to a television station, a message should accompany it explaining what type of audience is being sought. If the station runs the PSA, they will generally try to reach the audience that the park, recreation, and leisure service delivery system would like to address. Most likely the PSA will be placed on the air during the day, since prime time is heavily booked with commercials. Great care should be taken that the PSA does not sound like an advertisement. If it does, it is not as credible, and it does not have as much of a chance of being picked-up. A sample PSA is seen in Figure 11-3.

FIGURE 11-3

Sample PSA

PSA announcements can be as short as 10 seconds or as long as 60. For writing purposes, a good rule of thumb is to plan on 25 words as an equivalent to 10 seconds of air time on radio and 20 words for 10 seconds on television. Descriptive words should be used for radio, and artwork should accompany every 10 seconds to be broadcast on television. The message should be limited to key points, triple spaced, and typed in capital letters.

ROSEWOOD DEPARTMENT OF PARKS AND RECREATION
DATES (At least 10 days before airing)
ADDRESS, TELEPHONE

                                                FOR IMMEDIATE RELEASE
CONTACT: NAME   Expires: Date
PUBLIC SERVICE ANNOUNCEMENT
TIME: 20 seconds
WORDS: 50

AS THE WEATHER HEATS UP, COOL DOWN IN THE LEARN TO

SWIM PROGRAM AT THE CITY POOL. REGISTER JULY 6TH

THROUGH THE 12TH AT THE REC CENTER. LESSONS RUN JULY

6TH TO AUGUST 4TH WEEKDAY MORNINGS FROM 9:00 TO 10:30.

FOR MORE INFORMATION CONTACT THE ROSEWOOD

DEPARTMENT OF PARKS AND RECREATION.

The Media Kit

A media kit is a folder or an large envelope that contains recent news releases and other pertinent forms of information, like the information seen in Table 11-4. The kit is then placed on file to be used for future reference or at a moment's notice should the media or other interested party need information. Media kits may also accompany news releases, handed out at news conferences, given to advertising agencies, or produced at sales promotions. To remain fresh, the media kit is reviewed on a regular basis with fact sheets updated as needed and old releases, documents, and photographs replaced whenever necessary.

TABLE 11-4
_____

Media Kits
_____

Media kits hold recent news releases and other pertinent material, such as:

1. *Fact Sheets* that describe size, service, product, annual sales, number of people in the agency or organization, and programs sponsored by the park, recreation, and leisure service delivery system.

2. *Question and Answer Sheets* that cover a wide range of subjects in an easy to absorb format.

3. *Histories* or capsules that provide background information and show relationships.

4. *Documents* or reports, studies, and even books with short summaries attached.

5. *Photographs* with vertical and horizontal page-layout opportunities. Black and white, eight-by-ten inch glossies are generally preferred by newspapers, but five-by-seven's are acceptable. Magazines call for 35mm color slides. Television stations often have their own special requirements.

6. *Video tapes* and *audio cassettes* should not exceed eight to10 minutes. Because broadcast quality is needed, they are usually developed by professionals.
_____

In the Field...

Public Contacts and Interviews

Besides arranging for publicity, managers also do interviews and give speeches. When doing either, they prepare, arrive on time, and consider who they will be addressing. While speeches can be dressed up with a slide show or other visual aids, radio interviews demand descriptive phrases. Television requires that cameras and lights are ignored. These appearances are enhanced when the interviewee dresses simply. Bold patterns are avoided and solid colors are preferred, for example, as are bright white shirts and blouses and shiny jewelry. The interviewee also needs to be alert, yet, relaxed. This can be accomplished with occasional humor, and the audience always appreciates a smile which even shows in the voice on radio.

In every situation, goals are established and mock interviews are conducted. All questions are answered honestly and frankly. The best way to stay on track is to know the topic and to avoid questions that reach outside of the speaker's range of knowledge or area of expertise. A question can be deflected, for instance, by mentioning another source who might provide an answer. An interviewer can also be lead when the interviewee makes a clear position statement which represents the park, recreation, and leisure service delivery system on an issue. The speaker should be ready to summarize key points and make a final point which is backed with a small narration of no more than 30 seconds.

When the interviewee arrives for the interview a little early, it is sometimes possible to meet with the host and establish rapport. Sometimes the host will ask questions that may be addressed during the program, and the interviewee can mention topics that he or she would like to cover. Arriving too early, however, can be disruptive and hosts do not want to destroy spontaneity. When other guests are appearing, it is wise to meet them as well and to attempt to determine their point-of-view before going on the air. At his time, the producer or director is given slides or tape that will accompany the interview. After the interview, it is most appropriate to ask for a tape of the interview, though a charge is likely. After the interview, the host is thanked in person and the thank you letter follows.

In the Field...

Appearing on Radio and Television

1. *Know your message.* Although you will not have total control of the interview situation, know what you want to say before the interview begins. Review the agency's background information, and develop a list of important points that you wish to cover during the interview. Consider adding personal anecdotes about the impact of your agency on you, your family, or friends.

2. *Know the program.* Watch or listen to the program in advance of your appearance. Pay close attention to the interviewer's style, types of questions asked, physical layout of the set, and the program format. Does the interviewer appear well-prepared or uninformed? Is he/she casual, formal, charming, challenging...abrasive? Does the studio audience participate in the program? Does the interviewer take questions from telephone callers?

3. *Know your audience.* The program's time slot, content and commercial announcements will tell you a lot about the audience. Evening news programs are directed at a general audience, daytime talk shows tend to feature issues of concern to homemakers and retired persons, and weekend public affairs programs are targeted at a well-educated, upscale audience.

4. *Tailor your message.* Use the information you have obtained about the program to construct a message that is interesting and significant to your audience.

5. *Tailor your presentation.* Use the knowledge you acquired about the interviewer's personality and program's format to style your presentation. If you are appearing on an evening news program, be prepared to deliver the key points in less than three minutes. If you are the sole guest on a 30 minute talk show, make certain you have 30 minutes worth of information to deliver. "Call-in" programs offer you a unique opportunity to directly involve your audience in the campaign. Structure your presentation to be brief and allow for a maximum number of calls.

Source: Biles, Faye (ed). California Association of Health Physical Education Recreation and Dance (CAHPERD) Public Relation Training Packet (Sacramento: CAHPERD, April 1988.), pp. 10-11.

The News Conference

More powerful than a news release is the news conference which, if held at all, is held only for major announcements or intense issues that are of immediate interest and importance to a broader audience. This usually means that a news release will not suffice because a conversation between the presenter and the media is warranted. If, on-the-other-hand, a news conference is called when a news release would have been sufficient, the park, recreation, and leisure service delivery system will lose credibility with the media.

When required, all media in a locale are invited to attend. In this manner, they will all hear the major announcement at the same time, and they will all have an opportunity to ask questions of the important newsmaker. The speaker is well-prepared and is someone who can answer immediate questions, such as the executive director, an architect, or the chairman of the board. If it is not possible to hold the event at an on-the-scene location, visual materials, appropriate lighting, electric outlets, chairs and media tables are necessities. Media kits are available and are often placed near the refreshments, which are always located behind cameras. Because it is never a sure bet how many media will attend, other guests can be invited. If attendance is especially successful, there will need to be a method of control.

Special Events

Special events provide opportunities to create a positive image and to improve public relations with the community or target audience. They can also hurt the public image if guests are not treated properly. This process begins with traffic management. If parking is not available in the vicinity of the event, the event can start off badly for guests. Traffic patterns, as a result, need to be studied and rush hour must be avoided. Since guests should be greeted upon entering the facility, it is imperative that employees are scheduled to act as hosts. Registration procedures have to be painless, and lines need to move quickly. At this time, name tags are distributed. These are especially helpful when the guests are expected to mingle and introductions need to be made. Arrangements include plenty of refreshments, seats, and literature when needed. At the end of the event, personnel are posted near the doors to thank the guests as they depart. Assistance to cars is available for those who need it, and traffic aides should be on hand to keep traffic moving smoothly.

The VIP: Very-important-persons (VIPs) include speakers, celebrities, and other important guests who may require special services. These include airport arrival procedures, reconfirmed arrival dates, a hotel room, transportation to the event, special aids such as lecterns or audiovisual equipment, dinner reservations, reimbursement procedures, and special tours.

In The Field...

Evaluating the Media Program

Two to four times a year media coverage should be evaluated. By doing so, the manager identifies strengths and weaknesses of the program, making efforts to develop the former and improve upon the latter. When evaluating the program managers ask the following questions:

- Was the coverage positive?
- Was there anything that could have been done to improve a story?
- Could clearer information have been provided?
- Should an interview have taken place?
- Were the personnel well-trained?
- Were the goals of the agency achieved?
- If not, why?
- What changes need to be made?

SALES PROMOTION

Sales promotion is a marketing effort used by most agencies, organizations, and businesses to encourage the sale of a service or product without devaluing it (Nilson 1999:179). It helps to penetrate new markets, attract new customers, increase sales during seasonal declines, introduce new services or products, entice dealers to carry a product, and motivate consumers to complete the exchange at the point of purchase. Memberships, clothing items, privileges, and excursions are common items that are sold by park, recreation, and leisure service delivery systems. Typical short-term incentives used to encourage quick sales turn-over are demonstrations, contests, and bonuses. Quite commonly these promotions are combined with advertising and/or personal selling. Although this combination calls for a considerable amount of coordination, without the use of these other marketing tools, sales promotions are likely to fail. Managers see to it that park, recreation, and leisure service delivery systems set their objectives, select the right sales promotion tools, develop their program, pretest results, implement the plan, and evaluate the results

Developing the Sales Promotion Program

To define the full sales promotion program, experts recommend that managers or marketers decide (Kotler & Armstrong 1990:421):

1. on the size of the incentive. Generally speaking, the larger the incentive, the greater the sales response.

2. on the conditions for participation. This includes, for example, a limitation to one age group or one location.

3. how the promotion will be distributed and at what cost. For example, coupons could be distributed at the site, through the mail, or at special events in cooperation with partnering agencies and organizations.

4. the length of the promotion. If a promotion is too short, many prospective clients will not be able to take advantage of the incentive. If it is too long, the incentive could loose some its momentum and power.

5. the sales-promotion budget. This is done by estimating the cost or by using a percentage of the total sales promotion budget.

Selecting the Right Tools

Sales promotion includes consumer promotion, trade promotion, and sales-force promotion (Kotler & Armstrong 1990:421-444).

Consumer Promotions: Consumer promotion is a type of sales promotion intended to motivate consumer purchases through the use of consumer stimulants. These include samples, coupons, rebates, deals, premiums (free or reduced prices), contests, sweepstakes, games, rewards, displays, and demonstrations. Samples, for instance, are distributed or made available to consumers to encourage them to try a service or product. This extremely successful tool has become a cornerstone for launching new services or items. Surveys reveal that 94 percent of housewives find samples to be the preferred method of product awareness with 79 percent of respondents indicating that they are the main stimulus for purchasing a new product. Television advertising lags well behind at 40 percent (Hindle and Williamson 1994:160). When consumer promotion is combined with advertising, the advertising publicizes the promotion and the promotion creates excitement for the advertising campaign.

Trade-Promotions: Trade-promotion is a type of sales promotion that is directed to retailers and wholesalers to pique their interest in promoting a product to consumers by allowing shelf space, display areas, or other incentives. Trade-promotion tools used in sales promotion include dealer discounts, free goods, buying and merchandise allowances, cooperative advertising, push money, and some of the tools used for consumer promotions including contests. Dealer discounts encourage sales, and manufacturers are often offered free goods if they are willing to switch to a new product. Allowances give the retailer a discount in return for a exhibiting a display or poster featuring the product. Cooperative advertising items such as pens, memo pads, and calendars help to create an interest in the product and draw consumers to the retailer. Push money - cash or gifts - are given to dealers to induce them to "push" the product.

Salesforce Premotions: Salesforce promotion is devised to rouse the interests of the salesforce through various incentives designed especially for them. These usually include bonuses, contests, and sales rallies.

Pretesting and Evaluating the Results

Sales promotions can be pretested on a smaller scale or through customer ratings. For example, a sales promotion could be pre-tested at a particular outlet or customer focus groups could be asked to evaluate various sales promotion plans. Pre-tests allow objectives to be tested and save the park, recreation, and leisure service delivery system unnecessary expenses if the promotion does not appear to be effective. If the pretest is successful, the promotion is implemented and eventually evaluated. Results are analyzed by comparing sales on a before and after basis. For instance, a fitness facility might offer a promotion allowing one week's free use of the facility. If the promotion is successful there will be an increased sale of memberships. If no increase is indicated, this method will need to be revised or withdrawn. Sometimes, too, evaluations are made by comparing sales during the promotion with sales at another time of year. It should be remembered that sales promotions are usually devised for slower periods. If a normally slow time is compared against a more competitive time then appropriate accounting must be made for a fair evaluation of the promotion. In some cases, it is more effective to make comparisons to the same time period for the prior year.

PERSONAL SELLING

Personal selling is the direct person-to-person communication between the buyer and the seller. The activity encompasses attempts by the seller to convince a prospective customer to take a particular action, such as buying a membership, signing up for a trip, making a donation, or purchasing a particular service or product. To do this, the seller must distinguish either the service, quality, or price from other offers in the industry (Johnson 1999:12). This is best accomplished if the park, recreation, and leisure service delivery systems' values are understood by the seller (Nilson 1999: 172).

Those involved in personal selling range from the individual operating the gift shop to the well-defined sales team of a large organization. Even the actions of the entire staff have an impact. Whether selling a membership, introducing a new class, or greeting visitors on the telephone, the public is deriving an impression of the organization that encourages or discourages use. Therefore, the leader-manager incorporates the concepts of personal selling as a supplement to the public relations effort when training all staff.

There are a number of theories about selling persuasively, but one imperative is that the seller devotes personalized attention to the buyer. This involves ascertaining the buyer's needs and desires through two-way (not one-way) communication. In this way, personal selling is the only marketing instrument that can respond directly to the individual. The first direction of communication generally comes from the seller. At a health spa, the employee's appearance, including general fitness and outgoing nature, send a signal to the prospective buyer. If the appearance is not consistent with the park, recreation, and leisure service delivery system's purpose, the prospective customer is unlikely to be receptive or to communicate further.

To prepare for success, it takes detailed planning, organization, and practice. For example, the first stage or sales call is not used to demonstrate the boat's speed or the mountain bike's brake system, but to encourage the customer to describe their need, thus, beginning the two-way communications.. The demonstration and development of an expected date of sale, occur later or at the second appointment. The third stage or meeting is for the most important event - the sale to the marketing effort. If the salespeople are successful, whether selling kayaks, generating new memberships, or soliciting donations, then the park, recreation, and leisure service delivery system is likely to be successful.

Supervising Sales

The manager directs personal selling activities by working with the employees to keep the organization's values in the forefront while helping them to establish goals. Goals are set in terms of dollars or units when dealing with sales, donations, visitor days, volume, gross margin, net profit, expenses, calls, number of new accounts, amount of dealer display, space obtained, or other measurable quantities. Despite the development of goals, sales evaluation is not an easy matter nor is there one simple approach. Some sales efforts are investments in the future and are not intended to effect an immediate sale. In addition, adjustments are needed for various conditions and established geographic sales boundaries. Managers balance the advantages and the disadvantages that each person involved with sales faces. As a result, the sales volume goal for each person is almost always set on an individual basis. These individual ratings can make sales management somewhat subjective. Other subjective considerations include the salesperson's initiative, energy level, ambition, confidence, and dominance.

Though difficult to judge, it is the manager's duty to provide each individual with direction. Leader-managers also offer assistance and serve as motivators. To help this cause, many managers obtain information about an individual's sales activity through a variety of sources including the marketing reports of the individual's sales performance. This information is used to better direct each individual. Leader-managers assist sales personnel by keeping each individual informed of any changes in policies, developments, and strategies. Assistance also comes in the form of listening. The representative's input is valuable and encouraged because sales personnel serve as the "ear" of the organization. They are a major source of information regarding customer opinion, thereby, aiding the manager in providing more precise marketing efforts to the target market. And because personal motivation is so important, a reward system is usually devised by the manager to help encourage sales personnel to succeed. Sales personnel in travel agencies receive free trips, and the aerobic dance instructor who retains the most participants may receive a free vacation day. Whether managing a general staff or formal sales department, the personal selling effort is quite often the necessary ingredient that either brings the customer to the service or encourages the consumer to make the purchase.

ADVERTISING

Advertising is a paid communication designed to provide potential customers with information about a service or product through various forms of media including newspapers, magazines, radio, television, posters, billboards, flyers, direct mail, point-of-purchase displays, specialty items, and the Internet. The objectives of advertising are to generate awareness of the service or product; cause potential customers to switch over to it; influence customers to try it; and keep people cognizant of the service or product over the long term. In order for these objectives to be transformed into reality, advertisers will know about their service or product's values and benefits. They will also understand their customers and potential customers because the more specific and personal the advertisement is to the target audience, the better (Crandall 1996:212).

Selecting the right medium for the appropriate target market is integral to advertising. For instance, advertising on the Web works well when trying to reach a highly focused, narrowly targeted market (Eager and McCall 1999:98). The selection of the type of media is tailored to match target market boundaries, customer profile, and budget constraints (Bullaro & Edginton 1986:237). The target market's boundaries are defined by the market's geographic location. Will the advertising effort, for example, need to reach a national, state, or local market? The customer profile is based on the results of research on the target market. It paints a picture of the typical customer in a particular market segment by identifying age, income level, assets, family size, recreational preferences, etc. Is the customer more likely to tune into radio or television? What magazines are they likely to read? Budget constraints are more obvious. What can the organization afford to spend on the advertising? Some choices may be excellent but simply too expensive. Information about the various types of media are shown in Table 11-5.

TABLE 11-5

Resources for Advertising

If advertising is a part of the marketing mix, the following media resources may be used:

NEWSPAPERS: Newspapers offer one of the most popular and convenient forms of advertising. Within a few days notice an ad can be placed for a brief or extended period of time. With a capacity to reach a wide audience, markets can also be targeted through certain sections of the paper. Advertisements focusing on leisure are placed in Arts, Currents, Local, Sports, and Travel sections.

MAGAZINES: Magazines serve national, regional, or local markets. More expensive than newspapers, they offer an opportunity to reach various audiences according to reader interest. Backpacker and Outside magazines attract individuals who enjoy outdoor activities. Because magazines tend to be read at a more leisurely pace than newspapers, there is a better chance that the advertisement will be seen and considered.

BROADCAST MEDIA: Although it can be expensive, broadcast media can be aired to large radio and television audiences. Kept simple, they answer the major who, what, when, where, why and how much questions. Unlike print media, it cannot be read a second time so the message needs to be readily absorbed or periodically repeated. To save on cash outlays, "trades" are sometimes possible. For example, a radio or television station may agree to exchange or trade advertising time for free or discounted memberships, tickets, or other items. These items may also be given to the station as contest prizes as a means of obtaining affordable advertising.

DIRECT MAIL: Direct mail is a more selective advertising tool. Postcards, flyers, catalogs, and free samples are sent to individual homes or e-mail addresses where feasible. Mailing lists are drawn from membership and registration lists, club rosters, magazine subscription lists, or telephone directories. A number of firms, called list brokers, specialize in gathering and selling target marketing lists.

POINT OF PURCHASE DISPLAYS: Frequently used in sales promotion are point-of-purchase displays that help identify a service or product and draw attention to it. These signs and display racks vary in expense and serve to attract the attention of customers in visitor centers or potential members at sidewalk sales. Banner ads at retail web-sites bring attention to services and products.

SPECIALTY ITEMS: Specialty items are used in sales promotion or personal selling. Items such as pencils, memo pads, key rings, and calendars attract customers to the service or product. The message is then taken into the customer's home, car, pocket, and purse establishing a future reminder.

INTERNET: Advertising on the Web can reach narrow markets. The Web is home to thousands of public electronic bulletin boards - known as "newsgroups" that cover commercial, academic, and recreational interests, ranging from the conventional to the eccentric. In some cases, posting notes about the park, recreation, and leisure service delivery system to a newsgroup is a valuable advertising tool. Posting cost nothing and can broadcast a detailed message to a large number of targeted prospects.

RADIO: Radio focuses on special segments of the population through its programming, making it an excellent medium to target an audience. Because radio often serves as a background for other activities, however, listeners are likely to have short attention spans. This means that an advertisement or spot may be easily missed. On the other hand, because radio advertisements are replayed frequently at a low cost, regular listeners will usually hear the ad on another occasion. Radio advertising requires descriptive images or entertaining slogans that help to catch the listeners' attention. These ads can be prepared in a short time, thereby, requiring less lead time than television advertising.

TELEVISION: Television is probably the most adaptable and powerful form of advertising since it is capable of reaching the prospective client through sight and sound. Matching its appeal is an expensive price tag. Nonetheless, it has the ability to create trust and believability. And because it serves as an excellent means for physical demonstration, television is a plus for leisure market advertising. Its use of motion and color not only attracts interest, it creates opportunities for innovation. Overall, television advertising is more difficult to use to reach a particular target audience, but certain shows and times relate better to certain audiences.

POSTERS AND BILLBOARDS: Posters and billboards, often referred to as outdoor advertising, present a relatively inexpensive, yet, successful means of promotion, provided the message can catch the consumer's attention. Although they are widely used to broadcast a message to a local area, their use is criticized because it clutters the environment. Many leisure activities are dependent upon the environment and park, recreation, and leisure service delivery systems need to be careful not to alienate concerned individuals or to stray from their goals.

For the complicated endeavor of selecting the right advertising campaign, it is desirable to hire an advertising agency to coordinate the process whenever it is financially feasible. They recognize that there is a relationship between a customer and the service or product that develops in stages. These stages, known as the Hierarchy of Effects, include awareness, knowledge, liking, preference, conviction, and purchase (Hindle & Williamson 1994:19). The right advertising at each stage of the relationship is critical and best achieved through the use of an advertising agency.

One advertising agency suggests that the best way for managers to make use of an agency is to provide it with a brief description of the service or product, a workable timetable, a feasible budget, and a realistic objective against which the agency's work can be measured (Hindle & Williamson 1994:21). During the negotiation of the contract, the manager should make full use of bargaining power. After the work is completed, it is advisable for the manager to carefully check the agency's copy and artwork, giving final approval before distribution. One way to evaluate the success of the agency's work is simply stated: if sales go up while an advertisement is running, it is a good campaign (Nilson 1999: 186).

When it is not financially feasible to hire an outside agency, the manager may be required to write the copy. To reach the market, managers need to ignite emotion and imagination, while staying away from hype. This requires a basic understanding of the essential elements of a successful advertising campaign. First, the advertisement should attract attention. This is accomplished through innovative techniques, humor, interesting or surprising copy, color, borders, and eye-catching images. Second, after attention is garnered, the campaign needs to cultivate the customer's interest in the service or product. Third, the advertisement should stimulate desire in order to trigger the sale. Fourth, the advertisement must motivate the customer into action or the sale will never be made. Fifth, the advertisement should generate sales (Ellis and Norton 1988:303-304).

A Blessing or a Curse: Advertising creates controversy. It is criticized for being manipulative, cunning, unfocused, and crude. It is praised as a modern art form that has become vital to the country's economic and political systems.

The Negative View: The advertising industry has been reprimanded for absorbing billions of dollars to convey messages of little value. Messages that only cause consumers to desire materials and to make foolish purchases for the benefit of the seller. They charge that advertising creates a barrier to the competitive system by imposing monopolistic pricing and forced name-brand affiliation. Similar arguments are rendered regarding advertising's negative impact on political freedom. It is criticized, too, for talking down to the audience, for creating price inflation, and for generating an "I need" society. Complaints are most often focused on morality issues (Hindle & Williamson 1994:22). Much attention has been focused on advertisements that encourage teenagers to break rules.

The Positive View: Proponents argue that advertising is short lived and does not change basic value systems. They praise it for its quick and economical means of bringing information to the masses. They claim that advertising reduces prices by increasing demand, and that increased demand creates new jobs. Those in favor of the medium maintain that consumers ultimately do what they want anyway, but that advertising raises awareness and ambition. They argue that it supports free media coverage through the revenues that they create.

Advertising Standards

The potential for advertisers to disseminate misleading or untruthful material is a continuous problem for governments and regulatory authorities. The advertising industry, itself, is usually the first in line to maintain standards. In the United States the Federal Trade Commission judges whether advertising is unfair or fallacious. The question is "should advertisements be judged before or after they are shown?" The future of advertising lies within the constraints set by the industry's ability to self-regulate. The future is also dependent on its regulatory agencies, the courts, on the industries ability to listen to consumer reaction, and on management's ethical conduct.

COORDINATING THE MIX

All of the promotional tools explored in this chapter are utilized by park, recreation, and leisure service delivery systems of all sizes. Each entity will use them in different proportions. Publicity will be developed with an awareness of current advertising campaigns. Sales promotions and personal selling efforts will demand coordination, and the ratios of use will vary considerably. The agency's promotional mix will be determined by it's promotional objectives. Considerations include whether the organization is producing a service or a product, differences in internal and external environments, and the agency's strategy and overall chance for success. Other factors include the appropriateness of each promotional tool for the campaign desired. Public relations, publicity, and advertising create awareness; personal selling promotes desire and action; and sales promotion encourages the completion of the exchange. Each have their place in the promotional picture, but every picture is painted differently.

SUMMARY

- Promotion efforts inform and persuade the target market about the value of a service or product. Sometimes promotion is simply utilized to remind, familiarize, overcome inertia, or add a perceived value to an offering.

- Public Relations is a promotional activity that aims to generate a favorable public opinion about a service, product, individual, or institution. The public relations effort is broken into direct and indirect forms. Direct public relations involves one-on-one contact. Indirect forms of public relations involve publicity or forms of promotional communication that are free.

- Public relations is a continuous and cooperative effort of the entire staff, including part-time employees and volunteer staff.

- Publicity is a method of attaining free communication about a service or product. It is generated through traditional news stories in newspapers, radio, and television; articles in magazines and other publications; and appearances on talk and public service shows or other special events.

- News releases generally describe events that are informative, uncommon, exceptional, funny, emotional, or nostalgic. As media individuals search for fresh stories, the news release provides a convenient method to obtain them. There are four types of releases: the advance or announcement, the backgrounder, the feature, and the follow-up.

- A Fact Sheet or a Five Questions Sheet answers journalism's famous five questions: who, what, where, when, and why (and sometimes how much). Fact Sheets or a Five Questions Sheet are also helpful in preparing posters, brochures, and flyers.

- The media kit is used to clarify information. It contains recent news releases and other pertinent forms of information including fact sheets, question and answer sheets, histories or capsules, documents, reports, studies, books, and photographs.

- A news conference is held only for major announcements or intense issues that are of immediate interest and importance to a broader audience. All media are invited so that they can hear a major announcement or ask questions of an important news maker at the same time.

- Television and radio stations frequently broadcast public service announcements, better known as PSA's, for free. The broadcast industry prides itself in taking an interest in community needs and offering its services to nonprofit groups.

- For public contacts and interviews it is important to prepare, be on time, and consider who will be listening. Speeches can be dressed up with a slide show or other visual aids.

- Special events provide opportunities to create a positive image and improve public relations with the community or target audience. They can also hurt the public image if guests are not treated properly.

- Sales promotion is a marketing effort used by most agencies, organizations, and businesses to encourage the sale of a service or product. Short-term incentives include demonstrations, contests, and bonuses. These promotions usually encourage quick sales turn-over and are quite commonly used as a combined effort with advertising and/or personal selling.

- Advertising is a paid communication designed to provide potential customers with information about a service or product using media such as newspapers, magazines, web-sites, radio, television, direct mail, billboards, posters, flyers, displays, and specialty items. Objectives include awareness of the service or product; persuading individuals to switch over to it; stimulating first time uses; and maintaining long term service or product awareness.

- All of the promotional tools explored in this chapter are utilized by park, recreation, and leisure service delivery systems, but each entity will use them in different proportions. The agency's promotional mix will be determined by it's promotional objectives.

LEARNING ACTIVITIES

1. Identify the key components that comprise a comprehensive promotion plan for an agency. Now think of a particular agency, and decide which component you would emphasize and why.

2. Are you aware of or have you attended an event recently sponsored by a recreation agency? Think about what you enjoyed most about it. Now write either a news release or a public service announcement for this event answering the famous five questions. Try to incorporate the standard format and the symbols: # # #, -30-, and -more- into your release or announcement.

3. Your agency has just decided to promote the use of some underutilized resources, for instance, a beautiful park that is not as convenient or well known to the public. How would you or your staff utilize sales promotion and personal selling to draw attention to this hidden resource? Alternatively, how would you utilize these techniques in a fund-raising effort?

4. This year's budget provides a modest amount for advertising your program. How can you make the most of these advertising funds? What other aspects of promotion could you utilize to maximize the public's awareness of your programs?

REFERENCES

Bullaro, J. and Edginton, C. (1986) **Commercial Leisure Services**. New York: Macmillan Publishing Company.

Cohn, R. (2000) **The PR Crisis Bible**. New York: St. Martin Press.

Crandall, R. (1996) **Marketing Your Success**. Lincolnwood, Ill: Contemporary Books.

Eager, B. and McCall, C. (1999) **The Complete Idiot's Guide to Online Marketing**. Indianapolis: Que Publishing.

Ellis, T. and Norton, R. (1988) **Commercial Recreation**. St. Louis: Times Mirror/ Mosby College Publishing.

Harris, T. (1998) **Value-Added Public Relations**. Chicago: NTC Business Books.

Hindle, T. and Williamson, A.D. (1994) **Field Guide to Marketing**. Boston: Harvard Business School Press.

Johnson, R. (1999) **Twenty-five Ways to Improve Sales Without Spending An Extra Dime on Advertising**. Melo Park, CA: Crisp Pub, Inc.

Kotler, P. and Armstron, G. (1990) **Marketing**. Englewood Cliffs: Prentice-Hall.

Larkin, G. A. (1992) **12 Simple Steps to a Winning Market Plan**. Chicago: Probes Publishing Company.

Nilson, T. (1999) **Competitive Branding**. New York: John Wiley & Sons.

O'Sullivan, E. (1991) **Marketing For Parks, Recreation, and Leisure**. State College, PA: Venture Publishing.

Ramacitti, D. (1994) **Do-It-Yourself Publicity**. New York: AMACOM, a Division of American Management Association.

Seacord, S. (1999) **Public Relations Marketing**. Central Point, OR: The Oasis Press.

Yale, D. (1993) **Publicity Handbook**. Lincolnwood, Il.: NTC Business Books.

CHAPTER 12
THE LEGAL ASPECTS OF MANAGEMENT

Learning Objectives

After studying this chapter, you should be able to do the following:

1. Understand the importance of managing the legal environment.
2. Define the four sources of law.
3. Describe the various court systems.
4. Describe the elements of negligence and the likely defenses.
5. Describe the elements of product liability and the likely defenses.
6. Understand the variety of labor laws that impact employment practices.
7. Understand some practical matters such as the need for insurance and an attorney.

In the United States, the constitution sets forth that each individual has the right to life, liberty, and the pursuit of happiness. These basic rights and others found in the constitution and its amendments have generated legislation, regulations, and court cases that define standards for how organization's deal with employees, customers, competitors, local communities, and even foreign nations. As stewards, leader-managers have the responsibility to ensure that their agency or organization as a legal entity stays abreast of legal requirements and complies.

Understanding the political and social environments that impact the legal environment is another important duty of management. History shows that changes in legislation reflect an evolving relationship between society and employers. For instance, during the Industrial Revolution, society saw business as an exploiter that provided unsafe working conditions and looked only to its own profits. In response, laws were passed that protected workers from harsh employers. A more harmonious relationship between society and employers existed during times of economic expansion, such as boom years of both world wars and the 1980's. In the 1960s environmental awareness and obligations to health were at the forefront of societal concerns which resulted in many environmental laws that impacted employers.

The process of moving from a societal concern to the passage of new legislation generally follows a four stage process as shown in Figure 12-1. The first stage involves societal pressure and public awareness campaigns to enact change. For example, the Americans with Disabilities Act (ADA) was originally drafted by the National Council on Disability. Eventually every major disability organization and constituency group supported it. As a societal concern grows, the second stage commences when political leaders press the issue by introducing laws and regulations in various bodies of government. The third stage occurs if enough support justifies formal legislation. At this stage, managers comply with the law or face legal enforcement. This is a transition stage. The fourth stage obliges the organization to comply with the law (Baird et. al. 1987:586-587). Employers effect the creation of laws in stage one and two and the course of laws in stage three and four.

FIGURE 12-1

Developmental Stages of Laws

Societal Pressure
Public Awareness ← Laws Introduced ← Comply and Enforcement ← Settled Law

---

Leader-managers recognize that laws do not address all ethical and moral duties of an organization, but realize that laws are a good place to begin. In pursuit of this duty, they stay abreast of legal developments including executive orders, regulations, court decisions, and statutes that pertain to their operations. These laws guide and control many managerial decisions and actions. The laws that guide empower managers to make contracts, own property, or form corporations, for instance. Laws that control define managers responsibilities and duties to others. The ADA, for example, controls managerial actions by making it illegal to fire a person because of a disability unless the impairment prevents that individual from performing the basic functions of the job. When laws are challenged, courts further define laws and determine their constitutionality. In pursuit of full compliance with the law, managers in the park and recreation field stay attuned to liability, negligence, products liability, contracts, and employee and labor laws. They have a familiarity with the legal system, procedures, attorneys, insurance, and risk management. These topics are addressed in this chapter only to provide familiarity, and should not be relied upon in lieu of legal counsel. The advice of legal counsel is always necessary in these matters.

OVERVIEW OF THE LEGAL SYSTEM

The legal system in the United States is composed of separate executive, legislative, and judicial branches at the federal, state, and local levels. The executive branch administers and enforces statutes or laws. The legislative branch enacts statutes or ordinances, and these are subordinate only to constitutions. The judicial branch conducts civil and criminal trials, resolves legal disputes, interprets the meaning of legislation, and examines the actions of the executive and legislative branches to determine if the laws are constitutional. Table 12-1 lists examples of each branch at the three levels of government.

TABLE 12-1

An Overview of the Legal System

	EXECUTIVE	LEGISLATIVE	JUDICIAL
FEDERAL	President	Congress	U.S. Supreme Court
	Cabinet		U.S. Circuit Courts of Appeals
			U.S. District Courts
			U.S. Magistrates
STATE	Governor	General Assembly	State Supreme Court
	Administrative Agencies		Intermediate Appellate Courts
LOCAL	Major or City/ County Commissioners	City Council	City and County Courts

Source: Buckley, W. Torts and Personal Injury Law (Albany, New York: Delmar Publishers, Inc., 1993), pp. 4-5.

Types of Courts

The judicial branch is of particular importance because so much is determined from previous court decisions rendered by the two types of courts, trial and appellate. The first is represented by United States District Courts; local trial courts such as district, circuit, superior, municipal, city, county, magistrate; small claims courts; courts of common pleas; or justices of the peace. They are designed to decide particular lawsuits by hearing testimony, taking evidence, and determining who wins and loses at trial. When trials are conducted with a jury, they are called jury trials; without juries they are known as bench trials.

The decisions of the trial courts may be reviewed by the second type or the appellate courts who study the transcripts of the first to determine if the trial judge was correct in applying the law to the facts of the case. Any errors are called reversible because the appellate court is obliged to reverse the lower court's decision and remand or send back the case to the first court with instructions about how to resolve the issues involved. Some states have intermediate courts of appeals and all states have supreme courts that may hear appeals. Examples of appellate courts include the state supreme courts, United States Circuit Courts of Appeals, and United States Supreme Court. A lawsuit may be filed and heard in a particular court depending upon the court's jurisdiction or its authority to try or hear certain types of cases.

Sources of Law

The highest form of law is found in the nation's constitutions. The United States Constitution represents the supreme law of the land. Approximately two years after it was signed, ten amendments were ratified which are collectively known as the Bill of Rights. These address issues involving the basic rights of the individual such as the right to exercise free speech. Because many of these rights are stated in abstract terms, it has fallen upon the courts and the legislature to determine how the abstract is to be applied to various specific situations. Modeled after and subject to the Constitution are state constitutions which are the supreme source of law within the state. Following constitutions in importance, are statutes or legislative acts which are enacted by legislatures such as Congress on the federal level. Rules, passed by local legislative bodies, are known as ordinances. All statutory law must comply with the constitutions.

Created within the last 75 years, the third highest form of law, administrative regulations are rules that come from administrative agencies such as the Environmental Protection Agency. While these regulations cannot negate ordinances, they may carry as much weight. Known as enabling acts, they enable agencies to regulate a particular type of activity. For example, at the federal level, Congress has given the Department of Interior the power to regulate and manage federal public lands. Finally, the lowest rung on the legal ladder is common law which is composed of court decisions generally issued by state appellate courts. Centuries old, American common law is based upon English common law. It is beneficial because it is predictable and can serve as a guide as to how cases should be decided in the present and in the future. Called precedents, common law decisions direct courts in resolving legal questions based on previous opinions. This creates a uniformity which appellate courts are not inclined to change. The reluctance of the courts to alter precedents is called stare decisis which in Latin means "Let the decision stand." When precedents are overruled it can only be done by the courts making them or by higher courts. Though common law varies significantly between states, the laws may not contradict any of the higher forms of law.

Litigation

Litigation is simply another term for lawsuit or the dispute between individuals or parties which is to be resolved through the court system. Disputes may involve either civil or criminal law issues. Civil law involves the adjudication of private rights between two or more parties. Examples include negligence, libel, slander, breach of contract, infliction of mental distress, and civil fraud. Civil judgments usually impose monetary settlements. Criminal law imposes punishment on those found guilty of violations forbidden by legislative bodies. Examples include murder or burglary. Penalties include fines and imprisonment. Because criminal actions generally begin with the issue of an arrest warrant or the actual arrest, the federal or state government becomes a party to the case. Both types of law could effect managers in parks, recreation, and leisure service delivery systems, but generally criminal concerns fall on the agency's law enforcement division. Nonetheless, all managers must protect recreation areas from noncompliant visitor behavior.

Increased crime and vandalism in public parks has been a drain on public funds including loss of property, and has created a need for increased security to negate these activities. For example, the Forest Service reported an increase in law enforcement workload in recent years. Because of the seriousness of misconduct, allegations, and increased law enforcement responsibilities, the agency established a new staff for law enforcement and investigations. The restructuring of the law enforcement program was designed to strengthen the independence of investigations and to do away with any perceived or real interference (Forest Service 1994).

For our purposes civil law which includes tort law or liability and personal injury will be discussed in greater detail in this chapter. An understanding of this area of the law bears particular importance to managers in the field of recreation who must manage risk and make decisions that will prevent unnecessary injuries and help avoid expensive lawsuits for the agency. We will also explore contracts and employee and labor law in a separate section. Before exploring this area of the law, it is helpful to have a background in courtroom terminology.

Courtroom Terminology

Managers can find legal terms in Black's Law Dictionary. This widely recognized legal dictionary is found in most public libraries. To understand the nature of the trial, for example, knowledge of certain terminology is essential. In civil litigation, it is the plaintiff who is the party that has allegedly suffered a legal wrong and files a suit. In criminal litigation, it is the public who brings the accused to court. The defendant is the party who is being sued and is accused of committing a legal wrong against another. The plaintiff's legal claim is called a cause of action. If the plaintiff wins the lawsuit, the plaintiff receives a judgment against the defendant. In a civil lawsuit, where the judgment is designed to settle a dispute, the losing defendant is generally ordered to pay money or damages as restitution to the plaintiff. Criminal prosecutions, on the other hand, are intended to punish or convict the offender.

Both types of lawsuits involve a battle of the burden of proof. In civil actions the plaintiff must prove by over half the evidence that their version of the facts is correct. This is called presenting a prima facie case or proving by a preponderance of the evidence. In cases involving intent, the plaintiff must provide clear and convincing evidence which is more difficult. Criminal lawsuits call for the prosecutor to prove a case beyond a reasonable doubt. This burden of proof is even more onerous. Once the burden of proof is satisfied, the burden shifts to the defendant who is required to disprove the evidence presented in order to receive a dismissal. This is called the defendant's burden of rejoinder or burden of rebuttal. After the decision is made by the trial judge or the jury, the case may be appealed to an appellate court by the appellant or the petitioner who lost at trial. The party who won is referred to as the appellee or the respondent.

The Pretrial

Many civil cases never reach the trial stage. Prior to the trial, the court may require the parties to meet with the judge for one or more pretrial conferences in order to resolve various matters relating to the case. One of the purposes of such conferences is to avoid the unnecessary waste of time at trial. Information obtained during discovery will show the strengths and weaknesses of each party's position often encouraging a settlement. Discovery involves various methods available to attorneys for finding facts and information concerning a case prior to the trial or final hearing. This includes the use of depositions or oral pretrial questioning.

TORT LAW

Tort law is a major component of the legal system. It is designed to consider the rights and remedies that are due when a person has been injured because of another's carelessness or intentional misconduct. There are three categories of tort law: intentional torts, the tort of "negligence," and strict liability. They are categorized according to the nature of the defendant's conduct. The defendant or tortfeasor is the person who commits the tort.

Torts, like all forms of law, have experienced an interesting and lengthy history which can be traced to English and Western European common law. Tort law in the United States eventually grew to include a combination of English and American common law as well as statutory law. Its growth from common law to include statutory law effects modern public parks and recreation programs. For example, under its common law roots the government could do no wrong. This resulted in an exemption of public agencies from any tort liability under the doctrine of sovereign immunity. By passing statutes, many state legislatures have abolished this exemption, allowing claims to be made against the government including public parks and recreation programs. This authorization protects the public from unjust injury, and litigation encourages minimum standards, discourages violations of standards, and allows compensation for harm.

Intentional Torts

First, there are intentional torts which are as they sound. They involve an intentional decision to harm another person or the property of that person. There are several types of intentional torts which could effect the parks, recreation, and leisure environment. Some of these are battery (touching another without consent), assault (attempted battery), infliction of emotional distress (caused from anxiety, fright, or grief which results from another's flagrant conduct), trespass (unreasonable or unlawful interference with another's property, conversion (taking property from its rightful owner), commercial disparagement (when a misleading or false statement is made about another's business which discourages the public from patronizing it), and defamation by computer (when personal information about another is held in a computer system and is either misused or is incorrect, resulting in injury to that individual's reputation).

Diagnosis Intent: Some intentional torts are simple to diagnose. For example, Bob swings his fist at John saying, "Here's a free nose job." The intent is obvious and he succeeded in breaking his nose. Bob committed battery against John. Consider the following hypothetical case. During a softball game several spectators collect on the bleachers. One spectator makes fun of a batter who strikes out. The child's mother hears and responds by throwing a plastic mustard bottle at the spectator. Simultaneously she shouts, "Now who looks stupid?" The bottles misses the intended spectator, hits an innocent bystander, and spills mustard on his clothes. Her action resulted in injury to his person and to his property. The child's mother did not mean to injure him, but he did not consent to her actions. Three elements to this tort were satisfied. There was an unconsented physical contact; it was offensive or harmful; and the tortfeasor intended to touch another in an offensive or injurious manner. Although she did not intend to strike the defendant, she committed a battery against him. Her intent is said to be carried along by the object set in motion. This is referred to as a transferred intent. These elements would not be met if in a game of horseshoes, for instance, a horseshoe struck an opponent by accident.

Intent May Not Be Required: For some intentional torts, intent may not be required. In the following case, a camp director must contend with a six year old camper who is creating a minor disturbance. To rectify the situation, he threatens the camper by telling him that if he leaves his tent that day, he will make him walk barefoot over the hot coals of the campfire that night. In this situation, the camp director has no intention of causing the physical injury implied, but it is his intent to confine the camper. The manager in charge of the nonprofit organization running the camp learns that there is to be a lawsuit against his organization for false imprisonment. He discovers that there are four essential elements needed. They are confinement without consent; intent to confine; confinement for an appreciable length of time; and no reasonable means of escape. The manager reviews a report explaining the incident. He realizes that the first three elements were violated, but assumes that because there was no lock on the tent that there has been no intentional tort. The organization's attorney explains to him that there was, however, an implied threat of force which was intended to intimidate the young camper and caused him to be held captive against his will.

Emotional Distress: If a tortfeasor should reasonably know that the consequences of his or her outrageous behavior could cause emotional injury then this knowledge would take the place of intent. In our final intentional tort case, an employee in an amusement park was admonished by his supervisor for coming to work late on several occasions. The employee began to make phone calls to his supervisor's home late at night hoping to disturb her sleep and cause her to come to work late. The calls continue every night for a month causing the supervisor to become agitated enough to loose her sleep. Her work performance slumped, she came to work late, and lost her temper with her manager. The proud employee told other employees his success story which soon came back to his supervisor. She promptly reported the incident to her manager. Because his outrageous actions were intended to cause emotional anguish which was suffered by the supervisor, he was liable to his supervisor for intentional infliction of emotional distress. Intentional infliction of emotional distress contains three elements: outrageous conduct, intention to cause severe mental distress, and actual suffering by the victim as a consequence of the behavior.

Negligence

Negligence is the second category of tort law. It does not require intent for a wrongful act to be committed. Most tort action in parks, recreation, and leisure services is caused as a result of negligence. Negligence is the failure to use reasonable care to avoid injuring another or another's property under the circumstances. It is often associated with "carelessness," but the key term is "reasonableness."

Acting Unreasonalbly: To establish negligence the following question must be asked: Was the tortfeasor acting unreasonably under the circumstances? Then skills or abilities of the reasonable person must be matched to the defendant. A reasonable person in parks, recreation, and leisure services is assessed according to the average individual with the same skills and knowledge as determined through expert testimony of members of the profession.

Professional Responsibility: The public looks to instructors, coaches, leaders, managers, and other professionals to offer programs which will prevent an unreasonable risk of harm or injury to the participants. Becoming increasingly aware of its legal rights, the public has increasingly turned to the courts for legal remedies and compensation for injuries related to a professional's negligence. As a result, it is most important that managers in the field of recreation understand the duties that are imposed on them and their employees.

Elements of Negligence: For negligence to occur, courts look for the presence of five elements: duty, breach of duty, causation of injury, proximate cause, and damages which the plaintiff has the burden of proving.

Duty: Duty involves the obligation to use a standard of reasonable care to safeguard others against an unreasonable risk of harm when a duty is owed.

Breach of Duty: A breach of duty occurs when a normal standard of care is not met within the scope of duty. This can be caused through inappropriate action (negligent actions) or failure to act (negligent omissions).

Causation of Injury: Causation of injury means that a physical or mental injury must have occurred which was caused by the tortfeasor's breach of duty. This is examined through the "but for" causation test which asks: Would the injury have occurred but for this breach of duty?

Indirect Causation: Indirect causation occurs if there were several forces co-operating to produce the injury. In these cases a formula takes the place of the "but for" test.

Proximate Cause: Proximate cause exists if the tortfeasor's actions caused a reasonably foreseeable injury. If it were reasonably foreseeable then it is said that the tortfeasor proximately caused the harm.

Damages: Damages are the injury suffered by the plaintiff as a result of the defendant's tortious conduct. Losses are normally monetary and are designed to compensate the plaintiff for the negligent act. These are referred to as compensatory damages. If there was gross negligence or conduct which approaches willful and wanton misbehavior than additional punitive damage might be awarded.

Special Negligence Rules

Negligence theory has evolved special rules for certain well-defined activities. Two rules that managers in the recreation field should be aware of are vicarious and premises liability.

Vicarious Liability: When one person carries the responsibility or liability of another person acting in his or her behalf as in an employer/employee relationship this is known as vicarious liability. Under the doctrine of respondent superior, the employer must respond to the injured plaintiff for the employee's negligence when the employee was acting in the scope of employment. This does not include coming and going to work or activity done during time of employment that involves personal matters, nor does it apply to an independent contractor hired to do a special service.

Premises Liability: In premises liability, owners and occupiers of land owe special duties of reasonable care to individuals who are injured while visiting the premises. Duties grow stronger with each of the following classifications: trespasser who has no permission to be on the land; licensee who has permission to be on the land; and invitee such as customers. While there is less duty to tres-passers, there is still a duty of reasonable care to trespassing children, for ex-ample, who may be attracted to alluring but hazardous conditions without knowing of the impending danger. A swimming pool or an abandoned well on the agency's property falls into this category, referred to an attractive nuisance. The conditions are considered enticing and under this special rule, the landowner is liable for harm and must safeguard against it.

Defenses to Negligence: Once the plaintiff has established a prima facie case or provided proof of negligence, the burden shifts to the defendant who must provide evidence to disprove the plaintiff's case or point to the plaintiff's role in causing the injury. This is referred to as the defendant's burden of rejoinder or rebuttal. Even though the defendant may have been negligent, any wrongdoing on the part of the plaintiff in causing the injuries could cause reason for the defendant to be either totally or partially forgiven.

Four Major Defenses: There are four major defenses. In the first, the defendant is exonerated if it can be proven that the plaintiff also contributed toward the harm. This defense is called contributory negligence. In these cases the defen-dant is exonerated. Comparative negligence is similar to contributory negligence and has replaced it in most states. After it is shown that the plaintiff also con-tributed toward the harm, a calculation of percentages is made which adjusts the defendant's compensation owed for causing injuries. The third defense is as-sumption of risk. This is commonly used as a defense in recreational activities where the plaintiff voluntarily assumed a known risk with full appreciation of the dangers involved. This defense totally excuses the defendant's negligence and erases any liability to the plaintiff. In general, participants cannot be expected to assume risks which they do not understand. The instructor must warn partici-pants of risks and teach them to reduce the possibility of these risks. Finally, statutes of limitations restrict the time period within which a plaintiff may file suit against a defendant. Statutes vary in different states for each particular tort. This defense is criticized on the grounds that a plaintiff may not discover the injury until after the statute has run out.

In the Field...

Negligence Diagnosed

In *Salevan v. Wilmington Park, Incorporated* the plaintiff was struck in the back by a baseball while walking on the street past the defendant's ball park. It was discovered that an average of two to three foul balls go over the 10 foot fence and on to the street per game. The manager testified that about 68 baseball games were played at Wilmington Park each season.

The plaintiff claimed that the defendant as landowner had a duty to exercise reasonable care in the use of the land so as to prevent injury to travelers lawfully using the highway adjacent to the park. The plaintiff contended that the defendant had notice of the passage of balls and by not protecting against the danger he was negligent.

The court found that the defendant did not have a right to interfere with the rights of persons lawfully using the highways. Despite the precautions originally taken by the defendant, it was apparent that they were not enough to protect the public. In fact, the posted signs showed that the defendant was aware of the circumstances and danger. Judgment was entered for the plaintiff and a sum was determined to adequately compensate the plaintiff for the injuries received as a result of negligence.

Additional Defenses: Managers in recreation should be aware of the following additional defenses and act accordingly.

Act of God: This occurs when accidents involve natural events such as lightning. In actuality this is simply a matter of foreseeability. If a golf class is playing golf on a sunny day and lightning suddenly strikes a participant then their can be no negligence. If lightning was seen and the instructor directed the class to continue, the instructor would be negligent if someone were struck because the incident would have been foreseeable.

Exculpatory Agreements: Exculpatory agreements, better known as waivers and releases, may free the leisure service organization from liability. As a result, many public and commercial recreation entities require their participants to sign a release stating that they will not hold the entity responsible for accidents that may occur. Their effectiveness may depend on state laws which tend to vary. The advice of an attorney is recommended since a waiver is a contract that requires careful wording. It is recommended that a waiver stand alone so that clients are fully aware that they are expressly and voluntarily relinquishing their right to sue. And it will explicitly state that it protects the entity against liability for its ownnegligence (Sawyer 2001:13). In some cases, however, courts will simply not provide protection if the injury was caused from negligence. Whenever utilized, releases should be meticulously formulated and thoroughly explained to the participants before they sign them. Managers will see to it that employees provide appropriate time for clients to read waivers and to ask questions if necessary. Courts have found that if the participant did not understand the full legal ramifications of signing the release at the time that the release was signed, then the release is invalid. Signed waivers are placed in safe storage for five or more years, never less than a minimum period in accordance with the tolling of the state statute of limitations (Sawyer 1999:21).

Participation Agreement: Children cannot legally sign away their right to sue, and minors, usually up to age 18, may void the contract. Therefore managers will want to talk with their attorneys about formulating an agreement to participate that clearly informs the participant about the nature of the activity, inherent risks, possible injuries, and what is expected of them. A participation agreement is a useful approach which requires that the participants or parents of the participants understand the activity, its possible risks, how the risk might be avoided through safety rules or guidelines with which the participant agrees to comply, and a specific agreement that the person is allowed or agrees to participate.

Strict or Absolute Liability

The third category of torts, known as strict or absolute liability, is liability without intent, negligence, or fault. In these cases, the tortfeasor must take on the responsibility for injuring another under certain conditions. The most important type of strict liability is products liability. Recreation managers are mindful of this theory which requires that a manufacturer or seller of an unreasonably dangerous or defective product be held liable for injuries caused by the product. In these cases the intent to commit an absolute liability tort is not relevant.

Origins of Products Liability: Established as a distinct tort theory in the early 1960s, strict or absolute liability has become an economically significant branch of tort law. Its roots are found in early nineteenth-century English and American common law where an injured buyer of a defective product had the right to sue under contract rather than tort law. If a product failed to meet certain standards then there was a breach of warranty or guarantee. Only the purchaser could sue, however. If a buyer's friend was injured while using the defective product the friend could not sue for injury because the warranty or contract did not extend beyond the immediate buyer. This led to a long evolution of legal action which resulted in products liability. Because a contract is not required for products liability, cases now extend beyond the scope of buyer and seller. This turn of events represented society's decision to let the manufacturer and seller bear the economic responsibility for injuries caused from defectively made products (Buckley 1993:317). And because the liability is absolute, it means that the manufacturer or seller does not need to be negligent in order to be sued for a defective product.

In the Field...

WAIVERS MUST BE PROPERLY WORDED

Powell v American Health Fitness Center of Fort Wayne, Inc helps to illustrate the importance of a carefully worded waiver for liability protection. Freda Powell (694 N.E.2d 757 [Indiana, 1998]) signed the following exculpatory clause when she joined American Health Fitness Center of Fort Wayne, Incorporated:

17. Damages: By signing this agreement and using the Club's premises, facilities and equipment, Member expressly agrees that the club will not be liable for any damages arising from personal injuries sustained by Member...in, on, or about the Club, or as a result of using the Club's facilities and equipment. Member assumes full responsibility for any injuries, damages or losses which may occur to Member...in, on, or about the club premises or as a result of using the club's facilities and equipment...and does hereby fully and forever release and discharge the club...from any and all claims, demands, damages, rights of action, or causes of action present or future, whether the same be known or unknown, anticipated or unanticipated, resulting from or arising out of Member's...use or intended use of said Club premises, facilities or equipment.

After Freda Powell injured her foot using the whirlpool of the defendant's fitness center, she alleged negligence on the part of American Health. Because she had signed her membership agreement with the exculpatory clause, the defendant believed that there was no genuine issue of material fact and moved for summary judgment. Powell claimed, however, that she did not know that the defendant was disclaiming liability for injuries due to its own negligence. The court held that an exculpatory clause must specifically and explicitly refer to the negligence of the party seeking release from liability in order for a waiver to protect from liability. As a result, the waiver failed to protect the defendant from liability.

Source: Cotton, Doyice. "Health Clubs Not Protected Because of Poorly Worded Waivers," *The Exercise Standards and Malpractice Reporter* Volume 12 No. 5 (Canton, Ohio:PRC Publishing, Inc., October 1998), pp. 65-68.

Elements of Products Liability: The ultimate user or plaintiff who is injured by a defective product will generally sue the retailer, wholesaler, and manufacturer. The manufacturer has a duty to use due care to design a reasonably safe product, provide reasonably error-free manufacturing, inspect and test the product, furnish reasonably safe packaging and shipping, and assemble and inspect parts (Statsky 1990:439).

Differing Views of Products Liability: Some managers believe that as a result of products liability, products have become safer, manufacturing procedures have been improved, and labels and use instructions have become more explicit (Nace 1994:3)." This has been particularly beneficial for recreation enthusiasts of higher risk activities who are dependent upon and deserve safe effective equipment and their providers who strive to provide a safe environment. Safer helmets, for example, have saved the lives of bicyclists, motorcyclists, kayakers, and others. Some manufacturers, on the other hand, feeling the brunt of lawsuits, maintain that products liability actually deters production of beneficial goods and services. This theory of torts continues to evolve.

CONTRACTS

A contract is a legally binding promise or set of promises. Contracts do not have to be in writing, but to enter into one both parties must come to some formal agreement. The law requires the parties in a contract to perform the promises made. If they do not perform, it is called a breach. Remedies are available to the injured person. Each contract contains certain essential elements. These include an offer, acceptance of the offer, consideration, itemized terms, and no valid defenses. Because contracts are involved in many aspects of recreation management such as concessions, purchasing, and employment agreements, it is beneficial to have a basic understanding of these elements.

Basic Elements of a Contract

An offer is a proposition to trade promises. Acceptance is the agreement which can be made verbally or in writing. Sometimes silence can indicate acceptance and so can beginning the work proposed. Acceptance differs from a counteroffer which offers new terms. A contract will not exist unless the counteroffer is accepted, and an offer can be dropped at anytime before acceptance. Consideration is necessary to validate the contract. This means that both parties have received something or given up something. Most often this involves an exchange of goods or services for money. A contract must also state the terms or necessary details of the contract. This could include price or time among other details. If essential terms are missing then the contract could be voided. If only certain items are missing, the court could use other similar contracts to fill in the missing items. Certain defenses can nullify a contract as well. These include illegal purpose, incompetence to contract, fraud or duress, unconscionable provisions such as one party using unequal bargaining power, and violations of the statute of frauds as listed in each state's Statute of Frauds and Uniform Commercial Code (See Table 12-2).

TABLE 12-2

Suggestions Before Entering into a Contact

1. *Get It in Writing.* Most disagreements rise over terms. By putting the terms in writing both sides have a referral.

2. *Do Not Sign Unless Sure.* Be certain that the language and terms are understood.

3. *Change the Language to Fit the Terms.* If the terms are not expressly stated, the language should be rewritten. The terms should never simply be an understanding.

4. *Fill in the Blanks.* Never sign a blank agreement and always fill in blank spaces in a standardized contract to prevent them from being filled in at a later time.

5. *Know the Payment Schedule.* If the contract involves payments, it is important to know the full amount, all interest, other charges, the payment schedule, and penalties for late payment or failure to pay.

6. *Keep a Copy of the Contract.* Keep a copy of the contract with original signatures as evidence of the agreement.

Source: Milko, G, Ostberg, K, Rudy, T.M. (1991) *Everyday Contracts* (New York: Halt Publishing, 1991), pp. 17-18.

Contract Enforcement

If a contract has been breached, common law principles require that the party who breached the contract should pay for the losses incurred. In this case a punishment is not required, but remedies are required and the offending party compensates for damages that are a foreseeable result of the breach. In an excused counterperformance, the side who is living up to the agreement is excused from further performance. Other means of enforcement include recision and restitution, specific performance, tort action, and calculated fair market value. Recision involves returning an object which has not been paid for. If the object has been used, rent could be charged. Specific performance involves a court order to complete the contract. Tort action could result if the injury or property damaged was foreseeable. Suing in quasi-contract would allow partial payment for work done even if specific specifications were not met.

THE LAW AND THE EMPLOYEE

Leader-managers of park, recreation, and leisure service delivery systems have a legal and moral obligation to carry out fair employment practices. But even well-intended managers can be in violation of the law if they are not aware of legal requirements. Ignorance of the law will not serve as an excuse. Because a significant amount of the nation's legal activity focuses on employment practices, it is imperative that leisure service managers stay abreast of current laws and changes in laws. This can be accomplished through familiarity with the agency's policies and procedures, contemporary reading, and by developing working relationships with their agency's attorneys, personnel department, and labor relations specialists. This action can help the manager to anticipate or eliminate potential legal difficulties while increasing the goodwill of employees.

Equal Opportunity Employer

Equal Employment Opportunity (EEO) refers to the responsibility of organizations and managers to keep the work environment free from discrimination. EEO ensures equal employment opportunity to all without regard to race, religion, national origin, color, disability, veteran status, gender or age. All United States citizens have the right to obtain work, earn fair wages, and receive fair treatment and to be evaluated on the basis of their ability, work performance, and potential. The major foe to the accomplishment of these objectives is found in the existence of prejudice or bias. While EEO legislation does not legislate away prejudice, it does control the impact of prejudice by making discrimination illegal. To execute and invoke the Civil Rights Act, the Equal Employment Opportunity Commission (EEOC) was established.

Equal Employment Opportunity CommissionEstablished by Title VII of the Civil Rights Act of 1964, the U.S. Equal Employment Opportunity Commission (EEOC) began operating on July 2, 1965. The EEOC enforces the principal federal statutes prohibiting employment discrimination that are seen in Table 12-3. Individuals who believe they have been discriminated against in employment may file administrative charges with the EEOC. Commissioners may also initiate charges that the law has been violated. Through the investigation of charges, if the EEOC determines there is "reasonable cause" to believe that discrimination has occurred, it must then seek to conciliate the charge to reach a voluntary resolution between the charging party and the respondent. If conciliation is not successful, the EEOC may bring suit in federal court (EEOC 1997:1).

Whenever the EEOC concludes its processing of a case, or earlier upon the request of a charging party, it issues a "notice of right to sue" which enables the charging party to bring an individual action in court. The EEOC also issues regulatory and other forms of guidance interpreting the laws it enforces, is responsible for the federal sector employment discrimination program, provides funding and support to state and local fair employment practices agencies (FEPAs), and conducts broad-based outreach and technical assistance programs.

TABLE 12-3

Principle Federal Statutes Enforced by the EEOC

1. **Title VII of the Civil Rights Act of 1964, as amended**—prohibits employment discrimination on the basis of race, color, religion, sex, or national origin

2. **Age Discrimination in Employment Act of 1967, as amended (ADEA)**—prohibits employment discrimination against individuals 40 years of age and older

3. **Equal Pay Act of 1963 (EPA)**—prohibits discrimination on the basis of gender in compensation for substantially similar work under similar conditions

4. **Title I of the Americans with Disabilities Act of 1990 (ADA)**—prohibits employment discrimination on the basis of disability in both the public and private sector, excluding the federal government

5. **Civil Rights Act of 1991**—includes provisions for monetary damages in cases of intentional discrimination and clarifies provisions regarding disparate impact actions

6. **Section 501 of the Rehabilitation Act of 1973, as amended**—prohibits employment discrimination against federal employees with disabilities

Source: The U.S. Equal Employment Opportunity Commission *U.S. Equal Employment Opportunity Commission: An Overview* http://www.eeoc.gov/overview.html. November 1997.

Key Employment Legislation

Park, recreation, and leisure service managers understand how employee rights are protected and interpreted. An overview of key employment legislation follows.

Equal Pay Act of 1963

The Equal Pay Act of 1963 (EPA), as amended, prohibits sex-based wage discrimination between men and women in the same establishment who are performing substantially equal work under similar working conditions. Any employer not covered by Title VII, because of the size of the business, is covered by the EPA.

Title VII of the Civil Rights Act of 1964

Title VII of the Civil Rights Act of 1964(CRA), as amended (see also the Civil Rights Act of 1991), prohibits discrimination in hiring, promotion, discharge, pay, fringe benefits, and other aspects of employment, on the basis of race, color, religion, sex, or national origin. The law covers applications to private businesses with 15 or more employees, state and local governments, and public or private educational institutions. Employment agencies, labor unions, and apprenticeship programs are also covered. In addition to the protection of Title VII of the Civil Rights Act of 1964, Title VI of the Civil Rights Act prohibits discrimination on the basis of race, color, or national origin in programs or activities receiving Federal financial assistance. Title IX of the Educational Amendments of 1972 prohibits employment discrimination on the basis of sex in educational programs or activities which receive Federal assistance.

Age Discrimination in Employment Act of 1967

The Age Discrimination in Employment Act of 1967, as amended, prohibits age discrimination and protects applicants and employees 40 years of age or older from discrimination on account of age in hiring, promotion, discharge, compensation, terms, conditions, or privileges of employment. The law covers applicants, with 20 or more employees, state and local governments, educational institutions, employment agencies, and labor organizations.

Vietnam Era Veteran's Readjustment Assistance Act of 1974

Vietnam Era Veterans Readjustment Assistance Act of 1974 (VEVRA) prohibits job discrimination and requires affirmative action to employ and advance qualified Vietnam era veterans from August 5, 1964 to May 7, 1975 and qualified special disabled veterans.

Americans with Disabilities Act of 1990

Title I and Title V of the Americans with Disabilities Act of 1990 (ADA), as amended, prohibits discrimination on the basis of disability, and protects qualified applicants and employees with disabilities from discrimination in hiring, promotion, discharge, pay, job training, fringe benefits, and other aspects of employment. The law also requires that covered entities provide qualified applicants and employees with disabilities with reasonable accommodations that do not impose undue hardship.

The Civil Rights Act of 1991

The Civil Rights Act of 1991 amends and strengthens the Civil Rights Act of 1964. One of the key provisions is the expansion of remedies in discrimination cases to include compensatory damages for pain and suffering. This includes sexual harassment. In addition, the act shifts the burden of producing evidence to the employer if the plaintiff can identify a specific employment practice as the cause of discrimination. It extends protection to citizens employed in foreign facilities owned or controlled by a United States company; protects workers from intentional discrimination in all aspects of employment not just hiring and promotion; and allows seniority systems that intentionally discriminate against members of a protected group to be challenged (Cascia 1995:98-99; EEOC 1993:59-67).

Rehabilitation Act of 1973

The Rehabilitation Act prohibits discrimination on the basis of disability in programs conducted by Federal agencies, in programs receiving Federal financial assistance, in Federal employment, and in the employment practices of Federal contractors. The standards for determining employment discrimination under the Rehabilitation Act are the same as those used in title I of the Americans with Disabilities Act.

The Family and Medical Leave Act of 1993

The Family and Medical Leave Act of 1993 (FMLA) requires that public agencies, including state, local and federal employers, local education agencies (schools), and all businesses with 50 or more employees will be obliged to grant up to 12 weeks of unpaid leave per year to full-time employees and those who have worked 1250 hours during the year before the leave is to begin. Leave is provided for birth, adoption or foster care; care for a child, spouse, or parent with a serious health condition; or to care for the employee's own health condition if it prevents him or her from working. Employers must also promise that employees will return to equivalent jobs and continue to provide health benefits. The U.S. Department of Labor administers the law.

In the Field...

LIFEGUARD GOES TO COURT

In Faragher v. Boca Raton, No.97-282, United States Supreme Court (1998), the Supreme Court held the employer liable for the acts of a supervisory employee whose sexual harassment of subordinates created a hostile work environment that amounted to discrimination.

Lifeguard Beth Ann Faragher worked part time during the summers between 1985 and 1990 for the Marine Safety Section of the Parks and Recreation Department in Boca Raton, Florida under the immediate supervision of Bill Terry, David Silverman, and Robert Gordon. Terry and Silverman created a hostile working environment for Faragher and other female lifeguards by repeatedly subjecting them to uninvited, offensive touching and by making demeaning remarks about them and women in general. The city had adopted a sexual harassment policy in 1986, but failed to circulate it to the Marine Safety Division. As a result, the supervisors and lifeguards were unaware of the policy. Faragher and some of the female lifeguards complained informally to Gordon, but Terry was his supervisor and Silverman was of higher rank than he. Gordon believed that it was not his place to report the complaints and told one lifeguard that the city just didn't care. Faragher did not report the incidents to higher management, although two months before her resignation, a former lifeguard wrote a letter of complaint to the city's personnel director. After an investigation, the city found that Terry and Silverman had acted improperly and required them to choose between a suspension without pay or the forfeiture of annual leave.

In 1992, Faragher brought an action against Terry, Silverman, and the city asserting claims under Title VII of the Civil Rights Act of 1964. The federal district court found that the supervisors' conduct was discriminatory harassment serious enough to alter the conditions of the plaintiff's employment and constitute an abusive working environment. They also found that the city was liable for the harassment by its supervisory employees and awarded nominal damages to Faragher. When the city appealed, the appeals court reversed the judgment. The Supreme Court reversed the judgment of the appeals court, however, ordering that the judgment of the district court in favor of Faragher be reinstated.

The Supreme Court noted that Title VII was not intended to protect employees from isolated incidents or jokes, but from an environment that a reasonable person would find hostile or abusive. In implementing Title VII, the Supreme Court found it reasonable to hold an employer liable for sexual harassment by a supervisor, particularly when such misconduct is "made possible by abuse of his supervisory authority." While noting that an employer has the opportunity and responsibility to guard against misconduct by screening, training, and monitoring a supervisor's performance, the Court found that an employer could avoid such liability if the following two points could be established:

(a) that the employer exercised reasonable care to prevent and correct promptly any sexually harassing behavior, and (b) that the plaintiff employee unreasonably failed to take advantage of any preventive or corrective opportunities provided by the employer or to avoid harm otherwise.

In this case, however, Faragher and her colleagues were isolated from higher management, and the city did not have a policy in place that prevented harassment or eliminated it if it occurred. By taking reasonable care to prevent and promptly correct sexually harassing behavior, leader-managers help to protect the recreation entity from legal liability. Leader-managers will issue a no-tolerance educational statement with appropriate methods for reporting abuses that will not result in retaliatory measures.

Source: Kozlowski, James C. "One Lifeguard's Ongoing Struggle With Sexual Harassment" Parks & Recreation Vol 33 No 9, September (Ashburn, VA: National Recreation and Park Association, 1998), pp. 63-71.

EMPLOYEE RIGHTS

The Fair Labor Standards Act (FLSA) establishes minimum wage, overtime pay, record-keeping and child labor standards that affect over 100 million full- and part-time workers in the private sector and in federal, state and local governments. If these rights are violated the Department of Labor (DOL) can recover back wages either administratively or through court action.

Wages

Most employees are guaranteed a minimum wage. Only certain full-time students, student learners, apprentices, and workers with disabilities may be paid less than the minimum wage under special certificates issued by the DOL. An employer may claim a "tip credit" with respect to "tipped employees" which is 50 percent of the applicable minimum wage. Some camps allow tips for employees. In addition, unless exempted, overtime pay must be at least one and one half times the regular rate of pay for all hours worked over 40 in a workweek (U.S. Department of Labor 1999:1).

Child Labor

The child labor provisions of the FLSA are designed to protect the educational opportunities of youths and prohibit their employment in jobs and under conditions detrimental to their health and well being. To work in most jobs, an employee must be at least 16 years and at least 18 to work in non-farm jobs declared hazardous by the Secretary of Labor. Youths 14 and 15 years old may work outside school hours in some recreation positions which are non-hazardous for no more than three hours on a school day or 18 hours in a school week and 8 hours on a non-school day or 40 hours in a non-school week. In addition work may not begin before 7 a.m. or end after 7 p.m., except from June 1 through Labor Day, when evening hours are extended to 9 p.m. Youths aged 14 and 15 who are enrolled in an approved Work Exploration Program (WECEP) may be employed for up to 23 hours in school weeks and three hours on school days, including during school hours. Children of any age may deliver newspapers, perform in theatrical productions, and be employed in certain other activities (U.S. Department of Labor 1999:1).

Job Safety and Health Protection

Managers are expected to help maintain a safe and healthy work environment for employees and are familiar with and stay abreast of health-related legislation.

The Occupational Safety and Health Act of 1970

The Occupational Safety and Health Act (OSH Act), administered by DOL's Occupational Safety and Health Administration (OSHA), regulates safety and health conditions in most private industry workplaces (except those regulated under other federal statutes, e.g., the transportation industry). Many private employers are regulated through states operating under OSHA-approved plan. The Act also provides for mandatory civil penalties against employers for each serious violation and for optional penalties for each nonserious violation. Penalties may also be imposed for failure to correct violations . Besides providing penalties for violations, the Act encourages efforts by labor and management to recognize outstanding efforts in this area. In addition, a local OSHA office can offer advice on safety and health issues or refer managers to other sources for help. Free assistance in identifying and correcting hazards and improving safety and health management is available to employers through OSHA-supported programs in each State. These programs are usually administered by the State Labor or Health Department or State University (U.S. Department of Labor 1999:1).

Workers' Compensation Laws

Workers' Compensation Laws (WC), found in each state, have no mandates for safety. They are, instead, designed to protect employees by providing them with financial benefits should they suffer from a work-related injury or illness. This may include injuries incurred during employee recreation programs and those which do not involve fault or negligence. They also include injuries sustained while driving to various work sites and when the worker must reside at the worksite as in camp situations. WC laws cover part-time employees and some volunteers. Laws differ according to the state and not all states require participation of employers if they are self-insured. Because insurance goes up according to the number of accidents, the law encourages a safe work environment.

OTHER LABOR ACTS, REGULATIONS, AND EXECUTIVE ORDERS

Managers in parks, recreation, and leisure services have a basic understanding of other important acts, regulations, and executive orders. These are listed below, and managers pursue an awareness of state laws pertaining to their operation and state and local public employees.

Social Security Act of 1935

Social Security Act of 1935, passed in response to the Great Depression was initiated to compel employees to save for their retirement through a deduction in wages matched by their employer. Federal employees, the military, railroad personnel, and some state and local public employees do not participate in the program.

Unemployment Compensation Laws

Title IV of the Social Security Act obliged the states to enact these unemployment compensation laws which provide payments to workers who have been terminated through no fault of their own after working a specific amount of time. To receive payments, the employee must make a reasonable effort to find new employment in a similar line of work and be available for work provided the state employment service locates another position for the terminated employee. When the National Parks were closed in 1995 due to failed approval of the federal budget, many park employees were advised to file for unemployment compensation pending a lengthy government shutdown.

National Labor Relations Act of 1935

National Labor Relations Act of 1935, also known as the Wagner Act, was devised to give employees more bargaining power. Serving as the basic federal statement of policy toward labor-management relations, it restrains unfair labor practices by management. The National Labor Relations Board (NLRB) is charged with investigating unfair labor practices by management and also conducts elections designed to determine if employees wish to bargain collectively. The Labor-Management Relations Act of 1947 and 1974 (Taft-Hartley Act) and the Labor-Management Reporting and Disclosure Act of 1959 (Landrum-Griffin Act) protect employers from unfair union practices and regulate the internal affairs of unions.

Executive Order (EO) 10988

Executive Order (EO) 10988: Established by President John F. Kennedy in 1962 the EO recognized the rights of federal government employees— who had been excluded from the labor laws listed above— to organize and collectively bargain but not strike. Later orders amended this EO to include collective bargaining regulations and the creation of a Labor Relations Council.

Civil Service Reform Act

The Civil Service Reform Act, passed by Congress in 1978, replaced the Executive Orders above to become the law governing labor relations for federal employees. The independent, bipartisan Federal Labor Relations Authority (FLRA), modeled after the NLRB, was created to resolve disputes and interpret the Act relieving agency heads of this authority. Unlike the private-sector, however, the act still excluded salary, benefits, examination, and appointments from collective bargaining.

Privacy Act of 1974

The Privacy Act of 1974 gives the federal employee the right to privacy when it comes to the dissemination of employee records, knowledge of what information is on file in their records, and the right to respond to derogatory information.

PRACTICALITIES AND PREVENTATIVE MEASURES

Given the tendency of U.S. citizens to sue, providers of park, recreation, and leisure services will need to be prepared to manage the risks inherent in recreation programs, to investigate liability insurance premiums, and to seek legal advice when needed. Risk management and insurance plans are in place before an accident, and seeking the advice of an attorney before problems mount can save time, problems, and money later.

Risk Management

The leisure service manager assesses the risks that the organization is exposed to in fulfilling its mission and takes whatever action is necessary to combat or minimize the danger. This is called risk management. In general, there are three types of risks the manager considers. Unforeseeable natural risks include fires, floods, earthquakes, theft, etc.

Next, there is simply the risk of doing business or the possibility that the enterprise could fail or suffer losses due to contract loss, employee dishonesty, or change in the business environment, etc. Finally, there is the risk of liability to a customer or client who is injured by the service or product. This is of special concern to the park, recreation, and leisure manager who works in a risk-taking atmosphere where accidents do happen. A nation's capacity for taking risks varies. For instance, Japan is considered a risk-averse nation, whereas, the United States is considered a risk-taking nation (Greenfeld 1999:34). In this risk-taking environment, more Americans than ever are injuring themselves while testing their personal limits (Greenfeld 1999:32).

The most pronounced area of risk in recreation has been termed high-risk recreation. High-risk recreation activities are growing in popularity (Society of Park and Recreation Educators 1998:43). Thrill-seekers are skiing in unpatrolled back-country and BASE jumping from public and private sites even though it is illegal. Others are ice climbing, paragliding, and participating in more adventure activities and sports than ever before. Mountain sports, rock climbing, and snowboarding are all on the rise (Malkin and Rabinowitz 1998:36). According to American Sports Data, Incorporated (Greenfeld 1999:31), for example, snowboarding has gone up 113 percent with 5.5 million participants, while base-ball, touch football, and aerobics, on the other hand, have all seen a steady decline in participation. Thrill seekers and adventure enthusiasts, in turn, are injuring themselves at alarming rates (Greenfeld 1999:32). To control BASE jumping, park rangers are confiscating equipment and prosecuting for trespass. Recogniz-ing, too, that legal high-risk activities provide sensation seekers with a socially acceptable outlet, managers of park and recreation agencies are finding them-selves responsible for these activities. The risk management process includes four aspects: identifying risks, evaluating risks, selecting the proper approaches, and implementing procedures (Cotten 1993:58-61).

In the Field...

PROMOTING SAFETY

To promote river paddling safety, the National Livery Safety System devised informa-tive informative videos and posters, and an 85-page risk management manual to outfitters, management, and staff of livery operations. Paddling outfitters used the informative videos and posters to get participants off to a safer more informed start. Management studied the video, *So Take the Time... A Guide to Risk Management Training for Outfitters,* to provide a better, safer service to clients. The video provided information on assumption of risk, outfitter responsibility, accidents, water levels, staff training, and emergency plans.

The accompanying manual, *Introduction to Risk Management for Livery Opera-tors,* furnished *valuable* information on safe operations, waivers, American Whitewater Affiliation Safety Code, and safety audits which helped the manager examine canoeing through a risk management perspective. When managers and organization join pro-fessional associations with like interests, they generally are better able to stay abreast of developments in their fields that can help them improve safety and reduce risks.

Identifying the Risks

In the first step of the risk management process, the manager estimates the dam-age that could result from natural risks and from various disruptions to the nor-mal business routine. This involves an on-going process of accounting which includes an inventory of property and equipment. The manager also attempts to identify potential risks due negligence, intentional torts, contractual liability, discrimination, products liability, etc. When considering susceptibility to neg-ligence the manager needs to consider maintenance of facilities, the ratio of personnel to participants and personnel training.

Evaluating the Risks

The second step calls for an evaluation of the risks in terms of severity. Severity could include the seriousness or likelihood of harm as well as the numbers of individuals who could be injured.

Selecting Risk Approaches

After identifying and evaluating risks, a plan of action is necessary. The manager can eliminate the risk through discontinuance or avoidance; reduce the risk by limiting its frequency; or accept the risk by meeting the necessary standard of care. The necessary standard of care required for acceptance or limited frequency includes appropriate training for participants and personnel, suitable supervision of personnel, posted warnings of pending danger, proper maintenance of equip-ment, application of safety rules, a system of documentation, continuous moni-toring, and knowledge of the latest techniques and safety requirements. Another approach that the manager might take would be to transfer risk to an insurance company, a lessor, an independent contractor, or the participant. When a partici-pant signs a valid exculpatory agreement, commonly referred to as a waiver or release form, the risks of ordinary negligence are transferred from the organiza-tion to the participant.

Implementing the Risk Plan

The final step of the risk management process is implementation of the plan. This involves communicating and motivating employees, implementing the train-ing program, establishing policies and procedures, on-going risk evaluation, and contracting with others and/or purchasing suitable insurance.

INSURANCE MANAGEMENT

A variety of types of insurance policies are available to meet the needs of the park, recreation, recreation, or leisure service delivery service delivery system. There are three principal types of insurance to safeguard against loss: property, crime protection, and liability. The latter protects the agency against financial loss arising from personal injury or property damage for which the agency is liable. Because accidents can be related to the recreation field, liability insurance dominates this section.

Insurance Policies

Many county and municipal governments, agencies, and organizations have umbrella liability policies that cover all of their operations. Policies that have specific allocations allow operations with greater potential for risk to seek additional coverage of their own. Some insurance companies specialize in coverage pertaining to risk activities. Where liability and accident insurance is mandated by law, the park, recreation, and leisure service delivery system contracts for a broad liability policy and accident insurance for its employees. Liability insurance is available to cover employees, managers, and the board of directors in the event of a negligent act. Workmans' compensation insurance, discussed earlier in this chapter, provides benefits for employees who have been injured on the job. An agency or organization might choose to insure its volunteers or to arrange group rates. Personal liability insurance policies are sometimes available for employees through a group-coverage plan or through unions and professional associations. Agencies and organizations may choose to purchase accident insurance to cover participants' medical expenses, or they may advise participants to purchase their own accident insurance.

Higher Risks, Higher Rates: Insurance rates continue to escalate due to increased lawsuits and high jury awards. Some insurers have even refused to insure water parks, ski resorts, and amusements parks or certain high-risk activities like mountain climbing and river running. Even when insurance is available for higher risk outdoor-pursuits, it can be prohibitively expensive to buy on an on-going basis. Still, outfitters conducting activities on federal lands are generally required to carry specific liability insurance to obtain necessary permits. And customers and clients often expect insurance coverage from firms that they do business with. Some insurance companies offer limited coverage for specific trips or programs, but this can still be overwhelming. Entrepreneurs may decide to operate only a few trips a year, to subcontract, or to join forces with larger entities. Policies with large deductibles present another option. This form of insurance costs less and the savings in premiums could help pay the deductible or the amount that an entity pays in the event of a claim. Entrepreneurs have even turned to overseas ventures to escape high insurance fees (Ford 1993:264). Noninsurance or operating without insurance is not recommended.

Self-Insurance: Businesses may chose to self-insure. Self-insurance involves setting aside a certain sum of money against potential lawsuits. A self-insured business can offer to pay an injured person for an agreement not to sue. If a suit is litigated, damages are awarded out of the self-insurance fund. Large claims, however, could imperil the viability of the business. Additionally, the self-insured do not have the legal representation provided by an insurance company. In joint-pooling, an extension of self-insurance, several entities pool their funds to cover the risks of each. Risk management firms or an insurance company could be hired to administer the pool.

HIRING AN ATTORNEY

When the services of legal counsel are needed, park, recreation, and leisure service agencies and organizations may have an in-house attorney or an attorney on retainer who can help prevent or rectify legal matters. Managers may also turn to the personnel office for assistance. Unions typically offer legal service, but that service is directed to the employee. Some companies offer a prepaid legal plan entitling employees to a specified amount of time for legal services. Should it become necessary for a manager to retain an attorney for the entity, the process takes time, money, and effort. As a result, managers may put the process off too long, thereby, allowing a legal matter to escalate into a lawsuit. Preventive legal advice saves time, stress, money, and inconvenience because legal difficulties can often be resolved before they mushroom or at least kept under control. Communications are confidential so the manager should feel comfortable calling an attorney for legal advice when needed.

Attorneys provide for-profit managers with advice on the appropriate legal form for their business organization such as sole proprietorship, partnership, or incorporation. The first is the oldest and simplest form. It gives legal title and exclusive rights to one person, the owner, who is also responsible for certain stipulated legal responsibilities and liabilities. The second option represents an association between two or more persons who act as co-owners. The third is the most difficult to establish. Ownership is transferred through the purchase and sale of stock. This makes the corporation responsible for its own debts, and it is taxed on its own revenue.

The Selection

The challenge for the manager is not to find an attorney, but to select a competent one who specializes in the type of legal problem anticipated at a cost that can be afforded. The search is begun by seeking recommendations from other professionals, associates, and friends. Referral lists are available from professional associations, legal organizations, local bar associations, consumer information booklets, and legal clinics. Libraries also stock reference books that list attorneys by specialty. These include the Martindale-Hubbell Law Directory which profiles almost every active attorney in the United states, their areas of expertise, and their education; the Encyclopedia of Associations which lists legal organizations in specific fields; and the Lawyers Register by Specialities and Fields of Law, which lists attorneys by name. Referral agencies provide the names of eligible attorneys, but their method of selection varies. They may require only a minimum amount of experience, list any attorney who would like to be listed, or only list those attorneys who pay a fee.

Screening: After obtaining the names of several prospects, each attorney should be interviewed by telephone to see if they have handled similar cases, how recently, and how many. Potential attorneys should be interviewed in person to assess the potential for establishing a sound working relationship. This is followed with a call to the state attorneys' discipline agency and bar association to see if the selected attorney has committed any ethics violations.

The Charge

Fees charged are dependent upon the attorney's experience and the complexity of the task. Attorneys bill for research, locating witnesses, interviews, for time spent forming arguments, and the trial itself. To cover expenses several types of fee arrangements are possible including fixed, hourly, retainer, contingency, and statutory.

Fee Arrangements: When retaining an attorney, it is advisable to agree on a fee arrangement first. This includes understanding what the fixed fee would cover or not cover and, then, comparing it to an hourly charge. For an individual case, an estimate of the number of hours required is needed. The hourly rate can vary significantly depending on the attorney's experience and reputation. More important than the hourly fee, however, is the total cost. Billing is generally made by tenth of an hour or quarter-hour charges, and a ceiling can be agreed upon. A retainer involves a flat fee which is charged monthly, while contingency fees provide the attorney with a percentage of the damages awarded. Contingency arrangements are more often used in accident or negligence cases brought against the entity. Agreed upon ahead of time, the percentage of the contingency fee may range from 25-50 percent of the amount of the judgment actually collected. Statutory fees are set by state law.

Finalizing the Agreement: In consultation with the attorney, the manager assesses if court action is necessary or if there are other options. Managers learn when the matter is likely to be resolved, a likely time-table, and if it is possible to assist in any way to defray expenses. Billing terms are arranged as well as the information that will be itemized on the bill such as service rendered, date, time, and whether clerical services or other in-house costs will be charged. A letter of formal agreement confirms the arrangement and includes an estimate of costs and time. A termination clause should also be outlined in the letter.

SUMMARY

- As stewards, leader-managers have the responsibility to ensure that their agency or organization as a legal entity stays abreast of legal requirements and complies.

- Tort law is designed to consider the rights and remedies that are due when a person has been injured because of another's carelessness or intentional misconduct. There are three categories of tort law: intentional torts, the tort of negligence, and strict liability.

- A contract is a legally binding promise or set of promises. Contracts do not have to be in writing, but to enter into a contract, both parties must come to some formal agreement. The law requires the parties in a contract to perform the promises made.

- Leader-managers of park, recreation, and leisure service delivery systems have a legal and moral obligation to carry out fair employment practices.

- EEO ensures equal employment opportunity to all without regard to race, religion, national origin, color, disability, veteran status, gender or age. Park, recreation, and leisure service managers are responsible for providing a safe and healthy work environment, and they understand how employee rights are protected and interpreted.

- The leisure service manager assesses the risks that the organization is exposed to in fulfilling its mission and takes whatever action is necessary to combat or minimize the danger..

- There are three principal types of insurance to safeguard against loss: property, crime protection, and liability.

- The challenge for the manager is not to find an attorney, but to select a competent one who specializes in the type of legal problem anticipated at a cost that can be afforded.

LEARNING ACTIVITIES

1. For an entire day take notice of legal references in the newspaper, on television, and in your daily activities. Describe three of the references you noticed and the legal issues addressed. Would the legal issues have any impact on the role of a manager in the recreation field? Please explain.

2. Identify one or two federal laws that were enacted in the last fify years that impact the use of parklands. Describe the societal issue(s) that caused the law(s) to be enacted. Identify the primary groups or associations that either supported or opposed the enactment of the law(s). Please discuss the effectiveness of the legislation.

3. High-risk activities are controversial. Select one high-risk activity and either describe the likely positions of the proponents and the opponents of the activity, or interview individuals involved and describe their positions. Check with the local parks to determine if the activity is permitted in the parks, and if permitted, describe what steps have been taken to manage the risks. If not permitted, how is enforcement of the rule handled?

REFERENCES

Baird, L.S., Post, J.E., Mahon, J.F. (1987) **Management Functions.** New York: Harper & Row, Publishers.

Buckley, W. (1993) **Torts and Personal Injury Law.** Albany, New York: Delmar Publishers, Inc.

Bucher, C.A. (1987) **Management of Physical Education and Athletic Programs.** St. Louis: Times Mirror/Mosby College Publishing.

Cascio, W. (1995) **Managing Human Resources.** New York: McGraw-Hill.

Cotten, D. (1993) "Risk Management - A Tool for Reducing Exposure to Legal Liability," **Journal of Physical Education, Recreation, and Dance (JOPERD).** Vol 64, No 2. February 1993. Reston, VA: American Alliance for Health, Physical Education, Recreation, and Dance.

Equal Employment Opportunity Commission (EEOC) (1993) **EEOC Publication 355-218/90016.** Washington D.C.: U.S. Government Printing Office.

Ford, P. and Blanchard, J. (1993) **Leadership and Administration of Outdoor Pursuits.** State College, PA: Venture Publishing, Inc.

Greenfeld, K. (1999) "Life on the Edge Time," Vol 154 No 10 September 5. New York: Time, Inc.

Kinder, T. (1993) **Organizational Management for Athletic Programs.** Dubuque: Eddie Bowers Publishing, Inc.

Malkin, M. and Rabinowitz, E (1998) **Sensation Seeking and High-Risk Recreation Parks & Recreation.** Vol 33 No 7 Ashburn, VA: National Recreation and Park Association.

Nace, B. (1994) **Current Liability Law Enhances.** Safety NCAA News Vol 31 No 26.

Sawyer, T. (1999)" Assumption of Risk " **Journal of Physical Education, Recreation, and Dance (JOPERD).** Vol 70, No 3. March 1999. Reston, VA: American Alliance for Health, Physical Education, Recreation, and Dance.

Sawyer, T. (2001) "Release of Liability" **Journal of Physical Education, Recreation, and Dance (JOPERD)** Vol 72, No 1. January 2001. Reston, VA: American Alliance for Health, Physical Education, Recreation, and Dance.

Society of Park and Recreation Educators (1998) "Research Into Action: Meeting the Challenges of High-Risk Recreation **"Park & Recreation.** Vol 33 No 7 July. Ashburn: National Recreation and Park Association.

Statsky, W. Torts (1990) **Personal Injury Litigation.** St. Paul, MN: West Publishing Co.

U.S. Department of Labor (1999) "Child Labor (Nonagriculture)" **Small Business Handbook,** December www.dol.gov/dol/asp/ public/programs/handbook/childlbr.htm) December 1999.

U.S. Department of Labor (1999) "Laws, Regulations and Technical Assistance Services Overview" **Small Business Handbook.** www.dol.gov/dol/asp/public/ programs/ handbook/overview.htm December 1999.

U.S. Department of Labor (1999) "Minimum Wage and Overtime Pay," **Small Business Handbook,** www.dol.gov/dol/asp/ public/programs/handbook/minwage.htm December 1999.

U.S. Equal Employment Opportunity Commission "U.S. Equal Employment Opportunity Commission: An Overview" http://www.eeoc.gov/overview.html November 3, 1997.

U.S. Forest Service (1994) **Report of the Forest Service.** August 1994. Washington D.C. U.S. Government Printing.

CHAPTER 13

ENTREPRENEURIAL AND THE RECREATION BUSINESS

Learning Objectives

After studying this chapter, you should be able to do the following:

1. Appreciate the changes that have taken place in recreation and leisure service.

2. Understand the nature of commercial leisure services.

3. Appreciate the ability, perseverance, and dedication of the entrepreneur.

4. Understand and follow the steps to be taken in the development of a commercial business in general and in recreation in particular

5. Understand how to develop and manage a commercial enterprise in the expanding area of commercial recreation and leisure.

THE CHANGING NATURE
OF LEISURE SERVICES

Does every citizen have the right to receive public leisure service? Should leisure service be supported by public funds, either entirely or partially, as is the case with educational service? To answer these two questions, three sets of factors must be addressed. First, the social and economic circumstances during which policies and practices that governed public leisure in most of the 20th century should be understood. Secondly, the types and functions of the agencies through which the policies and practices governing leisure services should be examined. Thirdly, the ideologies behind these policies and the values of the decision-makers should be explored.

At the beginning of the 20th century drastic changes were taking place in the urban settings of both the United States and Canada. The social and economic conditions of this era helped to promote the adoption of the public recreation service. In order to ameliorate the declining conditions in most of the continent's inner cities, local recreational services were offered by voluntary organizations that, initially, received no government support. In addition there was a push to increase open spaces for urban centers. When New York City acquired Central Park the idea was quickly followed by many large cities in the United States and Canada. In both countries the role of the federal government to provide open space and to preserve natural areas was underscored with the establishment of national parks. Canadian provinces and American states followed suit.

The Great Society

During the first half of the 20th century, the idea of offering local recreational programs was adopted, and the role of local and state government in that endeavor increased. In the second half of the 20th century, local and state services were enhanced with the advent of President Lyndon Johnson's new ideology entitled the *Great Society*.

Funding social programs and protecting the environment, while maintaining a powerful military machine, was at best depleting the coffers of the Federal Government of the United States. Its inability early on to continue the previous level of support for the maintenance of national natural resources and for local services was compounded by the taxpayer's unhappiness which began to surface in the mid 1970's. The citizens of California spearheaded the tax revolt. In 1978, Proposition 13 became a Constitutional Amendment which kept state and local governments from increasing property tax, the main source of providing the previous level of public services.

As funds were shrinking on the federal, state, and local levels, public services were also being reduced. When pitted against other public services, such as education, law enforcement, and fire protection, public leisure service was low on the list of priorities.

In order to maintain their offerings many local departments of parks and recreation began to charge fees or to increase them. While some departments charged fees for direct services such as participating in activities and event, others began to charge for supplementary services such as parking on the premises.

Even with these measures which made public recreation less public, these departments as well as the state and federal agencies providing leisure services, continued to suffer from lack of adequate funds. Fiscal necessities led many leisure service agencies, whether local, state, or federal, to engage in activities that, only a few years before, were not considered part of their realm. Fundraising was one of these activities. This new technique is discussed in detail in other chapters. While to some extent successful, fundraising by these public leisure service agencies, did not correspond with the original intent to provide the public with *bone fide* public recreation.

Towards a Greater Society

Outwardly, it may seem that the typical citizen has lost interest in leisure services. However, statistics show a different story. Table 1-1 shows that the total spending on leisure pursuits continues to increase (See Page 6).

It is clear from the aforementioned table that a window of opportunity exists for the person who is still interested in engaging in some form of leisure services. While the financial support of public leisure services may be declining at this point in time, offerings through commercial agencies and or entrepreneurial enterprises are promising. This chapter is concerned with these two types of leisure services and should be differentiated as follows.

Commercial or Entrepreneurial Recreation

The commercial type of leisure service is one already established and is in need of qualified person. The entrepreneurial type refers to the innovative leisure service, which can to be established by one person, a team of entrepreneurs or an already established agency. Everyone involved in the enterprise should have prior knowledge that an element of risk is involved in the undertaking of an entrepreneurial task.

There are distinguishing features in each of these two types of leisure services. For instance one should think of the commercial type as the one which involves the creation of activities, facilities, and programs and or the involvement in the wholesaling and retailing of leisure experiences and goods. On the other hand, entrepreneurialship in a leisure service refers to the innovative yet risky ideas that requires the investment of time, talent, and or financial resources in a project that involves the creation of unique activities, facilities, and programs or the wholesaling and retailing of leisure experiences and goods (Bularo and Edginton, 1988:12). These two types of leisure services will be discussed separately in the following pages.

THE NATURE OF COMMERCIAL LEISURE SERVICES

Commercial leisure offerings have been around for many centuries. Commercial recreational offerings were witnessed in Ancient and Medieval China in the form of entertainment such as puppet and marionette shows (Garnet 1962: 225). The same was seen in Medieval Europe (Giels 1974: 112), and in Egypt (Lane 1836:). During the postbellum era, organized commercial spectator sport took place on this continent and established the foundation for the rise of modern organized sport (Dulles, 1965:146).

With the increased offerings of both public and semi-public recreation services, commercial offerings faded into the background. They were normally limited to tourism, amusement parks, and other aspects of entertainment. In today's world other leisure pursuits could be offered commercially as shown in the following section.

Classification of Commercial Recreation

There are basically two ways of classifying commercial leisure services. The first is related to both the production and distribution of recreational goods and products. For instance, a commercial enterprise engages in the production of fitness equipment, another engages in the wholesaling of these equipment, and a third engages in the retailing of such equipment.

Some commercial enterprises engage in one or more leisure services. Bullaro and Edginton consider the five areas to be within the realm of commercial recreational services as follows (1988:19):

Travel and Tourism	These agencies are responsible for transporting individuals to points of interest. The person engaged in these activities could manage a travel agency, operate a tour, serve as a tour guide, or provide transportation
Hospitality Services	These are housing and restaurant services, and the person engaged in these services could be employed in hotels, resorts, or food and beverage establishments.
Entertainment Services	These services are provided by movie theaters, night clubs, amusement parks, circuses, video arcades, professional sport, race tracks, bowling alleys, tennis and racquet clubs, and fitness centers.
Services in the Natural Environment	These are the services normally occur outdoors and includes instruction, interpretation, and counseling.
Retail Outlets	In the past few years, an increase interest in leisure goods and products has occurred. Thus the opportunities for management and sales of these goods and products exist today.

Crossley and Jamieson (1988) classify commercial recreation into three major groups as shown in the following section:

The Travel Industry	This is a complex network of transportation, carriers, travel agencies, hotels, and attractions.
The Hospitality Industry	This commercial recreation area includes the businesses that provide accommodations, food and beverage services, and related amenities.
Local Enterprises	These businesses provide leisure services and goods at the local level. Recreation providers include health and racquet clubs, golf courses, bowling alleys, and dance studios. Leisure product retailers and wholesalers include sporting goods, toys and arts, and craft equipment and material. Entertainment providers include theme parks, amusement parks, movie theaters, fairs, and festivals.

While there seems to be some agreement between these two approaches as to the classification of commercial recreation, additional areas of human activities have been added by Chubb and Chubb (1981) as follows:

- Shopping Facilities
- Food and Drink Services
- Dancing and sport establishments
- Amusement Parks
- Museums
- Traveling and Tourism
- Camps
- Hotels
- Resorts
- Farms
- Products
- Rental services

Kelly (1982) classifies commercial recreation enterprises differently as shown in the following list.

Travel	Direct Provider
	Arranger
	Support Services
Sport	Spectator service
	Participatory activities
	Television viewing
	Information and mass media
	Gambling, both legal and illegal
Popular Culture	Printed media
	Visual media
	Auditory media
The Arts	Performing arts
	Graphic arts
	Literary work
	Community theaters
	Instruction

After reviewing the above approaches, one might think that there is no agreement as to what constitutes commercial recreation. Yet evidently these enterprises do share one thing in common, these activities are pursued during one's free time. But how can a person become involved in one of these enterprises? The answer to this question is related to the ownership of the enterprise. Whether the enterprise is dealing with leisure services and goods or other kinds of services and goods, the ways through which it is established, owned, and run are the same.

Ownership of Commercial Enterprises

There are many ways in which a business is established, owned, and run. This section presents the four types of business ownerships in the United States and Canada, all of which are applicable to the ownership of commercial recreation businesses.

Sole Proprietorships: Sole proprietorship is the most common form of ownership in the business world, including most of the small commercial recreation businesses. A single person owns and operates this kind of enterprise, for which he or she is totally responsible.

Partnerships: In American and Canadian businesses, partnerships come in more than one form. Partnerships are formed when two or more persons form an association for which they share the responsibility, albeit of different degrees. In a **general partnership**, all co-owners share the responsibility for debts and contracts. In a **limited partnership**, some members have limited liability as to their capital investment while the other have an unlimited liability. A **joint venture** is created for a specific purpose, and is limited by certain time period.

Corporations: Since a corporation is not owned by a particular person or persons, it has its own legal status. Nonetheless, a corporation acts as business in that it can hold property, write contracts, and pay taxes. A corporation creates two types of stock shares. Common shares entitle the shareholder to a profit, and preferred shares entitle the shareholder to a position in terms of assets and profits. Shareholders may elect directors who then set the general policy of the corporation. The managers are charged with the every day operations of the corporation.

Cooperatives: These are associations formed by a group of people or businesses for the purpose of wielding greater market power in buying and selling. Members of the cooperative pay an annual fee. Although the members are not shareholders, they may receive some profits each year.

Advantages In Commercial Enterprises

Each of the four types of commercial recreational enterprises has its own advantages as well as disadvantages. The advantages and disadvantages of each type are discussed below.

Proprietorships: Perhaps the most important advantage to owning a solo proprietorship is the freedom to act as one pleases. There is also a very high incentive factor involved in owning one's own business. In addition an enterprise that is owned by one person normally does not require much capital to be established, depending on the nature of the business, and there is a possibility of saving on taxes. Furthermore, this type of commercial enterprise can be dissolved easier than the other types.

Partnerships: This business is also easy to form, but has more capital since two or more people are involved. The partners also bring into the business additional skills and talent not available to a single owner. When compared to corporations and cooperative, partnerships have greater freedom to act since they have less legal restriction imposed on them.

Corporations: Corporations provide some advantages for the owners in that they have limited liability to the amount invested, and their personal assets cannot be used to pay its debts. By selling more shares, a corporation can raise more capital. Members also have the advantage of selling their own shares

Cooperatives: Cooperatives are free to sell or to buy products and merchandise from different sources which enhances the chances for marketing. Furthermore, members of the cooperatives do not pay as much in taxes as members of a corporation.

Disadvantages In Commercial Enterprises

Accordingly disadvantages of the different types of commercial enterprises also vary. The disadvantages for each of the four types of businesses listed above are described on the next page.

Proprietorship: Typically a solo proprietorship takes a long time to be established. Moreover, such an enterprise may suffer from limited capital and unlimited personal financial liability in that the owner's personal assets could be attached for business debts. In case of the owner's death or incapacity, the business may be in jeopardy.

Partnerships: This form of business carries an unlimited financial liability for all partners. Thus, one partner's act can impact all the partners. While there is some constraint on capital, partnerships may also suffer from managing conflicts. In addition, transferring a partnership is somewhat complicated in this type of business enterprises.

Corporations: Besides the initial high cost of starting such an enterprise, sometimes corporations are double taxed. So in addition to corporate tax, income tax is also collected from shareholders.
Sometimes it is possible to legally avoid double taxation. Additionally, certain regulations, such as registering sold stock shares with the Securities and Exchange Commission, present a disadvantage to the person involved with a corporation.

Cooperatives: Perhaps the most important disadvantage of a cooperative is the fact that its members do not have much control over its management.

THE NATURE OF ENTREPRENEURIALSHIP

Entrepreneurialship refers to the spirit of initiative, innovation, and risk taking that may characterize a person or an agency. According to Ducker, entrepreneurialship, while mentioned in many management books, has not been seen as central to management from 1900 till 1985 when a book was published (1985:31).

Implicit in this statement is the possibility that, as mentioned at the beginning of this chapter, entrepreneurialship has been an important part of lifestyle in America prior to 1900. Today there is a nostalgic feeling which fills the air about the return to the enterprising spirit that built America. Many believe that it is time to revive the spirit of initiative, innovation, and risk taking in American lifestyle.

According to the **We**, the Newsletter of the San Diego Community College District, small businesses account for the creation of one in three jobs during good economic times and in some communities as high as nine out of 10 jobs during poor economic times (1993). Evidently its time has come. **The U.S. News and World Report** writes that the next two decades will herald a renaissance for the American entrepreneur. It suggests that more small businesses will be started in the following two decades than in the entire history of the United States (1993). If this is the case and the next two decades will be the golden age of entrepreneurialship, persons who are interested in recreation, parks, and leisure services should be prepared to join in and share some of this promised eldorado.

Entrepreneurialship in commercial recreation could mean two things. First for those who are interested in pursuing a career in this field and are imbued with the spirit of entrepreneurialship, a business either as a solo proprietorship or a partnership could be started. However, entrepreneurs should take into consideration the market needs where leisure pursuits are concerned. Secondly, for those who will be joining a corporation or a cooperative providing a leisure service, a spirit of initiative, innovation, and risk-taking should be used as their modus operandi. Clearly not every one is imbued with the spirit of entrepreneurialship. Perhaps a discussion of the characteristics of an entrepreneurial personally should be the starting point.

Characteristics of the Entrepreneur

Whether the person will start his or her own business, become a partner or try to be an innovative employee of a corporation or a cooperative, there are certain psychological traits that best describe an entrepreneur. After reviewing the literature on these traits, Crossley and Jamieson (1988) list entrepreneurs as being characterized by:

1. A high sense of morality
2. A sensitivity to good ideas
3. Mental toughness
4. A recognition of their limitations
5. An ability to take criticism

In studying the profile of some entrepreneurs, the above authors state that the entrepreneur is not really a big risk taker, but rather a realistic gambler who is more a doer than a planner, has little need for group affiliation, and would enter new ventures even without previous success. Even if the spirit is there, an important point should be taken into consideration by the entrepreneur as discussed in the next section.

Lessons To Be Learned

Starting a business is not an easy task because many factors need to be taken into account. Even if the finances are there, many experts believe that the psychological and social factors are as important as the fiscal ones. **The U.S. News and World Report** (1993) suggest lessons to be heeded and applied to the process of starting a small business as shown below.

Spiritual Versus Financial Goals	Due to the nature of the upcoming business atmosphere, the entrepreneur must think more in terms of personal accomplishment and self-realization than in material terms. A beginning small business not only must struggle to remain in the black, but it also requires endless hours of devotion. Unfortunately, the financial rewards from a small business will not match the corporate salaries of a bygone era.
Team Versus Individual Entrepreneurialship	In the world of business, industry, government, and international relations, a team entrepreneurial may fare better than a sole one. The more skills, provided that are complementary, the better are the chances for success. While the entrepreneurial spirit is being regained in this country, its old companion, rugged individualism, is something of the past.
The Career Entrepreneur	Similar to the life of the professional student who spends all his life studying and learning, the entrepreneur's life will be devoted to entrepreneurialship. This devotion requires more than the continuous attempt at improving the service or goods provided. This devotion includes the continuous endeavor to develop new services and goods.

Computer Literacy	Utilization of the most up-to-date technology can give the entrepreneur a definite edge. Today's entrepreneur needs to know how emerging information technologies can fit into his or her business and improve it. This does not mean that the entrepreneur needs to be a programmer as such, but rather that he or she should be familiar and comfortable with this new technology.
The Micro-marketing Approach	The idea that success comes from mass marketing is fading away. The suggestion in the past was to pursue as many customers as possible through the lowest common denominator. For today's enterprising business person, success lies in targeting a particular segment of the population. Serving a large segment of the population requires expertise, which is usually not available to a beginning entrepreneur. When the targeted segment is being served, an innovative approach to the service or the goods is a useful tool in the hands of the entrepreneur.
The Distinctive Feature	An entrepreneurialship will be successful if it has a distinctive feature about it. The distinctive feature along with a small segment of population to be served may work together to give the business an advantage that is typically enjoyed by a monopoly.
Time Pressure	Since the beginning of the 20th century, free time has steadily increased, and so has the pressure to utilize this free time. Suburban living for example has put pressure on parents who now find themselves driving their children from dance lessons to soccer games. A savvy entrepreneur could utilize this pressure of time to his advantage in that he or she could provide a service to help the parents and others feel freer from time constraints.
Location and Access	Since most customers would undoubtedly rather drive a short distance, the physical location of any service is of great importance. In the light of today's harsh economic situation, trendy addresses and stylish locations will not guarantee success for businesses. When the service is provided by phone, fax or computer, it is the quality of the information that matters rather than the size of the business.

Value Versus Price	Consumers are now focusing on the value of the service or the product. To the consumer value means that they get what they want at an appropriate price. The appropriate price of a service may not be the lowest one, but one that includes better, personalized and convenient features.
Networking Equals Success	While marketing has been the way of getting products and services moving in the past, today networking is just as crucial in doing the same. Networking means that the enterprise develop a one-on-one relationship with the customers either directly, through organizations, or via community involvement. The customers need to feel that the company they are dealing with has a persona, a character of its own.
Helping Customers and Clients	An important aspect in cultivating customers and clients is the willingness on part of the entrepreneur to be not only just a business person but also an advisor as well. This means he or she has to work harder to serve each and every customer or client. The idea is to provide both the service and or product and to be willing to spend the time in explaining the service or product to the customer or client.
Outgo Versus Income	By the very nature of the small business, control over the operational expense is crucial. The influence over the enterprise's income will not be through marketing as much as it will be through control of expenditure. Cutting cost should be valued over increasing prices, and frugality should be viewed by the entrepreneur as a permanent feature of any small business.
Employees as Variable Cost	Unfortunately, traditional personnel management practices have proved to be very costly for small businesses. This is due both to the cost of living increases as well as to the mandated benefits such as health insurance cost. Accordingly it is difficult to make the employees of small businesses a permanent feature of the enterprise. Alternative approaches to staffing may be possible. For instance the concept of commissions as well as

temporary and part-time help are suggested. These suggestions make personnel cost variable enough to correspond with the ups and downs of the business' performances.

Employees and Future Growth

Whether the employees work for a commission, or as part-timers or full-timers, loyalty can be established if they share in the action. The employees should be given a chance to share in the growth and profits of the business. Bonuses and shares are two methods of applying this proposal to the policy and practices of the business.

Right Size Versus Expansion

If in the last few years large corporations have found it necessary to downsize their work force, small business are better advised to continue with an adequate staff size for as long as possible. The concept that a business must grow or otherwise die is outdated. The answer is to find a niche, to have the right size of staff, and to improve the service or product. Large sized agencies lean towards standardization and not to customization, the *sine qua non* of the futuristic small business.

Hands on the Tiller

In the eyes of many business leaders today, the right approach, fiscal control, and right size are important features of a successful small business. Gone are the days when the board, the share- holders, and most lenders expected fast and vast returns. The get rich quick impulsers have been replaced by the savvy hands-on management. When dealing with banks and other financial institutions, this hands on approach will be useful.

Some Traditional Rules Are On

The upcoming two decades in entrepreneurship should not be considered a new era altogether but rather as a renewed era. New approaches will be laced with some old traditions. For example, the entrepreneur must rely on his own money to get started, focus on profitability, get up early, and go home late. He or she must treat people honestly and decently. Perhaps most importantly, the entrepreneur must have enough guts to start the business.

Although starting the business is a Herculean task, continuing in business requires the development of certain attitudes. According to Barrier, the entrepreneur can keep the juices flowing by doing the following (1994):

1. **A Genuine Commitment to Innovation**: Whether an entrepreneur or a company's executive, commitment to innovation is the key to being successful in business.

2. **Innovation should be Defined Broadly:** Innovation is not limited to the product or the service. Instead innovation should effect every thing that counts. For instance, whatever is innovative should be viewed as such by the entrepreneur, his clients or customers, and the enterprise's employees.

3. **Involvement of the Customers:** The customers should be asked about what they need and not what they want. In other words, the enterprise should address the customers as to what are their unmet needs and how they can be met.

4. **Slowness of Innovative Ideas:** Since innovative ideas are not easily accepted, these ideas should be allowed to flow freely from the beginning.

5. **Welcome of Small Innovations:** A small innovation may lead to a big one. Therefore, whatever the size and consequently the impact, each innovation should be assessed on its own merit and not necessarily on its wider impact.

THE DEVELOPMENT OF A COMMERCIAL LEISURE BUSINESS

Initially, the entrepreneur/business person has to choose between either starting a new business or joining an established one. One must choose wisely if the business is to succeed. Once a business started, its development revolves around two points, which this section discusses in detail. The first point that is important in the life of the enterprise is its daily operation. As important is the second point, which is related to the first one, i.e. the financial management of the business.

Starting A New Business

The mere desire to own a business, be it a recreation one or otherwise, is not sufficient to guarantee its success. In considering whether to start or join a business, and before proceeding any further, the entrepreneur/business person must consider these three basic elements:

1) Market need: A careful entrepreneur/business person does not depend on hunches or gut feelings to determine whether there is a need for his her service or product. In today's complex world, having a hunch on what the market needs could be, to say the least, a dangerous undertaking. The best approach in determining market need is through market research. Research pertaining to a particular market need may have been already conducted by a specialized firm, and its results can be obtained for a fee. A specialized firm could also be commissioned to conduct the required market research. While the cost may be high, the entrepreneur/business person usually finds that the result of the research is worth the cost. If the entrepreneur/ businessperson wishes to reduce the cost of the market research, he or she can conduct an initial research himself or herself through the perusal of business journals and magazines. Some journals and magazines conduct research on the market needs of certain services and products. A visit to the local public and research libraries to find out market need should be conducted anyway. Also, local governments sometimes conduct studies on local needs for certain services, and a visit to the local city hall may be very useful.

Although the initial conclusion may be in favor of starting or joining the business, another important step should be taken before embarking on the development of the project. A feasibility study should be conducted, the purpose of which is to increase the odds in favor of the success of the project.

2) Feasibility Study: Although a market need may have been established in the previous step, a feasibility study should be conducted to determine if the proposed project will realize a reasonable share of the market. The reasonable share is the one which will realize a profit, not necessarily immediately, but in the near future. The feasibility study usually produces a document which, according to Heralson (1986), touches on four specific points:

1. The determination whether the project will realize a return on the investment.

2. The formulation that produces the best idea about location, facilities, amenities, and possibly personnel.

3. The provision for general guidelines that could help in the management of the project.

4. The provision for possible resources that could help in the financing of the project.

3) Funding the Project: Seed money is needed to get the ball rolling. However, unless the entrepreneur/businessperson is financially able to support the project from A to Z, he or she will have to seek outside sources to secure the bulk of the funds needed to continue with the project. Most business projects require additional funds that can be secured through different sources such as :

1. Equity Loans: An equity loan can be provided through many sources such as banks, finance companies, and savings and loan associations. Although equity is a good source of financing a new project, interest paid on the amount borrowed is usually high.

2. Bank Loans: Banks are a good source for the financing of any new business project since the interest paid on a bank loan is usually not as high as loans from other sources. On the negative side, banks are usually conservative and require strict types of collateral.

3. Finance Companies' Loans: Since these companies are willing to accept risky projects, they provide loans at higher rates than the ones required by banks. Private recreation projects, particularly the ones that will provide service, are considered somewhat risky. Recreation projects that revolve around manufacturing products, such as sporting goods, are less risky in the eyes of the lenders. Nonetheless both types of recreation projects, service or products, may be met with some reluctance.

4. Savings and Loan Associations: The interest rates from these associations are also high. Their loans are usually secured against some property. Typically the loans is about 80% of the property value.

5. Insurance Companies: If the entrepreneur/businessperson has an insurance policy, he or she can borrow against the paid-up cash value of that policy. In this kind of financial arrangement, interest rates are usually lower than the ones provided by the financial institutions listed above.

6. Small Business Administration Loans: The Small Business Administration is a unit of the United States Government established for the specific purpose of helping small businesses. If the project is acceptable to the SBA, it will guarantee up to 90% of the loans acquired from the local bank.

7. Loans from Small Business Investment Companies: These companies, although privately owned, are chartered by the state. They can obtain low interest loans from the Federal Government to invest in small businesses.

Steps 1, 2 and 3 listed above are to be observed in starting a small business as well as in joining an existing person as shown in the next section.

Joining an Existing Business

Crossley and Jamieson (1988:91-4) suggest five possibilities when joining and or acquiring an existing business as shown in the following section.

Franchises These are agreements between the entrepreneur/businessperson, called the franchisee, and the original owner of an existing business, called the franchiser. The agreement may entail the selling of the franchiser service or product. The franchisee pays a fee and royalties to the original owner. Since the service or product has been tested and proved successful, the possibility of the franchisee success is very high,. Nonetheless, it is advisable that the franchisee give consideration to the company's history, reputation, and experience. Location of the new franchise is of prime importance as is the type of assistance and control rendered by the mother company. Commercial campgrounds are examples of recreational franchises.

Business Incubators	In this arrangement an existing business, be it large or small, will adopt a fledgling project providing it with space, services, management skills, and sometimes financial assistance. For example running a pro shop for a golf course is a business incubator. A new business can be successful under the auspices of an already established one. This is due to the reduced cost of overhead.
Buying an Existing Business	While there are advantages to buying an existing business, there are disadvantages to be considered before a decision is made. Granted buying an existing business will reduce lag time in receiving returns on investment, yet the facility itself may need costly renovation, which will eat up anticipated profits. Perhaps the most important question to be answered before buying an existing business is, Why is the owner selling it at this point?
Auxiliary Services	An entrepreneur / businessperson could become involved in an auxiliary service to an existing business. Instructors in a recreational program and guides in an outdoor adventure are examples of auxiliary services that are provided through contracting with persons who are not on the payroll of the existing business.
Public-Private Ventures	A number of public recreation, parks, and leisure service are contracting out some of the services that were once provided by them. For example, park maintenance could be contracted out.

As with starting a new business, the three steps previously suggested when considering the initiation of the new business should also be observed when joining an old business. These three steps are meant to: a) investigate market need for the particular service or product, b) conduct a feasibility study as to the possibility of success of the proposed project; and c) study the methods of financing or refinancing the project.

Also the same financial institutions used for funding new businesses could be used in joining an existing one. These are banks, savings and loan associations, insurance companies, U.S. Small Business Administration, and small business investment companies.

Operating A Business

According to Kelly (1985:72) businesses should be concerned with these four functions: planning, organizing, directing and controlling.

a) Planning: An initial plan of operation should be adopted by the entrepreneur/businessperson. The plan should include the objectives of the business as well as general guidelines for its operation. All people involved in the operation of the business should be familiar with the plan. The initial plan should be modified as the business grows and new approaches should be adopted to meet the new challenges. The plan, which includes the objectives and goals of the operation, should be evaluated periodically by the entrepreneur/businessperson as part of the operation of the business.

b) Organizing: The development of a structural outline for the operation of the business should be the next item after the plan. Such structure will specify who is responsible for what and who is responsible for making the decisions. In other words, organizing deals with division of labor and with the tasks that are charged to each person in the operation of the business. This step should be developed by the entrepreneur/businessperson as soon as the business begins to operate.

c) Directing: How to lead and motivate personnel is the third item in the operation of a business. Leading by example is one way of getting everyone to become involved in the operation of the business. Related to leadership in a business enterprise is the question of motivation. While the entrepreneur/businessperson may be self-motivated, as the owner of the business, other members of the enterprise should be motivated as well.

d) Controlling: Through standards, procedures, and periodic checks, the operation of the business is controlled. The idea behind control in business is not to hamstring any person who is engaged in the operation, but rather it is intended as a means of helping the business reach its stated goals. Control is utilized when the business is not achieving its goals as stated in its plan.

Financial Management

Since the purpose of any business is to make money, financial management of a new business is of great importance. As is the case with the operation of a business, financial management also requires a plan. The financial plan should evolve around revenues and expenditure. These two fiscal terms and their importance in the management of recreation, parks, and leisure services are found in Chapter Ten. A sound fiscal policy necessitates that both revenues and expenditure should be predicted and held in balance. Sound fiscal policy also requires the estimation of tax, overhead, insurance, debt, and other obligations. Control over expenditure is a must to realize reasonable profit. Accordingly, internal and external audits are used as specified in Chapter Ten. At this point two concepts that are important to a small business should be discussed.

Liquidity: This term defines the ability of the enterprise to generate enough cash to pay its bills. Liquidity can be measured periodically, let us say each month by comparing total revenues to total expenses within that period. Expenses include the cost of operation in the month such as labor, utilities, advertising, taxes, returned merchandise, and the cost of goods. A current ratio for the month is calculated by dividing the revenues by the current expenses. While a ratio of 2:1 is considered good, indicating that the current assets are twice that of liabilities, this objective is hard for new businesses to achieve. Therefore an adequate cash reserve must be available to cover expenses during the business initial period of operation.

Profitability: While the initial period may not net profits, the expectations is that profits will occur eventually. The entrepreneur/businessperson should develop a profit plan that leads to the improvement of the liquidity ratio allowing for a gradual increase in profits. Sales and cost estimates based on previous experiences would help in this endeavor. When estimating cost of operating the business, it is important to take into consideration elements such as inflation. The profit plan should be made an integral part of budgeting, which is discussed in detail in Chapter Ten.

The Cash Flow Statement: It is important that a cash flow statement be prepared monthly or quarterly. The purpose of the statement is to show the difference between revenues and expenses for the particular period, a month or three-months. An example of a periodic check is shown in Figure 10-3.

Needless to say cash flow will fluctuate from month to month or from period to period. Thus, there may be times when the entrepreneur/businessperson will have to decide whether to borrow additional cash to remain solvent for that period or to save the remaining amount to be used in the future.

Cash Management: This function represents the daily operational focus where accuracy measures are needed. A number of approaches are suggested. A collection process that accelerates the receipt of funds can be used to make them available. An analysis of the specific collection points could also be used. A zero balance accounts with remote or controlled disbursement points could be used. An audit system allows for control of the daily position in the movement of the funds.

The Balance Sheet: This sheet gives the financial condition of the enterprise over a long period of time such as six-month or a year. Chapter Ten discusses this concept in detail.

Pricing: The pricing of a commodity or a service is crucial to the success of the business. Pricing can be approached several ways. First is the cost-based pricing which requires sound knowledge of all costs. Second is the reaction- to-competition pricing which may lead to lowering the price in the face of competition. Thirdly is penetration pricing which intends to take a good share of the market.

Inventory Management: The purpose of inventory is to separate stocked commodity from being sold. At this point any stoppage or spurt of activity on one side will not affect the other side. This process will help in finding the right balance between the cost of carrying inventory in storing, insurance, and tied up funds on the one hand, and the cost of replenishing the stock on the other.

Accounts Receivable Management: Accounts receivable are related to the sales of commodity or service. In order to forecast accounts receivable, a simple formula is used:

$$\text{average collection period} = \frac{\text{accounts receivable}}{\text{sales of the year}} \times 365$$

The average collection period is applied to each month to determine the receivable balance.

Accounts Payable Management: Accounts should be paid on time as a measure of good faith.

Some businesses delay the payment of their accounts to earn more interest on their cash balances. This is a misguided policy since the reputation of the enterprise is more important than gaining a very small percentage on the cash balance. A bone fide inability to pay on time is usually acceptable to the other side.

Operating and Capital Budgets: While the operating budget is used for the day-to-day operation of the enterprise, the capital budget is the one included in the plan for future expansion. These two budgets should be handled as two separate entitles.

SUMMARY

- Leisure services, although started with volunteers who were trying to ameliorate the declining conditions of life in America's large cities, became part of the public services provided by the government.

- Commercial leisure services are old practices that can be traced to many ancient civilizations like China, India and Egypt. Although these services continued through the centuries, they were overshadowed by the services provided by the governments in many societies.

- With the shirking of public funds, commercial and entrepreneurial leisure services are increasing. These services can be classified in a number of ways: travel and tourism, hospitality services, entertainment services; services in the natural environment, and retail outlets.

- There are a number of ways to own a commercial business. Such as a sole proprietorship, a partnership, a corporation, and a cooperative. Each one of these types of ownership has its advantages and disadvantages.

- Entrepreneurialship is a special form of business in which there is a spirit of initiative, innovation, and risk taking. There is a trend to go in this direction in America today. But not every one could be described as an entrepreneur.

- Entrepreneurs are characterized by having a high sense of morality, sensitivity to ideas, and mental toughness as well as recognizing their own limitation.

- In starting a new business, three elements must be considered as follows: market need, feasibility study, and funding the project. A person can join an existing business by becoming a franchise; being part of a business incubator or an auxiliary service; joining a public-private venture; or buying an existing business.

- Operating a business requires planning, organizing, directing, controlling and above all financial management. This last one entails the understanding of liquidity, profitability, cash flow, cash management, the balance sheet, pricing, inventory management, account receivable and account payable management, operating and capital budgets as well as auxiliary revenues.

LEARNING ACTIVITIES

1. Invite a professor of Business Administration to talk about the advantages and disadvantages of owning a business.

2. Invite a professor of Business Administration to talk about the steps taken to start a business.

3. Invite a businessperson, preferably in the area of leisure services, to talk about his or her business.

4. Survey your city as to how many commercial leisure services exist.

5. Visit the Chamber of Commerce of your city to find out the possibility of starting a leisure business.

REFERENCES

Barrier, Michael (1994) "Innovation as a Way of Life," **Nation's Business.** Washington, D.C.: United States Chamber of Commerce Volume. 82 Number 7 p. 22.

Bullaro, John J. "Recreation and Leisure Service: Entrepreneurial Opportunities and Strategies," **Leisure Today**, February.

Bullaro, John J. and Christopher R. Edginton (1988**). Commercial Leisure Services: Managing for Profit, Service and Personal Satisfaction**. New York: Macmillan.

Chubb, Michael and Holly Chubb (1981). **One Third of Our Time?** New York: Wiley and Sons.

Crossley, John C and Lynn M. Jamieson (1988**). Introduction to Commercial and Entrepreneurial Recreation.** Champaign, IL: Sagamore Publishing.

Drucker, Peter F. (1985) **Management: Tasks, Responsibilities, Practices.** New York: Harper and Row, Publishers

Dulles, F.R. (1965) **A History of Recreation.** New York: Appleton-Century-Crofts.

Gernet, J. (1962) **Daily Life in China.** Stanford, CA: Stanford University Press.

Giels, J. and F. (1974) **Life in a Medieval Castle.** New York: Thomas Crowell.

Harelson, W. (1984) "The Economic Feasibility Study" in A.Epperson (Editor) **Private and Commercial Recreation.** State College, PA: Venture Publishing.

Kelly, John H. (1982) **Leisure.** Englewood Cliffs NJ: Prentice-Hall

Kelly, John H. (1985) **Recreation Business.** New York: Macmillan Publishing Company.

Kraus, Richard G. and Joseph E. Curtis (2000) **Creative Management in Recreation, Parks and Leisure Services.** St. Louis: McGraw-Hill.

Lane, E.W. (1836) {1973} **An Account of the Manners and Customs of Contemporary Egyptians.** New York: Dover.

San Diego Community College District (1993) "Entrepreneur Learn Small Business Basics" **WE**, San Diego, CA: SDCCD, November/December p.1.

Scott, Johnathon T.(1998) **Fundamentals of Leisure Business Success.** New York: The Hathorn Press

Sheffield, Emilyn and Ron Mendell(1987) "Entrepreneurship: A Review of Concepts and Research," **Leisure Today**, February.

U.S. News and World Report (1993) "Special Advertising Section," Volume 115, Number 18.

CHAPTER 14

EVALUATION, RESEARCH, AND LEISURE SERVICES

Learning Objectives

After studying this chapter, you should be able to do the following:

1. Appreciate the need for evaluation and research in parks, recreation, and leisure services.

2. Understand the purpose of evaluation in parks, recreation, and leisure services.

3. Comprehend the mechanisms of evaluation in parks, recreation and leisure services.

4. Differentiate between standard and criterion in evaluation and research in this field.

5. Appreciate the need for research in parks, recreation, and leisure services.

6. Understand the types, process, and uses of research in this field.

As indicated in the chapter on the leisure service profession, a body of knowledge is needed to underscore the significance of the profession and to help its causes. The body of knowledge of any profession is predicated on the recording of its experiences and the accumulation of knowledge therein. Two mechanisms, evaluation and research, are crucial to the development of a profession.

The needed enhancement of the profession through these two mechanisms can be met through systematic, carefully designed research and evaluation studies. Kraus and Allen suggest that the following specific needs can be accomplished when (1987:14):

1. New techniques and practices that upgrade leadership and management operations in the field are used;

2. knowledge of the motivational factors behind participation in organized recreation is applied; and

3. measurement of specific outcomes of organized recreation, documenting the importance of this service is utilized.

In this chapter, evaluation and research will be discussed. Their applications and utilization within and outside the parks, recreation, and leisure agency will also be presented.

EVALUATION AND THE LEISURE PROFESSION

Human beings are continuously using some form of evaluation in their lives. For instance, when reflecting on one's life, you evaluate past experiences with an eye on future events. Before a person crosses the street, an evaluation of the surrounding conditions takes place. After looking left then right and left again, a decision is made to proceed or not. These two examples show that evaluation is an ongoing process in the life of a human being. The same should be practiced by organizations and agencies including those dealing with parks, recreation, and leisure services. Yet as Murphy at al have observed, in this field "evaluation has undoubtedly been the weakest and the most disregarded of all the management functions" (1991:367). In this quote Murphy and his colleagues are referring to public leisure services. Possibly evaluation has been used more often in quasi-public and private agencies than is the case with the public ones.

Purpose of Evaluation

As expressed by Murphy et al, the above attitude on part of public agencies may be due to the fact that evaluation as a management tool brings about mixed feelings. For instance, the mere mention of evaluation may bring an aura of apprehension within certain parts of an agency. As a result, some resistance against it could build up easily and quickly. Therefore, it is incumbent upon the management of an agency dealing with parks, recreation, and leisure services to look into the motives behind the call for and resistance against evaluation. Feelings on both sides must be taken into consideration so that all parties are satisfied. For instance, are the ones suggesting the evaluation looking for improvement of that which currently exists? Or is it an attempt at proving or disproving something? Equally important is the emotion behind the resistance. Typically the persons whose area, program, sphere of influence, is being evaluated, will question the motive behind the evaluation. Those who are under the impression that the evaluation is to prove or disproving something are usually the ones who are involved in or affected by its outcome. Misconception about the purpose of evaluation may lead to undue and unnecessary apprehension, which should be dealt with immediately.

The management of an agency in leisure services should make it clear to all concerned the specific purpose or purposes of the evaluation. Granted, all evaluations have a general purpose, i.e. discovery, specific purpose or purposes may prevail at one point in time in the history of the agency making the evaluation necessary. If indeed the general purpose of the evaluative process is to improve, the question is to improve what? Granted the program is the core of what the agency does yet the program does not function in vacuum. Therefore all aspects of the agency may need evaluation. However, the evaluative process does not have to be conducted for all aspects of the agency at the same time.

For morale purposes, it may be useful to determine some of the reasons behind the need for an evaluation. Some reasons given for conducting an evaluation are listed below:

1. To determine the present status of a program, an area, or a facility

2. To assess progress toward achievement of objectives

3. To provide data on strengths and weaknesses (of offerings, etc.)

4. To provide information to justify change

5. To abide by a legal requirement to acquire or continue funding

6. To gain legitimacy in the political, economical, or social arena

7. To justify certain expenditure

8. To support expansion of service

Mechanisms of Evaluation

Although a "formal" evaluation may be scheduled, an "informal" evaluative process should be an ongoing fact in the daily life of the agency. In the past, evaluation was thought of as basically "formal" and "summative," to take place officially at the end of a particular period. Today, an "informal" and a "formative" evaluation emphasizing both the monitoring of the different functions of the agency as well its continual adjustment to meet new situations is suggested.

Emphasizing that the purpose of an evaluation is to improve certain areas, along with the determination that evaluation is a continuous process; the management of a parks, recreation, and leisure services should provide mechanisms through which all aspects of the agency are evaluated on an ongoing basis as well as periodically.

A number of evaluative processes have been tested over the years. In this section three processes currently being used to evaluate the performance of agencies dealing with services including leisure services are presented. Evaluative processes are different from evaluative instruments in that they are general rather than specific approaches to evaluation.

Information Systems: In the last few years, these systems have become the most important evaluative tools to be used by human service agencies. In order for this process to be useful in evaluating an agency, an integrated information system within the agency must be achieved. Such an integration cannot be installed in a few days or in a few weeks before the evaluation begins (Attkisson, 1978: 468). The development of an information system, which should become integrated overtime requires at least the following two steps:

1. The existence of plans that relate to the agency's goals and objectives, and

2. The presence of controls that assure efficient and effective action in pursuing these goals.

According to Attkisson (1978: 127) plans and controls, in turn, require specific types of information such as:

A) Planning and performance information, which can be found by answering the following questions:

What services will the agency render and to whom?

What resources will the agency use to provide the service?

How effectively is the agency doing its job?

How efficiently is the agency using its resources?

B) Processing of the information which can be revealed through the following mechanisms:

language and mathematical notations

publications of all sorts

mass media and telecommunication systems

computer programming

C) Vital information found within the agency such as the following:

size and rate of its growth

its specialization and complexity

its regulatory functions

accountability

Need Assessment: This evaluative process attempts to find out if there are unmet needs within an area or a geographic location. The concept of unmet need has several implications. Although the work of Siegel, Attkisson and Carsson, (1978:217) is directed towards health services, the steps they suggest can also be applied to leisure services. When it seems that the service is not meeting the needs in a certain community, a step by step operation can be taken as follows:

1. The determination of a comparison level which carries along with it an idea of the extent and saliency of the discrepancy.

2. The recognition of a problem which results in determining the discrepancy between what exists and what is deemed desirable. This step requires input from all concerned.

3. A satisfactory solution which means that the added offerings are viewed as capable of reducing the gap between what actually exists and what is deemed necessary.

4. The processes of problem identification and solution determination which occur within the values and attitudes and perspectives of the participants.

5. The assessment of resources which is a key factor in arriving at consensus about the relative priorities among unmet needs.

Outcome Evaluation: This tool may be difficult to apply in an agency dealing with parks, recreation, and leisure services. It may be hard for an agency's staff to agree on which outcome or outcomes of participation in recreational activities is or are desirable. Usually, the anticipated outcome or outcomes vary significantly from person to person. For instance, while relaxation may be the expected outcome for one person participating in a particular activity, another person, who is participating in the same activity, may look at companionship as the desirable outcome. Nonetheless, outcome assessment can be applied to the tangible aspects of the agency such as attendance, maintenance, and record keeping.

EVALUATION PROCEDURE

Although it is difficult, if not impossible, to develop a step-by-step procedure that will fit each evaluation's purpose, certain principles do apply as follows:

1. The general goals of the agency should be clearly stated;

2. Specific objectives as they relate to each section and function in the agency should be spelled out;

3. The instrument used in evaluating the agency must meet acceptable standards;

4. All products, records, and instruments used in the evaluation should be saved;

5. All data must be valid and analyzed by an expert or experts; and

6. The results of evaluation must be comprehensible and its recommendations usable.

The Evaluators

Benest and Foley (1984:113) suggest that whether the evaluation is done by the agency's staff or by an outside personnel team, each approach has advantages and disadvantages.

Internal Evaluators: The selection of evaluators from within the agency's staff may be more acceptable to the employees when compared to bringing in outside personnel. Moreover, internal persons are better informed about the mission, values, and operations of the agency than are external evaluators. Most importantly, internal persons are able to conduct an "informal-formative" evaluation, the ongoing evaluation as suggested at the beginning of this chapter.

On the negative side, there is a possibility that internal evaluators may not retain the objectivity required as they face the pressures to produce favorable results. Moreover, they may focus on the strengths and not on the weaknesses of the different aspects of the agency. Long standing policies and regulations may not be questioned by the internal group of evaluators. Perhaps more importantly are the skills and abilities of such a group who are not professional evaluators.

External Evaluators: External evaluators bring with them the possibility of objectivity as well the needed skills and abilities to conduct an evaluation. Moreover, the external evaluator usually brings with him or her a wealth of knowledge on the functions of similar agencies. More importantly, an external evaluator is not under the same pressure to produce results of a certain nature or succumb to accepting certain longstanding policies and regulations without questioning. For example, if an agency is dealing with an internal conflict, the external evaluator will not be party to either side, which is important in coming out with a solution.

On the negative side, external evaluators may face resistance from the staff for many reasons. They could be viewed as threat, unqualified, or uneducated to the inter-workings of the agency. External evaluators may put undue pressure on the staff to produce data or information, disrupting the flow of the operation of the agency. An external evaluator may accommodate the wishes of the agency and produce desirable, although skewed, results.

Pitfalls to Avoid

In order to achieve objectivity in the evaluation of leisure services, Benest and Foley suggest that the evaluators should be cognizant of a number of variables that may contaminate the results (1984:115):

1) **Conflict of Interest:** Whether "formal-summative" or "informal-formative," the evaluative process should be the property of all concerned. Although complete objectivity is an ideal, which many aspire but few achieve, nonetheless, the management should see to it that any conflict of interest is minimized. Benest and Foley recommend three steps to minimize conflict of interest: 1) Identify evaluation criteria at the outset of the program, 2) select measurable, verifiable criteria as much as possible; and 3) recognize the existence of conflict of interest.

2) **Cultural Biases:** This variable becomes pronounced with the use of external evaluators who may not know the "indigenous" culture of the agency. In other words, subjectivity on part of the evaluators may contaminate the results and subsequently the recommendations.

3) **Misuse of data:** Even if the results are totally objective, the possibility of misusing them exists. For instance, if the data show that there is a need or a trend, the power to be may ignore that altogether. Also, in the case that the results are not totally convincing in either direction, the power to be or the opposing side, could hang on the negative side. Such an attitude is understood in light of the half-filled, half-empty class explanation.

APPROACHES TO EVALUATION

What should the evaluation of an agency dealing with parks, recreation, and leisure services cover. In an early publication by the National Park and Recreation Association, it proposes the following six aspects (van der Smissen 1972).

I. <u>Philosophy and Goals</u>: There should be written statements of the agency's role in the lives of the individuals and the community.

II. <u>Administration:</u> The structure of the agency should reflect its purpose and methods of operation.

III. <u>Programming:</u> Specific objectives should be spelled out for each program element within the limits of the philosophy and goals of the agency.

IV. <u>Personnel:</u> The agency should acquire the services of well-qualified professionals and other staff members.

V. <u>Areas, facilities and equipment:</u> There should be a plan to develop areas and facilities and to maintain them in a reasonable condition.

VI. <u>Evaluation:</u> There should be a systematic evaluation for the total operation of the agency.

Shivers (1978: 333-4) suggests that an agency dealing with parks, recreation, or leisure services should concern itself with the evaluation of the following aspects:

1. Space, physical, plant, and equipment,

2. Programming,

3. Staff, and

4. Administration.

In another attempt at evaluating an agency rendering park, recreation, and leisure services; Robert Banes, who served as the President of the California Park and Recreation Commissioners and Board members and was also active in the Citizens/Board Members Section of the National Recreation and Park Association, developed, in cooperation in with another interested citizen, an instrument that revolves around the following points (1976):

1. Discipline of service, which covers facilities and programs;

2. Discipline of administration, which covers direction, management, and control;

3. Discipline of financial stewardship, which includes inside and outside audits, input on budget, staff and policy making body; and

4. Discipline of contribution to public welfare, which measures tangible accomplishments, decreases in activities detrimental to society, or perception of those who pay, use or otherwise observe the benefits.

Nolan (1984) stated that a systematic approach to a recreation program appraisal revolves around three points:

1. Input: This phase of evaluation describes the personnel and the resources used in implementing the program. Time and cost spent are also included in the description. For example, publicity, manpower and materials are to be included in the agency's program.

2. Process: How flexible is the program process in allowing for adjustment according to the needs of the participants? The techniques and procedures used in the program should be described in as much detail as possible. Their documentation is important for the next phase of evaluation.

3. Outcomes: A written report should includes the following information: a) intended goals of the program, b) results of what has occurred in relation to the goals, c) changes that have taken place in the participants as in attitude and or performance, and d) unanticipated outcome such as the possibility of future of expansion, etc.

Henderson and Bialeshki (1995) suggest that in evaluating leisure service all involved should be honest so, possible problems can be avoided.

STANDARDS AND CRITERIA

In order to evaluate something, the evaluator has to determine or set its value. How does the evaluator set its value? General standards and/or criteria are used in this endeavor. A standard is looked upon as an object which is considered by an authority or by general consent as the basis of comparison. A criterion, on the other hand, is a standard of judgement. The difference between these two evaluation terms will be discussed later.

Both standards and criteria are used in evaluating a parks, recreation, or leisure service agency. Some standards and criteria have evolved over the years, particularly where areas and facilities are concerned..

Nonetheless, it is clear that other aspects of the leisure agency will need other evaluation standards and criteria. For instance how will the agency go about evaluating the success of the program. Or will the staff's performance be evaluated? How satisfied are the participants with the program content? In the following section the process of developing standards and criteria, in general, is discussed.

Developing Standards and Criteria

Keeping in mind the concept of the integrated information system, which was discussed earlier, how could the evaluative process show that the stated goal or goals of the agency have been reached? If the purpose of the evaluative process is to find out if the agency is successfully reaching its own goals, it must first try and reach an agreement about the degree of that success. Kosecof and Fink (1982:66-67) recommend a number of possible ways to set standards and criteria for an objective evaluation of a service agency.

1. Experts: Sometimes an expert's judgement may be the only way to arrive at realistic standards. Their expertise, and not the realities within the agency, will create the needed standards and criteria.

2. Past Performance: If the performance is slightly better, similar, or even lower at evaluation, past performance is a good standard of measurement.

3. Comparisons: Standards based on comparison are easy to explain and understand. A comparison in parks, recreation, and leisure services could be based on national, regional, or local bases.

AREAS OF EVALUATION

Within the agencies dealing with parks, recreation, and leisure services, a number of areas need to be evaluated. These areas could be evaluated either singularly or altogether and periodically or on a continual basis. A list of these areas along with suggested standards is included below. These standards are derived from a number of resources, all of which are listed in the references at the end of this chapter. As was previously mentioned, standards are objects agreed upon by experts and judgements are standards of judgement. In the list below, standards agreed upon by experts are given for five areas which an agency dealing with parks, recreation, or leisure services is concerned. Criteria are added to these standards as follows:

I. Mission, Goals and Direction of the Agency

Standard I-1: A clear indication of the mission of the agency is provided.

Standard I-2: A clear definition of the agency's long term goals is provided.

Standard I-3: A clear indication of the agency's short-term goals is provided.

Standard I-4: A clear indication that all personnel of the agency's are involved and informed of the agency's mission and goals.

II. Leadership, Management and Administration of the Agency

Standard II-1: The Agency's structure reflects its mission, goals, and direction, and pinpoints work relationships.

Standard II-2: An overall manual is available concerning the leadership, management, and administration of the agency.

Standard II-3: Manuals describing both tasks and responsibilities in the different divisions of the agency are provided.

Standard II-4: A personnel manual is provided and is available to all who work in theagency including volunteers.

Standard II-5:   Procedures to keep the agency's staff and its governing body abreast of development are given.

Standard II-6:   A master plan of facilities and operations has been established and is reviewed periodically.

Standard II-7:   A workable system of communication either written or verbal, and personal has been established.

Standard II-8:   Cooperative community planning has been established with other service agencies.

Standard II-9:   A long range financial plan is instituted including forecast revenue and expenditure.

Standard II-10:   An annual budget is provided with frequent reporting on variances.

Standard II-11:   An established policy on handling of funds is provided and made known to the staff.

Standard II-12:   A procedure for the use of facilities by the public is supplied.

Standard II-13:   A plan for innovative fundraising is approved and implemented.

Standard II-14:   A system of audit is provided with the help of both internal and external personnel.

Standard II-15:   A plan for promoting the agency within the community is established.

Standard II-16:   A comprehensive system of archives, records, and statistics is in place.

Standard II-17:   A policy on the use and handling of equipment is provided.

Standard II-18:   A policy on the inventory and use of material is given.

Standard II-19:   A policy on the bidding and purchasing of equipment, materials and supplies is available.

Standard II-20:   A system of periodic and continual evaluation is in place, the results and recommendation of which are implemented.

III. Programming

Standard III-1: Specific objectives of each program element are provided.

Standard III-2: Quality and quantity of the program is observed in the program.

Standard III 3: Consultation with an advisory board and/or lay people will lead to the formation of the current program.

Standard III-3: Flexibility is observed in the management and leadership of the program to insure meeting different needs.

Standard III-4: The quality of the environment is being protected by the type of program offered.

Standard III-5: A system of reviewing grievances concerning the program is available.

IV. Personnel

Standard IV-1: A number of qualified professional staff members is hired which commensurate with the elements of the program.

Standard IV-2: A reasonable number of support staff is available in the agency.

Standard IV-3: Job descriptions are available for each position including positions held by the volunteers.

Standard IV-4: A written policy on personnel procedures is available and posted.

Standard IV-5: A recruitment program is in place to attract the best qualified persons for both professional and support staff.

Standard IV-6: An orientation program is available and is used with new staff members.

Standard IV-7: A program to assist staff development is provided and is implemented.

Standard IV-8: A workable system of supervision over both professional and support staff is provided.

Standard IV-9: An effective system for use and supervision of volunteers is provided.

V. Areas, Facilities, And Equipment

Standard V-1: A master plan for areas and facilities exists and is being followed.

Standard V-2: An efficient and effective management procedure for areas, facilities and Equipment exists.

Standard V-3: A policy concerning safety and cleanliness of areas and facilities is in place.

Standard V-4: A policy concerning the availability of areas and facilities id followed.

While these standards are used as the basis of evaluating agencies dealing with parks, recreation, and leisure services in general, specific standards are established by the Commission For Accreditation of Park and Recreation Agencies (CAPRA). These are listed in Appendix A.

RESEARCH AND THE LEISURE PROFESSION

Research differs from evaluation in both scope and purpose. Evaluation being practical in orientation, deals with applications and is usually limited in scope. For instance, the evaluation of a local agency is usually intended for local use. Research, on the other hand, has a wider application, is theoretical in orientation, and has a longer appeal. Both research and evaluation could be empirically oriented.

Many professionals often assume that research in leisure services is not in the domain of the practitioner. However, research by the practitioner has a wider application and is an important contribution to the enhancement of the body of knowledge in this field. In fact most books written by the scholars in the field are filled with examples derived from evaluations and applied research. Examples of these are given by Kraus and Allen (1987:16-18):

1) Recreation Programs, Services and Outcomes

   a) Surveys of program practices and trends

   b) Feasibility studies

   c) Participants needs assessment

   d) Program Benefits

   e) Examination of a program

2) Professionalism in leisure Service

   a) Survey of personnel at work

   b) Competency based studies

   c) Studies of recreation curricula

   d) Role of professional societies

   e) Staff productivity

3) Areas and Facilities

   a) Planning studies

   b) Experimentation with facilities

   c) Environmental impact studies

   d) Access to areas and facilities

4) Management Problems and Trends

   a) Research in fiscal practices

   b) Studies of vandalism

   c) Studies of community relations

   d) Examination of managerial practices

RESEARCH INSTRUMENTS

Over the years a number of instruments have proved to be beneficial in collecting data in research. The choice of the instrument will depend on the research design and its purpose, two points which will be discussed later. The following are some of these instruments:

Observation: In an informal-formative evaluation this instrument is effective. However, its informality tends to hamper its utility as an instrument in research.

Interviews: This technique helps reveal information that is often hard to otherwise detect. For instance, human feeling cannot be detected from paper and pencil questionnaires, but it can be detected in an interview.

Conferences: While an interview is a meeting with one person, a conference includes a varying amount of people. Like the interview, a conference is more apt to reveal a candidate's attitude toward certain questions than a questionnaire would give.

Self-appraisal: This technique could be used by the participants to analyze their own performance, interest, and/or information concerning a particular program.

Questionnaires: Generally questionnaires are the most used instruments in research. A questionnaire is a series of specific questions used to gather information on some of the practices within the agency.

Checklist: Proven to be useful in leisure research, these lists allow one to answer by using yes or no in the response. Judgements are not rendered in checklists.

Surveys: A survey relates to people, their behavior and their attitude. However the survey also could be used with programs, personnel, facilities and other elements of a leisure agency.

Records and Reports: Records and reports are very important data sources. It is incumbent on the management of a parks, recreation, and leisure service to develop an archival system that proves useful in future research.

Simulations: A simulation is an information collection technique that evaluators use to find out how well people perform. Sometimes, this technique is called a performance test. For example, a trained person pretends that he or she needs service, and the staff's response is analyzed to see if it is adequate.

Experimentation: This type of research dominates physical and biological science and is considered the most rigorous of all research techniques. Experimentation requires the testing of a hypothesis using two groups for comparison of results.

TYPES OF RESEARCH

A perusal of the major research journals in the field reveals that there are many types of research such as experimental, historical, and descriptive. Although all three are important to the body of knowledge in parks, recreation, and leisure services, this work concentrates on the descriptive research since this type seems to appeal the most to the professionals in the field. The basic designs used in this type of research include areas such as: surveys, case studies, time series, comparative, correlation, and evaluative research.

Surveys

The essence of a survey is the uniform collection of data which helps the researcher to generalize. The uniformity in survey research creates a problem in that the questions asked may mean different things to different respondents. Efforts, on the part of the researcher, should be directed towards maximizing both the validity and reliability of the instrument used in collecting the data. These two concepts will be explained in detail later.

Surveys have many uses in parks, recreation, and leisure services. For instance, a survey could be used in market research for a commercial agency as in the reaction of the buyer to a product or a service. A survey could also be used in finding public opinion and attitude toward a certain program or trend. Furthermore surveys could detect the emotions of the participants concerning certain programs and services.

Freedom from bias is an important variable in the success of surveys. The following are suggested to ensure such a freedom:

1. Careful construction of the instrument,

2. proper use of the instrument,

3. selection of the appropriate staff,

4. training of the staff on administering the instrument, and

5. flexible administration of the instrument in the field.

Case Studies

A case study is designed to study one person, one group, or one entity and to report on it. In the case of a leisure agency, it is usually an intensive investigation of a group or a program, utilizing many of the instruments that are listed above such as observation, interviews, conferences, and questionnaires.

Case studies are very useful tools in evaluative research. They have been used in clinical research for a long time, which means that they are also useful in therapeutic recreation. Diagnosis and guidance could be found through a case study if and when the recreation therapist is able to evaluate cause and effect relationships and prescribe a program for the individual. It is possible to apply case study techniques on a group of individuals under the care of a recreation therapist, and the findings may be used to develop a general theory having wider implications and broader applications.

Time Series

This type of research is also called a longitudinal study. Its design makes use of a research technique applied to the same person, group, or entity over a period of time. Kraus and Allen suggest the term **developmental research** be applied since its purpose is to measure change
(1987:58). They state that the environmental conditions in a state forest can be examined regularly through this technique.

The term **trend analysis** is also used to describe this type of research. It is possible that through longitudinal, time-series studies key trends are depicted at one point, which will show the direction that may take place in the future.

Comparative Research

There are two approaches in comparative research. The first approach is called cross-sectional research, and is designed to compare two or more programs or practices in the same entity using the same variable or variables. For instance, comparing enrollment in the afternoon offering to a similar offering in the evening may yield some results that can be useful to the agency and to other agencies as well.

The second type compares whole entities or sections thereof with sections from other entities. For example, flextime, which is followed by one agency, could be compared to traditional time, which is followed in another agency. The finding could be useful not only to the agencies involved but also to agencies in leisure services in general.

Correlational Research

This traditional research technique reveals the relationship between two variables. For instance, the relationship between enrollment in recreational offerings and fees would be of interest to the agency and to the profession in general. The question is: does this correlation reveal that enrollment decreases as fees increase. If this is the case, a negative correlation exists between these two variables.

On the other hand, a positive correlation could be revealed if more advertisement of the agency's program leads to more enrollment in recreational offerings.

Evaluative Research

This brings us a complete circle back to evaluation. Evaluative research is a tool of evaluating an agency dealing with parks, recreation, and leisure services. The elements to be evaluated have been described previously and include the mission and the objectives of the agency; its leadership, administration and management; its program; its personnel; and its areas, facilities, and equipment.

THE RESEARCH PROCESS

In carrying out a research project, a number of steps must be taken. Although there is no agreement on the exact number or nature of the steps, generally speaking, the following describes what a research project may entail.

1. Defining the nature of the research

2. Selecting a research design

3. Deciding on the research instruments to be used

4. Collecting the data

5. Analyzing the data

Research Design

The research design delineates the entire research undertaking from the planning to the carrying out of the study. Three elements in the design are of great importance to the researcher: the instrument or instruments to be used, the administration of these instruments, and the analysis of the data.

The Research Instrument

Regardless of what instruments are used, all evaluation tools and research must meet three important criteria: objectivity, validity and reliability.

Objectivity: This criterion should guarantee that the research is free from personal bias and self-interest. When conducting evaluation and research, it is essential that self-interest be set aside. While complete objectivity may be impossible, attempts should be made to reduce subjectivity as much as possible.

Validity: This criterion in evaluation and research refers to the extent to which the instrument measures what it is designed to measure. For instance, is the questionnaire used to measure what the person feels about a particular offering, or does it measure the mastery of the English language? There are many kinds of validity with which the evaluator and researcher should be acquainted.

Reliability: This criterion refers to the consistency of the instrument. For instance, if a measuring tape yields two totally different readings of the same field's width, a question should be raised as to the reliability of the measuring tape.

Collection of Data

Although selection of a design, development of the instrument and analysis of the data are considered the most technically difficult tasks in research and evaluation, data collection could become a logistic nightmare. In order to avoid such an outcome, a number of steps are suggested.

1. Selection of data collectors must be done very carefully. Educational background and experience as well as interpersonal skills are important ingredients of a competent worker.

2. Training of data collectors should include information on the instrument, a chance for practice and recording, and how to deal with potential problems.

3. Organization for data collection should include the needed clearances, a monitoring process, and a system of storing the data for the next step, their analysis.

Data Analysis

Data analysis depends on the type of data collected. A decision on the type of data is made apriori. For our purposes there are basically two types of data: quantitative and nonquantitative or qualitative data. While quantitative data can be easily measured in quantities such as amounts, weights, capacity, and test scores, the nonquantitative data deal with variables that cannot easily be put in numerical terms such as feelings and traits. In other words the nonquantitative depends on words rather than numbers.

In the construction of the instrument, the words used in responding can be turned into numbers. For instance, van der Smissen(1972) suggests numerical values for the criteria in her scale as follows:

-If the criterion is met	5 points
-If the criterion is almost met	3 points
-If the criterion is met to some degree	1 point
-If the criterion is not met	0 points

Manipulation of the quantitative data requires the understanding of statistics. There are basically two types of statistics: descriptive and inferential. Descriptive statistics provide central tendency, i.e., the mode, the median and the mean. While the mode is the most frequent score, the median is the most middle score, and the mean is the arithmetical average of all scores. The researcher should be acquainted with the uses of described statistics.

Inferential statistics are more sophisticated and require the service of a specialist. Perhaps the most important use of these statistics is hypothesis testing.

DOCUMENTATION AND FOLLOW-UP

Whether the document is for internal use (evaluation) or wide distribution (research), certain criteria should be met. First the document should include the following:

1. An introduction,

2. design strategy including the instrument(s) used,

3. information and or data collection techniques,

4. information and or data analysis, and

5. conclusion and recommendations.

It is hoped that the outcome of having a report (evaluation) or a paper (research) published and/or distributed will benefit not only the agency, but also leisure service in general. It has been advocated by the powers to be that the purpose of evaluation is to improve. The outcomes of evaluations should be used to improve not only the agency which is conducting the evaluation but also the whole field of parks, recreation, and leisure services. The same thing should be said about the value of research in this field.

SUMMARY

- The body of knowledge of any profession is enhanced when research and evaluation are conducted by its members.

- The purpose of evaluating an agency in parks, recreation, and leisure services is to improve the quality of the offerings rather than to prove anything.

- Evaluation should be both formal-summative which is rather official and periodic and informal-formative which is continuous and spontaneous.

- A number of evaluative processes could be followed. One is concerned with the information system in the agency, another with the needs assessment, and third with the outcome evaluation.

- The evaluation procedure requires evaluators either from within the agency or from external sources. Each approach has its advantages and disadvantages.

- Standards and criteria in evaluation could be developed or could be borrowed from previous research. Care should be taken that the criteria meet the rigors of objectivity, validity and reliability.

- While the impact of evaluation may be felt locally, the research should have wider use within the profession of leisure services.

- Numerous instruments are listed in this chapter as well as the process have to conduct and disseminate research finds.

LEARNING ACTIVITIES

1. Invite a professor from the Business Administration Department to talk about the evaluation process in the business world.

2. Visit your local Park and Recreation Department and interview the director about the process of evaluating the department.

3. Invite a professor of statistics to talk about the use of statistics in evaluation.

4. Scan one or two newspapers to find articles dealing with evaluation.

REFERENCES

Attkisson, C.C. and others (Editors) (1978) **Evaluation of Human Service Programs.** Orlando: Academic Press.

Attkisson, C.C. and others (1978) "Evaluation: Current Strength and Future Directions" in Attkisson, C.C. and others (Editors) **Evaluation of Human Service Programs.** Orlando: Academic Press.

Banes, R. and C. Novak (1976) **Guidelines for Evaluating and Agency Rendering Recreation, Park and Leisure Services.** La Mirad, CA: C & B Associates.

Benest,F.; J. Foley, and G. Welton (1984) **Organizing Leisure and Human Services.** Dubuque, IA: Kendall/Hunt.

Chambers, D.f., K.R. Wedel and M.K. Rodwell. (1992) **Evaluating Social Programs.** Boston: Allyn and Bacon

Henderson, Karla, and Debrah Bialeschki (1995) **Evaluating Leisure Services.** State College, PA: Venture Publishing.

Kosecoff, J. and Fink A. (1982) **Evaluation Basics: A Practitioner's Manual.** Beverly Hills, CA: Sage Publications.

Kraus, R and L. Allen (1987) **Research and Evaluation in Recreation, Parks and Leisure Studies.** Columbus, OH: Publishing Horizons

Murphy, J. et al (1991) **Leisure Systems: Critical Concepts and Applications.** Champaign, IL: Sagamore Publishing.

Nolan, M. (1984) "A Systemic Approach to Recreation Progam Appraisal" in J. Bannon (Editor) **Administrative Practice of Park, Recreation and Leisure Services.** Champaign, IL: Management Learning Laboratories.

Shivers, J. (1978) **Essentials of Recreational Services.** Philadelphia: Lea & Febiger.

Siegel, L.M., C.c. Attkisson and L. Carson (1978) "Need Identification and Program Planning in the Community Context" in Attkisson, C.C. and others (Editors) **Evaluation of Human Service Programs.** Orlando: Academic Press.

van der Smissen, B. (1972) **Evaluation and Self-study of Public Recreation and Park Agencies.** Arlington, VA: NRPA.

CHAPTER 15
CURRENT ISSUES AND FUTURE TRENDS

Learning Objectives

1. After reading this chapter, you should be able to do the following:

2. Distinguish between two types of issues in the leisure services and studies,

3. Appreciate the professional obligation of professionals and scholars in combating some of the problems faced by leisure services in general,

4. Become cognizant of the major problems faced by the leadership and management in leisure service agencies,

5. Become familiar with some of the solutions suggested for reducing the problems in leisure services, and

6. Understand the societal and economical factors that would affect the functions of a leisure agency where offerings and staffing are concerned.

Issues and trends in parks, recreation, and leisure should be of interest to the leaders and managers of their agencies. One group of issues and trends is related to leisure in general. For instance, there is a concern about the increase of violence and sex in the mass media. There is also a concern about the rise of sedentariness and "spectatoritis." Since gambling has become a source of income for many states, what does this mean to leisure behavior? Alcohol consumption, drug abuse, and smoking are on the rise, particularly among the young. As dis-

cussed earlier all these issues and concerns should be reviewed by both professionals and scholars since they are obligated to raise questions of societal significance, and these are, indeed, issues and concerns of national significance. As the
aforementioned issues and concerns do not have a direct bearing on the leadership and management of a leisure agency, they will not be discussed in detail
here. Other issues and concerns that affect the smooth functioning of an agency
dealing with parks, recreation, and leisure services will be presented.

ISSUES FACING THE LEISURE DELIVERY SYSTEM

The problems plaguing our society are not the only issues affecting parks, recreation, and leisure services. These services also have their own problems to
address. In this final chapter, the problems faced by them are presented.

  One of these problems concerns equity. A person who wants to enjoy a park,
participate in a recreational activity, or pursue a pastime may not have the means
to do so. Should the management of the agency help him or her to fulfill his or
her need? Are there other barriers to the participation in the agency's activities,
which could be alleviated with the help of the agency? In other words, the issue
of equal opportunity in leisure pursuits deserves as much of the professional's
attention as do the barriers to recreational participation.

  With participation in leisure pursuits at its peak, management of visitors and
users of parks, recreational facilities, and playing fields is another issue that will
be discussed in this section. As visitations increase, the manager needs to be
concerned with the possible abuse and destruction of these areas. The third problem involves agencies who charge fees as a means of increasing income. Since
this practice deprives some people from pursuing their desired activities, the
matter of "haves" versus "have not" occurs.

The Question of Equality

If our society has indeed entered the age of leisure, an important question needs
to be asked: Is leisure a right or a privilege? This should be followed by other
questions such as: Is there equality of opportunities in leisure pursuits? Are areas

and facilities evenly distributed among the different segments of the population? What are the barriers to recreational participation?

Today there is a tacit agreement over the meaning of the term leisure as encompassing three interrelated variables: free-time, recreational activities, and the participants' state of mind. With "human rights" gaining grounds in the second half of the 20th century, an issue is now being raised by professionals and scholars of leisure: Is leisure a right or a privilege? This debate intensified after the General Assembly of the United Nations adopted a universal declaration of human rights that included the right of each citizen to rest and leisure (U.N.1978) While it is almost universally agreed that leisure is a human right, studies show that such a right is not within the means of many citizens in many societies including the United States as shown in the following sections.

Gender Inequity: It is agreed that there are gender differences in playforms, games, and similar activities. These differences are in a sense universal (Ibrahim, 1991: 240). Of concern, however, are not these differences, but rather how will opportunities to participate in activities of one's choice be achieved. Studies within the United States and in other countries show that as the old rhyme states, "a man works from sun to sun, but a woman's work is never done", is indeed a fact. Even if the woman works outside the home, housework consumes a great part of her remaining hours.

As reported by Cordes and Ibrahim (1996: 168-9), some improvement in the societal attitudes where women and leisure are concerned, may have occurred. On the other hand, Henderson believes that these attitudes are far from being reversed. She suggests that not only is women's leisure unstructured and fragmented, but that many women in this society still feel they are not entitled to leisure (1990). Kelly and Freysinger concur with this analysis suggesting that significant inequities based on biological sex still exist (2000:152).

Class Distinction: In the early 1980's a study by Mitchell revealed that there are 9 different possible lifestyles, and of these 9 lifestyles two were labeled survivors and sustainers (1983). The author found that survivors and the sustainers, representing the poorest of the nine category, were not only need- driven, but they also had fewer opportunities for leisure pursuits than the other seven categories of life-styles.

Most of these needy people lived in the inner cities of America. Studies conducted in two large metropolitan areas in the United States, Los Angeles and Chicago, confirmed Mitchell's findings. Foley (1989) decried the appearance of what he called "recreational apartheid" in many parts of Los Angeles. The existence of dark parks was reported on five years earlier in the **Los Angeles Times** (1984). These parks were not fit to be called places where one could participate in recreational activities or engage in leisure pursuits. They were places filled with drug users and gang members. A similar situation occurred in Chicago. The situation in Los Angeles seems as bleak as it did a decade earlier. In 1995 the **Los Angeles Times** reported that one of the City's parks suffered "from problems common to parks in poor urban areas including drugs being dealt and used inside the park and control of certain areas by gangs."

Other barriers to participation in organized recreational activities include lack of transportation, lack of time, distance of the leisure place, along with some psychological factors that keeps the person from being involved in activities outside the home.

Suggestions for the Manager: The following would be of help to the manager.

1. Despite the recent trends in political philosophy, where public human services are concerned, the American people have taken care of the isolated and the needy, since the creation of the Republic, either through private or public means. Where inequity is concerned, a philosophic stand should be taken by the management of the agency as approved by its board (whether public, semi-public or private). The policy on diversity and inclusiveness should be spelled out to become part of the parcel of the structure and functions of the agency.

2. When it comes to leisure pursuits, the agency should provide equal opportunity to people who are at a relative disadvantage. Flextime and flexplace are new terms, the meaning behind which are the provision of opportunities, not only to work, but also to play. If America's huge corporations are allowing certain segments to change their arrival and departure time from the work place to suit their special needs and/or to work at home with the use of the new technologies, should not an agency dealing with parks, recreation and leisure service utilize these two new concepts? If the gas and electricity companies are using slide scales based on income to provide the poor with these two basic needs, why not apply the same

principle in a private agency providing recreation? It is becoming clear that the burden of improving life conditions for the underprivileged is not assigned to public agencies alone. The private sector also has to invest in the future of America.

3. The providers of public recreation should work cooperatively with local agencies, be they public, semi-public, or private, to reduce the impact of drug use and gang activities in leisure places. Perhaps, drug dealing and gang activities should be classified as acts of vandalism, which are discussed in the next section.

4. The management of an agency in parks, recreation or leisure service should consider establishing an extension program as part of its mission. The idea of extension service will be given at the end of this chapter.

Crowding and Carrying Capacity

These two issues have been of concern for the managers of outdoor recreation areas for a long time. Attempts were made on the National Level when the National Park Service designed the framework VERP, or the Visitor Experience and Resource Protection which incorporated two previous concepts: Limits of Acceptable change and Visitor Impact Management.

VERP revolves around nine basic elements: interdisciplinary approach, public involvement, clear objectives, use of overlay maps, potential zoning, application, standards, comparisons and strategies. This framework is still being applied in a number of units of the National Park Service (Manning 2001).

Crowding is a another issue of concern in outdoor recreation. While the use of a recreation site is a physical concept, crowding has a psychological, subjective meaning, therefore it is a judgement call on the part of the participant. Accordingly it is influenced by the characteristics of visitors, the characteristics of those encountered by them, and the situational variables such as the type of area, it's location, quality, and design (Manning et al., 2000). For example, one area located on the Angeles National Forest in Southern California is Frequently closed to additional visitation because of crowded conditions (U.S. Forest Service 2001).

Suggestions for the Manager: Here are ideas to be considered.

1) Crowding is a function of use level, ergo carrying capacity may have to be imposed.

2) Normative standards of what constitute crowding should be used to establish such levels.

3) Zoning to separate conflicting use may apply under certain circumstances.

4) Educational programs should be used to modify visitors' behavior.

5) Diverse outdoor recreation opportunities should be provided.

6) VERP, having been successful on the national level, could be used with needed modifications.

Conflict

Conflict over the use of open space, parkland, and outdoor recreation areas and facilities come from many directions. For example participants in one leisure pursuit may feel excluded when a particular area or facility is scheduled for another group. Preservationists for example who desire to keep an area in its pristine condition would be in conflict with those who believe in multiple use.

Conflict typically arises when participants engage in a traditional activity, e.g. skiing, encounter another group using newer technology such as snowmobiling. Another form of conflict is the in-group conflict which may occur among members of the same group.

Limits of Acceptable Change (LAC), Visitor Impact Management (VIM) and Visitor Experience and Resource Protection (VERP) are planning frameworks the purpose of which is to help natural resources planners and managers make sound decisions to reduce not only the negative impact of overuse and crowding, but also to reduce potential conflict.

Suggestions for the Manager: Following are ideas to be followed.

1) Utilization of normative theory described above to find out what is acceptable and unacceptable behavior in the site is a must.

2) Regulations should be made very clear to all groups using the site.

3) Designation and zoning of certain areas may be needed to separate groups.

4) Education and information should be used to underscore the agencies philosophy on conflict.

Visitor Management

Leisure places are visited by people of all ages, socioeconomic backgrounds, and lifestyles. In general, the managers of leisure places should take into consideration a number of factors in an attempt to provide an adequate visitor management program. Below are some of these factors.

1. The leisure place is characterized by informality which may affect the behavior of the visitor/participant.

2. The visitor to a leisure place or the participant in a leisure pursuit has certain expectations.

3. Most recreational activities are group oriented, a factor that has a bearing on leisure behavior.

4. It is rather difficult to provide an average profile of a visitor/ participant to a leisure place.

5. Persons with disabilities require the attention of the manager.

6. The profile of thrill seekers should be taken into consideration.

7. General provisions should be put in place to accommodate the needs of all visitors/participants in a parks, recreation, or leisure agency.

Suggestions for the Manager: The following are some suggestions for the manager concerning visitors to a park, recreation, and leisure area.

1. **Education and Information:** Many managerial problems that are related to visitor management can be solved with an effective education/information program. Roggenuch and Ham find that such a program is useful in outdoor settings (1986:M59). The program should be directed to the staff as well as to the users of the agency's services.

2. **Signs:** People tend to follow directions that are placed on signs, a tendency which should be utilized in visitor management of a leisure place. Signs are an important means of communication as they identify specific areas and provide the agency's regulations.

3. **Interpretive Service:** This service not only tells the background of the leisure place, but it also shapes the visitor's experience by involving him or her in its activities and thus enhancing appreciation of the place (Knudson, 1984: 396 and Jensen, 1985: 359).

4. **Control of Undesirable Actions:** As suggested earlier, a leisure place with an informal atmosphere is desirable. Nonetheless, certain behaviors on the part of many visitors/participants may create some adverse outcomes. While enforcement of the law may be used in extreme cases, careless thoughts, unskilled actions, and uniformed behavior should be controlled.

5. **Risk Recreation:** It seems that specific personality characteristics lead to certain behaviors which has some bearing on leisure behavior. A person with a type "T" personality has been identified as someone with a low physiological arousability, which makes him/her seek extra excitement. These risk seekers are found among both genders (Mills 1986). Many activities are being provided for them in public, semi-public, and private leisure agencies. In such a case, adequate supervision by well-qualified staff is a must. It is also important to have the needed insurance coverage.

6. **Special Population:** Planning facilities for the handicapped can be found in Chapter Six. The program for the handicapped should be built on the latest studies of the different handicapped populations. A qualified member of the staff should be charged with the overall supervision of the program.

Fees and Charges

Today, the management of a public park, recreation and leisure service must face whether to charge fees or not. Semi-public and private agencies have always charged for their services. For many years, providers of public recreation on the local, county, state, and national levels provided recreational opportunities either free of charge or at low cost to their visitors/participants. In the last few decades, fiscal crisis made local department charge fees for many of their services. Other public park and recreation agencies have also increased their nominal fees on certain offerings to such an extent that the public agency is hardly considered "public". Fees charged for the use of public facilities and areas can be classified into six categories:

Entrance fees: These are charged for the entry into large areas such parks.

Admission fees: These are charged for entry into a building having a program or event.

Rental fees: These are charged for the use of a facility or a variety of equipment.

Users fees: These are charged for the right to participate in an activity.

Permit fees: These are charged for the privilege of participation.

Special Service fees: These are charged for specific use.

Suggestions for the Manager: Since fees seem to be a permanent feature of a public park and recreation agency, the following two sets of recommendations should be considered when fees are being considered.

A. Establishing and Maintaining Fees: Public parks and recreation agencies follow these six principles (1964:256):

1. All fees and charges should be in conformity with the long term policy and regulations of the agency.

2. The fees and charges should be for an activity that meets public need and not as an income producing process.

3. Review of the fees and charges should be done periodically to see that they meet the policy and regulations of the agency.

4. The best business procedures and administrative controls should be utilized in managing fees and charges.

5. Leases and concessions should be considered a portion of fees and charges and managed accordingly.

6. Semi-public, nonprofit agencies should be charged a minimal cost for the use of public facilities.

B. Management Techniques: About twenty years later, Kraus and Curtis, realizing that fees and charges had become a fixture in the management of park, recreation, and leisure service agencies, suggested four ways of minimizing the impact of imposing fees on the visitor/participant (1982:232).

1. **Public Relations:** The charging of fees should be made in conjunction with the best public relations techniques which includes an announcement and explanation for the need to increase or impose fees.

2. **Gradual Increases:** Gradual increases tied to cost of living are easier to explain and more acceptable to the constituency of the parks, recreation, or leisure agency.

3. **Fee by fee consideration:** Each activity and or facility should be considered separately, and fees should be charged according to what is needed there.

4. **Annual Passes:** In the case of zoos, botanical gardens, and other natural resource areas, the annual pass increases both the identification with the facility as well with visitation to it.

Recent research shows that while increase in fees is acceptable in principle by users, it suffers from lack of general knowledge about the need to change and the good that can result (U.S. Forest Service 2001).

Vandalism

Vandalism is defined as the wanton, deliberate destruction of property. Although actions against vandalism have taken place in leisure places unfortunately it is on the increase in our nations' parks, recreation centers, and playing fields.

The notion that only young people commit acts of vandalism is not totally true, because there is evidence that many adults also vandalize public and private property. The other incorrect notion is that vandalism is done by poor, deprived persons. Many rich persons of different ages vandalize parks, recreation centers, and playing fields across this country (Sharpe and others, 1994 P.330). But why do people vandalize these places? Knudson (1984:500-501) suggests the following ten reasons:

Overuse destruction	Self-expression vandalism
Conflict vandalism	Spin-off vandalism
No-other-way-to-do-it vandalism	Slovenly vandalism
Inventive vandalism	Malicious vandalism
Curiosity vandalism	Thrill vandalism

On the other hand, believes there are psychosocial causes for vandalism. These include social decay, inadequate parenting, lenient courts, boredom, peer pressure, and developmental factors.

Target Areas: Vandals normally target certain areas in the park, recreation center, or playing field for their acts of vandalism. Sharpe and others have developed a list that shows that no leisure place or area is immune from vandalism. Buildings, restrooms, lights, tables, benches, grassy areas, blacktop areas, plants, trees, drinking fountains, sinks, fireplaces, and grills are subject to vandalism (1994: 343-349).

Suggestions For The Manager: It would be an unrealistic notion to suggest that an end to vandalism is possible. Since vandalism will remain a problem for the manager, perhaps the following suggestions can help to reduce it in the leisure place.

1. **Design of Facilities:** Facilities which are targets of vandals need an adequate design to help reduce the possibility of their destruction. For instance nicely built and well-maintained facilities may reduce the possibility of vandalism. Restrooms are frequent targets of vandals, and one way of reducing damage to these facilities is to hide the pipes behind their walls. In addition the use of electric dryers, heavy wired glass, and push button faucets discourages vandalism.

2. **User Fees:** There are mixed reports on the relationship between charging fees for the use of the facility and the acts of vandalism. In some cases, less acts of vandalism have been reported in areas where a user fee has been imposed. In other cases, the opposite has been reported (Sharpe and others, 1994:349). The collection of user fees is not intended, of course, to reduce vandalism. Yet if it proves useful in reducing vandalism, then user fees should be imposed as one measure to reduce these wanton acts.

3. **Surveillance:** According to Sharpe and others (1994: 350), surveillance is probably the best method of controlling vandalism in the leisure place. The use of patrols, which watch over the facility at varied schedules and patterns, could be useful. Adequate lighting and a comprehensive alarm system are also good methods of keeping vandalism down.

4. **Public Awareness and Involvement:** The participation of the person who uses the recreational facility is an important tool in combating vandalism and in helping to reduce these acts.

Current and future users of the agency's facilities should be provided with information and educational programs to combat vandalism. In addition to the above, Kraus and Curtis believe (2000; 293) that maintenance's fast and efficient response to repairing the damaged facilities as well as improved staffing and supervision may help in reducing vandalism.

Law Enforcement

A few years ago, law enforcement did not rank high among the duties of a manager or his/her staff in a parks, recreation, and leisure service agency. Today, with the radical and fast changes that are taking place in our society, the concept of law enforcement, and its aspects and procedures should be understood and followed by the staff in an agency dealing with park, recreation, and leisure services (See Chapter Twelve).

Jurisdiction: The authority given to enforce the law depends on the affiliation, type, and location of the agency. i.e., whether the agency is a public agency affiliated with the federal, state, or local government; a semi- public or a private agency. Moreover, law enforcement differs from one agency to another under the same type of government or affiliation. Other factors should also be considered in determining the jurisdiction required to enforce the law in an agency dealing with parks, recreation, and leisure services. Yet, generally speaking there are four types of jurisdiction according to Sharpe and others (1994: 398) as follows.

Exclusive Jurisdiction: This type of jurisdiction occurs when one body of government maintains sovereign authority in enforcing the law. For instance in our national parks, where this policy is followed, federal law is applied and supplants the laws in the states in which the park is located.

Concurrent Jurisdiction: This type of jurisdiction is followed when the legal rights are shared. This is seen when both federal and state laws are observed.

Proprietary Jurisdiction: If the agency is built on property held by a private owner, proprietary jurisdiction is applied. In such case, both the state laws and local ordinances are enforced, provided that they are not in conflict with federal laws.

Partial Jurisdiction: In some special cases, the federal government may give the state partial authority to enforce the law. Such arrangement could give complete authority to the state or concurrent authority with the federal government.

A Ranger Or Policeman: At one point in time, the resource manager was looked upon as a person with special talents, dedicated to providing the public with outdoor recreational experiences to be remembered for a long time. Today as the number of visitors to America's natural resources increases, so do the problems of the resource manager. As his or her duties expand beyond management, maintenance, and interpretation of the natural heritage of America, it has become increasingly necessary to enforce the law. The resource managers find themselves becoming more and more a police force, sometimes to the determent of other duties. For instance, does the need to carry a gun, as a measure of law enforcement, change the image of the resource manager which is described above?

Although the managers of America's natural resources must deal with many issues, the carrying of firearms is the top of the list. To these professional men and women, carrying arms is needed for their own protection and for the protection of the visitors to the natural resources. On October 13, 1995, when a female park worker gave a ride to person in a national park, the passenger pulled a stun gun on her and tried to handcuff her. She managed to escape and the search for him ended when he was apprehended hiding in the meadows two weeks later (Los Angeles Time, 1995: A25)

Liability: When law enforcement become part of the job responsibility, the resource manager must constantly be aware of the liability issues. Since park rangers are not commissioned law officials, they face a greater liability risk. In this case he or she is held more liable by criminal and civil laws. According to Sharpe and others, "a park officer making an illegal arrest may be sued by the private party and may even be arrested and charged for the deed" (1994:427). Law enforcement training of personnel in parks, recreation, and leisure agencies then becomes essential.

Suggestions for the Manager: This relatively new element of law enforcement that has entered the realm of the management of parks, recreational facilities, and playing fields should be taken seriously and cautiously. The following are suggestions for the manager in these fields.

1. **In-Service-Training:** In-service-training for existent staff and new staff should be provided on a continual basis. In some cases training in the use of firearms may be included. The in-service- training should include how to conduct a citizen' arrest, handle citations and conduct search, seizure and arrest.

2. **Patrols:** In large and small facilities, the formation of a patrol system could be very helpful. The visibility of a patrol is in itself a deterrent to unlawful acts. A patrol is also a measure of education and visitor assistance.

3. **Complaints and Citations:** While a complaint is a formal written charge by an officer or a private citizen, a citation is an order to appear before a magistrate or to post a bond in lieu of appearing.

4. **Education and Information:** Upon arrival the typical citizen should be informed about the type of crimes being committed in the park, recreational facility, or playing field. The information could be distributed as hand bills upon entering the facility or posted at the entrance.

Safety and Security

These two terms are sometime used interchangeably. Nonetheless, they are two different approaches to the reduction of accidents, injuries, and possible harm to the participants in recreational activities and leisure pursuits. While security incorporates the means of warding off violent acts, safety encompasses the re-duction of accidents in the natural resources, recreational facilities, and playing fields.

Hazards spots in parks, recreation facilities, and playing fields are dangerous not only to the consumer but also to the participant. Interestingly, they are more hazardous to the staff than to the participants. According to Sharpe and others, a study by the National Safety Council reveals that of all park-related injuries, 66 percent involve the maintenance personnel(1994:267). Many of the visitors to the leisure place are also subject to injuries unless good measures are taken.

Suggestions for the Manager: To minimize the possibility of injuries to visitors and staff, several activities should be included as important functions in the lei-sure place.

1. **A Safety and Security Program:** A program on safety and security should be included in the structure of the agency. Gold suggests that such a program include the following components (1991):

   Commitment and Policy

   Safety Committee and Coordinator

   Inspection

   Maintenance

   Site Development

   Site Management

   Public Information and Education

   Employee Training

   Research and Evaluation

2. **Inspection for Hazards:** Where safety is concerned, the United States Consumer Production Safety Commission provides two checklists. The first includes the playground maintenance checklist, which emphasizes the role of inspection in reducing hazards. The Commission suggests that an inspection be conducted frequently and regularly. The Commission further indicates that specific danger points should be checked on each tour.

   Visible cracks, bending, warping, rusting or breakage

   Deformed hooks, shackles, rings and links

   Worn hangers and chains

Missing seats

Loose bolts

Sharp edges

Broken supports, nails, steps and rungs

Splintered and deteriorated wood

Tripping hazards such as roots, rocks, etc.

Protruding sharp objects

3. **Security Checks:** Where security is concerned, Greenbaum suggests the following 18 security prevention strategies (1994) be observed:

Develop practical emergency preparedness

Devise an incident reporting system

Provide adequate vehicle access

Install exterior lights

Limit roof access

Place dumpsters away from buildings

Design parking lots to discourage cruising

Design secured areas for bikes

Use gates constructed of heavy material

Locate playgrounds in visible areas

Implement a neighborhood watch

Install an alarm system

Employ security guards

Develop incentive program to combat vandalism

Involve youth in program development

4. **Private Security:** Semi-public private leisure places and even public agencies may need to hire a private security agency. Companies that specialize in this type of work also responsible for checking the backgrounds of their employees and for their training. Sometimes retired police officers, with their background in law enforcement, are hired directly by the agency.

The Environment

Despite all the attempts to protect the environment from the impact of our ever growing human population, many problems have arisen at an alarming rate in the last few decades.

The Nature of the Ecosystems: An ecosystem is composed of two major systems: the aquatic and the terrestrial. The aquatic system is also composed of two systems: the fresh-water and the marine systems. On the other hand, the terrestrial systems consists of forests, tundra, and grasslands. The delicate balance among all these systems is being threatened by human activities including the participation in recreational and leisure pursuits.

Air Pollution: Fossil fuel and the clearing and burning of forests for agricultural purposes are creating a dramatic increase in carbon dioxide in the atmosphere. Will this practice lead to a warming trend? For instance, Southern Africa had a severe drought in 1996, as a consequence of the greenhouse effect. This condition, created by an increase in carbon dioxide, allows an excess of solar radiation to penetrate the atmosphere.

Attention was paid to the harmful effects of air pollution in 1963 when the Congress of the United States passed the Clear Air Act. This act was aimed at controlling air pollution from stationary sources, such as factories and electric power stations, and from mobile resources such as motor vehicles. Nonetheless, it became necessary to amend the Act along the way, In 1990, a new Clear Air Act was signed by the President of the United States. The aims of the new Act are to cut emissions of pollutants that created smog and acid rain and to reduce the depletion of the protective ozone layer.

The impact of the unhealthy air on recreational places has been devastating. For instance, the Associated Press reported that the number of trees damaged in Yosemite National Park by the ozone depletion has increased five folds in the previous 5 years (1990). Air pollution has decreased the visibility in the Grand Canyon, North Cascades National Park, and the Great Smokey Mountains.

Water Pollution: Aquatic systems cover over 70 percent of the earth's surface. The freshwater system is composed of streams and rivers, is rich in oxygen. Streams and rivers end in pools, bogs, ponds, and lakes which are not as rich in oxygen, but are rich in nutrients. With the building of approximately 50,000 dams in this country, very few rivers are left to flow purely or freely. While the reservoirs created behind these dams are appreciated sites for providing recreational opportunities, the poor quality of river water has affected other recreational pursuits. It is reported that two- thirds of the salmon, which existed in abundance in the rivers of the Northwest, have disappeared. The same is happening to wild trout. Perhaps with the disappearance of these fish, the lure of fishing will also start to fade (Cone 1990).

Noise Pollution: The human ear can tolerate up to 80 decibels. In today's mechanized world, this level can easily be surpassed. In every day activities, such as driving or working, residents of urban and rural areas are exposed to high levels of noise. Unfortunately high noise levels are happening more and more in our national, regional, and local recreational areas. The all-terrain vehicles in the Joshua Tree National Monument and the low flying helicopters in the Grand Canyon are examples of the high noise level being imported into these serene surroundings. In snow regions cross-country skiers can hardly tolerate the noisy snowmobiles.

Several managers in parks, recreation, and leisure services are faced with the continued controversy between the two groups of recreationists. One group seeks contemplation while the other searches for excitement and thrill.

The Estuarine Ecosystems: These systems occur when saltwater and fresh water mix as in swamps and marshes. An estuarine ecosystem is also part of the coast where the tide meets the current and over which the tide ebbs and flows as it meets the mouth of a river. These areas usually support varied species of fish, birds, and mammals. However, our burgeoning population continues to put pressure on the estuarine ecosystems. To satisfy peoples deserve for waterfront homes, some of Florida's swamps are being filled in and converted to waterfront homes. According to Pogatchnik (1990 A 16), an estimated 300,000 to 500,000 acres of wetland disappear annually.

The Marine Ecosystems: These systems can provide recreational opportunities for many people for many years to come if and only if these resources are used wisely. Unfortunately, the outlook for the preservation of these natural resources is not very optomistic as population growth is proceeding at a very high rate. For example, the populations along the East and the West coasts and the Gulf of Mexico more than doubled between 1940 and 1980 (Time Magazine 1988:45).

The impact of these masses is seen in the 10 tons of trash collected in one day in and around Southern California beaches (Perry 1990). A huge dead zone in the Gulf of Mexico, 300 miles long and 10 miles wide, is totally depleted of oxygen (Time Magazine 1988).

Terrestrial Ecosystems: Two types of vegetations distinguish the terrestrial ecosystem: trees and grass. Forests play a very important role in regulating the global climate in that they have a great capacity to absorb carbon dioxide. With the destruction of forests/jungles, an increase in the greenhouse effect is occurring. In addition, the disappearance of trees is depriving wildlife of its natural habitat. Excess carbon dioxide in the atmosphere is threatening the trees themselves. Two types of grassland exist in the United States: the tall grass prairies toward the east and the short grass prairies toward the west. Again most of these lands have become farms, factories, and residences as civilization seeks land for expansion.

Other than forests and grasslands, the deserts constitute 15% of the land mass on earth. Contrary to common belief, the deserts are not void of living creatures. This attitude towards the desert led to the destruction of many rare animals and fragile plants. Reportedly after a race that took place a few years ago in California on BLM land, desert tortoises with cracked shells and some kangaroo rats with bleeding ears were seen. Furthermore, other small animals were found crushed or buried alive in their burrows. Tiny desert plants that took hundreds of years to grow were destroyed in no time at all (California Magazine, 1989:105).

Suggestions for the Manager: As professionals, the managers of leisure places should be involved in helping to reduce the impact of human activities on the earth's natural resources. Furthermore, they should also make sure that their clientele's health is not affected by the hazardous materials currently plaguing contemporary living conditions. In a sense professionals are obligated to follow some practices, though seemingly minimal, that help to reduce the destructive impact on recreational use of these natural resources.

1. **Air Quality Management:** It is incumbent upon the professional in parks, recreation, and leisure services to see that the air quality is enhanced, not only at work, but also at all times. Ride sharing should be encouraged for those who work in the agency and for those coming to enjoy their leisure pursuits at the agency. Whenever

possible the use of an emission-free vehicle should be utilized by the agency. In areas where the air quality is in question, the participants should be encouraged to practice their physical activity indoors or to postpone it for a day or two.

2. **Noise Abatement:** Maintenance of the facilities and the surrounding areas could be deferred to times when visitation is at a minimum. Also the management should allocate certain quiet hours to which everyone should adhere. Moreover, specific days and hours should be allocated to the activities that produce high levels of noise on the premises.

3. **Water Pollution Management:** All water sources not ascertained must be tested frequently. Water taken from a lake, reservoir, or spring may require chlorination. Springs must be fenced, boxed, and covered. Also hand pumps must be boxed to prevent contamination.

4. **Waste Treatment:** While most of the leisure places connect directly to the local sewage treatment plant, those lacking a direct connection need an adequate waste treatment system. When pit toilets are used, a priori test is needed to determine the type of soil. Perc soil is suitable to accept an overflow, and a septic tank-drain field can be utilized. Since chemically sealed vault toilets have to be dumped out periodically, the cost should be taken into consideration.

5. **Fire Management:** While a controlled prescribed burn is important in land management, preparation for wildfires should also be part of an agency dealing with large pieces of land. Controlled burning has been used as a method of hazard reduction, nutrient release, and sanitation. A wildfire is a free burning phenomenon which could consume many acres. While nature plays a role in creating wildfires, smokers, children and campers cause about 25% of wildfires (Sharpe and others, 1994: 439).

6. **Carrying Capacity:** As a means of protecting the leisure site from overuse and the environment from deterioration, the concept of carrying capacity was introduced in the early 1930's. It was reintroduced in the 1960's. A number of factors should be taken into consideration in determining the carrying capacity of a leisure site, such as the general attractiveness of the site, the population around the site, and the economic level of the population.

7. **"No Trace" Ethics:** This concept is promoted through which the land, upon which one is experiencing nature, should be left in the same condition as it is found. This "no trace ethics" could become one of the features of a natural resource, be it local, regional or national.

FUTURE TRENDS AND MANAGEMENT

The trends in the leadership and management of leisure agencies presented in this section have evolved in reaction to the changes that have taken place in society in general and the leisure field in particular. Their importance in the leadership and management of an agency dealing with parks, recreation and leisure services will be discussed.

Time To Work And Play

Since the concept of flextime has been discussed earlier, it will not be discussed here. With the advent of high tech gadgets, not only work time may be reduced, but also the structure of work schedule, place, and input may be subject to change.

This trend will affect the leadership and management of a leisure service agency in two ways. The first impact will be on the scheduling of the agency's own activities and offerings, and the second will deal with its operations. Whether public, semi-public, or private, an agency offering services will have to conform to the work patterns in the society. Not long ago, scheduling any activity on a Sunday, unless related to the church's activities, was a taboo. In the last few decades, scheduling of sport events, concerts, parades and the like has changed to include Sunday. However, many public recreation centers and playing fields still are not available for the young and old on Sundays and other holidays. While a few evening programs are offered by some public recreation programs, most public parks are closed at sundown. Yet these facilities can be utilized very effectively if only adequate security and safety measures are implemented.

Outreach Programs

Many semi-public agencies such as the YMCA have had outreach programs for sometime. Many colleges and universities have opened up extension centers to reach those who can not come to the main campus. Unfortunately public recreation departments have not utilized this method effectively.

Public recreation service should extend into places where segments of the populations are isolated by choice or by the social order such as older people living in senior homes and others who are incarcerated, hospitalized, or under custodial care.

The United States Public Law 94-142, labeled Magna Carta of Disabled Americans, gave each person in that category the right to have a chance at an education. The professionals in leisure service could follow their own leisure magna carta for the disabled and out of reach Americans. This could be done in cooperation with other public, semi-public, and private organizations as shown in the following section.

Partnerships

As a result of shrinking public funding in the closing years of the 20th century joint power agreements between two or more separate entities in local governments are now used. These joint agreements grew in the 1980's. For example, the City of Pasadena and the County of Los Angeles now share the responsibility for operating recreational facilities and offering leisure activities in the area.

Partnerships are not limited to the cooperation between two local governmental units. Some arrangements are conducted between a local government unit and a semi-public agency as in the case of the Mount Kisco, New York. Here, the local government has entered into an agreement with the Boys' Club to share facilities and to share common staff (Kraus and Curtis, 2000:82).

Another example of partnership comes from California where the residents in 10 counties surrounding the San Francisco Bay area had a 400- mile corridor for a hiking trail in 1998. The efforts of the Bay Area Ridge Trail Council began in 1991. The Council received federal funds from the National Park Service, local governments, and private donations.

These examples point to the way of the future. While the insightful leadership of a leisure agency may lead it in this direction, careful management requires that certain procedures be followed.

Environmental Ethics

Although a number of environmental acts have been passed by the Congress of the United States, the aim of which is to protect the fragile environment from deteriorating further, environmental protection really falls within the realm of human behavior. Environmental ethics should become part of the program of any parks, recreation, or leisure agency. Aldo Leopold believes that the environment is not a commodity for humans to control, but rather it is a community to which we all belong (1966).

SUMMARY

- Leaders and managers in the leisure delivery system must become involved in finding creative solutions to the problems facing both the profession and the field.

- The question of equal opportunity for each citizen to enjoy leisurely pursuits, what the United Nations has declared a civil right, should be at the forefront of deliberation in national and regional meetings.

- Women and the poor need special attention when it comes to recreational opportunities. Suggestions have been provided for their inclusion.

- Visitor management is an issue faced by the leader/manager of a leisure place. Several suggestions have been given in this regard.

- Should fees and charges be used by public recreational agencies? It may be necessary to do so in this time of shrinking public funds? Suggestions are given on how to do so in the most effective way.

- Vandalism has plagued the leisure place for years. There are several types of vandalism, and the methods of combating them are provided in this chapter.

- Increased visitation to public, semi-public, and private recreational areas necessitates that law enforcement becomes part of the duties of the recreational professional's duties.

- Safety and security in parks, recreational areas and playing fields has become an integral part of the work of the leisure professionals.

- Our increasing population is being felt not only in wilderness areas, but also inside parks, recreation centers, and playgrounds. The manager and his staff should do their utmost to protect the environment. Suggestions are given in this section.

- Trends in this field include new approaches to time management at work and in play, increased partnership in management, development of extension services, and protection of the environment.

LEARNING ACTIVITIES

1. Invite a professor of sociology to discuss with your class the status of women and the poor in this country.

2. Visit a local park. Observe if any of the suggestions given in this chapter on visitor management are being followed.

3. Look at the park and recreation program in your community. Are there charges and fees for some activities? Are they reasonable?

4. Invite a police officer to class to discuss what the city or county is doing about the problem of graffiti.

5. Invite a park manager/ranger to class to discuss law enforcement, security, and safety provisions in the park.

6. Visit City Hall. Find out if your local government has a program designed to protect the environment in your area.

REFERENCES

Associated Press (1990) "Study finds Sharp Rise in Ozone Damage to Yosemite Pine trees," **Los Angeles Times**, July 12.

Bosserman, P. (1975) "The Evolution and Trends in Work and Non-work Time in the United States Society (1920-1970)", **Society and Leisure** 7 (1):89- 132.

Butler, George (1940) **Introduction to Community Recreation.** (1st Edition) New York: McGraw-Hill.

California Magazine (1989) "Vanishing California" (December)

Cone, M. (1990) "Lure of Fishing is Fading" **Los Angeles Times**, November 18.

Cordes, K. and H. Ibrahim (1996) **Applications to Recreation and Leisure.** St. Louis: Mosby Year-Book Inc.

Cross, G.S. (1986) "The Political Economy of Leisure in Retrospective: Britain, France and the Origin of the Eight Hour Day," **Leisure Studies.** 5(1):69-90.

Gold, S. (1995) "Inspecting Playgrounds for Hazard," **Parks and Recreation**, August, 1991.

Greenbaum, S. (1995) "Trends and Practices," **Parks and Recreation.** March: 49.

Henderson, K.(1990) The Meaning of Leisure to Women: An Integrative View of the Research, **Journal of Leisure Research** 22 :(3):228-43

Ibrahim, Hilmi (1991) **Leisure and Society: A Comparative Approach.** Dubuque , IA: Wm. C. Brown.

Jensen, C. (1985) **Outdoor Recreation in America.** Minneapolis, MN: Burgess Publishing.

Kelly, J.R. and V.J. Freysinger (2000) **21st Century Leisure.** Boston, MA: Allyn and Bacon.

Knudson, D. (1984) **Outdoor Recreation**. New York: Macmillan

Kraus, R. and J. Curtis (1982) **Creative Management in Recreation and Parks.** St. Louis, MO: Mosby.

Kraus, R. and J. Curtis (2000) **Creative Management in Recreation and Parks.** St. Louis, MO: McGraw-Hill

Leopold, Aldo.(1966) **A Sand County Almanac.** New York: Oxford University Press

Los Angeles Times (1995a) "Fugitive Arrested," October 27, A25.

Los Angeles Times (1995b) "A Park, Once Saved, Stumbles Again," November 4, B7.

Manning, R. (2001) "Visitor Experience and Resource Protection: A Framework for Managing the Carrying Capacity of National Parks." **Journal of Parks and Recreation Administration**. 19(1): 93-108.

Manning, R. et al. (2000) "Crowding in Parks and Outdoor Recreation: A Theoretical, Empirical, and Managerial Analysis." **Journal of Park and Recreation Administration** 18(4): 57-72.

Mills, J. (1986) "Living on the Edge," **Women's Sport and Fitness** (March):24.

Mitchell, Arnold Perry, C. (1990) On the Beach," **Los Angeles Times Magazine**, June 24.

Pogatchnik, S. (1990) "A Former Foe, Army Corps Now Fights for Wetlands", **Los Angeles Times** A1:16-17.

Roggenbuck, J. and S. Ham (1986) "Use of Information and Education in Recreation Management," in **The President's Commission on Americans Outdoors, A Literature Review.** Washington, D.C.: U.S. Government Printing Office.

Samuel, N (1986) Free Time in France: A Historical and Sociological Survey. **International Social Science Journal** 38:49-63.Sharpe,

Time (1988)" the Dirty Seas", vol 132, No. 5 : 44-50. August 1.

United Nations (1978) **Human rights: A Compilation of International Instruments.** New York: United Nations.

United States Forest Service: Pacific Southwest Research Station (2001) "Carrying and Social Capacity in the Wildland Interface" No.37 (July).

United States Forest Service: Pacific Southwest Research Station (2001) "Customer Service and Fee at Mono Basin Scenic Area" No. 37 (July).

Veblen, T. (1899) **The Theory of Leisure Class.** New York: New American Library (1953 Edition).

GLOSSARY

Account Number: The number assigned to an individual grant as part of a financial management system. **Account** Payable: The amount that an entity owes to a creditor, usually a supplier, not evidenced by a promissory note.

Account Receivable: The amount that is owed to an entity usually by one of its customers, as a result of the ordinary extension of credit.

Accounting: A systematic means of providing information on the economic and business affairs of an organization.

Accounting Period: The period of time over which an income statement summarizes the change in owners' equity.

Accounting System: The method of do recording the costs and income of a project, either by cash, accrual, or modified accrual basis.

Affirmative Action: The development and implementation of a plan to assure that steps are taken in the recruitment of employees to seek out applicants form "protected groups" .

Allowable Costs: The specific items of cost for which a grantee may be reimbursed.

Assets: An item of value by a business.

Audit: When applied to projects, an audit involves an examination of financial operations.

Award: A grant amount set forth in a notice of award.

Balance Sheet: A periodic financial statement which shows the financial status.

Block Grant: A grant from a government agency to a class of political subdivisions.

Budget: The list of itemized expenditures and income for a project for a special period of time (usually twelve months).

Budget Code: The list of itemized expenditures and income for an accounting system to designate different accounts and line items of expenditure, such as rent, postage, supplies, salaries, fringe benefits.

Budget Period: The interval (usually twelve months) form the beginning to the end of the time when costs may be incurred against a grant or contract.

Capital: Owners' equity or worth.

Capitalization: A grant awarded according to the number of persons to be served or trained

Cash Flow: The amount of money that is required to meet the expenses.

Certified Public Accountant (CPA): An independent professional accountant certified to practice by a state agency.

Compilation: When the accountant prepared monthly, quarterly, or annual statements.

Compliance: Refers to adherence to the rules, regulations, requirements and guidelines of a funder.

Continuation Grant: The amount granted to support a project that has been approved for more than one year.

Contract: A legally enforceable document that provides for the rights and duties of the grantee or grantor.

Contract Officer: The agency official who has the authority to develop negotiate, and enter into contracts.

Contractor: This term is used variably to refer to the organization under contract to a funder to perform a specific work or service; or to refer to the agency that awards the contract.

Cost Overrun: The amount of additional costs that are incurred beyond those that were originally estimated and approved in the budget in a proposal or contract.

Cost Sharing: The portion of the project costs which are contributed by the grantee.

Debits: In an accounting system, a debit is an entry on the left side of an account in a ledger.

Deficit: Negative retained earnings.

Demonstration Project: A project whose purpose is to demonstrate or test a method to provide a particular service, activity, or technique.

Depreciation: The process of systematically allocating the cost of an asset so that a proper matching of revenue and expenses may be obtained.

Direct Costs: Items of expense that can be specifically attributed to project objectives and activities, such as expenditures for salaries, fringe benefits, travel, supplies, rent equipment, postage, telephone, printing.

Disallowance: An expenditure made by the project that is not approved by the grantor or by an auditor.

Discretionary Funds: Funds which may or may not be spent that are allocated for a particular purpose.

Encumbrance: An obligated cost that has not yet actually been expended.

Equal Opportunity: The certifications that a grantee will not discriminate in employment.

Expenditure: The decrease in an asset or increase in a liability associated with the acquisition of goods or services.

Expenses: A decrease in owners' equity associated with activities of an accounting period.

Fee Simple: Absolute ownership unencumbered by any other interest.

Fiscal Year (FY): A twelve-month period that designates the beginning and end of the allocations.

Foundations: Nonprofit organizations that provide funds from an establishment source to support.

Freedom of Information Act: A federal act requiring federal agencies to release information in their possession regarding grants.

Fringe Benefits: The budget category that includes costs to the grantee associated with project personnel beyond their salaries, such as health insurance, social security taxes, pension plans, unemployment, and disability payments.

Gantt Chart: A timetable that shows in chart form the starting and ending time for each activity or task involved in a project.

Grant: An award made by a funding agency to a grantee to support a project or other work.

Grantee: The individual or organization to which grant monies are actually paid and which is technically responsible for their use.

Grantor: The government agency of foundation that awards a grant.

Grants Management Officer: The person designated by a funding agency to responsible for the financial and business aspects of a particular grant.

Income: Assets acquired through the sale of merchandise or services.

Journal: In an accounting system, the journal is known as the book of original entry in which the daily transactions of expense (debits) and income (credits) are entered.

Ledger: In accounting system, the ledger is the record book in which accounts are kept based on transferring (posting) information form the daily journal and shown on a monthly (or period) basis.

Liabilities: An accounting term that refers to debts such as bills that are owned, rent, salaries, utilities, and interest.

Limited Partnership: A partnership with two levels of partners, one or more general partners and one or more limited partners.

Management By Objectives (MBO): A managerial technique in which managers and other workers participate in a process to identify and implement goals.

Matching Funds: That portion of the project costs which are provided by the grantee in the form of cash or the value of in-kind contributions.

Net Income: The amount by which total revenues exceed total expenses for an accounting period; the bottom line.

Net Loss: Negative net income.

Notice of Award: A formal written notification used by federal granting agencies and others indicating approval of a grant, its amount, time period, and conditions and terms.

Overhead Cost: Product costs other than direct materials and direct labor. It includes, for example, supervision, building maintenance, and power.

Owners' Equity: The original capital stock plus the retained earnings.

Periodic Inventory: Involves business actually physically counting the quantities in inventory and adjusting their accounting records to reflect this information at regular, periodic intervals.

Periodicity: Provides for the regular summing up of the firm's activity and establishes the time for regular reporting on that activity.

Privacy Act: Federal legislation that prohibits the release of information by federal agencies that would invade the privacy of individuals.

Profit Margin Percentage: Net income expressed as a percentage of net sales.

Project Cost: The direct and indirect costs that are attributable to a grant supported activity. Some funders limit these costs to those included in the budget it approved when the grant was made (also see Allowable Costs).

Program Evaluation Review Technique (PERT): A management system to plan and control project activities (and their related costs) by scheduling the timing of all events and activities in a way that recognizes their interdependence and enables their completion in the shortest possible time.

Progress Payment: The amount of the grant or contract paid by the grantor according to a regularly scheduled payment plan.

Proposal: A written document submitted to a funder that provides a detailed description of the project's objectives, activities, methods, operating plans, and budget.

Regulations: Requirements of funding agency with respect to the rules that govern a particular program and with which grantees must be in compliance.

Revenue: The increase in owners' equity resulting from operations during a period of time, usually from the sale of goods or services.

Revenue Sharing: Refers to grants for unrestricted use from the federal government to states and local governments.

Review: A financial statement conducted by an independent accountant who issues a report giving a limited degree of assurances.

RFP (Request for Proposal): A formal written announcement from a funding agency inciting competitive proposals for an available contract that sets forth the specifications and scope of the work and the product that is being sought.

Site Visit: A formal visit to the site of a project by persons authorized by a funder to obtain firsthand information about a project, either prior to an award, during the project period, or in connection with renewal or continuation of funding.

Sponsor: Refers to the granting agency (see Grantor). Also used as an adjective, for example, in "sponsored research", to identify activities that are supported by sources outside the host organization.

Stipend: A payment made to an individual in a training program or participating in a project activity to defray the person's living and other costs associated with the period of training or participation, and not as a salary for services to be performed.

Subcontractor: The organization or person that a project contracts with to perform a particular service to the project. Subcontractors are generally subject to all the requirements imposed on the project itself by a funding agency.

Subgrantee: An organization to which a project makes a grant (as contrasted with a subcontract) to perform particular services for the project.

Terms and Conditions: All of the legal requirements that pertain to and are imposed on a grant or contract.

Third Party: An organization (or person) additional to the two main parties (the grantee and the grantor) involved in performing the work of a project usually as a subcontractor or a consultant performing contractual services.

Unobligated Balance: Unspent amount of funds that remain at the end of a budget period and against which there are no accrued expenses.

Voucher: A written order as part of a paper system to establish a record of requisitions, purchases of supplies and equipment, requests for travel and payments that require approval prior to being processed and paid.

Working Capital: The difference between current assets and current liabilities.

APPENDIX A

STANDARDS OF COMMISSION FOR ACCREDITATION OF PARKS AND RECREATION AGENCIES (CAPRA)

The following ten categories detail 156 standards that are required for a quality operation of a public park and recreation agency.

1.0 AGENCY AUTHORITY, ROLE AND RESPONSIBILITY

2.0 PLANNING

3.0 ORGANIZATION AND ADMINISTRATION

4.0 HUMAN RESOURCES

5.0 FINANCE (FISCAL POLICY AND MANAGEMENT)

6.0 PROGRAMS AND SERVICES MANAGEMENT

7.0 FACILITY AND LAND USE MANAGEMENT

8.0 SECURITY AND PUBLIC SAFETY

9.0 RISK MANAGEMENT

10.0 EVALUATION AND RESEARCH (EVALUATIVE RESEARCH)

INDEX